CHRISTIANITY AND CULTURE:
A BIBLIOGRAPHY WITH INDEXES

CHRISTIANITY AND CULTURE: A BIBLIOGRAPHY WITH INDEXES

MARTIN S. REED (EDITOR)

Nova Science Publishers, Inc.
New York

Senior Editors: Susan Boriotti and Donna Dennis
Coordinating Editor: Tatiana Shohov
Office Manager: Annette Hellinger
Graphics: Wanda Serrano
Editorial Production: Jennifer Vogt, Matthew Kozlowski, Jonathan Rose
         and Maya Columbus
Circulation: Ave Maria Gonzalez, Vera Popovich, Luis Aviles, Melissa Diaz,
        Nicolas Miro and Jeannie Pappas
Communications and Acquisitions: Serge P. Shohov
Marketing: Cathy DeGregory

Library of Congress Cataloging-in-Publication Data
Available Upon Request

ISBN 1-59033-395-0

Copyright © 2002 by Nova Science Publishers, Inc.
        400 Oser Ave, Suite 1600
        Hauppauge, New York 11788-3619
        Tele. 631-231-7269   Fax 631-231-8175
        e-mail: Novascience@earthlink.net
        Web Site: http://www.novapublishers.com

Printed in the United States of America

CONTENTS

Preface   vii

Title Index   ix

Bibliography   1

Author Index   187

Subject Index   201

PREFACE

In over 2,000 years, Christianity has made 'the' overwhelming impact on the culture of the Western world in particular. But culture has also helped to shape the development and form of Christianity since the interaction of two such powerful phenomena cannot help but change the other. This new book brings together over 1200 citations on Christianity and Culture which are indexed by subject, title and author for easy access.

TITLE INDEX

#

20 essays on inculturation, 170

32 articles evaluating inculturation of Christianity in Africa, 1

A

A blueprint for humanity: Paul Tillich's theology of culture, 21

A Christian America, 69

A Christian America: Protestant hopes and historical realities, 69

A Christian critique of American culture, 70

A Christian critique of culture, 108

A Christian look at secular society, 149

A Christian view of philosophy and culture, 143

A Christian's guide to Greek culture: the pseudo-nonnus commentaries on sermons 4, 5, 39 and 43, 65

A Church for all peoples: missionary issues in a world church, 1

A common sense theology: the Bible, faith, and American society, 49

A crisis of saints: essays on people and principles, 140

A far glory: the quest for faith in an age of credulity, 12

A free society reader: principles for the new millennium, 1

A handbook on inculturation, 144

A history of Christianity in the Balkans, 152

A history of Korean Buddhist culture and some essays: the Buddhist Pure Land & the Christian Kingdom of Heaven, 182

A history of the English parish: the culture of religion from Augustine to Victoria, 127

A local Church living for dialogue: Muslim-Christian relations in Mindanao-Sulu, Philippines: 1965-2000, 92

A measure of success: Protestants and public culture in antebellum Cleveland, 105

A millennium of Christian culture in Ukraine, 2

A Native American theology, 86

A new babel, a new pentecost: communicating the gospel in a mass mediated culture, 73

A peculiar people: the Church as culture in a post-Christian society, 32

A reason for hope, 44

A reason to hope, 48

A resurrected church: Christianity after the death of Christendom, 10

A spacious heart: essays on identity and belonging, 67

A spirituality of Catholic aborigines and the struggle for justice, 2

A study of the influence of Christianity upon Japanese culture,, 141

A universal faith? : peoples, cultures, religions, and the Christ: essays in honor of Frank de Graeve, 37

A visit to Vanity fair: moral essays on the present age, 81

A voice in the wilderness, 137

A world of difference, following Christ beyond your cultural walls, 75

Abrahamic faiths, ethnicity, and ethnic conflicts, 2

Accessory to murder: the enemies, allies, and accomplices to the death of our culture, 159

Adapting to America: Catholics, Jesuits, and higher education in the twentieth century, 93

Africa: the kairos of a synod: Sedos Symposium on Africa, April-May 1994, 3

African culture and the Christian church, 148

African culture and the Christian church: an
    introduction to social and pastoral
    anthropology, 148
African inculturation theology: Africanizing
    Christianity, 107
African parables: thoughts for Sunday readings
    (cycle A), 19
African parables: thoughts for Sunday readings
    (cycle B), 87
African theology in images, 120
African theology in its social context, 20
African traditional institutions and the Christian
    church: a sociological prologue to Christian
    inculturation, 120
African traditional religion and Christianity: the
    neglected dimensions, 118
Afrocentric or eurocentric? : our task in a
    multicultural South Africa, 170
After Christendom? : how the church is to behave
    if freedom, justice, and a Christian nation are
    bad ideas, 71
After Christianity: Christian survivals in post-
    Christian culture, 14
Against the night: living in the new dark ages, 34
Agape and Eros, 117
Agents of transformation: a guide for effective
    cross-cultural ministry, 95
All God's children and blue suede shoes:
    Christians & popular culture, 113
All quite beautiful, 177
All under heaven: transforming paradigms in
    Confucian-Christian dialogue, 13
Allen Tate and the Catholic revival: trace of the
    fugitive gods, 77
Ambulatio fidei: essays in honor of Otto W.
    Heick, 4
Ambushed by grace: the virtues of a useless faith,
    41
American Catholic arts and fictions: culture,
    ideology, aesthetics, 62
American declarations: rebellion and repentance
    in American cultural history, 21
American madonna: images of the divine woman
    in literary culture, 60
America's other Jesus, 72
An address to the members of the Protestant
    Episcopal Church in Virginia, 100
An African theology of mission, 113
An American Emmaus: faith and sacrament in
    the American culture, 47
An Arthur A. Cohen reader: selected fiction and
    writings on Judaism, theology, literature, and
    culture, 33

An enduring flame: studies on Latino popular
    religiosity, 5
An evaluation of the philosophy and pedagogy of
    ethical culture .., 9
An evil lost to view? : an investigation of post-
    evangelisation Andean religion in mid-
    colonial Peru, 108
An intrusive Gospel? : Christian mission in the
    postmodern world, 89
An unchanging faith in a changing world:
    understanding and responding to critical issues
    that Christians face today, 16
Ancient and modern perspectives on the Bible
    and culture: essays in honor of Hans Dieter
    Betz, 5
Annual bibliography of Christianity in India, 5
Anthropological insights for missionaries, 73
Anthropological reflections on missiological
    issues, 73
Anthropology for Christian witness, 89
Antisemitic, Zionist, social, and political
    pamphlets. Part 2], 6
Aotearoa New Zealand: defining moments in the
    gospel-culture encounter, 42
Apologia: contextualization, globalization, and
    mission in theological education, 153
Appropriate ecclesiology: through narrative
    theology to an African church, 80
Arm the children: faith's response to a violent
    world, 87
Art, modernity, and faith: towards a theology of
    art, 123
Artists, citizens, philosophers: seeking the peace
    of the city: an Anabaptist theology of culture,
    58
Arts, entertainment & Christian values: probing
    the headlines that impact your family, 8
Asante Catholicism: religious and cultural
    reproduction among the Akan of Ghana, 117
Asian arts and Christian hope, 114
Asian theological reflections on suffering and
    hope, 8
Aspects of Jewish culture in the Middle Ages, 8
Assumptions that affect our lives, 121
At this time [microform]: Lakota grieving, a
    pastoral response, 77
Athens and Jerusalem: an interpretative essay on
    Christianity and classical culture, 177
Augustine and sexuality: protocol of the forty
    sixth colloquy, 22 May 1983, 20
Augustine's City of God, 8
Australian theologies: themes and methodologies
    into the third millennium, 64

Authentic African Christianity: an inculturation model for the Igbo, 46

Authentic transformation: a new vision of Christ and culture, 153

Awakening: challenging the culture with girls, 32

Axiomatics and dogmatics, 22

B

Barbarian Europe, 148

Bearing the witness of the spirit: Lesslie Newbigin's theology of cultural plurality, 77

Becoming a Christian: the ecumenical implications of our common baptism, 11

Becoming Indian: the process of inculturation, 4

Belief and culture in the Middle Ages: studies presented to Henry Mayr-Harting, 11

Believer, Christian, Catholic: three essays in fundamental theology, 33

Believing in the future: toward a missiology of Western culture, 16

Beyond a Christian commonwealth: the Protestant quarrel with the American Republic, 1830-1860, 69

Beyond culture wars, 76

Beyond inculturation: can the many be one?, 4

Beyond modernity: reflections of a post-modern Catholic, 140

Beyond the dark night: a way forward for the church?, 65

Beyond the white noise: mission in a multicultural world, 110

Beyond theological tourism: mentoring as a grassroots approach to theological education, 13

Beyond victory, 6

Bible map, 13

Biblical exegesis and the formation of Christian culture, 184

Biblical interpretation and the church: text and context, 14

Biblical interpretation and the Church: the problem of contextualization, 14

Biblical proclamation for Africa today, 90

Black theology today: liberation and contextualization, 136

Border crossings: Christian trespasses on popular culture and public affairs, 32

Boundaries of our habitations: tradition and theological construction, 20

Breaking enmities: religion, literature, and culture in Northern Ireland, 1967-97, 65

Bridge-makers and cross-bearers: Korean-American women and the church, 87

Bridging the gap, 18

Bridging the schism: Christian divisions and culture wars, 19

Bright promise, failed community: Catholics and the American public order, 171

Bringing the church off the slippery slope: recovery from culture wars, 129

Buddhist-Christian empathy, 152

Building credible multicultural teams, 137

Building strong families: how your family can withstand the challenges of today's culture, 109

Bukidnon: politics and religion, 21

By word, work, and wonder: cases in holistic mission, 104

Byzantium-Rus-Russia: studies in the translation of Christian culture, 58

C

Called to be a faithful church in a plural world, 22

Can we talk? : sharing your faith in a pre-Christian world, 169

Caribbean theology, 179

Catholicism and Austrian culture, 23

Catholicism and secularization in America: essays on nature, grace, and culture, 23

Catholics and American culture: Fulton Sheen, Dorothy Day, and the Notre Dame football team, 102

Catolicismo y cultura: encuentro de intelectuales, 23

CCICA annual: publication of the Catholic Commission on Intellectual and Cultural Affairs, 24

Cease fire: searching for sanity in America's culture wars, 149

Celebrate life: hope for a culture preoccupied with death, 22

Celebrating Jesus Christ in Africa: liturgy and inculturation, 84

Change across cultures: a narrative approach to social transformation, 18

Changes in Korean society between 1884-1910 as a result of the introduction of Christianity, 25

Changing churches: the local church and the structures of change, 24

Changing conversations: religious reflection & cultural analysis, 25

Changing the way America thinks, 149

Charismatic Christianity as a global culture, 25

Charlotte Yonge (1823-1901) : novelist of the
Oxford Movement: a literature of Victorian
culture and society, 44

Chekhov and Russian religious culture: the
poetics of the Marian paradigm, 43

Chieftaincy, widowhood, and ngambi in
Cameroon, 41

Chinese ancestor practices in light of the
scriptures [microform], 122

Chinese culture and Christianity, 148

Chinese culture and Christianity, 154

Choices at the heart of technology: a Christian
perspective, 37

Christ & the modern mind, 25

Christ and context: the confrontation between
Gospel and culture, 25

Christ and culture in dialogue: constructive
themes and practical applications, 26

Christ and culture, 26, 38, 115, 144

Christ and the Caesars: the origin of Christianity
from romanized Greek culture, 10

Christ and the unicorn, 158

Christ in modern Athens, 15

Christ in the Philippines, 107

Christ is a Native American, 124

Christ, the African king: New Testament
christology, 101

Christain influence and culture change among the
Ngas people: the Tuwan experience, 63

Christendom awake: on re-energizing the church
in culture, 114

Christian America? : what evangelicals really
want, 150

Christian business values in an intercultural
environment, 26

Christian communities in the Arab Middle East:
the challenge of the future, 26

Christian ethics in a postmodern world, 48

Christian ethics in an African background: a
study of the interaction of Christianity and Ibo
culture, 78

Christian faith and the contemporary arts, 52

Christian librarianship: essays on the integration
of faith and profession, 26

Christian living in a pagan culture, 175

Christian missions and a new world culture, 9

Christian mothers, families, and new Nigeria:
foundations of Christian culture, 118

Christian philosophy, 27

Christian spirituality and the culture of
modernity: the thought of Louis Dupré, 27

Christian theology and scientific culture, 168

Christian theology of inculturation, 45

Christian worship and its cultural setting, 146

Christianity and African culture: conservative
German Protestant missionaries in Tanzania,
1900-1940, 55

Christianity and classical culture, 33

Christianity and classical culture: a study of
thought and action from Augustus to
Augustine, 33

Christianity and classical culture: the
metamorphosis of natural theology in the
Christian encounter with Hellenism, 124

Christianity and culture change in India, 141

Christianity and culture in our time, 125

Christianity and culture in the crossfire, 27

Christianity and culture versus the negro, 65

Christianity and culture, 27, 49, 57, 65, 81, 112,
125, 141

Christianity and culture: an introduction to
pastoral theology and ministry for the
bicultural community, 49

Christianity and culture: The idea of a Christian
society and Notes towards the definition of
culture, 49

Christianity and cultures: a mutual enrichment,
27

Christianity and European culture: selections
from the work of Christopher Dawson, 42

Christianity and Ibo culture, 78

Christianity and Igbo culture: a study of the
interaction of Christianity and Igbo culture, 78

Christianity and modern culture, 147

Christianity and paganism in the fourth to eighth
centuries, 100

Christianity and Russian culture in Soviet
society, 28

Christianity and Tamil culture, 74

Christianity and the African imagination: after
the African Synod: resources for inculturation,
148

Christianity and the African imagination: essays
in honour of Adrian Hastings, 28

Christianity and the classics: the acceptance of a
heritage, 28

Christianity and the culture of economics, 28

Christianity and the Eastern Slavs, 28

Christianity and the human body: a theology of
the human body, 29

Christianity and the Igbo rites of passage: the
prospects of inculturation, 119

Christianity and the intellectuals, 169

Christianity and the new age, 42

Christianity and the world of thought, 7

Christianity before Christ, or Prototypes of our faith and culture, 154

Christianity challenges the university, 29

Christianity confronts culture, 103

Christianity confronts culture: a strategy for crosscultural evangelism, 103

Christianity in Africa as seen by Africans, 44

Christianity in Africa: the renewal of non-Western religion, 11

Christianity in conflict: the struggle for Christian integrity and freedom in secular culture, 29

Christianity in culture: a study in dynamic Biblical theologizing in cross-cultural perspective, 89

Christianity in its social context, 29

Christianity in northern Mala^wi: Donald Fraser's missionary methods and Ngoni culture, 167

Christianity in the Roman world, 101

Christianity in world history: the meeting of the faiths of East and West, 94

Christianity in world perspective, 38

Christianity made in Japan: a study of indigenous movements, 112

Christianity, culture, and colonialism in Africa: organised religion and factors in developing culture--an analysis, 81

Christianity, mediaeval and modern: a study in religious change, 115

Christianity, social change, and globalization in the Americas, 29

Christianity: a social and cultural history, 30

Christians and chiefs in Zimbabwe: a social history of the Hwesa people, 103

Christians and politics beyond the culture wars: an agenda for engagement, 30

Christians in a pluralist society, 20

Christians must choose: the lure of culture and the command of Christ, 95

Christians, feminists, and the culture of pornography, 107

Christology in dialogue, 30

Christopaganism or indigenous Christianity?, 30

Christ's body: identity, culture, and society in late medieval writings, 11

Chronic fatigue syndrome, Christianity, and culture: between God and illness, 138

Chung-kuo wên hua yü Chi-tu chiao, 30

Church and Canadian culture, 31

Church and China, towards reconciliation?, 152

Church and culture change in Africa, 31

Church and culture in early medieval Armenia, 60

Church and culture in seventeenth-century France, 125

Church and culture: Singapore context, 31

Church and shrine, 45

Church and society in history, 120

Church authority in American culture: the second Cardinal Bernardin Conference, 31

Churches and social issues in twentieth-century Britain, 99

Citizens of Zion: the social origins of camp meeting revivalism, 51

Civilization in crisis: a Christian response to homosexuality, feminism, euthanasia, and abortion, 57

Claiming the city: politics, faith, and the power of place in St. Paul, 180

Clashing symbols: an introduction to faith and culture, 59

Closure in the Canterbury tales: the role of The parson's tale, 32

Clothes make the man: female cross dressing in medieval Europe, 76

Collected works of Georges Florovsky, 57

Comatose Christianity: a wake-up call for Christians, 22

Committed to conflict: the destruction of the church in Rwanda, 103

Communication and Lonergan: common ground for forging the New Age, 35

Communication, reconciliation: challenges facing the 21st century, 35

Confessing the faith: Christian theology in a North American context, 67

Confident witness--changing world: rediscovering the Gospel in North America, 35

Conflict or connection: interpersonal relationships in cross-cultural settings, 85

Confucianism, Buddhism, Daoism, Christianity, and Chinese culture, 157

Conjuring culture: biblical formations of black America, 151

Conquering the culture: the fight for our children's souls, 49

Conservative essays, 35

Constructive Christian theology in the worldwide church, 36

Consulting the faithful: what Christian intellectuals can learn from popular religion, 111

Contemporary culture and Christianity, 91

Contemporary Gospel accents: doing theology in Africa, Asia, Southeast Asia, and Latin America, 36

Contextualization of Christianity and Christianization of language: a case study from the highlands of Papua New Guinea, 133

Contextualization of theology: an evangelical assessment, 57

Contextualization: meanings, methods, and models, 73

Converging on culture: theologians in dialogue with cultural analysis and criticism, 36

Conversion to Christianity: historical and anthropological perspectives on a great transformation, 36

Coping with culture, 37

Cosmos, self, and history in Baniwa religion: for those unborn, 183

Counter culture and the vision of God, 83

Court and culture in Renaissance Scotland: Sir David Lindsay of the Mount, 48

Court and politics in papal Rome, 1400-1800, 38

Covenant and commitments: faith, family, and economic life, 153

Creed and deed: a series of discourses, 3

Crefydd a diwylliant,, 48

Cross-cultural Christianity: a textbook on cross-cultural communication, 39

Cross-cultural connections: stepping out and fitting in around the world, 50

Crosscurrents in indigenous spirituality: interface of Maya, Catholic, and Protestant worldviews, 39

Crosswinds: the reformation digest, 39

Cultural anthropology: a Christian perspective, 66

Cultural change and liberation in a Christian perspective, 47

Cultural information service, 40

Cultural interpretation: reorienting New Testament criticism, 15

Cultural revival and church planting: a Nigerian case study, 91

Cultural wars in American politics: critical reviews of a popular myth, 40

Culture and biblical hermeneutics: interpreting and applying the authoritative Word in a relativistic age, 92

Culture and Christianity: a view, 91

Culture and Christianity: the dialectics of transformation, 40

Culture and control in counter-reformation Spain, 40

Culture and evangelization: collection of Indian anthropological readings, 40

Culture and religion in some of their relations, 146

Culture and theology, 127, 178

Culture and theology: a sketch for a contemporary Christianity, 178

Culture in Christian perspective: a door to understanding & enjoying the arts, 140

Culture shift: communicating God's truth to our changing world, 72

Culture, Christianity & the Cross, 18

Culture, communication, and Christianity, 89

Culture, religion, and society: essays in honour of Richard W. Taylor, 41

Culture-protestantism: German liberal theology at the turn of the twentieth century, 139

D

Dakota cross-bearer: the life and world of a Native American bishop, 33

Dancing in the dark: youth, popular culture, and the electronic media, 41

Dangerous 'isms, 41

Darwinism and the divine in America: Protestant intellectuals and organic evolution, 1859-1900, 136

Date with destiny, a preamble to Christian culture, 151

De doctrina Christiana: a classic of western culture, 43

Defeating the dragons of the world: resisting the seduction of false values, 52

Deliver us from evil: restoring the soul in a disintegrating culture, 184

Developing a Christian worldview of the Christian in today's culture, 34

Developing a curriculum for the Northeast India Theological Seminary [microform], 129

Developing cross-cultural fellowship within a multiethnic group of Christians in Cayenne, French Guiana [microform], 155

Dialogue at the depth-level: inculturation of prayer in the Nigerian Church, 49

Different windows, 121

Dining with the devil: the megachurch movement flirts with modernity, 67

Dipo custom and the Christian faith: the nature of a people is in their traditions, culture, religion, and customs, 159

Disciples of liberty: the African Methodist Episcopal Church in the age of imperialism, 1884-1916, 96

Discipleship of the mind: learning to love God in the ways we think, 149

Discoveries, missionary expansion, and Asian cultures, 45

Discovering Christianity in African cultures, 25

Discovering the Bible in the non-biblical world, 91

Disquiet in the land: cultural conflict in American Mennonite communities, 88

Divine Heiress: the Virgin Mary and the creation of Christian Constantinople, 94

Divine representations: postmodernism and spirituality, 45

Does theological education make a difference?: Global lessons in mission and ministry from India and Britain, 179

Doing contextual theology: a festschrift in honour of Bruce John Nicholls, 45

Doing theology across cultures, 79

Doing theology in context: South African perspectives, 45

Doing theology with cultures of Asia, 46

Double image: biblical insights from African parables, 158

Down to earth: studies in Christianity and culture, 46

Drift from the Churches: attitude toward Christianity during childhood and adolescence, 85

E

Earth story, sacred story, 35

Earthing the Gospel: an inculturation handbook for pastoral workers, 7

East challenges West: towards a convergence of spiritualities, 152

Ecclesial praxis of inculturation: toward an empirical-theological theory of inculturizing praxis, 6

Echoes from the African Synod: the future of the African church from present and past experiences, 119

Effective inculturation and ethnic identity, 48

Emerging voices in global Christian theology, 50

En la lucha = In the struggle: a Hispanic women's liberation theology, 80

Encompassing others: the magic of modernity in Melanesia, 95

Encountering the West: Christianity and the global cultural process: the African dimension, 142

Enquiries into religion and culture, 42

Entertainment evangelism: taking the church public, 84

Environmental man, 90

Essays in order, 51

Essays in theology of culture, 82

Essays on nature and grace, 149

Ethics after Christendom: toward an ecclesial Christian ethic, 67

Ethiopian review of cultures, 51

Ethnic realities and the church: lessons from Kurdistan: a history of mission work, 1668-1990, 15

Europe, was it ever really Christian?: the interaction between gospel and culture, 177

Evangelicals and culture, 138

Evangelisation in the South African context, 10

Evangelization, culture, and Catholic identity, 52

Evangelizing the culture of modernity, 23

Evangelizzazione e culture: atti del Congresso internazionale scientifico di missiologia, Roma, 5-12 ottobre 1975, 52

Every-day topics, 74

Exiles in Babylon, 90

Eyes wide open: looking for God in popular culture, 137

F

Facing the OSU issue in the African Synod: a personal response, 120

Facing the reality of communication: culture, church, and communication, 130

Faith and appreciative awareness: the cultural theology of Bernard E. Meland, 111

Faith and culture in the Irish context, 53

Faith and culture: issues for the Australian Church, 53

Faith and culture: the role of the Catholic university, 53

Faith and fiction: interdisciplinary studies on the interplay between metaphor and religion, 53

Faith and morality in the secular age, 70

Faith challenged by history: reports, lectures, sermons, and Bible Studies, 120

Faith in a changing culture, 60

Faith in the centre: Christianity and culture, 53

Faith, culture, and the worshiping community, 174

Faith, culture, and the worshiping community: shaping the practice of the local church, 174

Faith, culture, India today: perspectives, 53

Faith, history, and cultures: stability and change in church teachings, 128

Faith, reason, and philosophy: lectures at the al-azhar, Qum, Tehran, Lahore, and Beijing, 105

Faith, scholarship, and culture in the 21st century, 53

FaithQuakes, 155

Fantasy explosion, 100

Fields of the Lord: animism, Christian minorities, and state development in Indonesia, 7

Filipino spirit world: a challenge to the church, 73

Filipino values and our Christian faith, 109

Focus!: the power of people group thinking: a practical manual for planning effective strategies to reach the unreached, 136

Foolishness to the Greeks: the Gospel and Western culture, 114

For the beauty of the earth: a Christian vision for creation care, 17

For the healing of the nations: the book of Revelation in an age of cultural conflict, 63

For the love of children: genetic technology and the future of the family, 125

For the nations: essays evangelical and public, 184

Freedom, justice, and Christian counter-culture, 50

From complicity to encounter: the church and the culture of economism, 34

From culture wars to common ground: religion and the American family debate, 58

From East to West: essays in honor of Donald G. Bloesch, 58

From Jerusalem to Antioch: the Gospel across cultures, 40

From Orpheus to Paul, 99

From sacrament to contract: marriage, religion, and law in the Western tradition, 180

From sacred lies to holy wisdom: a faith journey in a postmodern world, 23

Frontiers of the Reformation: dissidence and orthodoxy in sixteenth-century Europe, 82

Fully Christian...fully human: a model for the new evangelization, 59

Fundamentalism and American culture: the shaping of twentieth century evangelicalism, 1870-1925, 101

Fundamentalism in America: millennialism, identity, and militant religion, 106

G

Gay threads in the fabric of Western culture: dramatized biographies of famous gay men, 173

Gender and material culture: the archaeology of religious women, 61

Gender, culture, and Christianity: American Protestant mission schools in China, 1880-1930, 65

German culture and christianity.., 64

Gifts and strangers: meeting the challenge of inculturation, 62

Global communication: is there a place for human dignity?, 126

Global theology: the meaning of faith in the present world crisis, 4

God and culture: essays in honor of Carl F.H. Henry, 63

God does not foreclose: the universal promise of salvation, 174

God in South Africa: the challenge of the gospel, 116

God in the wasteland: the reality of truth in a world of fading dreams, 176

God is rice: Asian culture and Christian faith, 156

God, mystery, diversity: Christian theology in a pluralistic world, 85

God's call to mission, 147

God's federal republic: reconstructing our governing symbol, 52

God's global mosaic: what we can learn from Christians around the world, 24

God's gym: divine male bodies of the Bible, 110

God's word in culture, 178

God's wrathful children: political oppression and Christian ethics, 16

Going public: Christian responsibility in a divided America, 2

Gospel & culture: the papers of a consultation on the Gospel and culture, 64

Gospel and culture in Vanuatu: the founding missionary and a missionary for today, 128

Gospel and culture: an ongoing discussion within the ecumenical movement, 7

Gospel in context, 64

Gospel message and Hellenistic culture, 41

Gospel message and human cultures: from Leo XIII to John Paul II, 23

Gospel virtues: practicing faith, hope & love in uncertain times, 179

Governing the tongue: the politics of speech in early New England, 84

Grasping for the wind: the search for meaning in the 20th century, 177

Great awakenings: popular religion and popular culture, 56

H

Halloween, 140

Has democracy had its day?, 72

Health, medicine, and empire: perspectives on colonial India, 71

Hellenization revisited: shaping a Christian response within the Greco-Roman world, 72

Hidden people: how a remote New Guinea culture was brought back from the brink of extinction, 117

Hindu-Christian meeting point, within the cave of the heart, 2

History of Christianity in Oyo State of Nigeria: its influence in Yoruba culture/ Esther Feyisike, 74

Hope against darkness: the transforming vision of Saint Francis in an age of anxiety, 137

Hopes for English religion, 55

How does America hear the gospel?, 47

How now shall we live?, 34

How to run a Catholic foundation: increasing the impact of religious giving, 76

How to survive in a world of unbelievers: Jesus' words of encouragement on the night before his death, 99

How to win the culture war: a Christian battle plan for a society in crisis, 89

Human freedom an Indian culture: Christian ethical reflections, 167

Human rights and the conflict of cultures: Western and Islamic perspectives on religious liberty, 96

Humanities, 77

I

I will not bow, 122

Ideals and applications, 170

Identity and change: Nigerian philosophical studies, I, 78

Idolatry and its enemies: colonial Andean religion and extirpation, 1640-1750, 108

Illusions of our culture, 66

Image as insight: visual understanding in Western Christianity and secular culture, 108

Images or idols?: the place of sacred art in churches today, 172

In all things: religious faith and American culture, 78

In old New Orleans, 78

In search of meaning and identity: conversion to Christianity in Pakistani Muslim culture, 156

Inculturating North American theology: an experiment in foundational method, 61

Inculturation & Christian art: an Indian perspective, 49

Inculturation and African religion: indigenous and Western approaches to medical practice, 121

Inculturation and Filipino theology, 107

Inculturation and liturgy, 79

Inculturation and the challenges of modernity, 8

Inculturation in seminary formation, 79

Inculturation of Filipino-Chinese culture mentality, 184

Inculturation of the Jesus tradition: the impact of Jesus on Jewish and Roman cultures, 151

Inculturation theology of the Jerusalem Council in Acts 15: an inspiration for the Igbo Church today, 103

Inculturation through basic communities: an Indian perspective, 125

Inculturation: abide by the otherness of Africa and the Africans, 79

Inculturation: its meaning and urgency, 79

Inculturation: new dawn of the church in Latin America, 80

Inculturation: path to African Christianity, 170

Inculturation: the Eucharist in Africa, 168

Inculturation: the faith that takes root in African cultures, 79

Inculturation: where do we stand?, 80

Indigenization: how to grow black churches in white denominations, 47

Indigenous responses to western Christianity, 80

Into the vacuum: being the church in the age of barbarism, 145

Introduction to the New Testament, 88

Invitation to cross-cultural theology: case studies in vernacular theologies, 47

Is a culture of life still possible in the United States?, 80

Is it a lost cause?: having the heart of God for the church's children, 42

Israel: the culture, 150

Issues 2000: evangelical faith and cultural trends in the new millennium, 38

J

Jahrbuch für kontextuelle Theologien = Yearbook of contextual theologies, 81

Jane Austen and religion: salvation and society in Georgian England, 61

Jerusalem in Russian culture, 82

Jesus in the power of the spirit, 151

Jesus, an economic mediator: God's remedy for industrial and international ills, 41

Jing feng, 82

Journal of inculturation theology, 83

Joy, 113

Judaism as religion and culture, 85

K

Karl Barth's theology of culture: the freedom of culture for the praise of God, 122

Kerala Christian sainthood: collisions of culture and worldview in South India, 44

Key to the door, 123

Kierkegaard, religion, and the nineteenth-century crisis in culture, 123

Kikuyu traditional culture and Christianity: self examination of an African church, 17

King Lear and the naked truth: rethinking the language of religion and resistance, 90

Kingdom, cross, and community: essays on Mennonite themes in honor of Guy F. Hershberger, 87

Kinship and pilgrimage: rituals of reunion in American Protestant culture, 113

Korea and Christianity, 88

Korea struggles for Christ, 88

Korea's response to the West, 82

L

Lambs among wolves, 19

Language, religion, culture: in memory of Professor Witold Tyloch, 92

Learning about theology from the Third World, 48

Learning the language of Babylon: changing the world by engaging the culture, 39

Let the whole world sing: the story behind the music of Lausanne II, 9

Let your life speak: a study of politics, religion, and antinuclear weapons activism, 75

Liberating news: a theology of contextual evangelization, 38

Liberation theology: human hope confronts Christian history and American power, 139

Life and death matters: the practice of inculturation in Africa, 94

Lifeviews: understanding the ideas that shape society today, 153

Light from Paris: Cardinal Lustiger on faith and contemporary culture, 70

Light of revelation and non-Christians, 44

Lighten our darkness: toward an indigenous theology of the cross, 67, 68

Like a house on fire: renewal of the arts in a postmodern culture, 145

Literature and religious culture in seventeenth-century England, 9

Liturgical inculturation in the Anglican Communion: including the York statement, 96

Liturgical inculturation: sacramentals, religiosity, and catechesis, 30

Liturgies of the future: the process and methods of inculturation, 31

Liturgy and cultural religious traditions, 96

Liturgy and spirituality in context: perspectives on prayer and culture, 96

Liturgy in a multicultural community, 58

Living in color: embracing God's passion for diversity, 182

Living the discipline: United Methodist theological reflections on war, civilization, and holiness, 98

Living tradition: a changing life in Solomon Islands, 90

Logos: a journal of Catholic thought and culture, 98

Lonergan's challenge to the university and the economy, 105

Losing our virtue: why the church must recover its moral vision, 176

Lost in America: how you and your church can impact the world next door, 32

Love your enemy [sound recording] \: the Gospel call to nonviolence, 137

Love your God with all your mind: the role of reason in the life of the soul, 110

M

Maasai: between the Oreteti-tree and the tree of the cross, 172

Made in America: the shaping of modern American evangelicalism, 76

Main springs of Western civilisation, 148

Making all things new: dialogue, pluralism, and evangelization in Asia, 4

Making ethnic ways: communities and their transformations in Taita, Kenya, 1800-1950, 18

Making the good news relevant: keeping the Gospel distinctive in any culture, 79

Man & woman: alone & togethe [i.e. together], 37

Man in God's milieu, 90

Man, culture, and Christianity, 73

Manifesto for a global civilization, 58

Mankind's search for God, 101

Mansex fine: religion, manliness and imperialism in nineteenth-century British culture, 4

Many cultures, one nation: a festschrift for Beyers Naudé, 101

Marginality: the key to multicultural theology, 93

Martung upah: black and white Australians seeking partnership, 102

Marvels, monsters, and miracles: studies in the medieval and early modern imaginations, 102

Mary--mother of the African Church: a theological inculturation of Mariology, 117

Masculinity and spirituality in Victorian culture, 102

Material Christianity: religion and popular culture in America, 104

Meadows of howling, or, Abortion, feminism, and the culture of death, 17

Media, culture, and Catholicism, 106

Media, culture, and the religious right, 106

Medieval encounters: Jewish, Christian, and Muslim culture in confluence and dialogue, 106

Memory eternal: Tlingit culture and Russian Orthodox Christianity through two centuries, 84

Men's bodies, men's gods: male identities in a (post-) Christian culture, 106

Message of the Special Assembly of the Synod of Bishops for Africa, 107

Metaphors for God's time in science and religion, 70

Ministry and theology in global perspective: contemporary challenges for the church, 108

Ministry in an oral culture: living with Will Rogers, Uncle Remus, and Minnie Pearl, 142

Miracles and pilgrims: popular beliefs in medieval England, 55

Missiology and the social sciences: contributions, cautions, and conclusions, 109

Mission in a pluralist world, 109

Missions and money: affluence as a western missionary problem, 16

Missions: biblical foundations & contemporary strategies, 171

Models of contextual theology, 13

Modern poetry and the Christian tradition, 178

Modern sannyasins: Protestant missionary contribution to Ceylon Tamil culture, 75

Modernity: Christianity's estranged child reconstructed, 167

Morphologies of faith: essays in religion and culture in honor of Nathan A. Scott, Jr, 111

Mujerista theology: a theology for the twenty-first century, 81: Muscular Christianity: embodying the Victorian Age, 113

Music, body, and desire in medieval culture: Hildegard of Bingen to Chaucer, 74

Must God remain Greek?: Afro cultures and God-talk, 75

My Father's world: meditations on Christianity and culture, 141

Mysticism, Buddhist and Christian: encounters with Jan van Ruusbroec, 110

Mythmakers: gospel, culture, and the media, 57

N

Near the far bamboo: an insightful look at cross-cultural clashes through the eyes of a tentmaking missionary, 153

New library, 24

New paths in Muslim evangelism: evangelical approaches to contextualization, 122

New wine: the cultural shaping of Japanese Christianity, 131

Nigeria: people & culture, 115

Nigerian peoples and cultures, 115

Nine great American myths: ways we confuse the American dream with the Christian faith, 6

Nineteenth-century English religious traditions: retrospect and prospect, 116

No place for truth, or, Whatever happened to evangelical theology?, 176

O

Odyssey of the self-centered self, 56

On being the church in the United States: contemporary theological critiques of liberalism, 74

On deconstructing life-worlds: Buddhism, Christianity, culture, 100

On human dignity: political theology and ethics, 110

On the eve of the millennium: the future of democracy through an age of unreason, 118

One Christ, many religions: toward a revised Christology, 141

One church, many cultures: challenge of diversity, 56

One church, many tribes, 169

One faith, many cultures: inculturation, indigenization, and contextualization, 119

One faith, two peoples: communicating across cultures within the church, 102

Ordaining women: culture and conflict in religious organizations, 25

Organization man, organization woman: calling, leadership, and culture, 137

Our prodigal son, culture, 167

Our world in transition: making sense of a changing world, 117

Out of every tribe and nation: Christian theology at the ethnic Roundtable, 64

Outlines of a philosophy of religion based on psychology and history, 141

P

Paano maging Pilipinong Kristiano = Becoming a Filipino Christian, 92

Paganism in the Church, 135

Paradox lost: free will and political liberty in American culture, 1630-1760, 121

Paschal mystery of Christ: foundation for liturgical inculturation in Africa, 25

Pastoral care to the sick in Africa: an approach to transcultural pastoral theology, 12

Paul the Apostle to America: cultural trends and Pauline scholarship, 82

Peace culture amidst power conflicts: caste, class, race, state tensions, 24

People of the Book: Christian identity and literary culture, 81

People of the truth: a christian challenge to contemporary culture, 175

People on the way: Asian North Americans discovering Christ, culture, and community, 124

Perspectivas: Hispanic ministry, 125

Perspectives on Christianity in Korea and Japan: the Gospel and culture in East Asia, 125

Piety and power: gender and religious culture in the American colonies, 1630-1700, 95

Pinocchio nation: embracing truth in a culture of lies, 46

Please don't squeeze the Christian into the world's mold, 146

Pledges of jubilee: essays on the arts and culture, in honor of Calvin G. Seerveld, 126

Pluralism and oppression: theology in world perspective, 126

Points of view, 49

Polish literature in the culture of Christian Europe, 126

Pop culture wars: religion & the role of entertainment in American life, 137

Pope John Paul II on inculturation: theory and practice, 170

Popular Catholicism in a world church: seven case studies in inculturation, 126

Popular religion in America: the evangelical voice, 83

Popular religion, liberation, and contextual theology, 127

Post-modern pilgrims: first century passion for the 21st century world, 155

Postmodern times: a Christian guide to contemporary thought and culture, 171

Power religion: the selling out of the evangelical church?, 127

Power structures and and the church, 144

Praying for America, 147

Preaching and cultural identity: proclaiming the gospel in Africa, 90

Preaching to a church in crisis: a homiletic for the last days of the mainline church, 86

Preaching to every pew: cross-cultural strategies, 115

Preaching wisdom to the wise: three treatises, 116

Priests of culture: a study of Matthew Arnold & Henry James, 154

Primary documents in Reformation theology for Batak theological students [microform]: a class syllabus, 104

Problems and promises of Africa: towards and beyond the year 2000, 128

Processive revelation, 131

Professing the faith: Christian theology in a North American context, 68

Profiles in Protestant witness: the first fifty years of evangelical Christianity in the Philippines, 1898-1948, 128

Project for Orthodox renewal: seven studies of key issues facing Orthodox Christians in America, 128

Protestant evangelical literary culture and contemporary society, 15

Psychic conversion and theological foundations: toward a reorientation of the human sciences, 46

Public religion in American culture, 179

Pushing the faith: proselytism and civility in a pluralistic world, 129

Putting an end to worship wars, 169

Q

Quest for reality: Christianity and the counter culture, 129

R

Race and the cosmos: an invitation to view the world differently, 74

Radical monotheism and western culture: with supplementary essays, 115

Radical social movement and the radical church tradition, 139

Ramakrishna and Christ, or, The paradox of the incarnation, 168

Reaching a new generation: strategies for tomorrow's church, 138

Reaching out without dumbing down: a theology of worship for the turn-of-the-century culture, 42

Reaching the world next door: how to spread the gospel in the midst of many cultures, 75

Readings in Christian humanism, 130

Readings in missionary anthropology, 150

Readings on religion as news, 130

Reclaiming the sacred: the Bible in gay and lesbian culture, 130

Reclaiming the soul: the search for meaning in a self-centered culture, 17

Reconciliation: a community celebration: a case-study in inculturation for Igbo Catholics in Enugu State Nigeria, 52

Reconstructing the reality of images: Byzantine material culture and religious iconography, 11th-15th centuries, 122

Redeeming the dial: radio, religion, and popular culture in America, 69

Redemptorama: culture, politics, and the new evangelicalism, 56

Reflections in a mission mirror: ancient wisdom from younger churches, 2

Reformations: a radical interpretation of Christianity and the world, 1500-2000, 54

Reformed social ethics and the Korean church, 183

Reforming Protestantism: Christian commitment in today's world, 121

Religion and contemporary Western culture, 24

Religion and cooperation between civilizations: Islamic and Christian cultures in a global horizon, 105

Religion and culture in dialogue: a challenge for the next millenium, 131

Religion and culture in Germany (1400-1800), 145

Religion and culture in Renaissance England, 131

Religion and culture, 65, 131, 145

Religion and mass media: audiences and adaptations, 131

Religion and political culture in Jefferson's Virginia, 132

Religion and politics in Nigeria: a study in Middle Belt Christianity, 84

Religion and the arts: a journal from Boston College, 132

Religion and the cultural crisis in India and the West: an ecumenical inquiry, 3

Religion and the culture wars: dispatches from the front, 132

Religion and the modern mind, 37

Religion and the present crisis, 88

Religion and the variety of culture: a study in origin and practice, 142

Religion in Europe: contemporary perspectives, 132

Religion in Western culture: selected issues, 48

Religion, economics, and public policy: ironies, tragedies, and absurdities of the contemporary culture wars, 173

Religion, feminism, and the family, 132

Religion, politics, and the American experience: reflections on religion and American public life, 133

Religions in conflict: ideology, cultural contact, and conversion in late-colonial India, 37

Religious culture in the sixteenth century: preaching, rhetoric, spirituality, and reform, 119

Religious encounter and the making of the Yoruba, 123

Religious experience and interpretation: memory as the path to the knowledge of God in Julian of Norwich's Showings, 184

Religious poverty in Africa, 148

Religious values in Japanese culture, 20

Remarks on the internal evidence for the truth of revealed religion, 51

Remembering Esperanza: a cultural-political theology for North American praxis, 158

Repetition and the visions of secular culture, 155

Research on culture and values: the intersection of universities, churches, and nations, 134

Resident aliens: life in the Christian colony, 71

Resistance or submission: snatches of a Christian conversation, 134

Resistant peoples: the case of the pastoral Maasai of East Africa, 113

Restoring the faith: the Assemblies of God, pentecostalism, and American culture, 16

Resurrecting the Third Reich: are we ready for America's modern fascism?, 158

Rethinking Luther's theology in the contexts of the Third World, 134

Return to Babel: global perspectives on the Bible, 134

Re-visioning mission: the Catholic Church and culture in postmodern America, 38

Revivalism and cultural change: Christianity, nation building, and the market in the nineteenth-century United States, 166

Revolution of spirit: ecumenical theology in global context: essays in honor of Richard Shaull, 134

Rewriting the Bible: the real issues: perspectives from within Biblical and religious studies in Zimbabwe, 134

Right thinking and sacred oratory in Counter-Reformation Rome, 104

Risky business: brotherhood in American culture, 136

Roaring lambs: a gentle plan to radically change our world, 19

Romanced to death: the sexual seduction of American culture, 44

Romania: orthodox identity at a crossroads of Europe, 19

Rome in late antiquity: AD 313-604, 91

Roots of Western culture: pagan, secular, and Christian options, 46

Ruskin's God, 177

Russian culture at the threshold of the third millenium of Christianity, 140

Russian culture in modern times, 140

Russian Orthodoxy and political culture transformation, 174

S

Sacred communities: Jewish and Christian identities in fifteenth-century Germany, 11

Sacred place, chosen people: land and national identity in Welsh spirituality, 97

Saint Paul at the movies: the apostle's dialogue with American culture, 82

Saints and sinners: the American Catholic experience through stories, memoirs, essays, and commentary, 141

Saints' lives and women's literary culture c. 1150-1300: virginity and its authorizations, 181

Sambahaginan: an experience in community development work, 142

Santo Domingo and after: the challenges for the Latin American Church, 143

Say you want a revolution: we now find ourselves transported into a deceptive and deadly 90's culture, 83

Screen christologies: redemption and the medium of film, 44

Screen saved: peril and promise of media in ministry, 5

Scribe of the kingdom: essays on theology and culture, 114

Sea of dreams, 145

Seasons of celebration: ritual in Eastern Christian culture, 63

Seeking God in contemporary culture, 175

Selections from the essays of Thomas Henry Huxley, 77

Self-definition in early Christianity: protocol of the thirty-seventh colloquy, 6 January 1980, 146

Selling Catholicism: Bishop Sheen and the power of television, 99

Shakespeare and the loss of Eden: the construction of family values in early modern culture, 11

Shaking the sleeping beauty: arousing the church to its mission, 66

Shape a circle ever wider: liturgical inculturation in the United States, 58

Silver thread: the ups and downs of a Mennonite family in mission, 1895-1995, 147

Sinners in the hands of an angry church: finding a better way to influence our culture, 107

Slaves, women & homosexuals: exploring the hermeneutics of cultural analysis, 175

Small arms, big impact: a challenge to the churches: a report of the Consultation on Microdisarmament, 149

Social facts and forces, 63

Social, cultural, economic & religious life of a transformed community: a study of the Paite tribe, 94

Society and culture in North-East India: a Christian perspective, 151

Someone or nothing? : Nishitani's religion and nothingness as a foundation for Christian-Buddhist dialogue, 17

Something to believe in: Is Kurt Vonnegut the exorcist of Jesus Christ Superstar?, 147

SoulTsunami [sound recording]: sink or swim in new millennium culture, 155

SoulTsunami: sink or swim in new millennium culture, 156

Speaking of God, 76

Spirit at work: discovering the spirituality in leadership, 152

Spirit scapes: mapping the spiritual & scientific terrain at the dawn of the new millennium, 122

Spiritual encounters: interactions between Christianity and native religions in colonial America, 152

Spiritual interrogations: culture, gender, and community in early African American women's writing, 10

Spiritual life in the Good Ol' USA: story-essays on popular culture and Christianity, 70

Spiritual saturnalia, 117

Spiritual warfare: the invisible invasion, 75

St. Martín de Porres: the, 60

Stay tuned: what every parent should know about media, 123

Still bored in a culture of entertainment: rediscovering passion & wonder, 180

Strange virtues: ethics in multicultural world, 3

Strangers & pilgrims: female preaching in America, 1740-1845, 18

Struggles of faith: essays, 59

Studies in world Christianity, 155

Studies on theology and Naga culture, 156

Summer in the seed, 153

Sun and cross: the development from Megalithic culture to early Christianity in Ireland, 154

Surviving the media jungle, 24

Symbol and ceremony: making disciples across cultures, 185

T

T.S. Eliot and ideology, 8

Talitha, qumi!, 157

Talking about cultural diversity in your church: gifts and challenges, 5

Talking back to civilization: Indian voices from the Progressive Era, 157

Tao, reception in East and West, 157

Teaching moral values, 173

Televangelism and American culture: the business of popular religion, 144

Ten strategies for preaching in a multimedia culture, 169

Tending the flock: congregations and family ministry, 158

Text & experience: towards a cultural exegesis of the Bible, 159

The (magic) kingdom of God: Christianity and global culture industries, 20

The African church, today and tomorrow, 113

The African Synod: hope for the continent's liberation, 118

The American Puritan elegy: a literary and cultural study, 68

The Aquinas review of Thomas Aquinas College, 159

The attic Moses: the dependency theme in some early Christian writers, 135

The attitude towards labor in early Christianity and ancient culture, 61

The believer as citizen: John Courtney Murray in a new context, 77

The Bible in cross-cultural perspective, 97

The Bible tells me so: uses and abuses of Holy Scripture, 74

The biblical basis for evangelization: theological reflections based on an African experience, 112

The bread for today and the bread for tomorrow: the ethical significance of the Lord's Supper in the Korean context, 86

The bursting of new wineskins: reflections on religion and culture at the end of affluence, 130

The bush was blazing but not consumed: developing a multicultural community through dialogue liturgy, 93

The Caribbean: enculturation, acculturation, and the role of the churches, 179

The Catholic church and American culture: reciprocity and challenge, 159

The Catholic counterculture in America, 1933-1962, 56

The Catholic milieu, 154

The Catholic side of Henry James, 59

The challenge of our culture, 39

The Challenge of our culture: Clarence Tucker Craig, editor .., 39

The change of conversion and the origin of Christendom, 89

The changing face of the church, 159

The changing of the guard: the vital role Christians must play in America's unfolding political and cultural drama, 65

The choice: America at the crossroads of ruin and revival, 168

The Christian approach to culture, 21

The Christian confronts his culture, 58

The Christian druids: on the filid or philosopher-poets of Ireland, 108

The Christian frame of mind, 168

The Christian heritage, 57

The Christian intellectual, 124

The Christian mind: how should a Christian think?, 15

The Christian myth: origins, logic, and legacy, 99

The Christian tradition, 159

The Christian's handbook of science and philosophy, 139

The church & world mission, 66

The Church and civilization, 47

The Church and culture since Vatican II: the experience of North and Latin America, 160

The church and culture: challenge and confrontation: inculturation and evangelization, 127

The church and cultures, 99

The church and cultures: an applied anthropology for the religious worker, 98

The church and cultures: new perspectives in missiological anthropology, 99

The Church and homosexuality: a preliminary study, 160

The church and inculturation: a century of Roman Catholicism in Eastern Nigeria, 170

The church and the culture war: secular anarchy or sacred order, 96

The church and the future of Africa: problems and promises, 160

The church and the new world mind, 160

The church as counterculture, 160

The church between Gospel and culture: the emerging mission in North America, 161

The Church in Africa and her evangelising mission towards the year 2000

The Church in Africa: 1450-1950, 70

The church in dialogue: culture and traditions, 20

The Church in exile: God's counter culture in a non-Christian world, 167

The Church in response to human need, 161

The church on the world's turf: an evangelical Christian group at a secular university, 18

The church unbound, 64

The Ciskei--a Bantu homeland: a general survey, 161

The civilization of Christianity, 105

The clash between Christianity and cultures, 104

The clash of civilizations: an intrusive gospel in Japanese civilization, 93

The comfort trap: spiritual dangers of the convenience culture, 10

The Community of the Holy Spirit: a movement of change in a convent of nuns in Puerto Rico, 142

The completion of the project of the West, and it romantic sequel: essays in the history of western culture, 100

The compromised church: the present evangelical crisis, 162

The consuming passion: Christianity & the consumer culture, 162

The contemporary faces of Satan, 84

The contextualization of the gospel in Chile [microform], 172

The cosmic center, 97

The cosmic center: the supremacy of Christ in a secular wasteland, 97

The crisis of faith and morality of the Igbo Christians of Nigeria, 3

The critique of modernity: theological reflections on contemporary culture, 70

The cross and the crisis, 147

The cross-cultural process in Christian history: studies in the transmission and appropriation of faith, 173

The cultural concept of Christianity, 22

The culture of economism: an exploration of barriers to faith-as-praxis, 34

The culture of interpretation: Christian faith and the postmodern world, 98

The culture war in America: a society in chaos, 138

The deadliest monster: a Christian introduction to worldviews, 9

The death cry of an eagle: the rise and fall of Christian values in the United States, 116

The death of truth, 162

The development of the doctrine of the Holy Spirit in the Yoruba (African) indigenous Christian movement, 119

The Devil and Doctor Dwight: satire and theology in the early American Republic, 176

The devil's gauntlet: the church and the challenge of society, 67

The disciplined life-style, 158

The discovery of humankind: an essay on the Christian understanding of community, 138

The drumbeat of life: jubilee in an African context, 9

The dust of death, 67

The Dynamic character of Christian culture: essays on Dawsonian themes, 162

The earth is God's: a theology of American culture, 48

The emancipation of Russian Christianity, 162

The enchantment of sociology: a study of theology and cul ture, 56

The encyclopedia of apocalypticism, 162

The end of Christendom and the future of Christianity, 68

The enduring revolution: a battle to change the human heart, 34

The essence of Christianity, 54

The essence of faith according to Luther, 54

The ethical dimension of community: the African model and the dialogue between North and South, 21

The Evangelical forfeit: can we recover?, 146

The extermination of Christianity: a tyranny of consensus, 143

The fabric of theology: a prolegomenon to Evangelical theology, 95

The Failure of the American Baptist culture: a symposium, 163

The fate of man in the modern world, 12

The Filipino in the seventies, 64

The final roar, 19

The first nations: a Canadian experience of the gospel-culture encounter, 105

The formation of Christendom, 42

The formulation of Christianity by conflict through the ages, 163

The fundamental ideas of Christianity, 21

The future people: Christianity, modern culture and the future, 18

The globalisation of charismatic Christianity: spreading the gospel of prosperity, 33

The globalization of communications: some religious implications, 7

The Globalization of theological education, 163

The God of stones and spiders: letters to a church in exile, 34

The gold coast church and the ghetto: Christ and culture in mainline Protestantism, 176

The good of affluence: a theology for people seeking God in a culture of modern capitalism, 144

The gospel according to the marginalized, 149

The Gospel and the American dream, 147

The Gospel as good news for African cultures: a symposium on the dialogue between faith and culture, 163

The Gospel in a pluralist society, 114

The great dissent: John Henry Newman and the liberal heresy, 123

The great rebellion, 129

The guru in Indian Catholicism: ambiguity or opportunity of inculturation?, 38

The highest culture and Christianity, 98

The historic reality of Christian culture, 42

The historic reality of Christian culture: a way to the renewal of human life, 43

The Human person and philosophy in the contemporary world, 163

The illuminating icon, 170

The illustrated story of Christian Ireland: from St Patrick to the peace process, 154

The impact of Christianity on the Igbo religion and culture, 118

The Impact of the church upon its culture, 163

The influence of Greek ideas on Christianity, 71

The invisible God: the earliest Christians on art, 55

The irrelevance and relevance of the Christian message, 167

The Italian influence on Western law and culture, 130

The Jesuits: cultures, sciences, and the arts, 1540-1773, 164

The Labor of God: an Ignatian view of church and culture, 164

The law and the gospel, 131

The least of these: race, law, and religion in American culture, 37

The liberated imagination: thinking Christianly about the arts, 141

The life of prayer in a world of science: Protestants, prayer, and American culture, 1870-1930, 120

The life of Selina Campbell: a fellow soldier in the cause of restoration, 98

The light in the city: why Christians must advance and not retreat, 122

The limits of ancient Christianity: essays on late antique thought and culture in honor of R.A. Markus, 164

The Lord's Table: Eucharist and Passover in early Christianity, 54

The making of sages: biblical wisdom and contemporary culture, 111

The many faces of Jesus Christ: intercultural christology, 90

The McDonaldization of the church: consumer culture and the church's future, 47

The message of mainstream Christianity in Malawi: an analysis of contemporary preaching, 138

The mirror of simple souls, 127

The missionary congregation, leadership & liminality, 139

The missionary movement in Christian history: studies in the transmission of faith, 173

The modern God, 176

The moment and late writings, 86

The mystical language of sensation in the later Middle Ages, 139

The new catholicity: theology between the global and the local, 144

The New Left church [essays], 48

The new left Church, 48

The new paganism, 95

The new tolerance: how a cultural movement threatens to destroy you, your faith, and your children, 104

The Nigerian church: evangelisation through inculturation: pastoral letter, 164

The nineteenth-century church and English society, 88

The novel, spirituality and modern culture, 55, 164

The one and the many, 140

The One, the Three, and the many: God, creation, and the culture of modernity, 67

The other side of 1984: questions for the churches, 114

The Oz syndrome: finding contentment in your family, 118

The pagan temptation, 109

The paths of Kateri's kin, 171

The poor woman: a critical analysis of Asian theology and contemporary Chinese fiction by women, 182

The post-Christian mind: exposing its destructive agenda, 15

The practice of piety: Puritan devotional disciplines in seventeenth-century New England, 68

The proclamation of the good news: a study of Lk 24 in Tiv context, 3

The proclamation of the Gospel in a pluralistic world, 57

The prodigal hugging church: a scandalous approach to mission for the 21st century, 183

The Protestant presence in twentieth-century America: religion and political culture, 69

The Puritan conversion narrative: the beginnings of American expression, 22

The reflection of theology in literature: a case study in theology and culture, 100

The resilience of Christianity in the modern world, 157

The restoration of perfection: labor and technology in medieval culture, 121

The revolt against God, 175

The revolution in religion, 54

The rise of Baptist republicanism, 151

The road to reality: coming home to Jesus from the unreal world, 184

The sacred pipe: an archetypal theology, 154

The Samoan culture and the Christian gospel, 84

The savage my kinsman, 49

The scandal of a crucified world: perspectives on the Cross and suffering, 165

The scandal of the evangelical mind, 116

The Scottish Highlands: the churches and Gaelic culture, 106

The secular saint: a case for evangelical social responsibility, 175

The secularization of sin: an investigation of the Daedalus complex, 54

The seven cities of the apocalypse and Greco-Asian culture, 183

The seven cities of the Apocalypse and Roman culture, 183

The slippery earth: Nahua-Christian moral dialogue in sixteenth-century Mexico, 21

The sociology of Singapore religion: studies in Christianity and Chinese culture, 31

The span of the cross: Christian religion and society in Wales, 1914-2000, 110

The spectacle of worship in a wired world: electronic culture and the gathered people of God, 142

The spirit of Chinese culture, 176

The spirit of Christ and the spirit of fundamentalism [sound recording], 19

The spiritual society: what lurks beyond postmodernism?, 10

The story of civilization, 47

The strange new word of the Gospel: re-evangelizing in the postmodern world, 165

The struggle of the Gods: a study in Christianity and the African culture, 86

The subversion of Christianity, 50

The teacher, 169

The teaching minister, 179

The ten words that will change a nation: the Ten commandments, 144

The Theology of Christian resistance: a symposium, 165

The theology of the cross and Marx's anthropology: a view from the Caribbean, 124

The Third World and Bernard Lonergan: a tribute to a concerned thinker, 165

The total image: or, Selling Jesus in the modern age, 121

The transformation of culture: Christian social ethics after H. Richard Niebuhr, 145

The transforming vision: shaping a Christian world view, 173

The transition from Shamanism to Russian Orthodoxy in Alaska, 111

The Trinity and culture, 99

The Trinity in a pluralistic age: theological essays on culture and religion, 165

The Trinity in Asian perspective, 93

The universal God: justice, love, and peace in the global village, 178

The Venetian upper clergy in the 16th and early 17th centuries: a study in religious culture, 97

The Venetian upper clergy in the sixteenth and early seventeenth centuries: a study in religious culture, 98

The vitality of the Christian tradition, 166

The way of the (modern) world, or, Why it's tempting to live as if God doesn't exist, 60

The web of text and the web of God: an essay on the third information transformation, 129

The West and Islam: towards a dialogue, 165

The wolf shall dwell with the lamb: a spirituality for leadership in a multicultural community, 93

The Word among us: contextualizing theology for mission today, 166

The word made strange: theology, language, culture, 107

The world is too much with us: The world of the early Christians, 85

The world to come: from Christian past to global future, 61

The world--love it or leave it?, 47

Theological foundations, 46

Theology and aspects of Igbo culture, 103

Theology and lived Christianity, 166

Theology as cultural critique: the achievement of Julian Hartt, 179

Theology in folk culture: the theological significance of Haitian folk religion, 112

Theology in the Philippine setting: a case study in the contextualization of theology, 157

Theology of culture, 167

Theories of culture: a new agenda for theology, 157

Theory and practice of inculturation: an African perspective, 120

Theory of social involvement: a case study in the anthropology of religion, state, and society, 3

Things hidden since the foundation of the world, 62

Things that count: essays moral and theological, 106

Thinking the faith: Christian theology in a North American context, 68

Third World theologies: commonalities and divergences, 166

Through the tempest: theological voyages in a pluralistic culture, 62

Times enmeshed: gender, space, and history among the Duna of Papua New Guinea, 155

Times of the trinity: a proposal for theistic cosmology, 93

To be at home: Christianity, civil religion, and world community, 138

To change the world: Christology and cultural criticism, 139

To live ancient lives: the primitivist dimension in Puritanism, 17

To understand the world, to save the world: the interface between missiology and the social sciences, 156

Tocqueville's civil religion: American Christianity and the prospects for freedom, 85

Tough faith, 122

Toward a contemporary Christianity, 178

Toward a theology of inculturation, 148

Toward an African Christianity: inculturation applied, 74

Towards a mature African Christianity, 103

Towards an African narrative theology, 71

Towards an inculturated local theology in the diocese of Crookston, Minnesota [microform], 181

Towards theory and practice of pastoral counseling in Africa, 12

Transculturation: the cultural factor in translation and other communication tasks, 147

Transforming culture: a challenge for Christian mission, 95

Transforming our days: spirituality, community, and liturgy in a technological culture, 59

Transition and permanence, Chinese history and culture: a festschrift in honor of Dr. Hsiao Kung-ch`üan, 169

Truth and authority in modernity, 114

Truth under fire: a call to Christian thought and action in all of life, 178

Turkey of the Ottomans, 60

Turn back the night, 93

Twelve religions and modern life, 43

Twilight of a great civilization: the drift toward neo-paganism, 73

Two cities, two loves: Christian responsibility in a crumbling culture, 16

Two different worlds: Christian absolutes and the relativism of social science, 60

Two kingdoms: the Church and culture through the ages, 32

U

Uncompleted mission: Christianity and exclusivism, 45

Understanding and practising inculturation, 176

Understanding modern theology, 75

Understanding today's youth culture, 111, 112

Uneasy in Babylon: Southern Baptist conservatives and American culture, 69

Unfamiliar paths: the challenge of recognizing the work of Christ in strange clothing: a case study from France, 14

Unholy devotion: why cults lure Christians, 21

Unity and plurality: mission in the Bible, 94

V

Veiled and silenced: how culture shaped sexist theology, 144

Vernacular Christianity: essays in the social anthropology of religion presented to Godfrey Lienhardt, 171

Versions of deconversion: autobiography and the loss of faith, 9

Violence and miracle in the fourteenth century: private grief and public salvation, 64

Visionary science: a translation of Tillich's, 167

Voices from the margin: interpreting the Bible in the Third World, 171, 172

Voices in the Holy Land, 172

W

Wait for me: rediscovering the joy of purity in romance, 153

Waking from the American dream: growing through your disappointments, 104

Wandering in the wilderness, 12

Wang Yang-ming and Karl Barth: a Confucian-Christian dialogue, 86

We dare to dream: doing theology as Asian women, 174

West Africa: Christ would be an African too, 126

Western civilization and the natives of South Africa, 143

What doth the Lord require of thee?, 184

What ever happened to commitment?, 43

What is Christianity?, 70

What on earth are we doing?: finding our place as Christians in the world, 56

What's God got to do with the American experiment?, 177

When all the gods trembled: Darwinism, Scopes, and American intellectuals, 35

When nations die [sound recording], 14

When nations die: ten warning signs of a culture in crisis, 15

When the empire strikes out: are we repeating the pattern of past civilizations?, 63

When the kings come marching in: Isaiah and the new Jerusalem, 111

When time shall be no more: prophecy belief in modern American culture, 17

When tolerance is no virtue: political correctness, multiculturalism & the future of truth & justice, 59

Where in the world is the church?: a Christian view of culture and your role in it, 76

Where resident aliens live: exercises for Christian practice, 71

Where the nations meet: the church in a multicultural world, 135

Whirled views: tracking today's culture storms, 119

Whitebread Protestants: food and religion in American culture, 141

Who moved my church? : a story about discovering purpose in a changing culture, 113

Who's watching the playpen?, 12

Why America needs religion: secular modernity and its discontents, 94

Why Christianity works, 85

Why is Christianity true? Christian evidences, 112

Why we live in community, 7

Why you can't stay silent: a biblical mandate to shape our culture, 108

Will Evangelicalism survive its own popularity?, 83

Will Western civilization survive: challenging readings for contemporary times, 178

Winning the values war in a changing culture: thirteen distinct values that mark a follower of Jesus Christ, 5

With heart and mind: a personal synthesis of scholarship and devotion, 125

Without help or hindrance: religious identity in American culture, 50, 51

Women and fundamentalism: Islam and Christianity, 61

Women and men in spiritual culture, XIV-XVII centuries: a meeting of South and North, 181

Women and religion in medieval and Renaissance Italy, 181

Women and the New Testament: an analysis of Scripture in light of New Testament era culture, 102

Women caught in the conflict: the culture war between traditionalism and feminism, 66

Women of faith in Victorian culture: reassessing the angel in the house, 181

Women on the move: a Christian perspective on cross-cultural adaptation, 81

Women overseas: a Christian perspective on cross-cultural adaptation, 81

Women's poetry and religion in Victorian England: Jewish identity and Christian culture, 143

Word alive! : learning, loving, and living the Christian faith in the context of modern culture, 145

Word crimes: blasphemy, culture, and literature in nineteenth-century England, 101

World catechism or inculturation?, 182

World order and religion, 182

Worldly amusements: restoring the Lordship of Christ to our entertainment choices, 179

Worldwide perspectives: understanding God's purposes in the world from Genesis to Revelation, 182

Worshipping God as Africans: report on the AFALMA-Namibia Workshop and Festival, Windhoek, 7-12 December 1993, 182

Writings in the philosophy of culture, 168

.

BIBLIOGRAPHY

"Christen und Gewürze": Konfrontation und Interaktion kolonialer und indigener Christentumsvarianten / Klaus Koschorke (Hg.). Published/Created: Göttingen: Vandenhoeck & Ruprecht, c1998. Related Authors: Koschorke, Klaus. Description: 298 p.; 24 cm. ISBN: 3525559607 Notes: Papers presented at a symposium held Feb. 14-16, 1997 in Freising, Germany. Includes bibliographical references. German and English, with summaries in English, German, and Spanish. Subjects: Christianity and culture--History--Indigenous peoples--Religion--Imperialism--Acculturation--Congresses. Series: Studien zur aussereuropäischen Christentumsgeschichte (Asien, Afrika, Lateinamerika); Bd. 1. LC Classification: BR115.C8 C4442 1998

32 articles evaluating inculturation of Christianity in Africa / Teresa Okure ... [et al.]. Published/Created: Kenya: AMECEA Gaba Publications, c1990. Related Authors: Okure, Teresa. Description: xii, 259 p.: ill.; 22 cm. ISBN: 9966836039 Contents: Some pre-and post Vatican II documents -- Biblical, theological, cultural & missiological bases -- Music and dance in Christian worship -- Culture-based Christian art -- Features of African traditional prayer. Notes: Spine Inculturation of christianity in Africa. Includes bibliographical references. Subjects: Christianity and culture--Africa, Sub-Saharan--Papal documents. Christianity and the arts--Christianity--Civilization --Africa, Sub-Saharan. Series: AMECEA Gaba Publications spearhead; 112-114 LC Classification: BR1430 .A15 1990

A Church for all peoples: missionary issues in a world church / edited by Eugene LaVerdiere. Published/Created: Collegeville, Minn.: Liturgical Press, c1993. Related Authors: LaVerdiere, Eugene. Description: 104 p.; 23 cm. ISBN: 0814621414 : Notes: Papers originally presented at a symposium: The Church: salvation and mission, Oct. 1991. Includes bibliographical references and index. Subjects: Catholic Church--Missions--Theory--Christianity and culture--Congresses. LC Classification: BV2160 .C48 1993 Dewey Class No.: 266/.2 20

A free society reader: principles for the new millennium / edited by Michael Novak, William Brailsford, and Cornelius Heesters. Published/Created: Lanham, Md.: Lexington Books, c2000. Related Authors: Novak, Michael. Brailsford, William. Heesters, Cornelius. Description: xix, 414 p.; 24 cm. ISBN: 0739101439 (alk. paper) 0739101447 (pbk.: alk. paper) Notes: Includes bibliographical references and index. Subjects: Catholic Church--Doctrines. Sociology, Christian (Catholic) Economics-- Democracy--Religious aspects--Catholic Church. Christianity and culture. Series: Religion, politics, and society in the new millennium LC Classification: BX1753 .F73 2000 Dewey Class No.: 261 21

A garden of many colours: the report of the Archbishop's Commission on Multicultural Ministry and Mission: presented to the Synod of the Anglican Diocese of Melbourne. Published/Created: Melbourne: Diocesan Registry, Anglican Diocese of Melbourne, 1985. Description: 191 p.: ill.; 21 cm. Notes: "March 1985." Includes bibliographical references. Subjects: Anglican Church of Australia. Anglican Communion--Australia. Christianity and culture. Pluralism (Social sciences)--Australia. Australia--Church history. LC Classification: BX5714 .A64 1985 Dewey Class No.: 283/.94 20

A millennium of Christian culture in Ukraine / [board of editors, Andrew Sorokowski (editor in chief), Rostyslav Hluvko, Daria Darewych]. Published/Created: London: Ukrainian Millenium Committee in Great Britain, 1988. Related Authors: Sorokowski, Andrew. Hluvko, Rostyslav. Darevych, Dariia. Description: 197 p.: ill. (some col.); 31 cm. ISBN: 0951318411 Notes: Includes bibliographies. Subjects: Christianity and the arts--Ukraine. LC Classification: NX663.S65 M55 1988 Dewey Class No.: 700/.1/04 19

A spirituality of Catholic aborigines and the struggle for justice / [editors Joan Hendriks, Gerry Hefferan]. Published/Created: [Kangaroo Point, Brisbane Qld.]: Aborigines & Torres Strait Islander Apostolate, c1993. Related Authors: Hendriks, Joan. Hefferan, Gerry. Description: 128 p.: ill.; 30 cm. ISBN: 0646142909 Notes: Includes bibliographical references (p. 125-126). Subjects: Catholic Church--Australia--Queensland. Australian aborigines--Torres Strait Islanders--Religion. Australian aborigines--Torres Strait Islanders--Land tenure. Land tenure--Religious aspects--Christianity. Liturgical adaptation--Catholic Church. Christianity and culture--Australia--Queensland. Christianity and justice--Catholic Church. Queensland--Church history. LC Classification: BX1686.Q44 S67 1993 Dewey Class No.: 282/.089/9915 21

Aaseng, Rolf E. Reflections in a mission mirror: ancient wisdom from younger churches / by Rolf E. Aaseng. Published/Created: Minneapolis, Minn.: Kirk House Publishers, c1998. Description: 72 p.; 22 cm. ISBN: 1886513074 Notes: Includes bibliographical references. Subjects: Blacks--South Africa--Religion--Social life and customs. Christianity and culture. Missions--Theory. LC Classification: BR1450 .A19 1998 Dewey Class No.: 299/.698 21

Abhishiktananda, Swami, 1910-1973. Hindu-Christian meeting point, within the cave of the heart / Abhishiktananda [i.e. H. Le Saux]. Edition Information: Rev. ed. Published/Created: Delhi: ISPCK, 1976. Description: xiii, 128 p.; 23 cm. Notes: Translation of La rencontre de l'hindouisme et du christianisme. First published in 1969 by Institute of Indian Culture, Bombay. Includes bibliographical references and index. Subjects: Christianity and other religions--Hinduism. Hinduism--Relations--Christianity. LC Classification: BR128.H5 L4313 1976 Dewey Class No.: 261.2

Abrahamic faiths, ethnicity, and ethnic conflicts / edited by Paul Peachey, George F. McLean, John Kromkowski. Published/Created: Washington, D.C.: Council for Research in Values and Philosophy, 1997. Related Authors: Peachey, Paul, 1918- McLean, George F. Kromkowski, John, 1939- Description: p. cm. ISBN: 1565181034 (lib. ed.) 1565181042 (pbk.) Notes: Includes bibliographical references and index. Subjects: Abraham (Biblical patriarch) Ethnicity--Nationalism--Ethnic relations--Religious aspects. Religions--Relations. Judaism. Christianity. Islam. Series: Cultural heritage and contemporary change. Series I, Culture and values; vol. 7 LC Classification: BL65.E75 A37 1997 Dewey Class No.: 291.1/4 21

Adams, Lawrence E., 1953- Going public: Christian responsibility in a divided America / Lawrence E. Adams. Published/Created: Grand Rapids, Mich.:

Brazos Press, c2002. Description: 192 p.: ill.; 23 cm. ISBN: 1587430304 (pbk.) Notes: Includes bibliographical references (p. 181-188) and index. Subjects: Christianity and politics--United States. Christianity and culture--United States. LC Classification: BR526 .A32 2002 Dewey Class No.: 261.7/0973 21

Adappur, Abraham, 1926- Religion and the cultural crisis in India and the West: an ecumenical inquiry / Abraham Adappur; with a foreword by C. Subramaniam. Published/Created: New Delhi: Intercultural Publications, 2000. Description: xxviii, 482 p.; 23 cm. ISBN: 8185574472 Notes: Includes bibliographical references (p. [433]-446) and index. Subjects: Christianity and culture. Christianity--India. Ecumenical movement. Multiculturalism--Religious aspects. India--Religion. LC Classification: BR115.C8+

Adeney, Bernard T., 1948- Strange virtues: ethics in multicultural world / Bernard T. Adeney. Published/Created: Downers Grove, Ill.: InterVarsity Press, c1995. Description: 286 p.; 24 cm. ISBN: 0830818553 (alk. paper) Notes: Includes bibliographical references (p.[259]-281) and index. Subjects: Christianity and culture. Ethics, Comparative. Christian ethics. LC Classification: BR115.C8 A33 1995 Dewey Class No.: 241 20

Adibe, Gregory E. M. The crisis of faith and morality of the Igbo Christians of Nigeria / by Gregory E.M. Adibe. Published/Created: [Onitsha, Nigeria: G. Adibe], 1992. Description: xv, 195 p.; 21 cm. Notes: Includes bibliographical references (p. 177-187) and index. Subjects: Catholic Church--Nigeria. Igbo (African people)--Religion. Christianity and culture. LC Classification: BX1682.N5 A25 1992 Dewey Class No.: 276.69/0825/08996332 21

Adler, Felix, 1851-1933. Creed and deed: a series of discourses. Published/Created: New York, Arno Press, 1972 [c1877] Description: iv, 243 p. 22 cm. ISBN:

0405040512 Contents: Immortality.-- Religion.--The new ideal.--The priest of the ideal.--The form of the new ideal.--The religious conservatism of women.--Our consolations.--Spinoza.--The founder of Christianity.--The anniversary discourse. Appendix: The evolution of Hebrew religion.--Reformed Judaism, I, II, III. Subjects: Religion--Addresses, essays, lectures. Ethics--Addresses, essays, lectures. Ethical culture movement-- Addresses, essays, lectures. LC Classification: BL50 .A33 1972 Dewey Class No.: 200

Africa: the kairos of a synod: Sedos Symposium on Africa, April-May 1994 / edited by Walter von Holzen, Seán Fagan. Published/Created: Rome: Sedos, [1994] Related Authors: Von Holzen, Walter. Fagan, Seán. Description: 183 p.; 21 cm. Notes: English and French. Includes bibliographical references (p. [170]-179). Subjects: Catholic Church--Africa-- Congresses. Christianity and culture-- Congresses. Women in Christianity-- Africa--Congresses. Africa--Religion-- Congresses. LC Classification: BX1675.A1 S43 1994 Dewey Class No.: 282/.6/09049 20

Aigbe, Sunday A., 1957- Theory of social involvement: a case study in the anthropology of religion, state, and society / Sunday A. Aigbe. Published/Created: Lanham: University Press of America, c1993. Description: 266 p.: ill., map; 24 cm. ISBN: 0819188735 (cloth: alk. paper) Notes: Includes bibliographical references (p. [239]-262) and index. Subjects: Assemblies of God--Nigeria. Pentecostal churches--Nigeria. Church and state-- Nigeria--History--20th century. Missions-- Theory. Christianity and culture. Nigeria-- Church history. LC Classification: BX8765.5.A45 N63 1993 Dewey Class No.: 261.8/09669 20

Akaabiam, Terwase H. The proclamation of the good news: a study of Lk 24 in Tiv context / Terwase H. Akaabiam. Published/Created: Frankfurt am Main; New York: P. Lang, 1999. Description: xi,

184 p.; 21 cm. ISBN: 0820443638 Notes:
Includes bibliographical references (p.
171-184). Subjects: Bible. N.T. Luke
XXIV--Socio-rhetorical criticism. Tiv
(African people)--Religion. Christianity
and culture--Nigeria. Series: Europäische
Hochschulschriften. Reihe XXIII,
Theologie; Bd. 673. LC Classification:
BS2595.2 A38 1999 Dewey Class No.:
226.4/06/0899636 21

Alderson, David, 1968- Mansex fine: religion,
manliness and imperialism in nineteenth-
century British culture / David Alderson.
Published/Created: Manchester, England;
New York: Manchester University Press;
New York: Distributed in the USA by St.
Martin's Press, c1998. Description: ix, 207
p.: ill.; 23 cm. ISBN: 0719052750 Notes:
Includes bibliographical references (p.
171-197) and index. Subjects: Gender
identity--Great Britain--History--19th
century. Sex--Religious aspects--History--
19th century. Masculinity--Religious
aspects--Christianity--History of doctrines-
-mperialism--History--Great Britain--
Religion--Civilization--19th century. LC
Classification: BR759

Amaladoss, M. (Michael), 1936- Becoming
Indian: the process of inculturation /
Michael Amaladoss. Published/Created:
Rome: Centre for Indian and Inter-
Religious Studies and Dharmaram
Publications, Bangalore, 1992.
Description: 114 p.; 23 cm. Notes:
Running The process of inculturation.
"Chavara lectures, no. 1"--T.p. verso.
Includes bibliographical references.
Subjects: Christianity and culture.
Christianity--India. LC Classification:
BR115.C8 A44 1992

Amaladoss, M. (Michael), 1936- Beyond
inculturation: can the many be one? /
Michael Amaladoss. Published/Created:
Delhi: Jointly published by Indian Society
for Promoting Christian Knowledge for
Vidyajyoti Education & Welfare Society,
1998. Related Authors: Vidyajyoti
Education & Welfare Society (Delhi,
India) I.S.P.C.K. (Organization)
Description: xv, 148 p.; 22 cm. ISBN:

8172144377 Summary: Dialog between the
Gospel and culture; with reference to India.
Notes: Includes bibliographical references.
Subjects: Bible--Criticism, interpretation,
etc. Christianity and culture--India.
Christianity--India. LC Classification:
BR115.C8 A445 1998 Dewey Class No.:
261/.0954 21

Amaladoss, M. (Michael), 1936- Making all
things new: dialogue, pluralism, and
evangelization in Asia / Michael
Amaladoss. Published/Created: Maryknoll,
N.Y.: Orbis Books, c1990. Description: x,
203 p.; 24 cm. ISBN: 0883446774 (pbk.) :
Notes: Includes bibliographical references
(p. 189-203). Subjects: Catholic Church--
Missions. Missions--East Asia. Missions--
Theory. Christianity and culture.
Christianity and other religions. East Asia--
Religion. Asia--Religion. LC
Classification: BV2183 .A52 1990 Dewey
Class No.: 261/.0954 20

Ambler, R. A. Global theology: the meaning of
faith in the present world crisis / Rex
Ambler. Published/Created: London: SCM;
Philadelphia: Trinity Press International,
1990. Description: 90 p.; 23 cm. ISBN:
033402434X Notes: Includes
bibliographical references (p. 84-90).
Subjects: Human ecology--Religious
aspects--Christianity. Christianity and
international affairs. Economics--Religious
aspects--Christianity. World politics--
1985-1995. East and West. North and
South. Christianity and culture. LC
Classification: BT695.5 .A46 1990 Dewey
Class No.: 261.8 20

Ambulatio fidei: essays in honor of Otto W.
Heick / Edited by Erich R. W. Scultz.
Published/Created: Waterloo: Waterloo
Lutheran University, 1965. Related
Authors: Heick, Otto William, 1895-
Schultz, Erich R. W., ed. Description: viii,
92 p.: illus., port.; 23 cm. Contents: Otto
W. Heick, a tribute, by J. R. Houser.--On
rereading Cicero's De senectute, by W. E.
Gwatkin, Jr.--The Decalogue in rabbinic
Judaism and early Christianity, by U. S.
Leupold.--The Holy Spirit in the church,
by O. P. Kretzmann.--An amendment to

Brunner's concept of the humanum, by J. F. Little.--For such a time as this, by D. W. Hay.--The ethics of Samuel Sprecher, by W. P. Allbeck.--Culture and religion, by C. W. Kegley.--Implications of the personalistic era for theological education, by A. J. Siirala.--A bibliography of books, articles, and book reviews by Otto W. Heick (p. 86-92) Notes: Addenda (3 leaves) inserted. Bibliographical footnotes. Subjects: Heick, Otto William, 1895- --Bibliography. Christianity. Festschriften. LC Classification: BR50 .W37 Dewey Class No.: 208

An enduring flame: studies on Latino popular religiosity / edited by Anthony M. Stevens-Arroyo and Ana María Díaz-Stevens. Edition Information: 1st ed. Published/Created: New York: Bildner Center for Western Hemisphere Studies, c1994. Related Authors: Stevens Arroyo, Antonio M. Díaz-Stevens, Ana María, 1942- Description: 219 p.; 24 cm. ISBN: 0929972074 (hbk.) 0929972082 (pbk.) Notes: Includes bibliographical references and index. Subjects: Hispanic Americans--Religious life and customs. Hispanic Americans--Religion. Hispanic Americans--Ethnic identity. Christianity and culture--United States. Religion and sociology--United States. Series: PARAL studies series; v. 1 LC Classification: BR563.H57 E64 1994 Dewey Class No.: 306.6/089/68073 20

Ancient and modern perspectives on the Bible and culture: essays in honor of Hans Dieter Betz / edited by Adela Yarbro Collins. Published/Created: Atlanta, Ga.: Scholars Press, c1998. Related Authors: Betz, Hans Dieter. Collins, Adela Yarbro. Description: xv, 452 p.: port.; 23 cm. ISBN: 0788505211 (cloth: alk. paper) Notes: Essays based on a conference presented at the University of Chicago, Oct. 8-10, 1996. Includes bibliographical references (p. 398-430) and indexes. Subjects: Bible--Socio-rhetorical criticism--Congresses. Religion and culture--Mediterranean Region--History Congresses. Christianity and culture--History--20th century Congresses. Philosophy and religion--Mediterranean Region--History Congresses. Philosophy, Ancient--Congresses. LC Classification: BS521.9 .A53 1998 Dewey Class No.: 220.6/7 21

Anderson, Leith, 1944- Winning the values war in a changing culture: thirteen distinct values that mark a follower of Jesus Christ / Leith Anderson. Published/Created: Minneapolis, Minn.: Bethany House, c1994. Description: 203 p.; 23 cm. ISBN: 1556613407 : Subjects: Christianity--20th century. Christianity and culture. Moral conditions. Christian life. Values. North America--Moral conditions. LC Classification: BR481 .A53 1994 Dewey Class No.: 277.3/0829 20

Andriacco, Dan. Screen saved: peril and promise of media in ministry / Dan Andriacco. Published/Created: Cincinnati, Ohio: St. Anthony Messenger Press, c2000. Description: 153 p.: ill.; 22 cm. ISBN: 0867164182 Notes: Includes bibliographical references (p. 145]-150). Subjects: Christianity and culture--United States. Mass media--Religious aspects--Christianity. Mass media--Influence.

Angrosino, Michael V. Talking about cultural diversity in your church: gifts and challenges / Michael Angrosino. Published/Created: Lanham, Md.: AltaMira Press, c2001. Description: x, 116 p.; 23 cm. ISBN: 0759101809 (alk. paper) 0759101795 (pbk.: alk. paper) Notes: Includes bibliographical references (p. [113]-116). Subjects: Christianity and culture. Multiculturalism--Religious aspects--Christianity--Case studies. LC Classification: BR115.C8 A54 2001 Dewey Class No.: 261.5 21

Annual bibliography of Christianity in India. Published/Created: Bombay: Heras Institute of Indian History and Culture, 1982- Related Authors: Heras Institute of Indian History and Culture. Description: v.; 25 cm. No. 1 (1981)- Current Frequency: Annual Notes: SERBIB/SERLOC merged record Subjects: Christianity--India--Bibliography--Periodicals. LC

Classification: Z7778.I4 A56 BR1155
Dewey Class No.: 016.2 19

Anshen, Ruth Nanda, ed. Beyond victory /
planned and edited by Ruth Nanda Anshen.
Published/Created: New York: Harcourt,
Brace, [1943] Description: 291 p.; 22 cm.
Contents: Anshen, Ruth N. The rights of
man.--Shotwell, J. T. The nature of peace.-
-Hambro, C. J. World organization.--
MacIver, R. M. The interplay of cultures.--
Toynbee, A. J. Has Christianity a future?--
Montague, W. P. Religion after the war.--
Mead, Margaret, The family in the future.--
Friedrich, C. J. War and government.--
Hansen, Alvin. Economic organization for
peace. Winan, J. G. International labor
organization and furture social policy.--
Karpovich, Michael. Russia in the new
world.--Meiklejohn, Alexander. Education
and the future.--Conant, J. B. Science and
society in the postwar world.--Nehru,
Jawaharlal. The end of imperialism.--
Hamilton, W. H. The end of the political
frontier.--Hu, Shih. Force as an instrument
of law and government.--Emerson, Rupert.
The future role of the former colonial
peoples.--Arnold, Thurman. Free enterprise
and planned organization.--Wallace, H. A.
The people's cause.--Beveridge, W. H.
Freedon in social security.--Anshen, Ruth
N. The nature of man. Subjects:
Reconstruction (1939-1951) International
cooperation. Series: [Science of culture
series, v. 3] LC Classification: D825 .A56

Anshen, Ruth Nanda, ed. Beyond victory,
planned and edited by Ruth Nanda Anshen.
Published/Created: Freeport, N.Y., Books
for Libraries Press [1971, c 1943]
Description: 291 p. 23 cm. ISBN:
0836923030 Contents: The rights of man,
by R. A. Anshen.--The nature of peace,
by J. T. Shotwell.--World organization, by
C. J. Hambro.--The interplay of cultures,
by R. M. MacIver.--Has Christianity a
future? By A. J. Toynbee.--Religion after
the war, by W. P. Montague.--The family
in the future, by M. Mead.--War and
government, by C. J. Friedrich.--Economic
organization for peace, by A. Hansen.--
International Labor Organization and
future social policy, by J. G. Winant.--

Russia in the new world, by M.
Karpovich.--Education and the future, by
A. Meiklejohn.--Science and society in the
post-war world, by J. B. Conant.--The end
of imperialism, by J. Nehru.--The end of
the political frontier, by W. H. Hamilton.--
Force as an instrument of law and
government, by Hu Shih.--The future role
of the former colonial peoples, by R.
Emerson.--Free enterprise and planned
organization, by T. Arnold.--The people's
cause, by H. A. Wallace.--Freedom in
social security, by W. H. Beveridge.--The
nature of man, by R. N. Anschen. Notes:
"Originally published as volume III in the
Science and culture series." Subjects:
Reconstruction (1939-1951)--Addresses,
essays, lectures. International cooperation--
Addresses, essays, lectures. LC
Classification: D825 .A56 1971 Dewey
Class No.: 940.531/44

Anthony, Francis-Vincent. Ecclesial praxis of
inculturation: toward an empirical-
theological theory of inculturizing praxis /
Francis Vincent Anthony.
Published/Created: Roma: LAS, c1997.
Description: 342 p.: ill.; 24 cm. ISBN:
882130373X Notes: Includes
bibliographical references (p. [309]-336).
Subjects: Christianity and culture. Series:
Biblioteca di scienze religiose (Libreria
Ateneo salesiano); 136. LC Classification:
BR115.C8 A56 1997

Antisemitic, Zionist, social, and political
pamphlets. Part 2. Published/Created:
1843-1947. Description: 49 items.
Subjects: Antisemitism--Europe.
Antisemitism--United States. Zionism.
Europe--Ethnic relations. United States--
Ethnic relations. Israel--Emigration and
immigration. LC Classification: Collection
Level Cataloging

Apel, Pat. Nine great American myths: ways
we confuse the American dream with the
Christian faith / Pat Apel. Edition
Information: 1st ed. Published/Created:
Brentwood, Tenn.: Wolgemuth & Hyatt,
Publishers, 1991. Description: xi, 279 p.;
23 cm. ISBN: 1561210641 Notes: Includes
bibliographical references and index.

Subjects: National characteristics, American. Christianity--United States. Christianity and culture. Myth. United States--Civilization. United States--History--Religious aspects--Christianity. LC Classification: E169.1 .A577 1991 Dewey Class No.: 261/.0973 20

Aragon, Lorraine V., 1954- Fields of the Lord: animism, Christian minorities, and state development in Indonesia / Lorraine V. Aragon. Published/Created: Honolulu: University of Hawai'i Press, c2000. Description: xii, 383 p.: ill., maps; 24 cm. ISBN: 0824821718 (cloth: alk. paper) 0824823036 (pbk.: alk. paper) Notes: Includes bibliographical references (p. 335-367) and index. Subjects: Christianity and culture--Indonesia--Sulawesi Tengah History--20th century. Sulawesi Tengah (Indonesia)--Church history. Sulawesi Tengah (Indonesia)--Religion--20th century. LC Classification: BR1221.S84 A73 2000 Dewey Class No.: 275.98/4082 21

Arbuckle, Gerald A. Earthing the Gospel: an inculturation handbook for pastoral workers / Gerald A. Arbuckle. Published/Created: Maryknoll, N.Y.: Orbis Books, c1990. Description: 236 p.: ill.; 24 cm. ISBN: 088344643X Notes: Includes bibliographical references(p. [221]-236). Subjects: Christianity and culture. Missions--Theory. Evangelistic work--Philosophy. Ethnology--Religious aspects--Christianity. LC Classification: BR115.C8 A67 1990 Dewey Class No.: 266/.001 20

Ariarajah, S. Wesley. Gospel and culture: an ongoing discussion within the ecumenical movement / S. Wesley Ariarajah. Published/Created: Geneva: WCC Publications, c1994. Related Authors: World Council of Churches. Description: xv, 50 p.; 21 cm. ISBN: 282541140X Notes: Includes bibliographical references. Subjects: Christianity and culture. Ecumenical movement. Series: Gospel and cultures pamphlet; 1 LC Classification: BR115.C8 A68 1994 Dewey Class No.: 261 20

Armerding, Hudson T. Christianity and the world of thought, edited by Hudson T. Armerding. Contributors: Beatrice Batson [and others] Published/Created: Chicago, Moody Press [1968] Related Authors: Batson, E. Beatrice. Description: 350 p. 24 cm. Notes: Includes bibliographies. Subjects: Christianity and culture. LC Classification: BR115.C8 A7 Dewey Class No.: 261

Arnold, Eberhard, 1883-1935. Why we live in community / Eberhard Arnold; with two interpretive talks by Thomas Merton; foreword by Basil Pennington. Edition Information: 3rd English ed. Published/Created: New York: Plough Pub. House, 1995. Related Authors: Merton, Thomas, 1915-1968. Description: xv, 73 p.; 18 cm. ISBN: 0874860687 (pbk.) Notes: "Why we live in community is a translation of Warum wir in Gemeinschaft leben, an essay published in Eberhard Arnold's journal Die Wegwarte I:10/11 (October/November 1925) and again in III:8/9 (May/June 1927), in Sannerz, Germany"--T.p. verso. Includes bibliographical references. Subjects: Hutterian Brethren--Doctrines. Christian communities. Christianity and culture. Christianity and politics. Nonviolence--Religious aspects--Christianity. LC Classification: BX8129.B65 A74 1995 Dewey Class No.: 289.7/3 20

Arthur, C. J. (Christopher John), 1940-. The globalization of communications: some religious implications / Chris Arthur. Edition Information: [1st ed.] Published/Created: Geneva, Switzerland: WCC Publications; London: World Association for Christian Communication, c1998. Related Authors: World Council of Churches. World Association for Christian Communication. Description: 69 p.; 21 cm. ISBN: 2825412880 (pbk.) Contents: Physics and metaphysics of globalization -- Globalization defined -- Global village? world civilization? information revolution? -- A turning point in human history -- Religion in an era of globalization -- The suffering of strangers -- Dealing with a "pollution of information" -- A positive perspective on religious diversity -- Some questions of religious identity -- The world of the "image junkie" -- The power of zero -- Challenges facing religious communications, some questions for discussion -- Profile of the World Association for Christian Communication. Notes: Includes bibliographical references. Subjects: Religion and culture. Christianity and culture. Information technology--Religious aspects. LC Classification: IN PROCESS (COPIED) (lccopycat)

Arts, entertainment & Christian values: probing the headlines that impact your family / Jerry Solomon, general editor. Published/Created: Grand Rapids, MI: Kregel Publications, c2000. Related Authors: Solomon, Jerry, pastor. Description: 191 p.; 22 cm. ISBN: 0825420326 Notes: Includes bibliographical references (p. [185]-191). Subjects: Mass media--Religious aspects--Christianity. Christianity and culture. LC Classification: P94 .A77 2000 Dewey Class No.: 261.5/2 21

Asher, Kenneth George. T.S. Eliot and ideology / Kenneth Asher. Published/Created: Cambridge [England]; New York, NY, USA: Cambridge University Press, 1995. Description: ix, 196 p.; 24 cm. ISBN: 0521452848 (hardback) Notes: Includes bibliographical references (p. 167-189) and index. Subjects: Eliot, T. S. (Thomas Stearns), 1888-1965 --Political and social views. Eliot, T. S. (Thomas Stearns), 1888-1965 --Religion. Literature and society--England--History--20th century. Christianity and literature. Series: Cambridge studies in American literature and culture; 86 LC Classification: PS3509.L43 Z598 1995 Dewey Class No.: 821/.912 20

Asian theological reflections on suffering and hope / edited by Yap Kim Hao. Published/Created: Singapore: Christian Conference of Asia, 1977. Related Authors: Yap, Kim Hao. Description: 79 p.: ill.; 24 cm. Notes: "MC(P) no. 661/1/77"--Cover. Subjects: Suffering--Religious aspects--Christianity. Hope.

Theology, Doctrinal--East Asia. Series: Asia focus LC Classification: BT732.7 .A85 1977

Aspects of Jewish culture in the Middle Ages: papers of the eighth annual conference of the Center for Medieval and Early Renaissance Studies, State University of New York at Binghamton, 3-5 May, 1974 / edited by Paul E. Szarmach. Published/Created: Albany: State University of New York Press, 1979. Related Authors: Szarmach, Paul E. State University of New York at Binghamton. Center for Medieval and Early Renaissance Studies. Description: xxi, 208 p.: ill.; 23 cm. ISBN: 0873951654 Notes: Includes bibliographical references. Subjects: Jews--History--70-1789--Historiography--Christianity and antisemitism--History--To 1500--Jews--Spain--Judaism and art--Grail--Spain--History--Arab period, 711-1492--Congresses. LC Classification: DS124 .A74 Dewey Class No.: 909/.04/924

Augustine's City of God. Published/Created: Nashville, Tenn.: Broadman & Holman Publishers, c1998. Related Authors: Broadman & Holman Publishers. Description: viii, 102 p.; 21 cm. ISBN: 080549345X Notes: Includes bibliographical references (p. 101-102). Subjects: Augustine, Saint, Bishop of Hippo. De civitate Dei. Kingdom of God. Apologetics. Christianity and culture. Series: Shepherd's notes. Christian classics LC Classification: BR65.A65 A84 1998 Dewey Class No.: 239/.3 21

Azevedo, Marcello de Carvalho. Inculturation and the challenges of modernity / Marcello de Carvalho Azevedo. Published/Created: Rome: Centre "Cultures and Religions," Pontifical Gregorian University, 1982. Jesuits. Description: xii, 63 p.; 25 cm. Notes: Papers from a seminar sponsored by the Jesuits and held in Jerusalem, June 16-21, 1981. Bibliography: p. 57-63. Subjects: Christianity and culture. Series: Inculturation; 1. LC Classification: BR115.C8 A94 1982

Bacon, Leonard, 1802-1881. The American church: a discourse in behalf of the American Home Missionary Society: preached in the cities of New York and Brooklyn, May, 1852 / by Leonard Bacon. New York: Printed for the Society, by Baker, Godwin & Co., 1852. Related Authors: YA Pamphlet Collection (Library of Congress) Description: 23 p.; 24 cm. Subjects: Christianity and culture. LC Classification: YA 12937

Bacon, Samuel Frederick, 1908- An evaluation of the philosophy and pedagogy of ethical culture ... by Samuel Frederick Bacon. M. A. Published/Created: Washington, D.C., The Catholic university of America, 1933. Description: viii, 182 p., 1 l. 23 cm. Notes: Vita. "This examination of the philosophy and the pedagogy of ethical culture [is] from the Catholic standpoint."-p. 167. Thesis (Ph. D.)--Catholic university of America, 1934. Bibliography: p. 169-176. Subjects: Catholic Church--Education. Ethical culture movement. Moral education. Religious education. Christianity and other religions--Ethical culture movement. LC Classification: BJ1581 .B2

Bakare, Sebastian. The drumbeat of life: jubilee in an African context / Sebastian Bakare. Published/Created: Geneva: WCC Publications, c1997. Related Authors: World Council of Churches. Description: ix, 52 p.; 21 cm. ISBN: 2825412295 Subjects: World Council of Churches. Assembly (8th: 1998: Harare, Zimbabwe) Christianity and culture--Christianity--Africa--Religion. Series: Risk book series; no. 80 LC Classification: BR115.C8 B34 1997 Dewey Class No.: 276/.0829 21

Baker, Archibald G. (Archibald Gillies), b. 1875. Christian missions and a new world culture, by Archibald G. Baker. Chicago, New York, Willett, Clark & company, 1934. Description: xiii, 322 p. diagrs. 21 cm. Subjects: Missions. Culture. Christianity and other religions. Psychology, Religious. LC Classification: BV2063 .B3 Dewey Class No.: 266

Bakke, Corean, 1938- Let the whole world sing: the story behind the music of Lausanne II / Corean Bakke. Published/Created: Chicago: Cornerstone Press Chicago, c1994. Description: xvi, 251 p.: ill.; 23 cm. ISBN: 0940895188 Notes: Includes indexes. Part 2 contains 59 "hymns and praise songs from traditional Western sources and from the non-Western church"--P. [187]; in part melodies and in part close score; various languages. Subjects: International Congress on World Evangelization (2nd: 1989: Manila, Philippines) Church music--Congresses. Hymns--History and criticism--Congresses. Hymns. Ethnicity--Religious aspects--Christianity--Congresses. Christianity and culture--Congresses. LC Classification: ML3001 .B16 1994 Dewey Class No.: 264/.2 20

Baldwin, J. F. The deadliest monster: a Christian introduction to worldviews / J.F. Baldwin. Published/Created: Eagle Creek, Or.: Coffee House, c1998. Description: 272 p.; 23 cm. ISBN: 0966317602 Notes: Includes bibliographical references (p. 255-271). Subjects: Christianity and other religions. Christianity and culture. Ideology--Religious aspects. LC Classification: BR127 B29 1998 Dewey Class No.: 261.2 21

Barbour, John D. Versions of deconversion: autobiography and the loss of faith / John D. Barbour Published/Created: Charlottesville: University Press of Virginia, 1994. Description: 238 p.; 24 cm. ISBN: 0813915465 Notes: Includes bibliographical references (p. [219]-233) and index. Subjects: Ex-church members--Case studies. Apostasy--Case studies. Apostasy--Comparative studies. Autobiography--Religious aspects--Christianity. Autobiography--Religious aspects. Series: Studies in religion and culture (Charlottesville, Va.) LC Classification: BV820 .B37 1994 Dewey Class No.: 280/.092/2 20

Barbour, Reid. Literature and religious culture in seventeenth-century England / Reid Barbour. Published/Created: Cambridge;

New York: Cambridge University Press, 2002. Description: viii, 282 p.; 24 cm. ISBN: 0521006643 Notes: Includes bibliographical references (p. 251-275) and index. Subjects: English literature--Early modern, 1500-1700--History and criticism. Christianity and literature--England--History--17th century. Religion and literature--England--History--17th century. Protestantism and literature--History--17th century. Great Britain--History--Charles I, 1625-1649. England--Church history--17th century. LC Classification: PR438.R45 B37 2001 Dewey Class No.: 820.9/3823 21

Bascom, Tim, 1961- The comfort trap: spiritual dangers of the convenience culture / Tim Bascom. Published/Created: Downers Grove, Ill.: InterVarsity Press, c1993. Description: 163 p.; 21 cm. ISBN: 0830816585 (alk. paper) Notes: Includes bibliographical references (p. [161]-163). Subjects: Bascom, Tim, 1961- Christianity and culture. Christian life. United States--Moral conditions. LC Classification: BR115.C8 B38 1993 Dewey Class No.: 248.4 20

Bassard, Katherine Clay, 1959- Spiritual interrogations: culture, gender, and community in early African American women's writing / Katherine Clay Bassard. Published/Created: Princeton, N.J.: Princeton University Press, c1999. Description: 183 p.; 24 cm. ISBN: 0691016399 (hardcover: alk. paper) 069101647X (pbk.: alk. paper) Notes: Includes bibliographical references (p. [165]-175) and index. Subjects: Wheatley, Phillis, 1753-1784 --Religion. American literature--African American authors--History and criticism. American literature--Women authors--History and criticism. American literature--19th century--History and criticism. Christianity and literature--United States--History. Women and literature--United States--History. Spirituals (Songs)--History and criticism. African American women--Religious life. African American women in literature. Community life in literature. Spiritual life in literature. Religion and literature. Series: Princeton studies in culture/power/history

LC Classification: PS153.N5 B33 1999 Dewey Class No.: 810.9/382 21

Bate, Stuart C. Evangelisation in the South African context / Stuart C. Bate. Published/Created: Rome: Centre "Cultures and Religions," Pontifical Gregorian University, 1991. Description: xiii, 117, [1] p.; 24 cm. ISBN: 8876526358 Notes: Includes bibliographical references (p. 105-[118]). Subjects: Theology, Doctrinal--South Africa. Christianity--South Africa. Christianity and culture. Evangelistic work--South Africa. Series: Inculturation; 12 LC Classification: BT30.S5 B37 1991 Dewey Class No.: 261/.0968 20

Baue, Frederic W., 1946- The spiritual society: what lurks beyond postmodernism? / Frederic W. Baue. Published/Created: Wheaton, Ill.: Crossway Books, 2001. Description: p. cm. ISBN: 1581342535 (pbk.: alk. paper) Notes: Includes bibliographical references and index. Subjects: Christianity and culture. LC Classification: BR115.C8 B385 2001 Dewey Class No.: 261 21

Bauer, Bruno, 1809-1882. Christ and the Caesars: the origin of Christianity from romanized Greek culture / by Bruno Bauer; English translation by Frank E. Schacht. Published/Created: Charleston, SC: A. Davidonis, c1998. Description: 359 p.: ill.; 24 cm. ISBN: 0966997700 Subjects: Church history--Primitive and early church, ca. 30-600. Church and state--History. LC Classification: BR166 .B3813 1998 Dewey Class No.: 270.1 21

Bayer, Charles H. A resurrected church: Christianity after the death of Christendom / Charles H. Bayer. Published/Created: St. Louis, Mo.: Chalice Press, c2001. Description: ix, 181 p.: ill.; 23 cm. ISBN: 0827232233 (pbk.: alk. paper) Notes: Includes bibliographical references (p. 177-181). Subjects: Christianity and culture. LC Classification: BR115.C8 B39 2001 Dewey Class No.: 270.8/3 21

Beatty, Charles, 1715?-1772. The journal of a two months tour; with a view of promoting religion among the frontier inhabitants of Pennsylvania, and of introducing Christianity among the Indians to the westward of the Alegh-geny [sic] Mountains. To which are added, remarks on the language and customs of some particular tribes among the Indians, with a brief account of the various attempts that have been made to civilize and convert them from the first settlement of New England to this day. Published/Created: London, Printed for W. Davenhill and G. Pearch, 1768. Description: 110 p. Notes: Microfilm. Ann Arbor, Mich., University Microfilms, 1962. Subjects: Indians of North America--Missions.Pennsylvania--Description & travel.Ohio--Description & travel. Series: American culture series, 189:2. LC Classification: Microfilm 01291 reel 189, no. 2 E

Beckwith, Sarah, 1959- Christ's body: identity, culture, and society in late medieval writings / Sarah Beckwith. Published/Created: London; New York: Routledge, 1993. Description: xii, 199 p.; 23 cm. Notes: Includes bibliographical references (p. 166-184) and index. Subjects: Jesus Christ--Crucifixion. Body, Human--Religious aspects--Christianity. Christian art and symbolism--Medieval, 500-1500. Devotional literature--History and criticism. LC Classification: BT450 .B39 1993 Dewey Class No.: 248/.094/0902 20

Becoming a Christian: the ecumenical implications of our common baptism / edited by Thomas F. Best & Dagmar Heller. Published/Created: Geneva: WCC Publications, c1999. Related Authors: Best, Thomas F. Heller, Dagmar, 1959- World Council of Churches. Commission on Faith and Order. Description: 106 p.; 22 cm. ISBN: 2825413151 Notes: "Records the reflection and experience of some twenty Christians--liturgists, theologians, church musicians, pastors--who gathered at a Faith and Order consultation held in Faverges, France, in 1997"--Introd. "Bibliography on baptism and its

ecumenical significance": p. [98]-104. Includes bibliographical references. Subjects: Baptism and Christian union. Christianity and culture. Series: Faith and order paper; no. 184

Bediako, Kwame. Christianity in Africa: the renewal of non-Western religion / Kwame Bediako. Published/Created: Edinburgh: Edinburgh University Press; Maryknoll, N.Y.: Orbis Books, c1995. Description: xii, 276 p.; 22 cm. ISBN: 1570750483 Notes: Includes bibliographical references and index. Subjects: Christianity--Africa. Christianity and culture. LC Classification: BR1360 .B39 1995 Dewey Class No.: 276 20

Belief and culture in the Middle Ages: studies presented to Henry Mayr-Harting / edited by Richard Gameson and Henrietta Leyser. Published/Created: Oxford; New York: Oxford University Press, 2001. Related Authors: Mayr-Harting, Henry. Gameson, Richard. Leyser, Henrietta. Description: xvi, 370 p.: ill.; 24 cm. ISBN: 0198208014 Notes: Includes bibliographical references and indexes. Subjects: Christianity and culture--Europe--History--Middle Ages, 600-1500. Europe--Church history--600-1500. LC Classification: BR252 .B45 2001 Dewey Class No.: 274/.03 21

Bell, Dean Phillip, 1967- Sacred communities: Jewish and Christian identities in fifteenth-century Germany / Dean Phillip Bell. Published/Created: Boston: Brill Academic Publishers, 2001. Description: xi, 301 p.: map; 23 cm. ISBN: 0391041029 Notes: Includes bibliographical references (p. 261-283) and index. Subjects: Jews--Germany--History--1096-1800. Christianity and culture--Germany. Social history--Medieval, 500-1500. Germany--Ethnic relations--Social conditions. Series: Studies in Central European histories LC Classification: DS135.G31 B45 2001 Dewey Class No.: 943/.004924 21

Belsey, Catherine. Shakespeare and the loss of Eden: the construction of family values in early modern culture / Catherine Belsey. Published/Created: New Brunswick, NJ:

Rutgers University Press, 1999. Description: xvii, 203 p.: ill.; 22 cm. ISBN: 0813527635 (cloth: alk. paper) Notes: Includes bibliographical references and index. Subjects: Shakespeare, William, 1564-1616 --Criticism and interpretation. Shakespeare, William, 1564-1616 --Political and social views. Family--Religious aspects--Christianity--History of doctrines--16th century--17th century. Domestic drama, English--History and criticism. Loss (Psychology) in literature. Drama--Psychological aspects. Social values in literature. Fall of man in literature. Family in literature. Family in art. LC Classification: PR3069.F35 B45 2000 Dewey Class No.: 822.3/3 21

Benne, Robert. Wandering in the wilderness; Christians and the new culture. Published/Created: Philadelphia, Fortress Press [1972] Description: viii, 115 p. 21 cm. ISBN: 0800601173 (pbk.) Notes: Bibliography: p. 113-115. Subjects: Christianity--20th century. Church renewal. LC Classification: BR121.2 .B383 Dewey Class No.: 262/.001

Benoit, David, 1955- Who's watching the playpen? / David Benoit. Published/Created: Oklahoma City: Hearthstone Pub., c1995. Description: 195 p.: ill.; 21 cm. ISBN: 1575580004 Notes: Includes bibliographical references (p. 191-195). Subjects: Family--Religious aspects--Christianity. New Age movement. Christianity and culture--United States. LC Classification: BV4526.2 .B45 1995 Dewey Class No.: 261/.0973 21

Berdiaev, N¯ikolai Aleksandrovich, 1874-1948. The fate of man in the modern world, by Nicholas Berdyaev ...translated by Donald A. Lowrie. Published/Created: New York, Milwaukee, Morehouse publishing co [c1935] Related Authors: Lowrie, Donald Alexander,tr. Description: 3 p. l., 120 p. 19 cm. Subjects: Civilization--Philosophy. Collectivism. Nationalism. Sociology, Christian. LC Classification: CB425 .B37

Berdiaev, Nikolai Aleksandrovich, 1874-1948. The fate of man in the modern world, by Nicholas Berdyaev ... translated by Donald A. Lowrie. Published/Created: London, Student Christian movement press [1935] Related Authors: Lowrie, Donald Alexander,tr. Description: 131 p. 20 cm. Contents: A judgment on history--the war.--Dehumanization.-- New forces in the world's life.--Culture and Christianity. Subjects: Civilization--Philosophy.Collectivism.Nationalism.Soci ology, Christian. LC Classification: CB425 .B37 1935a

Berger, Peter L. A far glory: the quest for faith in an age of credulity / Peter L. Berger. Edition Information: 1st Anchor Books ed. Published/Created: New York: Anchor Books, 1993. Description: vi, 218 p.; 20 cm. ISBN: 0385469799 (pbk.) : Subjects: Faith. Sociology, Christian. Christianity and culture. LC Classification: BV4637 .B38 1993 Dewey Class No.: 234/.2 20

Berger, Peter L. A far glory: the quest for faith in an age of credulity / Peter L. Berger. Published/Created: New York: Free Press; Toronto: Maxwell Macmillan Canada; New York: Maxwell Macmillan International, c1992. Description: x, 218 p.; 22 cm. ISBN: 0029029309 : Subjects: Faith. Sociology, Christian. Christianity and culture. LC Classification: BV4637 .B38 1992 Dewey Class No.: 234/.2 20

Berinyuu, Abraham Adu. Pastoral care to the sick in Africa: an approach to transcultural pastoral theology / Abraham Adu Frankfurt am Main; New York: P. Lang, c1988. Description: xi, 136 p.; 21 cm. ISBN: 3820416609 Notes: Bibliography: p. 132-136. Subjects: Church work with the sick--Africa, Sub-Saharan. Christianity and culture. Christianity and other religions--African. Africa, Sub-Saharan--Religion. Series: Studien zur interkulturellen Geschichte des Christentums; Bd. 51. LC Classification: BV4335 .B435 1988 Dewey Class No.: 259/.4/096 19

Berinyuu, Abraham Adu. Towards theory and practice of pastoral counseling in Africa /

Abraham Adu Berinyuu. Published/Created: Frankfurt am Main; New York: P. Lang, c1989. Description: vii, 140 p.; 21 cm. ISBN: 363142146X Notes: Includes bibliographical references (p. 136-140). Subjects: Pastoral counseling--Psychotherapy--Religion and culture-- Psychoanalysis and culture-- Africa, Sub-Saharan. Psychotherapy-- Religious aspects--Christianity. Series: Europäische Hochschulschriften. Reihe XXVII, Asiatische und afrikanische Studien; Bd. 15. LC Classification: BV4012.2 .B37 1989 Dewey Class No.: 253.5/096 20

Berthrong, John H., 1946- All under heaven: transforming paradigms in Confucian-Christian dialogue / John H. Berthrong. Published/Created: Albany: State University of New York Press, c1994. Description: viii, 273 p.; 24 cm. ISBN: 079141857X (alk. paper) 0791418588 (pbk.: alk. paper) Notes: Includes bibliographical references (p. 235-260) and index. Subjects: Christianity and other religions--Confucianism. Confucianism--Relations--Christianity. Christianity--Philosophy. Philosophy, Confucian. Neo-Confucianism. Series: SUNY series in Chinese philosophy and culture LC Classification: BR128.C43 B46 1994 Dewey Class No.: 261.2/9512 20

Bevans, Stephen B., 1944- Models of contextual theology / Stephen B. Bevans. Edition Information: Rev. and expanded ed. Published/Created: Maryknoll, NY: Orbis Books, 2002. Description: p. cm. ISBN: 1570754381 (pbk.) Notes: Includes bibliographical references and index. Subjects: Theology--Methodology. Christianity and culture. Series: Faith and cultures series LC Classification: BR118 .B44 2002 Dewey Class No.: 230/.01 21

Bevans, Stephen B., 1944- Models of contextual theology / Stephen B. Bevans. Published/Created: Maryknoll, N.Y.: Orbis Books, c1992. Description: xiv, 146 p.; 24 cm. ISBN: 0883448149 (pbk.) : Notes: Includes bibliographical references (p. 113-139) and index. Subjects: Theology--

Methodology. Christianity and culture. Series: Faith and cultures series LC Classification: BR118 .B44 1992 Dewey Class No.: 230/.01 20

Beyond theological tourism: mentoring as a grassroots approach to theological education / edited by Susan B. Thistlethwaite, George F. Cairns. Published/Created: Maryknoll, N.Y.: Orbis Books, c1994. Related Authors: Thistlethwaite, Susan Brooks, 1948- Cairns, George F. Description: viii, 174 p.: ill.; 24 cm. ISBN: 088344965X (pbk.) : Notes: Includes bibliographical references (p. 167-174). Subjects: Chicago Theological Seminary. Theology--Study and teaching--Illinois--Chicago. Mentoring in church work--Illinois--Chicago. Christianity and culture. Man (Theology) LC Classification: BV4070.C489 B48 1994 Dewey Class No.: 207/.1/1 20

Bible map. Published/Created: [Jerusalem?]: Carta, [1979?] Description: 18 maps: col.; 91 x 65 cm. or smaller, on sheets 68 x 99 cm. and 99 x 68 cm., folded to 34 x 25 cm. Scale Information: Scales differ. Partial Contents: No. 10. Palestine in the time of the Apocrypha -- No. 11. Jesus in his land -- No. 12. Jesus in Galilee -- No. 13. The journeys of the Apostles -- No. 14. The spread of the early church -- No. 15. The growth of Christianity -- No. 16. Palestine in the time of the Old Testament -- No. 17. Palestine in the time of the New Testament -- No. 18. Chronological table [not a map]. Notes: Relief shown by shading. Relief also shown by gradient tints on some maps. In lower left corner of each map: [Copyright] Carta. Includes ill. Some maps include text and 1 or 2 insets (some of Jerusalem). Subjects: Bible--Geography--Maps. Palestine--History--To 70 A.D.--Maps. Middle East--History--To 622--Maps. Mediterranean Region--History--Maps. Rome--History--Empire, 30 B.C.-284 A.D.--Maps. Greece--History--To 146 B.C.--Maps. Jerusalem--History--Maps. LC Classification: G7480 svar .K28 Geographic Class No.: 7480 7501 7421 5672 M4 6701 6811 7504 J4

Biblical interpretation and the church: text and context / edited by D.A. Carson. Published/Created: Grand Rapids, Mich.: Published on behalf of the World Evangelical Fellowship by Baker Book House; Carlisle, UK: Paternoster Press, 1993. Related Authors: Carson, D. A. World Evangelical Fellowship. Description: 240 p.; 23 cm. ISBN: 0801025281 (pbk.) 0853643806 (cover) Notes: Originally published: Exeter: Paternoster Press, c1984. Includes bibliographical references and indexes. Subjects: Bible--Hermeneutics. Church. Christianity and culture. LC Classification: BS476 .B495 1993 Dewey Class No.: 220.6/01 20

Biblical interpretation and the Church: the problem of contextualization / edited by D.A. Carson. Published/Created: Nashville: T. Nelson Publishers, 1985, c1984. Related Authors: Carson, D. A. Description: 240 p.; 22 cm. ISBN: 0840775016 (pbk.) : Contents: A sketch of the factors determining current hermeneutical debate in cross-cultural contexts / D.A. Carson -- The Church and the kingdom of God / R.T. France -- The Church in the Gospel of Matthew / Gerhard Maier -- Interpreting the biblical models of the Church / Edmund P. Clowney -- Principalities and powers / Peter T. O'Brien -- The Church in African Theology / Tite Tiénou -- The Church in the liberation theology of Gutiérrez / Emilio A. Nuñez -- Social justice / Russell P. Shedd. Notes: Originally published: Exeter: Paternoster Press, c1984. Includes indexes. Bibliography: p. 225-233. Subjects: Bible--Hermeneutics. Church. Christianity and culture. LC Classification: BS476 .B495 1985 Dewey Class No.: 220.6/01 19

Binion, Rudolph, 1927- After Christianity: Christian survivals in post-Christian culture / Rudolph Binion. Published/Created: Durango, Colo.: Logbridge-Rhodes, c1986. Description: 136 p.; 24 cm. ISBN: 0937406414: 0937406406 (pbk.): 0937406422 (lim. ed.) : Notes: Includes bibliographies and index.

Subjects: Future life--Christianity--History of doctrines. Sin, Original--History of doctrines. Truth (Christian theology)--History of doctrines. Secularization (Theology)--History of doctrines. Civilization, Modern. Religion in literature. Literature, Modern--History and criticism. LC Classification: BT902 .B56 1986 Dewey Class No.: 209/.04 19

Bjork, David E. Unfamiliar paths: the challenge of recognizing the work of Christ in strange clothing: a case study from France / David E. Bjork. Published/Created: Pasadena, CA: William Carey Library, c1997. Description: xix, 172 p.: ill.; 22 cm. ISBN: 0878082786 Notes: Includes bibliographical references (p. 159-166) and indexes. Subjects: Missions--Theory--France--Case studies. Christianity and culture. France--Church history--1945- LC Classification: BV2063 .B53 1997 Dewey Class No.: 266/.00944 21

Black and Catholic: the challenge and gift of black folk: contributions of African American experience and thought to Catholic theology / Jamie T. Phelps, editor. Published/Created: Milwaukee, Wis.: Marquette University Press, [1997]. Related Authors: Phelps, Jamie T. (Jamie Therese), 1941- Description: 183 p.: ill.; 22 cm. ISBN: 0874626293 (pbk.) Notes: Includes bibliographical references and index. Subjects: Catholic Church--United States--Doctrines. Afro-American Catholics. Afro-Americans--Religion. Christianity and culture--United States. United States--Church history. Series: Marquette studies in theology; #5 LC Classification: BX1407.N4 B56 1997 Dewey Class No.: 282/.73/08996073 21

Black, Jim Nelson. When nations die [sound recording] / Jim Nelson Black. Wheaton, IL: Tyndale House Publishers, 1994. Description: 2 sound cassettes (ca. 180 min.): analog, Dolby processed. ISBN: 0842374337 : Summary: Jim Black deftly illustrates ten key problems facing America today and uses striking cross-cultural examples to show that every great civilization--from the ancient Greeks and

Romans to the Soviet Union--has faced the same problems. Notes: Subtitle on container: America on the brink: ten warning signs of a culture in crisis. Cast: Narrated by the author. Subjects: History--Religious aspects--Christianity. Christianity and culture. Civilization--Philosophy. Civilization, Modern--20th century. United States--Moral conditions. LC Classification: RZA 4036

Black, Jim Nelson. When nations die: ten warning signs of a culture in crisis / Jim Nelson Black. Published/Created: Wheaton, Ill.: Tyndale House, c1994. Description: xx, 280 p.; 24 cm. ISBN: 0842380051 : Notes: Includes bibliographical references (p. 271-276) and index. Subjects: History--Religious aspects--Christianity. Christianity and culture. Civilization--Philosophy. Civilization, Modern--20th century. United States--Moral conditions. LC Classification: BR115.H5 B47 1994 Dewey Class No.: 261 20

Blamires, Harry. The Christian mind: how should a Christian think? / by Harry Blamires. Published/Created: Ann Arbor, Mich.: Vine Books, 1997. Description: [v], 213 p.; 21 cm. ISBN: 1569550441 (alk. paper) Notes: Originally published: London: S.P.C.K., 1963. Subjects: Christian life--Anglican authors. Secularism. Christianity--20th century. Christianity and culture. LC Classification: BV4501.2 .B5558 1997 Dewey Class No.: 230 21

Blamires, Harry. The post-Christian mind: exposing its destructive agenda / Harry Blamires. Published/Created: Ann Arbor, Mich.: Vine Books, c1999. Description: 209 p.; 21 cm. ISBN: 1569551421 (alk. paper) Subjects: Christianity and culture. Christian life--Anglican authors. LC Classification: BR115.C8 B495 1999 Dewey Class No.: 239/.7 21

Bleeker, Claas Jouco, 1898- Christ in modern Athens; the confrontation of Christianity with modern culture and the non-Christian religions, by C. J. Bleeker.

Published/Created: Leiden: E.J.Brill, 1965. Description: xii, 152 p.; 21 cm. Notes: Bibliographical footnotes. Subjects: Christianity and other religions. Christianity--20th century. LC Classification: BR127 .B57

Blincoe, Robert. Ethnic realities and the church: lessons from Kurdistan: a history of mission work, 1668-1990 / Robert Blincoe; foreword by Ralph D. Winter. Published/Created: Pasadena, Calif.: Presbyterian Center for Mission Studies, c1998. Description: 265 p.: ill., 1 map; 21 cm. ISBN: 0965253325 Notes: Includes bibliographical references (p. 247-255) and index. Subjects: Presbyterian Church--Missions--Kurdistan--History. Christianity and culture--Kurdistan. Kurdistan--Ethnic relations. LC Classification: BV3173.K87 B58 1998 Dewey Class No.: 266/.515667 21

Blodgett, Jan, 1954- Protestant evangelical literary culture and contemporary society / Jan Blodgett. Published/Created: Westport, Conn.: Greenwood Press, 1997. Description: x, 181 p.; 24 cm. ISBN: 0313303959 (alk. paper) Notes: Includes bibliographical references (p. [163]-175) and index. Subjects: Christian fiction, American--History and criticism. Popular literature--Publishing--United States--History 20th century. Christian literature--Publishing--United States--History 20th century. Christianity and literature--United States--History--20th century. Literature and society--United States--History--20th century. American fiction--Protestant authors--History and criticism. American fiction--20th century--History and criticism. Evangelicalism--United States--History--20th century. Protestantism and literature. Evangelicalism in literature. Literary form. Series: Contributions to the study of religion, 0196-7053; no. 51 LC Classification: PS374.C48 B58 1997 Dewey Class No.: 813/.509382 21

Blount, Brian K., 1955- Cultural interpretation: reorienting New Testament criticism / Brian K. Blount. Published/Created: Minneapolis: Fortress Press, c1995.

Description: x, 222 p.: ill.; 22 cm. ISBN: 0800628594 (alk. paper) Notes: Includes bibliographical references (p. 213-217) and indexes. Subjects: Jesus Christ--Trial. Bible. N.T.--Criticism, interpretation, etc.--History 20th century. Bible. N.T.--Hermeneutics. Bible. N.T.--Social scientific criticism. Bible. N.T. Mark XIV, 53-65--Criticism, interpretation, etc. Sociolinguistics. Christianity and culture. LC Classification: BS2361.2 .B56 1995 Dewey Class No.: 225.6/09/04 20

Blumhofer, Edith Waldvogel. Restoring the faith: the Assemblies of God, pentecostalism, and American culture / Edith L. Blumhofer. Published/Created: Urbana: University of Illinois Press, c1993. Description: x, 281 p., [10] p. of plates: ill.; 23 cm. ISBN: 0252016483 0252062817 (pbk.: acid-free paper)) Notes: Includes bibliographical references (p. [275]) and index. Subjects: Assemblies of God--United States--History. Pentecostalism--United States--History. Popular culture--Religious aspects--Christianity. Popular culture--United States--History--20th century. United States--Church history--20th century. LC Classification: BX8765.5.A4 B59 1993 Dewey Class No.: 289.9/4 20

Boa, Kenneth. An unchanging faith in a changing world: understanding and responding to critical issues that Christians face today / Kenneth D. Boa and Robert M. Bowman, Jr. Published/Created: Nashville: Oliver Nelson, c1997. Related Authors: Bowman, Robert M. Description: xii, 404 p.; 23 cm. ISBN: 0785273522 Notes: Includes bibliographical references (p. [345]-388) and indexes. Subjects: Christianity and culture--Theology, Doctrinal--Evangelicalism--United States. LC Classification: BR115.C8 B52 1997 Dewey Class No.: 261 21

Boesak, W., 1948- God's wrathful children: political oppression and Christian ethics / Willa Boesak. Published/Created: Grand Rapids, Mich.: William B. Eerdmans Pub. Co., c1995. Description: xxi, 264 p.; 23 cm. ISBN: 080280621X (alk. paper)

Notes: Includes bibliographical references (p. 243-264). Subjects: Black theology. Liberation theology. Retribution-- Anger--Revenge--Religious aspects--Christianity. Christianity and politics. Christian ethics--Reformed authors. South Africa--Race relations--Church history. LC Classification: BT82.7 .B64 1995 Dewey Class No.: 230/.089/96 20

Boice, James Montgomery, 1938- Two cities, two loves: Christian responsibility in a crumbling culture / James Montgomery Boice. Published/Created: Downers Grove, Ill.: InterVarsity Press, c1996. Description: 279 p.; 23 cm. ISBN: 0830819878 (alk. paper) Notes: Includes bibliographical references (p. [265]-271) and indexes. Subjects: Augustine, Saint, Bishop of Hippo. De civitate Dei. Christianity and culture--United States. Kingdom of God. United States--Civilization--20th century. United States--Church history--20th century. LC Classification: BR526 .B56 1996 Dewey Class No.: 261/.0973 20

Bonk, Jon, 1945- Missions and money: affluence as a western missionary problem / Jonathan J. Bonk. Published/Created: Maryknoll, N.Y.: Orbis Books, c1991. Description: xxi, 170 p.; 24 cm. ISBN: 0883447185 : Notes: Includes bibliographical references (p. 156-168) and index. Subjects: Missions--Theory. Wealth--Religious aspects--Christianity. Christianity and culture. East and West. Missions. Series: American Society of Missiology series; no. 15 LC Classification: BV2063 .B63 1990 Dewey Class No.: 266/.0231722 20

Bosch, David Jacobus. Believing in the future: toward a missiology of Western culture / David J. Bosch. Edition Information: 1st U.S. ed. Published/Created: Valley Forge, Pa.: Trinity Press International; Leominster Herefordshire, England: Gracewing, 1995. Description: x, 69 p.; 19 cm. ISBN: 1563381176 (Trinity) 0852443331 (Gracewing) Notes: Includes bibliographical references (p. 65-69). Subjects: Missions--Theory. Christianity and culture. Missions--History. Mission of the church. Series: Christian mission and modern culture LC Classification: BV2063 .B648 1995 Dewey Class No.: 266/.001 20

Bottignole, Silvana. Kikuyu traditional culture and Christianity: self examination of an African church / Silvana Bottignole. Edition Information: English ed. Published/Created: Nairobi: Heineman Educational Books, 1984. Description: ix, 233 p.: ill.; 21 cm. Notes: Translation of: Una chiesa africana si interroga. Bibliography: p. 135-143. Subjects: Catholic Church. Diocese of Nyeri (Kenya) Kikuyu (African people)--Religion. Kenya--Church history. LC Classification: BX2740.K4 B6713 1984 Dewey Class No.: 282/.67626 19

Bouma-Prediger, Steven. For the beauty of the earth: a Christian vision for creation care / Steven Bouma-Prediger. Published/Created: Grand Rapids, Mich.: Baker Academic, c2001. Description: 234 p.: ill., maps; 23 cm. ISBN: 0801022983 (pbk.) Notes: Includes bibliographical references (p. 213-226) and indexes. Subjects: Human ecology--Religious aspects--Christianity. Series: Engaging culture LC Classification: BT695.5 .B69 2001 Dewey Class No.: 261.8/362 21

Bowers, Russell H., 1951- Someone or nothing?: Nishitani's religion and nothingness as a foundation for Christian-Buddhist dialogue / Russell H. Bowers, Jr. Published/Created: New York: Peter Lang, c1995. Description: 251 p.; 24 cm. ISBN: 0820428329 (alk. paper) Notes: Includes bibliographical references (p. [213]-244) and index. Subjects: Nishitani, Keiji, 1900- Christianity and other religions--Buddhism. Buddhism--Relations--Christianity. Religion--Philosophy. Series: Asian thought and culture; vol. 27 LC Classification: BR128.B8 B67 1996 Dewey Class No.: 261.2/43 20

Boyd, Jeffrey H. Reclaiming the soul: the search for meaning in a self-centered culture / Jeffrey H. Boyd. Published/Created: Cleveland, Ohio: Pilgrim Press, 1996. Description: xxv, 159

p.; 23 cm. ISBN: 0829810803 (pbk.: alk. paper) Notes: Includes bibliographical references (p. 137-153) and index. Subjects: Soul. Psychiatry and religion. Christianity--Psychology. LC Classification: BT741.2 .B683 1996 Dewey Class No.: 233/.5 20

Boyer, Paul S. When time shall be no more: prophecy belief in modern American culture / Paul Boyer. Published/Created: Cambridge, Mass.: Belknap Press of Harvard University Press, 1992. Description: xiv, 468 p., [16] p. of plates: ill., map; 25 cm. ISBN: 067495128X (alk. paper) : Notes: Includes bibliographical references (p. [341]-444) and index. Subjects: Bible--Prophecies. Millennialism--United States. Twentieth century--Forecasts. Prophecy (Christianity) United States--Religion--1945- United States--Religious life and customs. Series: Studies in cultural history LC Classification: BR526 .B58 1992 Dewey Class No.: 231.7/45/0973 20

Bozeman, Theodore Dwight, 1942- To live ancient lives: the primitivist dimension in Puritanism / Theodore Dwight Bozeman. Published/Created: Chapel Hill: Published for the Institute of Early American History and Culture, Williamsburg, Virginia, by the University of North Carolina Press, c1988. Related Authors: Institute of Early American History and Culture (Williamsburg, Va.) Description: x, 413 p.; 24 cm. ISBN: 0807817856 (alk. paper) Notes: Includes index. Bibliography: p. [369]-401. Subjects: Puritans--New England. Primitivism--Religious aspects--Christianity. New England--Church history. Massachusetts--Church history. LC Classification: F7 .B75 1988 Dewey Class No.: 974/.02 19

Bradley, Terris Wade, 1934- Meadows of howling, or, Abortion, feminism, and the culture of death / Terris Wade Bradley. Published/Created: London Miami: Minerva, 2000. Description: 180 p.; 20 cm. ISBN: 0754113620 Notes: Abortion, feminism and the culture of death. Subjects: Abortion--Religious aspects--

Christianity. Feminism--Religious aspects-
-Christianity. Family--Religious aspects--
Christianity. Pro-life movement--United
States. Pro-choice movement--United
States. Misogyny--Moral and ethical
aspects. LC Classification: HQ767.25 .B73
2000

Bradshaw, Bruce. Bridging the gap / Bruce
Bradshaw; foreword by Paul G. Hiebert.
Published/Created: Monrovia, Calif.:
MARC, c1993. Description: vi, 183 p.: ill.;
24 cm. ISBN: 0912552840 Notes: Includes
bibliographical references (p. 177-183).
Subjects: Mission of the church. Holism.
Church and the world. Christianity and
culture. Missions. Series: Innovations in
mission; 5th LC Classification: BV601.8
.B69 1993 Dewey Class No.: 266/.001 20

Bradshaw, Bruce. Change across cultures: a
narrative approach to social transformation
/ Bruce Bradshaw. Published/Created:
Grand Rapids, Mich.: Baker Academic,
2001. Description: p. cm. ISBN:
0801022894 (pbk.) Notes: Includes
bibliographical references and index.
Subjects: Social change. Discourse
analysis, Narrative. Christianity and
culture. LC Classification: HM831 .B72
2001 Dewey Class No.: 303.4 21

Brady, Veronica. The future people:
Christianity, modern culture and the future
[by] Veronica Brady. Published/Created:
Melbourne, Spectrum, 1971. Description:
161 p. 22 cm. ISBN: 0909837104 Notes:
Includes bibliographical references.
Subjects: Christianity and culture.
Christianity--20th century. LC
Classification: BR115.C8 B7 Dewey Class
No.: 248/.48/2

Bramadat, Paul A. The church on the world's
turf: an evangelical Christian group at a
secular university / Paul A. Bramadat.
Published/Created: Oxford; New York:
Oxford University Press, 2000.
Description: viii, 205 p.; 24 cm. ISBN:
0195134990 (alk. paper) Notes: Includes
bibliographical references (p. 183-199) and
index. Subjects: Inter-Varsity Christian
Fellowship. Christian college students--

Religious life-- Christianity and culture--
Ontario Hamilton. Series: Religion in
America series (Oxford University Press)
LC Classification: BV970.I6 B73 2000
Dewey Class No.: 306.6/6761/0971352 21

Bravman, Bill. Making ethnic ways:
communities and their transformations in
Taita, Kenya, 1800-1950 / Bill Bravman.
Published/Created: Portsmouth, NH:
Heinemann, c1998. Description: xiv, 283
p.; 25 cm. ISBN: 0325001057 (alk. paper)
0325001049 (pbk.: alk. paper) Notes:
Includes bibliographical references (p.
259-278) and index. Subjects: Taita
(African people)--Ethnic identity—
History--Religion. Ethnicity--Christianity
and culture--Community life--Kenya--
Taita Hills. Taita Hills (Kenya)--Social
conditions--Ethnic relations. Series: Social
history of Africa, 1099-8098 LC
Classification: DT433.545.T3 B73 1998
Dewey Class No.: 305.8/0096762 21

Breese, Dave, 1926- Culture, Christianity & the
Cross / Dave Breese. Published/Created:
Colton, Calif.: World Prophetic Ministry,
c1998. Description: 32 p.; 21 cm. LC
Classification: MLCS 99/3597 (B)

Brekus, Catherine A. Strangers & pilgrims:
female preaching in America, 1740-1845 /
Catherine A. Brekus. Chapel Hill, NC:
University of North Carolina Press, c1998.
Description: x, 466 p. ISBN: 0807824410
(cloth: alk. paper) 0807847453 (pbk.: alk.
paper) Notes: Papers presented at several
seminars and conferences. Includes
bibliographical references P. [425]-452)
and index. Subjects: Preaching--United
States--History--18th century--19th
century. Sermons, American--Women
authors--History and criticism. Women in
Christianity--United States--History--18th
century--19th century. United States--
Church history--18th century--19th
century. Series: Gender & American
culture. LC Classification: BV4208.U6
B74 1998 Dewey Class No.:
251/.0082/0973 21

Brent, Allen. Cultural episcopacy and
ecumenism: representative ministry in

church history from the Age of Ignatius of Antioch to the Reformation, with special reference to contemporary ecumenism / by Allen Brent. Published/Created: Leiden; New York: E.J. Brill, 1992. Description: xiv, 250 p.; 25 cm. ISBN: 9004094326 (alk. paper) Notes: Includes bibliographical references (p. [217]-228) and indexes. Subjects: Indigenous church administration--Church polity--History of doctrines. Bishops--Appointment, call, and election--History. Anglican Communion--Missions. Episcopacy and Christian union. Christianity and culture. Series: Studies in Christian mission, 0924-9389; v. 6 LC Classification: BV2082.I5 B74 1992 Dewey Class No.: 262/.12/09 20

Bria, Ion. Romania: orthodox identity at a crossroads of Europe / Ion Bria. Published/Created: Geneva, Switzerland: WCC Publications, c1995. Description: ix, 54 p.; 21 cm. ISBN: 2825411752 Notes: Includes bibliographical references. Subjects: Biserica Ortodoxa Româna. Orthodox Eastern Church--Romania. Christianity and culture. Romania--Church history. Series: Gospel and cultures pamphlet; 3 LC Classification: BX695 .B75 1995 Dewey Class No.: 281.9/498 21

Bridging the schism: Christian divisions and culture wars: a collection of papers presented at the Lord Byron Foundation's fourth annual conference held in Chicago in May 1998. London, England; Aiken, S.C.: Lord Byron Foundation for Balkan Studies, c1999. Description: 89 p.; 28 cm. ISBN: 1892478021 Notes: Includes bibliographical references. Subjects: Orthodox Eastern Church--Christianity and culture--Eastern question (Balkan)--Europe, Eastern--Church history--United States--Foreign relations--Congresses. LC Classification: BX215

Briner, Bob. Lambs among wolves / Bob Briner; foreword by Michael W. Smith. Published/Created: Grand Rapids, Mich.: Zondervan Pub. House, c1995. Description: 156 p.: ill.; 21 cm. ISBN: 0310488109 (hardcover: acidd-free paper) Subjects: Christianity and the arts--United

States. Christianity and culture. Christian biography-- Evangelicalism--United States--Moral conditions--Church history--20th century. LC Classification: BR115.A8 B75 1995 Dewey Class No.: 261.5/7 20

Briner, Bob. Roaring lambs: a gentle plan to radically change our world / Bob Briner. Published/Created: Grand Rapids, Mich.: Zondervan Pub. House, c1993. Description: 187 p.; 22 cm. ISBN: 0310591104 (hardcover) Subjects: Church and the world. Christian life. Christianity and the arts--United States. Christianity and culture. LC Classification: BR115.W6 B73 1993 Dewey Class No.: 261/.1 20

Briner, Bob. The final roar / Bob Briner. Published/Created: Nashville, Tenn.: Broadman & Holman, c2000. Description: xxviii, 164 p.: ports; 23 cm. ISBN: 0805423613 Notes: Includes bibliographical references (p. 163-164). Subjects: Church and the world. Evangelicalism--United States. Christianity and culture. LC Classification: BR115.W6 B72 2000 Dewey Class No.: 261/.0973 21

Brinsmead, Robert D. The spirit of Christ and the spirit of fundamentalism [sound recording] / R.D. Brinsmead. Published/Created: Fallbrook, CA: Verdict Publications, p1985. Description: 1 sound cassette: analog. Summary: Presents a lecture by Robert D. Brinsmead concerning religious fundamentalism and its effects on society and culture. Subjects: Christianity. Religious fundamentalism. Series: Verdict audio report; no. 10 LC Classification: RYC 1436

Brosnan, Declan, 1929- African parables: thoughts for Sunday readings (cycle A) / Declan Brosnan. Published/Created: Tamale, Ghana: Tamale Institute of Cross Cultural Studies, 1988. Related Authors: Tamale Institute of Cross Cultural Studies. Description: vi, 63 p.; 23 cm. Notes: Cover title. Subjects: Parables. Homiletical illustrations. Preaching--Africa. Storytelling--Religious aspects--Christianity. Storytelling--Africa. Series: Culture and ministry series; no. 1.

Occasional papers (Tamale Institute of Cross Cultural Studies) LC Classification: ACQUISITION IN PROCESS (COPIED)

Brown, Delwin, 1935- Boundaries of our habitations: tradition and theological construction / Delwin Brown. Albany, N.Y.: State University of New York Press, c1994. Description: xii, 215 p.; 23 cm. ISBN: 0791419657 0791419665 (pbk.) Notes: Includes bibliographical references (p. 151-212) and index. Subjects: Tradition (Theology) Hermeneutics--Theology--Methodology. Postmodernism--Religious aspects--Christianity. Christianity and culture. Series: SUNY series in religious studies LC Classification: BT90 .B76 1994 Dewey Class No.: 230/.01 20

Brown, Neil. Christians in a pluralist society / Neil Brown. Published/Created: Manly, N.S.W., Australia: Catholic Institute of Sydney, 1986. Description: 145 p.; 20 cm. ISBN: 0908224117 Notes: Includes bibliographical references and index. Subjects: Christianity and politics. Religious pluralism--Christianity. Pluralism (Social sciences) Liberalism. Social ethics. Christian ethics--Catholic authors. Series: Faith and culture; 12. LC Classification: BR115.P7 B694 1956 Dewey Class No.: 261.7 20

Brown, Peter Robert Lamont. Augustine and sexuality: protocol of the forty sixth colloquy, 22 May 1983 / Peter Brown; Mary Ann Donovan, editor. Published/Created: Berkeley, Calif.: Center for Hermeneutical Studies in Hellenistic and Modern Culture, c1983. Related Authors: Donovan, Mary Ann. Description: 41 p.; 21 cm. ISBN: 0892420359 : Notes: Includes bibliographical references. Subjects: Augustine, Saint, Bishop of Hippo--Sex--Religious aspects--Christianity--History of doctrines Early church, ca. 30-600--Congresses. Series: Colloquy (Center for Hermeneutical Studies in Hellenistic and Modern Culture); 46. LC Classification: BT708 .B76 1983 Dewey Class No.: 241/.66 19

Brumbaugh, Thoburn Taylor, 1896- Religious values in Japanese culture [by] T. T. Brumbaugh, S.T.M. Published/Created: Tokyo, Kyo bun kwan (Christian literature society of Japan) 1934. Related Authors: Christian Literature Society of Japan. Description: 2 p. l., viii, 154 p., 1 l. 20 cm. Notes: Bibliography: p. [141]-144; "References": p. [145]-154. Subjects: Christianity and other religions. Japan--Religion. Japan--Civilization. LC Classification: BL2201 .B7 Dewey Class No.: 290.956

Buckley, Francis J. The church in dialogue: culture and traditions / Francis J. Buckley. Published/Created: Lanham, Md.: University Press of America, c2000. Description: 294 p.; 23 cm. ISBN: 0761816755 (pbk.: alk. paper) Notes: Includes bibliographical references and index. Subjects: Catholic Church--Doctrines. Christianity and culture. LC Classification: BX1795.C85 B83 2000 Dewey Class No.: 261 21

Budde, Michael L. The (magic) kingdom of God: Christianity and global culture industries / Michael Budde. Published/Created: Boulder, Colo.: Westview Press, 1997. Description: viii, 177 p.; 24 cm. ISBN: 0813330750 (cloth: alk. paper) Notes: Includes bibliographical references (p. 153-168) and index. Subjects: Catholic Church--Membership. International business enterprises--Religious aspects Christianity. Advertising. Mass media. Marketing. Christianity and culture. Identification (Religion) Evangelistic work. Christian education. Cultural industries. LC Classification: BR115.E3 B83 1997 Dewey Class No.: 261 21

Bujo, Bénézet. African theology in its social context / Bénézet Bujo; translated from the German by John O'Donohue. Published/Created: Maryknoll, N.Y.: Orbis Books, c1992. Description: 143 p.; 21 cm. ISBN: 088344805X Notes: Includes bibliographical references: (p. 131-143). Subjects: Theology, Doctrinal--Africa, Sub-Saharan. Christianity and culture.

Series: Faith and cultures series LC Classification: BT30.A4 B8413 1992 Dewey Class No.: 230/.0967 20

Bujo, Bénézet. The ethical dimension of community: the African model and the dialogue between North and South / Bénézet Bujo. Published/Created: Nairobi, Kenya: Paulines Publications Africa, 1998. Description: 237 p.; 21 cm. ISBN: 9966213368 Notes: Includes bibliographical references (p. [228]-232). Subjects: Social ethics--Africa. Christian ethics--Africa. Christianity and culture--Africa. Africa--Social conditions--Moral and ethical aspects. LC Classification: HN780.Z9 M6313 1998 Dewey Class No.: 303.3/72/096 21

Bukidnon: politics and religion / edited by Alfonso de Guzman II, Esther M. Pacheco. Published/Created: Quezon City: Published for the Institute of Philippine Culture by the Ateneo de Manila, c1973. Related Authors: Guzman, Alfonso de. Pacheco, Esther M. Cullen, Vincent G. Bukidnon Description: xvi, 114 p.: maps; 23 cm. Contents: Cullen, V. G. Bukidnon animism and Christianity.--Biernatzki, W. E. Bukidnon datuship in the upper Pulangi River valley.--Claver, F. F. Dinawat Ogil. Notes: Includes bibliographies. Subjects: Bukidnon (Philippine people) Bukidnon, Philippines--Politics and government. Bukidnon, Philippines--Religion. Series: IPC papers; 11. LC Classification: DS666.B8 B84 Dewey Class No.: 959.9/7

Bulman, Raymond F., 1933- A blueprint for humanity: Paul Tillich's theology of culture / Raymond F. Bulman. Published/Created: Lewisburg: Bucknell University Press, c1981. Description: 248 p.: port.; 22 cm. ISBN: 0838750001 Notes: Includes index. Bibliography: p. 225-236. Subjects: Tillich, Paul, 1886-1965. Christianity and culture. LC Classification: BR115.C8 B84 Dewey Class No.: 230

Burkhart, Louise M., 1958- The slippery earth: Nahua-Christian moral dialogue in sixteenth-century Mexico / Louise M. Burkhart. Published/Created: Tucson:

University of Arizona Press, c1989. Description: xii, 242 p.: ill.; 24 cm. ISBN: 0816510881 (alk. paper) Notes: Includes index. Bibliography: p. 215-233. Subjects: Nahuas--Religion. Nahuas--Missions--History--16th century. Christianity and culture--History. LC Classification: F1219.3.R38 B78 1989 Dewey Class No.: 303.4/8272/046 19

Bush, Harold K. (Harold Karl), 1956- American declarations: rebellion and repentance in American cultural history / Harold K. Bush, Jr. Published/Created: Urbana: University of Illinois Press, c1999. Description: xiii, 224 p.: ill.; 24 cm. ISBN: 0252024281 0252067355 (pbk.) Notes: Includes bibliographical references (p. [187]-217) and index. Subjects: American literature--History and criticism. Christianity and literature--United States--History. National characteristics, American, in literature. Literature and history--United States--History. Puritan movements in literature. Culture conflict in literature. Repentance in literature. Myth in literature. United States--Civilization. LC Classification: PS166 .B87 1999 Dewey Class No.: 810.9/3823 21

Busséll, Harold L. Unholy devotion: why cults lure Christians / Harold L. Bussell; foreword by Ronald Enroth. Published/Created: Grand Rapids, Mich.: Zondervan Pub. House, c1983. Description: 128 p.; 21 cm. ISBN: 0310372518 (pbk.) Notes: Bibliography: p. 127-128. Subjects: Cults. Christian sects. Christianity--20th century. Christianity and culture. LC Classification: BL85 .B93 1983 Dewey Class No.: 280/.09/04 19

Cailliet, Émile, 1894- The Christian approach to culture. Published/Created: Nashville, Abingdon-Cokesbury Press [1953] Description: 288 p. 24 cm. Subjects: Culture. Christianity--Philosophy. LC Classification: BR115.C8 C29 Dewey Class No.: 261

Caird, John, 1820-1898. The fundamental ideas of Christianity, by John Caird. With a memoir by Edward Caird.

Published/Created: Glasgow, J.
MacLehose 1899. Related Authors: Caird,
Edward, 1835-1908. Description: 2 v.
front. (port.) 21 cm. Notes: The Gifford
lectures on natural theology delivered to
the University of Glasgow in sessions
1892-3 and 1895-6. Microfiche (Negative).
Louisville, Ky., Lost Cause Press, 1975. 9
fiches 10.5 x 15 cm. Subjects: Caird, John,
1820-1898. Christianity. Series: [British
culture series; ser.7, no. 9] LC
Classification: BR121 .C25

Caldwell, Patricia. The Puritan conversion
narrative: the beginnings of American
expression / Patricia Caldwell.
Published/Created: Cambridge; New York:
Cambridge University Press, 1983.
Description: x, 210 p.; 24 cm. ISBN:
0521254604 Notes: Includes index.
Bibliography: p. 199-204. Subjects:
Puritans--New England--History--17th
century. American prose literature--
Colonial period, ca. 1600-1775 History and
criticism. Christian literature, American--
Puritan authors--History and criticism.
Spiritual life--Christianity--History of
doctrines--17th century. Conversion--
Christianity--History of doctrines--
Puritans--England--History--Colonies in
literature. United States--Intellectual life--
England--Church history--17th century.
New England--Church history. Series:
Cambridge studies in American literature
and culture LC Classification: BX9354.2
.C34 1983 Dewey Class No.: 248.2/4/0974
19

Calhoun, Arthur W. (Arthur Wallace), 1885-
1979. The cultural concept of Christianity /
by Arthur Wallace Calhoun.
Published/Created: Grand Rapids, Mich.:
Wm. B. Eerdmans Pub. Co., 1950. Related
Authors: Rogers, Bruce, 1870-1957,
former owner. Pforzheimer Bruce Rogers
Collection (Library of Congress)
Description: 155 p.; 23 cm. Notes: "The
type face is Justowriter Centaur, a new
type face designed especially for the
Justowriter by Bruce Rogers"--Colophon.
Subjects: Culture. Civilization, Christian.
LC Classification: BR115.C8 C3

Called to be a faithful church in a plural world.
Section three: Lambeth Conference 1998,
July 18-August 9, Lambeth Palace,
Canterbury, England. Published/Created:
Harrisburg, Pa.: Morehouse Pub., c1999.
Description: viii, 51 p.; 23 cm. ISBN:
081921809X (pbk.) Notes: Includes
bibliographical references. Subjects:
Anglican Communion--Congresses.
Anglican Communion--Doctrines--
Congresses. Religious pluralism--
Christianity--Congresses. Christianity and
culture--Congresses. LC Classification:
BX5021 .L6 1998b Dewey Class No.: 283
21

Carlson, Ron. Comatose Christianity: a wake-
up call for Christians / Ron Carlson.
Published/Created: Nashville, Tenn.:
Christian Communications, c1989.
Description: 162 p.; 22 cm. ISBN:
0892253460 : Notes: Includes
bibliographical references. Subjects:
Christianity and culture. Christianity--20th
century. Secularism. LC Classification:
BR115.C8 C325 1989 Dewey Class No.:
261 20

Carnes, John Robb, 1924- Axiomatics and
dogmatics / John R. Carnes.
Published/Created: New York: Oxford
University Press, 1982. Description: xiv,
127 p.: ill.; 23 cm. ISBN: 0195203771
Notes: Includes indexes. Bibliography: p.
123-124. Subjects: Theology--
Methodology. Axioms. Knowledge,
Theory of (Religion) Language and
languages--Religious aspects--Christianity.
Theology, Doctrinal. Series: Theology and
scientific culture; v. 4 LC Classification:
BR118 .C23 1982 Dewey Class No.: 230
19

Carr, Steven A. Celebrate life: hope for a
culture preoccupied with death / Steven A.
Carr & Franklin A. Meyer. Edition
Information: 1st ed. Published/Created:
Brentwood, Tenn.: Wolgemuth & Hyatt,
1990. Related Authors: Meyer, Franklin A.
Description: xii, 269 p.: ill.; 23 cm. ISBN:
0943497140 Notes: Includes
bibliographical references. Subjects: Life
and death, Power over--Religious aspects

Christianity. Human ecology--Religious aspects--Christianity. Man (Christian theology) Hope--Religious aspects--Christianity. Christianity and culture. Christian ethics. Social ethics. Church and social problems--United States. LC Classification: BJ1469 .C37 1990 Dewey Class No.: 261 20

Carrier, Hervé, 1921- Evangelizing the culture of modernity / Hervé Carrier. Published/Created: Maryknoll, N.Y.: Orbis Books, c1993. Description: viii, 168 p.; 21 cm. ISBN: 088344898X (paper) : Contents: The church's perception of modernity -- Modernity as a culture to evangelize -- Inculturation -- Can we still hear a counter-cultural prophet? -- Toward a new convergence of science and religion? -- Christians and the modern conception of cultural rights -- The new evangelization facing agnostic culture. Notes: Includes bibliographical references (p. 151-164) and index. Subjects: Evangelistic work--Philosophy. Civilization, Modern--1950- Christianity and culture. Series: Faith and cultures series LC Classification: BV3793 .C3713 1993 Dewey Class No.: 261 20

Carrier, Hervé, 1921- Gospel message and human cultures: from Leo XIII to John Paul II / Hervé Carrier; translated by John Drury. Published/Created: Pittsburgh, Pa.: Duquesne University Press, c1989. Description: xiii, 178 p.; 23 cm. ISBN: 0820702072 (pbk.) 0820702064 (hard) Notes: Translation of: Evangile et cultures. Includes index. Bibliography: p. 159-169. Subjects: Catholic Church--Doctrines--History. Christianity and culture--History. Series: Institute for World Concerns series LC Classification: BX1795.C85 C3713 1989 Dewey Class No.: 261 19

Casanova, Judith Boice. From sacred lies to holy wisdom: a faith journey in a postmodern world / Judith Boice Casanova. Published/Created: Claremont, Calif.: Pinch Publications, c1998. Description: 159 p.; 21 cm. ISBN: 0966325575 Notes: Includes bibliographical references. Subjects: Theology, doctrinal--Popular works.

Christianity and culture. LC Classification: BT78 .C27 1998 Dewey Class No.: 230 21

Catholicism and Austrian culture / edited by Ritchie Robertson and Judith Beniston. Published/Created: Edinburgh: Edinburgh University Press, c1999. Related Authors: Beniston, Judith. Robertson, Ritchie. Description: xiii, 191 p.: ill.; 24 cm. ISBN: 0748613072 Notes: Includes bibliographical references. Subjects: Catholic Church--Austria. Christianity and culture--Austria. Austria--Religious life and customs. Series: Austrian studies; 10 LC Classification: BX1515 .C38 1999 Dewey Class No.: 282/.436 21

Catholicism and secularization in America: essays on nature, grace, and culture / edited by David L. Schindler; [contibutors] Louis Bouyer ... [et al.]. Published/Created: Huntington, Ind.: Our Sunday Visitor; Notre Dame, Ind.: Communio Books, c1990. Related Authors: Schindler, David L., 1943- Bouyer, Louis, 1913- Description: 236 p.; 21 cm. ISBN: 0879734507 Notes: "Most of the papers of this volume were presented in essentially the same form during a recent conference on 'Nature, Grace, and Culture: On Being Catholic in America'"--p. 9. Includes bibliographical references. Subjects: Nature--Religious aspects--Christianity--Congresses. Grace (Theology)--Congresses. Secularism--Congresses. Christianity and culture--Congresses. Catholics--United States--Congresses. LC Classification: BT695.5 .C38 1990

Catolicismo y cultura: encuentro de intelectuales / organizado por la Subcomisión Episcopal de Universidades y el Comité del XIV Centenario del III Concilio de Toledo; [Joseph Ratzinger ... et al.]. Edition Information: 1. ed. Published/Created: Madrid: Conferencia Episcopal Española, 1990. Related Authors: Ratzinger, Joseph. Subcomisión Episcopal de Universidades. Comité del XIV Centenario del III Concilio de Toledo. Description: 125 p.: ports.; 19 cm. Notes: Meeting held in Madrid, Feb. 24-25, 1990. Includes bibliographical references.

Subjects: Catholic Church--History--1965---Congresses. Christianity and culture--Congresses. LC Classification: BX1390 .C37 1990

Cavarnos, Constantine. New library / by Constantine Cavarnos. Published/Created: Belmont, Mass.: Institute for Byzantine and Modern Greek Studies, c1989- Related Authors: Cavarnos, John P. (John Peter) Description: v. <1-3: ill.; 22-23 cm. ISBN: 0914744828 (pbk.: v. 1) 091474481X (hard: v. 1) Notes: Includes bibliographical references and indexes. Subjects: Greece--Civilization--Book reviews. LC Classification: DF741 .C38 1989 Dewey Class No.: 949.5 20

CCICA annual: publication of the Catholic Commission on Intellectual and Cultural Affairs. Published/Created: Notre Dame, Ind.: The Commission, [1982- Related Authors: Catholic Commission on Intellectual and Cultural Affairs (U.S.) Description: v.; 23 cm. 1982- Current Frequency: Annual Notes: Title from cover. SERBIB/SERLOC merged record Subjects: Catholic Church--Doctrines--Periodicals. Christianity and culture--Periodicals. LC Classification: BX801 .C36974

Cell, Edward, 1928- comp. Religion and contemporary Western culture; selected readings. Published/Created: Nashville, Abingdon Press [1967] Description: 399 p. 26 cm. Notes: Includes bibliographies. Subjects: Christianity and culture. LC Classification: BR115.C8 C4 Dewey Class No.: 261/.08

Center journal Published/Created: [Notre Dame, Ind.: Center for Christian Studies, c1981- Related Authors: Center for Christian Studies (South Bend, Ind.) Description: v.; 23 cm. Vol. 1, no. 1 (winter 1981)- Ceased with vol. 4, no. 4 (fall 1985). Current Frequency: Quarterly ISSN: 0730-0069 Notes: SERBIB/SERLOC merged record Indx'd selectively by: Religion index one. Periodicals 0149-8428 1981- Subjects: Christianity--20th century--Christianity and culture--Periodicals. LC Classification: BR121.2 .C38 Dewey Class No.: 209/.04

Chagall, David. Surviving the media jungle / David Chagall. Published/Created: Nashville, Tenn.: Broadman & Holman, c1996. Description: xvi, 192 p.; 23 cm. ISBN: 0805462635 (pb) Subjects: Mass media--Moral and ethical aspects. Mass media--Religious aspects--Christianity. Manipulative behavior. Christianity and culture. Mass media and children--United States. United States--Moral conditions. LC Classification: P94 .C44 1996 Dewey Class No.: 302.23 20

Chandler, Paul Gordon. God's global mosaic: what we can learn from Christians around the world / Paul-Gordon Chandler; foreword by John Stott. Published/Created: Downers Grove, Ill.: InterVarsity Press, c2000. Description: 142 p.; 21 cm. ISBN: 0830822518 (pbk.: alk. paper) Notes: Originally published: Divine mosaic. London: SPCK/Triangle, 1997. Includes bibliographical references (p. [141]-142). Subjects: Christianity and culture. Multiculturalism--Religious aspects--Christianity. LC Classification: BR115.C8 C414 2000 Dewey Class No.: 270.8/2 21

Chandy, K. K., 1908- Peace culture amidst power conflicts: caste, class, race, state tensions / K.K. Chandy. Published/Created: Delhi: Christavashram: ISPCK, 2000. Related Authors: I.S.P.C.K. (Organization) Description: xxx, 468 p.; 23 cm. ISBN: 8172145551 Summary: Propagation of non-violence in community based on Christian faith; includes social conflict in India. Subjects: Nonvoilence--Religious aspects--Christianity. Social conflict--India. LC Classification: BT736.4+

Changing churches: the local church and the structures of change / Michael Warren, editor. Published/Created: Portland, Or.: Pastoral Press, c2000. Related Authors: Warren, Michael, 1935- Description: 262 p.: ill.; 23 cm. ISBN: 1569290334 (pbk.) Notes: Includes bibliographical references. Subjects: Church. Sociology, Christian.

Christianity and culture. LC Classification: BV625 .C48 2000 Dewey Class No.: 262/.2 21

Changing conversations: religious reflection & cultural analysis / edited by Dwight N. Hopkins & Sheila Greeve Davaney. Published/Created: New York: Routledge, 1996. Related Authors: Hopkins, Dwight N. Davaney, Sheila Greeve. Description: 262 p.; 23 cm. ISBN: 0415914329 (alk. paper) 0415914337 (pbk.: alk. paper) Notes: Includes bibliographical references. Subjects: Christianity and culture. Sociology, Christian. LC Classification: BR115.C8 C416 1996 Dewey Class No.: 261/.0973 21

Charismatic Christianity as a global culture / edited by Karla Poewe. Published/Created: Columbia, S.C.: University of South Carolina Press, c1994. Related Authors: Poewe, Karla O. Description: xiv, 300 p; 24 cm. ISBN: 0872499960 (alk. paper) Notes: Includes bibliographical references (p. [259]-291) and index. Subjects: Pentecostalism. Series: Studies in comparative religion (Columbia, S.C.) LC Classification: BR1644 .C43 1994 Dewey Class No.: 270.8/2 20

Chaves, Mark. Ordaining women: culture and conflict in religious organizations / Mark Chaves. Published/Created: Cambridge, Mass.: Harvard University Press, 1997. Description: x, 237 p.; 21 cm. ISBN: 0674641450 (alk. paper) Notes: Includes bibliographical references (p. [207]-227) and index. Subjects: Ordination of women--United States. Women in Christianity. Religion and sociology. Women clergy. United States--Church history--20th century. LC Classification: BV676 .C46 1997 Dewey Class No.: 262/.14/0820973 21

Chibuko, Patrick Chukwudezie. Paschal mystery of Christ: foundation for liturgical inculturation in Africa / Patrick Chukwudezie Chibuko. Published/Created: Frankfurt am Main; New York: P. Lang, c1999. Description: xvi, 197 p.; 21 cm. ISBN: 3631355602 (pbk.) 082044703X

(US) Notes: Includes bibliographical references. Subjects: Catholic Church--Africa--Liturgy. Paschal mystery. Christianity and culture--Africa. Series: Studien zur interkulturellen Geschichte des Christentums; Bd. 120. LC Classification: BX1977.A35 C45 1999 Dewey Class No.: 264/.02/00966 21

Chidili, Barth. Discovering Christianity in African cultures / Barth Chidili. Published/Created: Uthiru, Nairobi, Kenya: Pann Printers, 1993. Description: ix, 161 p.: ill.; 21 cm. Notes: Includes bibliographical references (p. 150-161). Subjects: Catholic Church--Africa--History. Christianity--Africa. Christianity and culture. Africa--Religious life and customs. LC Classification: BR1360 .C47 1993 Dewey Class No.: 276 20

Choi, Myung-Keun, 1945- Changes in Korean society between 1884-1910 as a result of the introduction of Christianity / Myung-Keun Choi. Published/Created: New York: Peter Lang, 1997. Description: xv, 321 p.: map; 24 cm. ISBN: 0820425494 (alk. paper) Notes: Includes bibliographical references (p. [297]- 315). Subjects: Church and social problems--Korea--History--19th century. Social change--Korea--History--19th century. Korea--Social conditions. Korea--Church history--19th century. Series: Asian thought and culture, 0893-6870; vol. 20 LC Classification: HN730.5.A8 C448 1997 Dewey Class No.: 306/.09519 21

Christ & the modern mind. Edited by Robert W. Smith. Published/Created: Downers Grove, Ill., InterVarsity Press [1972] Related Authors: Smith, Robert Wayne, 1926- ed. Description: viii, 312 p. illus. 22 cm. ISBN: 0877848637 Notes: Includes bibliographical references. Subjects: Christianity and culture--Addresses, essays, lectures. Learning and scholarship--Addresses, essays, lectures. LC Classification: BR115.C8 C44 Dewey Class No.: 261.5

Christ and context: the confrontation between Gospel and culture / edited by Hilary D.

Regan and Alan J. Torrance; with Antony Wood. Published/Created: Edinburgh: T&T Clark, c1993. Related Authors: Regan, Hilary D. Torrance, Alan J. Wood, G. A. Description: 269 p.; 22 cm. ISBN: 0567292355 Contents: Introduction / Alan J. Torrance -- The future of theology in a complex world / Daniel Hardy -- The truth looks different from here / Janet Martin Soskice -- Joy in the midst of suffering / Gustavo Gutiérrez -- Christ in feminist context / Elisabeth Moltmann-Wendel -- Christian witness and the transformation of culture: society in transition / John de Gruchy -- Christ in cosmic context / Jürgen Moltmann -- The 'One world': a challenge to western Christianity / Johann Metz -- The Spirit of God in creation and reconciliation / Daniel Hardy. Notes: "This collection of essays and interactive responses emerged from an international theological symposium ... which took place in Dunedin, New Zealand"--Pref. Includes bibliographical references and indexes. Subjects: Jesus Christ--Person and offices--Congresses. Christianity and culture--Congresses. LC Classification: BR115.C8 C442 1993 Dewey Class No.: 261 21

Christ and culture in dialogue: constructive themes and practical applications / edited by Angus J.L. Menuge, general editor ... [et al.]. Published/Created: St. Louis. Mo.: Concordia Academic Press, c1999. Related Authors: Menuge, Angus J. L. Description: 332 p.; 23 cm. ISBN: 0570042739 Notes: Includes bibliographical references. Subjects: Christianity and culture. Two kingdoms (Lutheran theology) Lutheran Church--Doctrines. LC Classification: BX8065.2 .C48 1999 Dewey Class No.: 261 21

Christian business values in an intercultural environment / edited by Norlin Rueschhoff and Konrad Schaum. Published/Created: Berlin: Duncker & Humblot, c1989. Related Authors: Rueschhoff, Norlin G. Schaum, Konrad. Description: 188 p.: ill.; 24 cm. ISBN: 3428067924 Notes: Includes bibliographical references. Subjects: Corporate culture--United States--Congresses. Corporate culture--Europe--

Congresses. Management--Religious aspects--Christianity--Congresses. Economics--Religious aspects--Christianity--Congresses. Intercultural communication--Congresses. Series: Volkswirtschaftliche Schriften, 0505-9372; Heft 393 LC Classification: HD58.7 .C488 1989

Christian communities in the Arab Middle East: the challenge of the future / edited by Andrea Pacini. Published/Created: Oxford: Clarendon Press; New York: Oxford University Press, 1998. Related Authors: Pacini, Andrea. Description: xiii, 365 p.: ill., maps; 24 cm. ISBN: 0198293887 (alk. paper) Notes: Includes bibliographical references (p. [327]-339) and index. Subjects: Christianity--Arab countries. Christianity and culture--Arab countries. Christianity and other religions--Islam. Islam--Relations--Christianity. Arab countries--Church history. LC Classification: BR1067.A7 C45 1998 Dewey Class No.: 305.6 21

Christian librarianship: essays on the integration of faith and profession / edited by Gregory A. Smith; foreword by Donald G. Davis, Jr. Published/Created: Jefferson, N.C.: McFarland & Co., c2002. Related Authors: Smith, Gregory A., 1972- Description: p. cm. ISBN: 0786413298 (alk. paper) Contents: A brief introduction to Christianity and its worldview / John Allen Delivuk -- The cultural mandate, the pursuit of knowledge, and the Christian librarian / Gregory A. Smith -- The Master we serve: the call of the Christian librarian to the secular workplace / Donald G. Davis, Jr. and John Mark Tucker -- The theological library: in touch with the witnesses / John B. Trotti -- The impact of the Christian faith on library service / Stanford Terhune -- A philosophy of Christian librarianship / Gregory A. Smith -- Library encounters culture / Roger W. Phillips -- Multiculturalism and libraries: a biblical perspective / John Allen Delivuk -- Beauty for ashes: Christian librarians facing a fragmented profession / Geo Warren -- And ne'er the Twain shall meet? personal vs. professional ethics / D.

Elizabeth Irish -- Intellectual freedom and evangelical faith / Donald G. Davis, Jr. -- A Christian approach to intellectual freedom in libraries / James R. Johnson -- Nothing new under the sun? public libraries and Sunday opening in the nineteenth century / Graham Hedges -- Keeping Sunday special in the contemporary workplace culture / Rod Badams -- The role of the library in the character formation of the Christian college student / Gregory A. Smith -- Partnership in library development: the mission focus of Christian librarians / William Fraher Abernathy and Kenneth D. Gill -- Afterword: the future of Christian librarianship / Gregory A. Smith. Notes: Includes bibliographical references and index.

Christian philosophy / edited by Thomas P. Flint. Published/Created: Notre Dame, Ind.: University of Notre Dame Press, c1990. Related Authors: Flint, Thomas P. Conference on Christian and Theistic Philosophy (1988: University of Notre Dame) Description: xix, 226 p.; 24 cm. ISBN: 0268007764 : Contents: Faith seeks, understanding finds--Augustine's charter for Christian philosophy / Norman Kretzmann -- Justice, mercy, supererogation, and atonement / Richard L. Purtill -- Providence and the problem of evil / Eleonore Stump -- Can anybody in a post-Christian culture rationally believe in the Nicene Creed? / Alan Donagan -- The remembrance of things (not) past-- philosophical reflections on Christian liturgy / Nicholas Wolterstorff -- Love and absolutes in Christian ethics / J.L.A. Garcia -- Taking St. Paul seriously--sin as an epistemological category / Merold Westphal. Notes: Papers presented at the Conference on Christian and Theistic Philosophy held Feb. 25-27, 1988, at the University of Notre Dame. Subjects: Christianity--Philosophy--Congresses. Series: University of Notre Dame studies in the philosophy of religion; no. 6 LC Classification: BR100 .C53 1990 Dewey Class No.: 190 20

Christian spirituality and the culture of modernity: the thought of Louis Dupré / edited by Peter J. Casarella and George P. Schner. Published/Created: Grand Rapids, Mich.: W.B. Eerdmans, c1998. Related Authors: Casarella, Peter J. Schner, George P., 1946- Description: xii, 352 p.; 24 cm. ISBN: 0802845908 (pbk.: alk. paper) 080283812X (hardcover: alk. paper) Notes: "Major publications of Louis Dupré": p. 346-347. Includes bibliographical references and index. Subjects: Dupré, Louis K., 1925- Christianity--Philosophy--History. LC Classification: BR100 .C536 1998 Dewey Class No.: 230 21

Christianity and culture in the crossfire / edited by David A. Hoekema and Bobby Fong. Published/Created: Grand Rapids, Mich.: Calvin Center for Christian Scholarship: W.B. Eerdmans Pub. Co., 1997. Related Authors: Hoekema, David A. Fong, Bobby. Description: ix, 194 p.; 23 cm. ISBN: 0802843239 (pbk.: alk. paper) Notes: Includes bibliographical references. Subjects: Christianity and culture. Christianity and culture--United States. Multiculturalism--Religious aspects-- Christianity. Postmodernism--Religious aspects--Christianity. Feminism--Religious aspects--Christianity. LC Classification: BR115.C8 C445 1997 Dewey Class No.: 261 21

Christianity and cultures: a mutual enrichment / edited by Norbert Greinacher and Norbert Mette. Published/Created: London: SCM Press; Maryknoll, NY: Orbis Books, c1994. Related Authors: Greinacher, Norbert, 1931- Mette, Norbert, 1946- Description: x, 142 p.; 22 cm. ISBN: 0883448777 (USA) 0334030250 (UK) Partial Contents: Transformations of faith: documents of intercultural learning in the Bible / Sylvia Schroer -- Inculturation of faith or identification with culture? / Robert Schreiter -- From theological vandalism to theological romanticism / Giancarlo Collet -- Coptic Christianity / Maurice Assad -- The process of developing the Church in Zaire / F. Kabasele Lumbala -- Christianity in

Pakistan / Mariam Francis. Notes: Includes bibliographical references. Subjects: Christianity and culture. Series: Concilium (Glen Rock, N.J.); 1994/2. LC Classification: BR115.C8 C446 1994 Dewey Class No.: 261 20

Christianity and Russian culture in Soviet society / edited by Nicolai N. Petro. Published/Created: Boulder: Westview Press, 1989. Related Authors: Petro, Nicolai N. Description: xi, 244 p.; 23 cm. ISBN: 0813377420 (alk. paper) : Notes: Includes bibliographical references and index. Subjects: Christianity--Soviet Union. Christianity and culture. Church and state--Soviet Union--History. Soviet Union--Civilization. Soviet Union--Church history. Series: CCRS series on change in contemporary Soviet society LC Classification: BR936 .C49 1989 Dewey Class No.: 274.7/.082 20

Christianity and the African imagination: essays in honour of Adrian Hastings / edited by David Maxwell with Ingrid Lawrie. Published/Created: Leiden; Boston: Brill, 2002. Related Authors: Hastings, Adrian. Maxwell, David, 1963- Lawrie, Ingrid. Description: xii, 421 p.: ill.; 25 cm. ISBN: 9004116680 (cloth: alk. paper) Notes: Includes bibliographical references (p. [367]-406) and index. Subjects: Christianity--Africa. Christianity and culture--Africa. Series: Studies on religion in Africa.; 23 LC Classification: BR1360 .C475 2002 Dewey Class No.: 276 21

Christianity and the classics: the acceptance of a heritage / Wendy E. Helleman, editor. Published/Created: Lanham, [MD]: London: University Press of America, c1990. Related Authors: Helleman, Wendy E., 1945- Description: 219 p.; 24 cm. ISBN: 0819175773 (alk. paper) 0819175781 (pbk.: alk. paper) Notes: "Co-published by arrangement with the Institute for Christian Studies, Ontario, Canada"-- verso of t.p. Includes bibliographical references (p. [205]-210) and index. Subjects: Christianity and other religions-- Greek. Christianity and other religions--

Roman. Christianity and culture. Christian literature--Classical influences. Classical literature--Appreciation. Philosophy, Ancient--Influence. Greece--Religion. Rome--Religion. LC Classification: BR128.G8 C47 1989 Dewey Class No.: 261.5 20

Christianity and the culture of economics / edited by Donald A. Hay and Alan Kreider. Published/Created: Cardiff: University of Wales Press, 2001. Related Authors: Hay, Donald A. Kreider, Alan, 1941- Description: x, 194 p.; 22 cm. ISBN: 0708317111 0708317049 (pbk.) Notes: Includes bibliographical references and index. Subjects: Economics--Religious aspects--Christianity. Consumption (Economics)--Religious aspects-- Christianity. Series: Religion, culture, and society LC Classification: BR115.E3 C535 2001 Dewey Class No.: 261.8/5 21

Christianity and the Eastern Slavs. Published/Created: Berkeley: University of California Press, c1993-1995. Related Authors: Gasparov, B. Raevskaia-Kh´iuz, O. (Ol´ga) Description: 3 v.; 24 cm. ISBN: 0520079450 (v. 1: alk. paper) Contents: v. 1. Slavic cultures in the Middle Ages / edited by Boris Gasparov and Olga Raevsky-Hughes -- v. 2. Russian culture in modern times / edited by Robert P. Hughes and Irina Paperno -- v. 3. Russian literature in modern times / edited by Boris Gasparov ... et al. Notes: English and Russian; summaries in English. Based on papers delivered at two international conferences held in May 1988 at the University of California--Berkeley and the Kennan Institute for Advanced Russian Studies to commemorate the millennium of the Christianization of Kievan Rus'. Includes bibliographical references and index. Subjects: Orthodox Eastern Church- -Slavic countries--Congresses. Slavs, Eastern--Civilization--Congresses. Christianity and culture--Congresses. Russian literature--History and criticism-- Congresses. Millennium of Christianity in Kievan Rus, 988-1988 Congresses. Russia (Federation)--Civilization--Congresses. Series: California Slavic studies; vol. 16-

18. LC Classification: DK4 .C33 vol. 16, etc. Dewey Class No.: 947 s 947 20

Christianity and the human body: a theology of the human body: proceedings of the ITEST Workshop, October, 2000. Published/Created: St. Louis, Mo.: ITEST Faith/Science Press, c2001. Related Authors: Institute for Theological Encounter with Science and Technology. Description: iii, 264 p.: ill.; 23 cm. ISBN: 1885583095 Partial Contents: A theology of the body: body, genes and culture: who's holding the leash? / Michael Hoy -- Theological meaning in genetic research and evolutionary theory / Carolyn Schneider -- Interpreting nature and Scripture: a new proposal for their interaction / Jitse M. van der Meer -- Notes: Includes bibliographical references and index. Subjects: Body, Human--Religious aspects--Christianity--Man (Christian theology)--Human genetics--Religious aspects--Christianity--Congresses. LC Classification: BT741.2 .I84 2000 Dewey Class No.: 233/.5 21

Christianity and western civilization: Christopher Dawson's insight-- can a culture survive the loss of its religious roots?: papers presented at a conference sponsored by the Wethersfield Institute, New York City, October 15, 1993. Published/Created: San Francisco: Ignatius Press, 1995. Related Authors: Wethersfield Institute. Description: 122 p.; 21 cm. ISBN: 0898705347 (pbk.) Subjects: Dawson, Christopher, 1889-1970 -- Congresses. Civilization, Christian--Congresses. Civilization, Western--Congresses. Christianity--Influence--Congresses. Series: Proceedings of the Wethersfield Institute; v. 7. LC Classification: BR115.C5 C48 1995 Dewey Class No.: 270/.09182/1 20

Christianity challenges the university / edited by Peter Wilkes. Published/Created: Downers Grove, Ill.: InterVarsity Press, c1981. Related Authors: Wilkes, Peter, 1937- Description: 97 p.; 21 cm. ISBN: 0877844747 Contents: The christian world view / Peter Wilkes -- Man, naked ape and nothing more? / Wayne M. Becker -- Christian doubts about economic dogmas / J. David Richardson -- The reliability of the Scriptural documents / Keith Schoville -- Christianity, modern medicine, and the whole person / A.A. MacKinney -- And then / Peter Wilkes. Notes: "Lectures presented in the Great Hall of the Memorial Union at the University of Wisconsin, Madison"--Foreword. Includes bibliographies. Subjects: Christianity and culture--Addresses, essays, lectures. LC Classification: BR115.C8 C447 Dewey Class No.: 261.5 19

Christianity in conflict: the struggle for Christian integrity and freedom in secular culture / edited by Peter Williamson and Kevin Perrotta. Published/Created: Ann Arbor, Mich.: Servant Books, c1986. Related Authors: Williamson, Peter, 1951- Perrotta, Kevin. Center for Pastoral Renewal (U.S.) Description: xxvi, 147 p.; 21 cm. ISBN: 0892832924 (pbk.) Notes: Based on addresses presented at a conference entitled, "Allies for Faith and Renewal," held in Ann Arbor, Mich., May 1985, sponsored by the Center for Pastoral Renewal. Includes bibliographies. Subjects: Christianity--20th century--Congresses. Series: A Pastoral renewal book LC Classification: BR481 .C494 1986 Dewey Class No.: 270.8/28 19

Christianity in its social context; Gerald Irvine (editor). Published/Created: London, S.P.C.K., 1967. Related Authors: Irvine, Gerald, ed. St. Anne's Society. Description: [6], 128 p. 22 cm. Notes: "Papers ... given in the summer of 1965 as a course of lectures under the ... title of The sociology of Christian formulations before St. Anne's Society." Subjects: Christianity and culture--Addresses, essays, lectures. Sociology, Christian--Addresses, essays, lectures. Series: Theological collections, 8 LC Classification: BR115.C8 C45 Dewey Class No.: 261/.08

Christianity, social change, and globalization in the Americas / edited by Anna Peterson, Manuel Vásquez, Philip Williams. Published/Created: New Brunswick, N.J.:

Rutgers University Press, c2001. Related Authors: Peterson, Anna Lisa, 1963- Vásquez, Manuel A. Williams, Philip J., 1959- Description: xii, 259 p.: maps; 23 cm. ISBN: 081352931X (hardcover: alk. paper) 0813529328 (pbk.: alk. paper) Notes: Includes bibliographical references (p.241-253) and index. Subjects: Christianity and culture--El Salvador. Christianity and culture--Peru. Latin Americans--United States--Religion. El Salvador--Social conditions--20th century. El Salvador--Church history--20th century. Peru--Social conditions--20th century. Peru--Church history--20th century. United States--Church history--20th century. LC Classification: BR625.S2 C47 2001 Dewey Class No.: 261.8/098 21

Christianity: a social and cultural history / Howard Clark Kee ... [et al.]. Edition Information: 2nd ed. Published/Created: Upper Saddle River, NJ: Prentice Hall, c1998. Related Authors: Kee, Howard Clark. Description: vii, 600 p.: ill., maps; 23 cm. ISBN: 0135780713 (pbk.) Notes: Includes bibliographical references (p. 581-590) and index. Subjects: Church history. Sociology, Christian--History. Christianity and culture--History. LC Classification: BR148 .C48 1998 Dewey Class No.: 270 21

Christianity: a social and cultural history / Howard Clark Kee ... [et al.]; epilogue by Dana L. Robert. Published/Created: New York: Macmillan, c1991. Related Authors: Kee, Howard Clark. Description: viii, 792 p.: ill., maps; 25 cm. ISBN: 0023624310 Notes: Includes bibliographical references (p. 765-775) and index. Subjects: Church history. Sociology, Christian--History. Christianity and culture--History. LC Classification: BR148 .C48 1991 Dewey Class No.: 270 20

Christians and politics beyond the culture wars: an agenda for engagement / edited by David P. Gushee. Published/Created: Grand Rapids, Mich.: Baker Books, c2000. Related Authors: Gushee, David P., 1962- Description: 255 p.; 23 cm. ISBN: 0801022312 (pbk.) Notes: Papers

presented at a conference held in Oct. 1998 at Union University. Includes bibliographical references and index. Subjects: Christianity and politics-- Congresses. Christianity and politics-- United States--Congresses. LC Classification: BR115.P7 C38163 2000 Dewey Class No.: 261.7/0973 21

Christology in dialogue / edited by Robert F. Berkey and Sarah A. Edwards. Published/Created: Cleveland, Ohio: Pilgrim Press, 1993. Related Authors: Berkey, Robert F. Edwards, Sarah A., 1921- Description: viii, 390 p.; 23 cm. ISBN: 0829809562 (acid-free paper) Notes: Includes bibliographical references (p. 389-390). Subjects: Jesus Christ-- History of doctrines--Early church, ca. 30- 600. Jesus Christ--History of doctrines-- 20th century. Christianity and culture. Christianity and other religions. LC Classification: BT198 .C455 1993 Dewey Class No.: 232 20

Christopaganism or indigenous Christianity? / Edited by Tetsunao Yamamori and Charles R. Taber. Published/Created: South Pasadena, Calif.: William Carey Library, [1975] Related Authors: Yamamori, Tetsunao, 1937- Taber, Charles Russell. Milligan College. Description: 262 p.; 23 cm. ISBN: 0878084231 Notes: Consists of 12 lectures delivered at the symposium sponsored by Milligan College. Bibliography: p. [251]-262. Subjects: Missions--Congresses. Christianity and culture--Congresses. LC Classification: BV2391 .M54 1974 Dewey Class No.: 266

Chung-kuo wên hua yü Chi-tu chiao. Published/Created: 16 i. e. 1927. ? 1971?] Related Authors: Ch`ing nien hsieh hui. Shu pao pu. Description: 1, 69 p. 18 cm. Notes: Romanized. Subjects: Christianity and culture.China--Civilization. LC Classification: BR115.C8 C47 1971

Chupungco, Anscar J. Liturgical inculturation: sacramentals, religiosity, and catechesis / Anscar J. Chupungco. Published/Created: Collegeville, Minn.: Liturgical Press, c1992. Description: 174 p.; 23 cm. ISBN:

0814661203 Notes: "Sequel to the author's Liturgies of the future"--Back cover. "A Pueblo book." Includes bibliographical references. Subjects: Catholic Church--Liturgy--Education--Catechetics. Christianity and culture. Sacramentals. LC Classification: BX1970 .C5715 1992 Dewey Class No.: 264/.02 20

Chupungco, Anscar J. Liturgies of the future: the process and methods of inculturation / Anscar J. Chupungco. Published/Created: New York: Paulist Press, c1989. Description: 220 p.; 21 cm. ISBN: 0809130955 : Notes: Includes bibliographical references. Subjects: Catholic Church--Liturgy. Christianity and culture. LC Classification: BX1970 .C572 1989 Dewey Class No.: 264/.02 20

Church and Canadian culture / Robert E. VanderVennen, editor. Published/Created: Lanham, Md.: University Press of America, c1991. Related Authors: VanderVennen, Robert E. Institute for Christian Studies. Description: vii, 224 p.; 23 cm. ISBN: 0819184209 (alk. paper) 0819184217 (pbk.: alk. paper) Notes: "Co-published by arrangement with the Institute for Christian Studies, Ontario, Canada"--T.p. verso. Contributions from a conference sponsored by the Institute for Christian Studies in Oct., 1988. Includes bibliographical references (p. [203]-215) and index. Subjects: Christian sects--Canada--Christianity and culture--Congresses. LC Classification: BR570 .C48 1991 Dewey Class No.: 277.1 20

Church and culture change in Africa, edited by David J. Bosch. Published/Created: Pretoria, N. G. Kerk-boekhandel [1971] Related Authors: Bosch, David Jacobus, ed. South African Society for Missionary Studies. Description: 100 p. 21 cm. Notes: "Papers read at the third annual meeting of the South African Society for Missionary Studies, 1971." Includes bibliographical references. Subjects: Sociology, Christian--Africa--Addresses, essays, lectures. Christianity and culture--Addresses, essays, lectures. LC Classification: BT738

.C49 Dewey Class No.: 261

Church and culture: Singapore context / edited by Bobby E.K. Sng, Choong Chee Pang. Published/Created: Singapore: Graduates' Christian Fellowship, c1991. Related Authors: Sng, Bobby E. K. (Bobby Ewe Kong) Choong, Chee Pang. Graduates' Christian Fellowship (Singapore) Description: viii, 130 p.; 23 cm. ISBN: 9810025092 Contents: Gospel and culture / Bobby E.K. Sng -- Understanding Chinese religion / Chua Toh Chai -- Chinese festival, customs, and rites / Chen Ai Yen -- Ancestral/parental-children ties in the Old Testament and their possible bearings of filial piety / John Chew -- Filial piety / Choon Chee Pang -- Church and the inculturation of the gospel / John Chew -- Understanding Tamil culture / Robert Solomon -- Church, ethnicity, and culture / Bobby E.K. Sng. Notes: Includes bibliographical references. Subjects: Christianity and culture. China--Religion. LC Classification: BR115.C8 C48 1991 Dewey Class No.: 261/.095957 20

Church authority in American culture: the second Cardinal Bernardin Conference / Catholic Common Ground Initiative; introduction by Philip J. Murnion. Published/Created: New York: Crossroad Pub., 1999. Description: p. cm. ISBN: 0824517881 (pbk.) Notes: "A Herder & Herder book." Includes bibliographical references. Subjects: Catholic Church--United States--History--20th century. Church--Authority--History of doctrines--20th century Congresses. Christianity and culture--United States--History--20th century--Congresses. LC Classification: BX1746 .C275 1998 Dewey Class No.: 262/.8/08822 21

Clammer, J. R. The sociology of Singapore religion: studies in Christianity and Chinese culture / by John Clammer. Published/Created: Singapore: Chopmen Publishers, 1991. Description: 125 p.; 24 cm. ISBN: 9971681498 (pbk.) 997168148X (hard) Notes: Includes bibliographical references and index. Subjects: Religion and sociology--

Singapore. Chinese--Singapore--Religion. Singapore--Religion. Series: Asia Pacific monograph; no. 4 LC Classification: BL2085 .C57 1991 Dewey Class No.: 306.6/095957 20

Clapp, Rodney. A peculiar people: the Church as culture in a post-Christian society / Rodney Clapp. Published/Created: Downers Grove, Ill.: InterVarsity Press, c1996. Description: 251 p.; 21 cm. ISBN: 0830819908 (pbk.: alk. paper) Notes: Includes bibliographical references (p. [213]-248) and index. Subjects: Church. Christianity and culture. LC Classification: BV600.2 .C554 1996 Dewey Class No.: 262 20

Clapp, Rodney. Border crossings: Christian trespasses on popular culture and public affairs / Rodney Clapp. Published/Created: Grand Rapids, Mich.: Brazos Press, c2000. Description: 224 p.; 23 cm. ISBN: 1587430037 (paper) Notes: Includes bibliographical references (p. 209-222). Subjects: Christianity and culture--United States. United States--Religion--1960- LC Classification: BR115.C8 C52 2000 Dewey Class No.: 261/.0973 21

Claussen, Janet. Awakening: challenging the culture with girls / Janet Claussen. Published/Created: Winona, Minn.: Saint Mary's Press, c2001. Description: 141 p.: 28 cm. ISBN: 088489696X (pbk.) Notes: Includes bibliographical references. Subjects: Church group work with teenage girls. Christianity and culture--Study and teaching. Culture. Teenage girls. Catholics. Christian life. Conduct of life. Series: Voices (Winona, Minn.) LC Classification: BX2347.8.Y7 C53 2001 Dewey Class No.: 259/.23 21

Clegg, Tom (Thomas T.) Lost in America: how you and your church can impact the world next door / by Tom Clegg and Warren Bird. Published/Created: Loveland, Colo.: Group, c2001. Related Authors: Bird, Warren. Description: 176 p.: ill.; 24 cm. ISBN: 076442257X Notes: Includes bibliographical references. Subjects: Evangelistic work--Christianity and

culture--United States. LC Classification: BV3790 .C567 2001 Dewey Class No.: 266/.00973 21

Closure in the Canterbury tales: the role of The parson's tale / edited by David Raybin and Linda Tarte Holley. Kalmamazoo, Mich.: Medieval Institute Publications, Western Michigan University, 2000. Related Authors: Raybin, David. Holley, Linda Tarte, 1940- Description: xxi, 268 p.; 24 cm. ISBN: 1580440118 (casebound: alk. paper) 1580440126 (paperbound: alk. paper) Notes: "Bibliography of scholarship treating The Parson's Tale": p. 209-252. Includes bibliographical references and index. Subjects: Parson's tale. Chaucer, Geoffrey, d. 1400 --Technique--Religion. Repentance--Christianity--History of doctrines--Middle Ages, 600-1500. Christianity and literature--England--History--To 1500. Repentance in literature. Clergy in literature. Rhetoric, Medieval. Closure (Rhetoric) Sin in literature. Series: Studies in medieval culture; 41 LC Classification: PR1868.P43 C57 2000 Dewey Class No.: 821/.1 21

Clouse, Robert G., 1931- Two kingdoms: the Church and culture through the ages / Robert G. Clouse, Richard V. Pierard, Edwin M. Yamauchi. Published/Created: Chicago: Moody Press, c1993. Related Authors: Pierard, Richard V., 1934- Yamauchi, Edwin M. Description: 672 p.: ill., maps; 23 cm. ISBN: 0802485901 Notes: Includes bibliographical references (p. [605]-638) and indexes. Subjects: Church history. Christianity and culture. LC Classification: BR145.2 .C56 1993 Dewey Class No.: 261/.09 20

Cobb, John B. Postmodernism and public policy: reframing religion, culture, education, sexuality, class, race, politics, and the economy / John B. Cobb, Jr. Published/Created: Albany: State University of New York Press, c2002. Description: xvi, 206 p.; 23 cm. ISBN: 0791451658 (alk. paper) 0791451666 (pbk.: alk. paper) Notes: Includes bibliographical references (p. [193]-198) and index. Subjects: Postmodern theology.

Christianity and politics. Postmodernism--Political aspects. Series: SUNY series in constructive postmodern thought LC Classification: BT83.597 .C63 2002 Dewey Class No.: 146/.7 21

Cochran, Mary E. Dakota cross-bearer: the life and world of a Native American bishop / by Mary E. Cochran; with an introduction by Raymond A. Bucko and Martin Brokenleg. Published/Created: Lincoln: University of Nebraska Press, c2000. Description: xx, 252 p.: ill., map; 23 cm. ISBN: 0803215118 Notes: Includes bibliographical references (p. [225]-243) and index. Subjects: Jones, Harold S., 1911- Episcopal Church--Bishops--Biography. Santee Indians--Biography. Santee Indians--Religion. Santee Indians--History. Racism--Religious aspects--Episcopal Church. Christianity and culture--Great Plains. LC Classification: E99.S22 J65 2000 Dewey Class No.: 283/.092 B 21

Cochrane, Charles Norris, 1889-1945. Christianity and classical culture; Published/Created: New York, Oxford University Press, 1957. Description: vii, 523 p. 21 cm. Subjects: Civilization, Christian.Civilization, Greco-Roman.Church history--Primitive and early church. LC Classification: BR170 .C6 1957

Cochrane, Charles Norris, 1889-1945. Christianity and classical culture; a study of thought and action from Augustus to Augustine, by Charles Norris Cochrane ... Published/Created: London, New York [etc.] Oxford University Press, 1944. Description: vii p., 1 l., 523 p. 22 cm. Notes: "Revised and corrected". Bibliographical foot-notes. Subjects: Civilization, Christian. Civilization, Greco-Roman. Church history--Primitive and early church, ca. 30-600. LC Classification: BR170 .C6 1944 Dewey Class No.: 270.1

Cochrane, Charles Norris, 1889-1945. Christianity and classical culture: a study of thought and action from Augustus to Augustine / by Charles Norris Cochrane.

Published/Created: Oxford: The Clarendon Press, 1940. Description: vii, 523 p.; 23 cm. Notes: Includes bibliographical references and index. Subjects: Civilization, Christian. Civilization, Greco-Roman. Church history--Primitive and early church, ca. 30-600. LC Classification: BR170 .C6

Coffey, David (David Michael) Believer, Christian, Catholic: three essays in fundamental theology / David Coffey. Published/Created: Manly, N.S.W., Australia: Catholic Institute of Sydney, 1986. Description: 74 p.; 20 cm. ISBN: 0908224109 Notes: Inclues bibliographical references. Subjects: Catholic Church--Doctrines. Catholic Church--Apologetic works. Theology, Doctrinal. Christianity and other religions. Christianity and culture. Series: Faith and culture; 11. LC Classification: BX1751.2 .C574 1986 Dewey Class No.: 230/.2 20

Cohen, Arthur Allen, 1928- An Arthur A. Cohen reader: selected fiction and writings on Judaism, theology, literature, and culture / edited by David Stern and Paul Mendes-Flohr. Published/Created: Detroit: Wayne State Unviersity Press, c1998. Related Authors: Stern, David, 1949- Mendes-Flohr, Paul R. Description: 573 p.: ill.; 23 cm. ISBN: 0814322824 (pbk.) Notes: Includes bibliographical references (p. 549-573). Subjects: Judaism. Judaism--Relations--Christianity. Christianity and other religions--Judaism. Holocaust (Jewish theology) Jews--Intellectual life. Literature, Modern--History and criticism. LC Classification: BM45 .C5835 1998 Dewey Class No.: 296 21

Coleman, Simon. The globalisation of charismatic Christianity: spreading the gospel of prosperity / Simon Coleman. Published/Created: Cambridge, U.K.; New York: Cambridge University Press, 2000. Description: xii, 264 p.; 23 cm. ISBN: 0521660726 (hardback) Notes: Includes bibliographical references (p. 241-258) and index. Subjects: Christianity and culture--Sweden--Uppsala--Case studies. Globalization--Religious aspects--

Christianity--Case studies. Faith movement (Hagin)--Pentecostalism--Sweden--Uppsala--History--20th century. Uppsala (Sweden)--Church history--20th century. Series: Cambridge studies in ideology and religion; 12 LC Classification: BR1018.U66 C65 2000 Dewey Class No.: 306.6/804 21

Collier, Jane, 1936- From complicity to encounter: the church and the culture of economism / Jane Collier, Rafael Esteban. Published/Created: Harrisburg, Pa.: Trinity Press International, c1998. Related Authors: Esteban, Rafael, 1939- Description: x, 118 p.: ill.; 18 cm. ISBN: 1563382601 (pbk.) Notes: Includes bibliographical references (p. 112-118). Subjects: Catholic Church--Missions--Theory. Christianity and culture. Economics--Religious aspects--Catholic Church. Series: Christian mission and modern culture LC Classification: BV2180 .C588 1998 Dewey Class No.: 261.8/5 21

Collier, Jane, 1936- The culture of economism: an exploration of barriers to faith-as-praxis / Jane Collier. Published/Created: Frankfurt; New York: P. Lang, c1990. Description: xii, 407 p.; 21 cm. ISBN: 3631425635 Notes: Includes bibliographical references (p. 378-407). Subjects: Economics--Moral and ethical aspects--Religious aspects--Christianity. Economic man. Series: Studien zur interkulturellen Geschichte des Christentums; Bd. 65 LC Classification: HB72 .C555 1990 Dewey Class No.: 330.1 20

Colson, Charles W. Against the night: living in the new dark ages / Charles Colson with Ellen Santilli Vaughn. Published/Created: Ann Arbor, Mich.: Vine Books/Servant Publications, 1999. Related Authors: Vaughn, Ellen Santilli. Description: p. cm. ISBN: 1569551448 (alk. paper) Notes: Includes bibliographical references and index. Subjects: Christianity and culture. Christian life--Biblical teaching. LC Classification: BR115.C8 C54 1999 Dewey Class No.: 261/.0973/09048 21

Colson, Charles W. Developing a Christian worldview of the Christian in today's culture / Charles Colson and Nancy Pearcey. Published/Created: Wheaton, Ill.: Tyndale House, [2001] Related Authors: Pearcey, Nancy. Description: xx, 366 p.; 21 cm. ISBN: 0842355871 Notes: Includes bibliographical references (p. [353]-364). Subjects: Christianity and culture. LC Classification: BR115.C8 C545 2001 Dewey Class No.: 261 21

Colson, Charles W. How now shall we live? / Charles Colson and Nancy Pearcey. Published/Created: Wheaton, Ill.: Tyndale House Publishers, c1999. Related Authors: Pearcey, Nancy. Description: xiv, 574 p.; 24 cm. ISBN: 0842318089 (hardcover: alk. paper) Notes: Includes bibliographical references (p. [493]-559) and index. Subjects: Christianity and culture. Christianity--20th century. Christian life. LC Classification: BR115.C8 C554 1999 Dewey Class No.: 261 21

Colson, Charles W. How now shall we live? / Charles Colson and Nancy Pearcey & Bill Henry. Edition Information: Collegiate ed. Published/Created: Nashville, Tenn.: LifeWay Press, c2000. Related Authors: Pearcey, Nancy. Henry, Bill. Description: 136 p.: ill.; 28 cm. ISBN: 0633004561 Subjects: College students--Religious life. Apologetics. Christianity and culture. LC Classification: BV4531.2

Colson, Charles W. The enduring revolution: a battle to change the human heart / Charles Colson. Published/Created: Uhrichsville, Ohio: Barbour, c1996. Description: 61 p.; 17 cm. ISBN: 155748936X Subjects: Christianity and culture. Liberty--Religious aspects--Christianity. LC Classification: BR115.C8 C55 1996 Dewey Class No.: 261 21

Colson, Charles W. The God of stones and spiders: letters to a church in exile / Charles Colson with Ellen Santilli Vaughn. Published/Created: Wheaton, Ill.: Crossway Books, c1990. Related Authors: Vaughn, Ellen Santilli. Description: 221 p.; 23 cm. ISBN: 0891075712 : Notes: Cover

The God of stones & spiders. Includes index. Subjects: Christianity--United States. Christianity and culture. Church and social problems--United States. United States--Civilization--1970- United States--Church history--20th century. United States--Moral conditions. LC Classification: BR526 .C64 1990 Dewey Class No.: 270.8/29 20

Communication and Lonergan: common ground for forging the New Age / edited by Thomas J. Farrell and Paul A. Soukup. Published/Created: Kansas City, MO: Sheed & Ward, c1993. Related Authors: Farrell, Thomas J. Soukup, Paul A. Description: xxxvii, 377 p.; 23 cm. ISBN: 1556126239 (alk. paper) : Notes: Includes bibliographical references (p. 330-362) andindex. Subjects: Lonergan, Bernard J. F.--Contributions in religious aspects of communication. Communication--Religious aspects--Christianity. Series: Communication, culture & theology LC Classification: BV4319 .C538 1993 Dewey Class No.: 254/.3 20

Communication, reconciliation: challenges facing the 21st century / edited by Philip Lee. Published/Created: Geneva: WCC Publications; London: World Association for Christian Communication, c2001. Related Authors: Lee, Philip J. World Council of Churches. World Association for Christian Communication. Description: xii, 96 p.; 22 cm. ISBN: 2825413410 Partial Contents: Introduction: Breaking the chains of inhumanity: stories on the way to reconciliation / Carlos A. Valle -- Creating a "culture of dialogue" in a multicultural and pluralist society / S. Wesley Ariarajah -- Communication, reconciliation and religion in America / William F. Fore -- Communication and reconciliation with truth / Dafne Sabanes Plou. Notes: Includes bibliographical references. Subjects: Communication--Religious aspects--Christianity. Reconciliation--Religious aspects--Christianity. Local Call/Shelving: P96.I5 C66 2001

Confident witness--changing world: rediscovering the Gospel in North America / edited by Craig Van Gelder. Published/Created: Grand Rapids, Mich.: Eerdmans, c1999. Related Authors: Van Gelder, Craig. Description: xvii, 313 p.: ill.; 23 cm. ISBN: 0802846556 (paper: alk. paper) Notes: Proceedings of a conference held in 1996. Includes bibliographical references. Subjects: Missions--North America. Christianity and culture. Missions--Theory. Evangelistic work--North America. North America--Religion--20th century. Series: The Gospel and our culture series LC Classification: BV2760 .C53 1999 Dewey Class No.: 266/.0097 21

Conkin, Paul Keith. When all the gods trembled: Darwinism, Scopes, and American intellectuals / Paul K. Conkin. Published/Created: Lanham, Md.: Rowman & Littlefield Publishers, c1998. Description: xi, 185 p.: ill.; 24 cm. ISBN: 0847690636 (cloth: alk. paper) Notes: Includes bibliographical references and index. Subjects: Scopes, John Thomas--Trials, litigation, etc. Darwin, Charles, 1809-1882. Religion and science--United States--History--20th century. Human evolution--Religious aspects--Christianity--History 20th century. United States--Intellectual life--20th century. United States--Religion--1901-1945. Series: American intellectual culture LC Classification: BL245 .C66 1998 Dewey Class No.: 291.1/75 21

Conlon, James, 1936- Earth story, sacred story / James Conlon; foreword by Thomas Berry. Published/Created: Mystic, Conn.: Twenty-Third Publications, c1994. Description: viii, 147 p.; 23 cm. ISBN: 0896225836 : Notes: Includes bibliographical references (p. 137-144). Subjects: Human ecology--Religious aspects--Christianity. Nature--Religious aspects--Christianity. Christianity and culture. LC Classification: BT695.5 .C66 1994 Dewey Class No.: 261.8/362 20

Conservative essays / Maurice Cowling ... [et al.]; edited by Maurice Cowling. Published/Created: London: Cassell, 1978.

Related Authors: Cowling, Maurice.
Description: 198 p.; 23 cm. ISBN:
0304300446 Contents: Cowling, M. The
present position.--Jones, A. and Bentley,
M. Salisbury and Baldwin.--Utley, T. E.
The significance of Mrs. Thatcher.--
Letwin, S. R. On Conservative
individualism--Norman, E. Christianity
and politics.--Casey, J. Tradition and
authority.--Scruton, R. The politics of
culture.--Minogue, K. On hyperactivism in
modern British politics.--Griffiths, R.
British conservatism and the lessons of the
Continental right.--Worsthorne, P. Too
much freedom.--Biffen, J. The
conservatism of Labour.--Peyton, J. "To
free men alone belongs the privilege of
being governed by their servants."--Gale,
G. The popular communication of a
Conservative message.--Cowling, M.
Conclusion. Notes: Includes
bibliographical references. Subjects:
Conservative Party (Great Britain)--
Addresses, essays, lectures. Conservatism--
Great Britain--Addresses, essays, lectures.
LC Classification: JN1129 .C72 1978
Dewey Class No.: 320.9/41/0857

Constructive Christian theology in the
worldwide church / edited by William R.
Barr. Published/Created: Grand Rapids,
Mich.: Eerdmans, c1997. Related Authors:
Barr, William R., 1934- Description: xviii,
553 p.; 24 cm. ISBN: 0802841430 (pbk.:
alk. paper) Notes: Includes bibliographical
references and indexes. Subjects:
Theology, Doctrinal. Christianity and
culture. LC Classification: BT80 .C65
1997 Dewey Class No.: 230 21

Contemporary Gospel accents: doing theology
in Africa, Asia, Southeast Asia, and Latin
America / edited by Daniel Carro and
Richard F. Wilson. Published/Created:
Macon, Ga.: Mercer University Press,
c1997. Related Authors: Carro, Daniel.
Wilson, Richard Francis, 1953- Baptist
World Alliance. Description: xv, 142 p.; 23
cm. ISBN: 0865545057 (alk. paper) Notes:
Papers presented at a Baptist World
Alliance seminar held in Aug. 1995 in
Buenos Aires, Argentina. Includes
bibliographical references. Subjects:

Baptists--Developing countries--Doctrines-
-History--20th century--Congresses.
Christianity and culture--Developing
countries--History of doctrines--20th
century--Congresses. LC Classification:
BX6331.2 .C67 1997 Dewey Class No.:
230/.6/09 20

Contextual theology for Lesotho: a report based
on a workshop held at the Anglican Centre,
Maseru, Lesotho, on 7 and 8 December,
1987. Published/Created: Maseru, Lesotho:
Transformation Resource Centre, [1988]
Related Authors: Transformation
(Organization) Description: 26 p.; 21 cm.
Notes: "September, 1988." Subjects:
Christianity and culture--Congresses.
Lesotho--Religion--Congresses. LC
Classification: BR115.C8 C59 1988

Converging on culture: theologians in dialogue
with cultural analysis and criticism / edited
by Delwin Brown, Sheila Greeve Davaney,
& Kathryn Tanner. Published/Created:
Oxford; New York: Oxford University
Press, 2001. Related Authors: Brown,
Delwin, 1935- Davaney, Sheila Greeve.
Tanner, Kathryn, 1957- American
Academy of Religion. Description: xiii,
202 p.; 25 cm. ISBN: 019514466X (alk.
paper) 0195144678 (pbk.: alk. paper)
Notes: Includes bibliographical references
and index. Subjects: Christianity and
culture--Congresses. Theology, Doctrinal--
Methodology--Congresses. Series:
Reflection and theory in the study of
religion. LC Classification: BR115.C8
C594 2001 Dewey Class No.: 261 21

Conversion to Christianity: historical and
anthropological perspectives on a great
transformation / edited and with an
introduction by Robert W. Hefner.
Published/Created: Berkeley: University of
California Press, c1993. Related Authors:
Hefner, Robert W., 1952- Description: x,
326 p.; 24 cm. ISBN: 0520078357 (cloth:
alk. paper) 0520078365 (pbk.: alk. paper)
Partial Contents: World building and the
rationality of conversion / Robert W.
Hefner. Notes: Includes bibliographical
references and index. Subjects:
Conversion--Christianity--History.

Christian converts. Missions--
Anthropological aspects. Religion and
politics. Religion and culture. LC
Classification: BV4916 .C67 1993 Dewey
Class No.: 248.2/4 20

Conway, Ruth. Choices at the heart of
technology: a Christian perspective / Ruth
Conway. Published/Created: Harrisburg,
Pa.: Trinity Press International, c1999.
Description: xii, 125 p.; 19 cm. ISBN:
1563382873 Notes: Includes
bibliographical references (p. 119-125).
Subjects: Technology--Religious aspects--
Christianity. Series: Christian mission and
modern culture LC Classification:
BR115.T42 C66 1999 Dewey Class No.:
261.5/6 21

Cook, Anthony E., 1964- The least of these:
race, law, and religion in American culture
/ Anthony E. Cook. Published/Created:
New York: Routledge, 1997. Description:
vii, 256 p.; 24 cm. ISBN: 0415916461 (alk.
paper) 041591647X (pbk.: alk. paper)
Notes: Includes bibliographical references
(p. 231-247) and index. Subjects: King,
Martin Luther, Jr., 1929-1968. Dewey,
John, 1859-1952. Christianity and politics-
-United States--History--20th century.
Liberalism--United States--Philosophy--
History--20th century. LC Classification:
BR115.P7 C646 1997 Dewey Class No.:
320.51/3/0973 21

Cook, Kaye V. Man & woman: alone & togethe
[i.e. together] / Kaye Cook & Lance Lee.
Published/Created: Wheaton, Ill.: Victor
Books, c1992. Related Authors: Lee,
Lance (Lance L.) Description: 288 p.: ill.;
24 cm. ISBN: 0896931811 Notes: "A
BridgePoint book." "Gender roles, identity,
and intimacy in a changing culture"--
Cover. Includes bibliographical references
(p. 270-283) and index. Subjects: Sex role-
-Religious aspects--Christianity. Man-
woman relationships--Religious aspects--
Christianity. LC Classification: BT708
.C66 1992 Dewey Class No.: 261.8/343 20

Cooper, Charles Champlin, 1874- comp.
Religion and the modern mind, edited by
Charles C. Cooper. Published/Created:

New York, Harper, 1929. Description: vi,
227 p. 20 cm. Partial Contents: An
adventure in religion, by C. C. Cooper.--
Religion from the standpoint of
agnosticism, by H. E. Barnes.--Religion
from the standpoint of science, by H. D.
Curtis.--Religion from the standpoint of
psychology, by E. S. Ames.--Religion from
the standpoint of philosophy, by M. R.
Gabbert.--Religion from the standpoint of
the ethical culture movement, by J. L.
Elliott. Subjects: Religion. LC
Classification: BL48 .C6

Coping with culture / edited and introduced by
Egbe Ifie. Published/Created: Ibadan:
Oputoru Books, c1999. Related Authors:
Ifie, Egbe. Description: xi, 440 p.: ill.,
maps; 26 cm. ISBN: 9783491350 Notes:
Includes bibliographical references (p.
440). Subjects: Social change--Africa.
Mythology, African. Christianity--Africa.
Folklore--Africa. Language and culture--
Africa. Africa--Civilization. Nigeria--
Civilization. Africa--Religion. LC
Classification: DT14 .C655 1999 Dewey
Class No.: 960 21

Copley, A. R. H. (Antony R. H.), 1937-
Religions in conflict: ideology, cultural
contact, and conversion in late-colonial
India / Antony Copley. Published/Created:
Delhi; New York: Oxford University Press,
1997. Description: xvii, 279 p.: ill., maps;
22 cm. ISBN: 0195636767 Notes: Includes
bibliographical references (p. [259]-269)
and index. Subjects: Protestant churches--
Missions--India. Church and social
problems--Christianity and culture--India.
Christianity and other religions--Hinduism.
Hinduism--Relations--Christianity. LC
Classification: BV3265.2 .C67 1997
Dewey Class No.: 266/.02341054 21

Cornille, C. (Catherine) A universal faith?:
peoples, cultures, religions, and the Christ:
essays in honor of Frank de Graeve /
Catherine Cornille & Valeer Neckebrouck.
Published/Created: Louvain: Peeters Press;
[Grand Rapids, Mich.]: W.B. Eerdmans,
[1992] Related Authors: Neckebrouck, V.
Description: x, 198 p.; 20 cm. ISBN:
9068314297 (pbk.) Notes: Includes

bibliographical references. Subjects: Graeve, F. de. Christianity and culture. Christianity and other religions. Religions--Relations. Series: Louvain theological & pastoral monographs; 9 LC Classification: BR115.C8 C6 1992 Dewey Class No.: 261.2 20

Cornille, C. (Catherine) The guru in Indian Catholicism: ambiguity or opportunity of inculturation? / Catherine Cornille. Published/Created: Louvain: Peeters Press, [1991]. Description: vi, 214 p.; 21 cm. ISBN: 9068313096 Notes: Includes bibliographical references (p. [203]-205) and index. Subjects: Christianity and culture. Christianity and other religions--Hinduism. Hinduism--Relations--Christianity. Series: Louvain theological & pastoral monographs; 6 LC Classification: BR115.C8 C67 1991 Dewey Class No.: 262/.1 20

Costas, Orlando E. Liberating news: a theology of contextual evangelization / by Orlando E. Costas. Published/Created: Grand Rapids, Mich.: Eerdmans, c1989. Description: xiv, 182 p.; 22 cm. ISBN: 0802803644 : Notes: Includes bibliographical references (p. 150-182). Subjects: Evangelistic work. Missions--Theory. Christianity and culture. Liberation theology. LC Classification: BV3793 .C65 1989 Dewey Class No.: 269/.2 19

Cote, Richard G., 1934- Re-visioning mission: the Catholic Church and culture in postmodern America / Richard G. Cote. Published/Created: New York: Paulist Press, c1996. Description: vi, 191 p.; 23 cm. ISBN: 0809136457 (pbk.: alk. paper) Notes: Includes bibliographical references (p. 173-191). Subjects: Catholic Church--United States--History--Civilization--20th century. Catholic Church--Missions--Christianity and culture--United States. Missions--Theory. Series: Isaac Hecker studies in religion and American culture LC Classification: BX1406.2 .C68 1996 Dewey Class No.: 282/.73/09049 20

Couch, Mal. Issues 2000: evangelical faith and cultural trends in the new millennium / by Mal Couch. Published/Created: Grand Rapids, MI: Kregel Publications, 1999. Description: p. cm. ISBN: 0825423635 Notes: Includes bibliographical references. Subjects: Christianity and culture--History--20th century. Christianity--20th century. LC Classification: BR115.C8 C635 1999 Dewey Class No.: 230/.04624 21

Court and politics in papal Rome, 1400-1800 / edited by Gianvittorio Signorotto and Maria Antonietta Visceglia. New York: Cambridge University Press, 2002. Related Authors: Signorotto, Gianvittorio. Visceglia, Maria Antonietta. Description: p. cm. ISBN: 0521641462 Notes: Includes bibliographical references and index. Subjects: Catholic Church. Collegium Cardinalium--History. Papal courts--History. Christianity and politics--Catholic Church--History. Series: Cambridge studies in Italian history and culture LC Classification: BX1818 .C68 2002 Dewey Class No.: 262/.135 21

Covert, William Chalmers, 1864-1942. Christ and culture, by William Chalmers Covert. Published/Created: New York, R. R. Smith, 1930. Description: ix, 91 p. 19 cm. Notes: Lectures delivered March 1930, on the Thomas F. Smyth foundation, Columbia Theological Seminary, Decatur, Georgia. cf. Statement. Subjects: Christianity. Culture. LC Classification: BR115.C8 C6 Dewey Class No.: 261.6

Cragg, Kenneth. Christianity in world perspective. Published/Created: London, Lutterworth, 1968. Description: 227 p. 23 cm. ISBN: 071881357X Notes: Bibliographical footnotes. Subjects: Christianity and culture. Christianity and other religions. Christianity--Essence, genius, nature. LC Classification: BR115.C8 C68 1968b Dewey Class No.: 260

Cragg, Kenneth. Christianity in world perspective. Published/Created: New York, Oxford University Press, 1968. Description: 227 p. 23 cm. Subjects:

Christianity and culture. Christianity and other religions. Christianity--Essence, genius, nature. LC Classification: BR115.C8 C68 Dewey Class No.: 260

Craig, Clarence Tucker, 1895- ed. The Challenge of our culture: Clarence Tucker Craig, editor ... Published/Created: New York, London, Harper & Brothers [1946] Description: xi p., 1 l., 205 p. 20 cm. Contents: The authors (p. ix-xi)-- Introduction: The faith by which we see, by C. T. Craig.--Men among machines, by Joseph Haroutunian.--Rivalries for power, by E. J. F. Arndt.--Racism and color caste, by B. G. Gallagher.--Personal tensions in modern life, by W. M. Horton.--The spirit of our culture, by A. N. Wilder.-- Secularism in the church, by J. H. Nichols. Notes: Prepared under the direction of Commission I-A of the Interseminary committee, C. T. Craig, chairman. cf. Pref. Issued with The church and organized movements. New York [c1946] "Further reading" at end of each chapter except the first. Subjects: Culture. Christianity--20th century. Church and social problems. LC Classification: BV600 .I55 vol. 1 Dewey Class No.: 261

Craig, Clarence Tucker, 1895-1953, ed. The challenge of our culture. Published/Created: Freeport, N.Y., Books for Libraries Press [1972, c1946] Description: xi, 205 p. 23 cm. ISBN: 0836927656 Notes: Original ed. issued as v. 1 of The Interseminary series. Includes bibliographies. Subjects: Culture-- Christianity--20th century--Church and social problems--Addresses, essays, lectures. Series: Interseminary series, v. 1. LC Classification: BR115.C8 C69 Dewey Class No.: 261.8

Crist, Terry M., 1965- Learning the language of Babylon: changing the world by engaging the culture / Terry M. Crist. Published/Created: Grand Rapids, Mich.: Chosen Books, c2001. Description: 189 p.; 23 cm. ISBN: 0800792882 (pbk.) 0800792874 (cloth) Notes: Includes bibliographical references (p. 183-185) and index. Subjects: Evangelistic work--United States. Christianity and culture--United States. LC Classification: BV3793 .C68 2001 Dewey Class No.: 261/.0973 21

Cross-cultural Christianity: a textbook on cross-cultural communication / by Atchenemou Hlama Clement ... [et al.]. Edition Information: 2nd ed. Published/Created: Jos, Nigeria: Nigeria Evangelical Missionary Institute, 1996. Related Authors: Clement, Atchenemou Hlama. Description: 136 p.: ill.; 21 cm. ISBN: 9782668699 Notes: Includes bibliographical references (p. 124-125). Subjects: Missions--Cross-cultural studies. Intercultural communication--Religious aspects Christianity. Christianity and culture--Nigeria. Missions--Study and teaching--Nigeria. LC Classification: BV2063 .C76 1996 Dewey Class No.: 266 21

Crosscurrents in indigenous spirituality: interface of Maya, Catholic, and Protestant worldviews / edited by Guillermo Cook. Published/Created: Leiden; New York: E.J. Brill, 1997. Related Authors: Cook, Guillermo. Description: xvi, 329 p.: ill., map; 25 cm. ISBN: 9004106227 (alk. paper) Notes: Includes bibliographical references (p. [327]-329) and index. Subjects: Catholic Church. Mayas-- Religion. Maya philosophy. Christianity and culture--Spiritual life--Latin America. Protestantism. Series: Studies in Christian mission, 0924-9389; v. 18 LC Classification: F1435.3.R3 C76 1997 Dewey Class No.: 200/.89/97415 21

Crosswinds: the reformation digest. Published/Created: Sunnyvale, CA: Coalition on Revival, c1992- Related Authors: Grimstead, Jay. Coalition on Revival (U.S.). Description: v.: ill.; 28 cm. Vol. 1, no. 1 (winter 1992)- Current Frequency: Quarterly ISSN: 1065-6863 Notes: Title from cover. Editor: Jay Grimstead. SERBIB/SERLOC merged record Subjects: Christianity and culture-- Church and the world--Periodicals. LC Classification: BR115.C8 C76 Dewey Class No.: 261/.05 20

Crowe, Jerome. From Jerusalem to Antioch: the Gospel across cultures / Jerome Crowe. Published/Created: Collegeville, Minn.: Liturgical Press, c1997. Description: xx, 160 p.; 21 cm. ISBN: 0814624324 Notes: Includes bibliographical references. Subjects: Bible. N.T. Acts--Criticism, interpretation, etc. Bible. N.T. Epistles of Paul--Criticism, interpretation, etc. Jerusalem in the Bible. Christianity and culture--Middle East. Church history--Primitive and early church, ca. 30-600. Missions--Middle East. Missions--History--Early church, ca. 30-600. Jerusalem--Church history. Antioch (Turkey)--Church history. LC Classification: BS2545.J4 C76 1997 Dewey Class No.: 270.1 21

Cultural identity in Latin America and in Europe: a colloquium on the occasion of the retirement of Prof. Dr. Jacques van Nieuwenhove on February 5, 1993 / edited by Arnulf Camps and Berma Klein Goldewijk. Published/Created: Kampen: Uitgeverij Kok, 1996. Related Authors: Nieuwenhove, Jacques van. Camps, Arnulf, 1925- Goldewijk, Berma Klein. Description: vii, 93 p.; 24 cm. ISBN: 9024271401 Notes: "Bibliography [of] Jacques van Nieuwenhove": p. 88-92. Includes bibliographical references. Subjects: Christianity and culture--Latin America. Christianity and culture--Europe. Group identity--Latin America. Group identity--Europe. Liberation theology. Series: Kerk en theologie in context; nr. 32. LC Classification: IN PROCESS

Cultural information service. Published/Created: [New York, CIStems, Inc.] Description: ill. 29 cm. Current Frequency: monthly (except July and Aug.) ISSN: 0097-952X Notes: SERBIB/SERLOC merged record Subjects: Christianity and culture--Periodicals. LC Classification: BR115.C8 C84 Dewey Class No.: 261.8/3

Cultural wars in American politics: critical reviews of a popular myth / Rhys H. Williams, editor. Published/Created: New York: Aldine de Gruyter, c1997. Related Authors: Williams, Rhys H. Description:

xii, 299 p.: ill.; 24 cm. ISBN: 0202305635 (cloth: acid-free paper) 0202305643 (pbk.: acid-free paper) Notes: Includes bibliographical references and index. Subjects: Culture conflict--Politics and culture--United States--History--20th century. Christianity and politics--Protestant churches. Protestants--United States--Political activity. Series: Social problems and social issues LC Classification: E169.12 .C77 1997 Dewey Class No.: 973.92 21

Culture and Christianity: the dialectics of transformation / edited by George R. Saunders. Published/Created: New York: Greenwood Press, 1988. Related Authors: Saunders, George R., 1946- Description: xiii, 217 p.: maps; 24 cm. ISBN: 0313261180 (lib. bdg.: alk. paper) Notes: Includes index. Bibliography: p. [195]-210. Subjects: Christianity and culture. Series: Contributions to the study of anthropology, 0890-9377; no. 2 LC Classification: BR115.C8 C85 1988 Dewey Class No.: 261 19

Culture and control in counter-reformation Spain / Anne J. Cruz and Mary Elizabeth Perry, editors. Published/Created: Minneapolis: University of Minnesota Press, c1992. Related Authors: Cruz, Anne J., 1941- Perry, Mary Elizabeth, 1937- Description: xxiii, 267 p.; 23 cm. ISBN: 0816620253 (hard: alk. paper): 0816620261 (pbk.: alk. paper) : Notes: Includes bibliographical references and index. Subjects: Counter-Reformation--Spain. Control (Psychology)--Religious aspects--Christianity. Spain--Civilization--1516-1700. Series: Hispanic issues; 7. LC Classification: BX1585 .C84 1992 Dewey Class No.: 306.6/8246/09031 20

Culture and evangelization: collection of Indian anthropological readings / edited by R.E. Hedlund and Beulah Herbert. Published/Created: Madras, India: Church Growth Research Centre: Also available at Evangelical Literature Service, [198-?] Related Authors: Hedlund, Roger E. Herbert, Beulah. Description: 164 p.: ill.; 23 cm. Notes: Includes bibliographical references. Subjects: Christianity and culture. Evangelistic work--Anthropology--India--Social life and customs. LC Classification: BR115.C8 C848 1980

Culture, religion, and society: essays in honour of Richard W. Taylor / edited by Saral K. Chatterji and Hunter P. Mabry. Published/Created: Delhi: Published for the Christian Institute for the Study of Religion and Society, Bangalore, by ISPCK, 1996. Related Authors: Taylor, Richard Warren, 1924- Chatterji, Saral Kumar, 1932- Mabry, Hunter P. Christian Institute for the Study of Religion and Society, Bangalore. I.S.P.C.K. (Organization) Description: x, 310 p.; 22 cm. ISBN: 817214170X Summary: Contributed articles. Notes: Includes bibliographical references. Subjects: Christianity and culture. Christianity--India. India--Religion. India--Social conditions. LC Classification: BR115.C8 C87 1996

Currie, Thomas W. Ambushed by grace: the virtues of a useless faith / Thomas W. Currie III. Published/Created: Allison Park, Pa.: Pickwick Publications, c1993. Description: x, 75 p.; 22 cm. ISBN: 1556350171 Notes: Includes bibliographical references. Subjects: Liberty--Religious aspects--Christianity. Grace (Theology) Faith. Christianity and culture. Relevance. Series: Princeton theological monograph series; 32 LC Classification: BT810.2 .C84 1993 Dewey Class No.: 230 20

Dah, Jonas N. (Jonas Nwiyende), 1940- Chieftaincy, widowhood, and ngambi in Cameroon / Jonas N. Dah. Pforzheim, Germany: [s.n.], 1995. Description: iv, 44 p.; 21 cm. Notes: Cover title. Includes bibliographical references. Subjects: Chiefdoms--Widowhood--Divination--Christianity and culture--Cameroon. LC Classification: GN865.C26 D34 1995

Dancing in the dark: youth, popular culture, and the electronic media / by Quentin J. Schultze ... [et al.]. Published/Created: Grand Rapids, Mich.: W.B. Eerdmans Pub. Co., c1991. Related Authors: Schultze, Quentin J. (Quentin James), 1952- Calvin Center for Christian Scholarship. Description: xii, 348 p.: ill.; 23 cm. ISBN: 0802805302 : Notes: "Calvin Center for Christian Scholarship." Includes bibliographical references (p. 310-341) and index. Subjects: Mass media and youth--United States. Popular culture--United States. Popular culture--Religious aspects--Christianity. LC Classification: HQ799.2.M35 D36 1990 Dewey Class No.: 302.23/083 20

Dangerous 'isms / hosted by the Southaven Church of Christ, Southaven, Mississippi; B.J. Clarke, lectureship director. Published/Created: Pulaski, TN (217 E. Jefferson, Pulaski 38478): Sain Publications, c1997. Related Authors: Clarke, B. J. Southaven Church of Christ (Southaven, Miss.) Description: 758 p.: ill.; 22 cm. Notes: Includes bibliographical references. Subjects: Apologetics. Christianity and other religions. Christianity and culture. Philosophy and religion. Series: Power lectures; 1997 LC Classification: BT1105 .D36 1997 Dewey Class No.: 239/.9 21

Daniélou, Jean. Gospel message and Hellenistic culture. Translated, edited, and with a postscript by John Austin Baker. Published/Created: London, Darton, Longman & Todd; Philadelphia, Westminster Press [1973] Description: x, 540 p. 24 cm. ISBN: 0664209610 (Westminster) Notes: Translation of Message évangélique et culture hellénistique aux IIe et IIIe siècles. Bibliography: p. [507]-513. Subjects: Christianity and other religions--Greek. Hellenism. Theology, Doctrinal--History--Early church, ca. 30-600. Greece--Religion. Series: His A history of early Christian doctrine before the Council of Nicaea, v. 2 LC Classification: BR128.G8 D313 Dewey Class No.: 230/.1

Darby, James Ezra, 1856- Jesus, an economic mediator: God's remedy for industrial and international ills / by James E. Darby. Published/Created: New York, Chicago [etc.]: Fleming H. Revell company c1922.

Description: 256 p.; 21 cm. Subjects: Jesus Christ--Teachings. Christianity and economics. Series: Christ and culture collection. LC Classification: BS2417.E3 D3

Davidson, Allan K. Aotearoa New Zealand: defining moments in the gospel-culture encounter / Allan K. Davidson. Published/Created: Geneva, Switzerland: WCC Publications, c1996. Related Authors: World Council of Churches. Description: xii, 63 p.; 21 cm. ISBN: 2825412058 Notes: Includes bibliographical references. Subjects: Christianity--Christianity and culture--New Zealand--Church history. Series: Gospel and cultures pamphlet; 12 LC Classification: BR1480 .D37 1996 Dewey Class No.: 279.3 21

Dawn, Marva J. Is it a lost cause?: having the heart of God for the church's children / Marva J. Dawn. Published/Created: Grand Rapids, Mich.: W.B. Eerdmans Pub., c1997. Description: 256 p.; 23 cm. ISBN: 0802843735 (pbk.: alk. paper) Notes: Includes bibliographical references (p. 250-255). Subjects: Church work with children--Christian education of children--Christianity and culture--United States--Church history--20th century. LC Classification: BR526 .D37 1997 Dewey Class No.: 261.8/3423 21

Dawn, Marva J. Reaching out without dumbing down: a theology of worship for the turn-of-the-century culture / Marva J. Dawn. Published/Created: Grand Rapids, Mich.: W.B. Eerdmans, 1995. Description: xi, 316 p.; 24 cm. ISBN: 0802841023 (pbk.: alk. paper) Notes: Includes bibliographical references (p. 308-316). Subjects: Public worship. Christianity and culture. LC Classification: BV15 .D38 1995 Dewey Class No.: 264/.001 20

Dawson, Christopher, 1889-1970. Christianity and European culture: selections from the work of Christopher Dawson / edited by Gerald J. Russello. Published/Created: Washington, D.C.: Catholic University of America Press, 1998. Related Authors:

Russello, Gerald J., 1971- Description: xxxiii, 262 p.; 22 cm. ISBN: 0813209145 (pbk.: alk. paper) Notes: Includes bibliographical references and index. Subjects: Christianity and culture--Europe--Church history. LC Classification: BR735 .D38 1998 Dewey Class No.: 261/.094 21

Dawson, Christopher, 1889-1970. Christianity and the new age / by Christopher Dawson; introduction by John J. Mulloy. Published/Created: Manchester, N.H.: Sophia Institute Press, c1985. Description: xv, 113 p.; 19 cm. ISBN: 0918477026: 0918477018 (pbk.) : Notes: Reprint. Originally published: London: Sheed & Ward, 1931. Includes bibliographical references and index. Subjects: Christianity and culture. Christianity--20th century. Christianity, Modern--20th century. Humanism. Civilization, Secular. LC Classification: BR115.C8 D29 1985 Dewey Class No.: 261 19

Dawson, Christopher, 1889-1970. Enquiries into religion and culture, by Christopher Dawson ... Published/Created: New York, Sheed & Ward, 1933. Description: xi, 347 p. fold. tab. 23 cm. Partial Contents: Civilisation and morals.--The mystery of China.--Rationalism and intellectualism.--Islamic mysticism.--On spiritual intuition in Christian philosophy.--St. Augustine and his age.--Christianity and sex.--Religion and life.--The nature and destiny of man. Notes: Essays, most of which are reprinted from various sources. cf. Introd. Subjects: Religion. Civilization. LC Classification: BL55 .D27 Dewey Class No.: 204

Dawson, Christopher, 1889-1970. The formation of Christendom, by Christopher Dawson. New York, Sheed and Ward [1967] Description: x, 309 p. 22 cm. Notes: Bibliographical footnotes. Subjects: Civilization, Christian, Medieval. Christianity and culture--History--Middle Ages, 600-1500. LC Classification: BR115.C5 D363 Dewey Class No.: 261

Dawson, Christopher, 1889-1970. The historic reality of Christian culture; a way to the renewal of human life. Published/Created:

New York, Harper [1960] Description: 124 p. 22 cm. Notes: Includes bibliography. Subjects: Christianity and culture. Civilization, Christian. Series: Religious perspectives, v. 1 LC Classification: BR115.C8 D3 Dewey Class No.: 261

Dawson, Christopher, 1889-1970. The historic reality of Christian culture: a way to the renewal of human life / by Christopher Dawson. Westport, Conn.: Greenwood Press, 1976, c1960. Description: 124 p.; 23 cm. ISBN: 0837190010 Notes: Reprint of the ed. published by Routledge and Kegan Paul, London, which was issued as v. 1 of Religious perspectives. Includes index. Includes bibliographical references and index. Subjects: Christianity and culture. Civilization, Christian. Series: Religious perspectives; v. 1. LC Classification: BR115.C8 D3 1976 Dewey Class No.: 261

Dayal, Har, 1884-1939. Twelve religions and modern life, by Har Dayal. Published/Created: Edgware (Middlsex) Eng., Modern culture institute [1938] Related Authors: Modern Culture Institute (Edgeware, England) Description: 250 p. 17 cm. Notes: An attempt "to indicate some elements of permanent value in twelve religious systems from the standpoint of modern humanism". cf. Pref. "First published in 1938." Subjects: Religions. Humanism--20th century. Positivism. LC Classification: BL85 .D37

Dayton, Edward R. What ever happened to commitment? / Edward R. Dayton. Published/Created: Grand Rapids, Mich.: Zondervan Pub. House, c1984. Description: 234 p.; 21 cm. ISBN: 0310231612 (pbk.) Notes: Includes indexes. Bibliography: p. 217-224. Subjects: Evangelicalism--United States. Christianity and culture. Commitment to the church. United States--Church history. LC Classification: BR1642.U5 D4 1984 Dewey Class No.: 280/.4 19

De doctrina Christiana: a classic of western culture / edited by Duane W.H. Arnold and Pamela Bright. Published/Created: Notre Dame: University of Notre Dame Press,

c1995. Related Authors: Arnold, Duane W. H. Bright, Pamela, 1937- Description: xx, 271 p.; 24 cm. ISBN: 0268008744 (alk. paper) Notes: Includes bibliographical references (p. 247-260) and indexes. Subjects: Augustine, Saint, Bishop of Hippo. De doctrina Christiana. Bible--Criticism, interpretation, etc.--History--Early church, ca. 30-600. Theology--History--Early church, ca. 30-600. Series: Christianity and Judaism in antiquity; v. 9 LC Classification: BR65.A6552 D63 1995 Dewey Class No.: 230/.14 20

De Sherbinin, Julie W. Chekhov and Russian religious culture: the poetics of the Marian paradigm / Julie W. de Sherbinin. Published/Created: Evanston, Ill.: Northwestern University Press, 1997. Description: xiii, 189 p.: ill.; 25 cm. ISBN: 0810114046 (cloth: alk. paper) Notes: Includes bibliographical references (p. 153-184) and index. Subjects: Chekhov, Anton Pavlovich, 1860-1904 --Knowledge Christianity. Mary, Blessed Virgin, Saint--In literature. Mary Magdalene, Saint--In literature. Mary, of Egypt, Saint--In literature. Christianity in literature. Series: Studies in Russian literature and theory LC Classification: PG3458.Z9 C454 1997 Dewey Class No.: 891.73/3 21

De Vos, Craig Steven, 1964- Church and community conflicts: the relationships of the Thessalonian, Corinthian, and Philippian churches with their wider civic communities / Craig Steven de Vos. Published/Created: Atlanta, Ga.: Scholars Press, c1999. Description: x, 332 p.; 22 cm. ISBN: 0788505637 (cloth: alk. paper) Notes: Originally presented as the author's thesis (Ph. D.)--Flinders University of South Australia, 1997. Includes bibliographical references (p. [305]-332). Subjects: Christianity and culture--Greece--Thessalonik̄e--History Early church, ca. 30-600. Christianity and culture--Greece--Corinth--History--Early church, ca. 30-600. Christianity and culture--Greece--Philippi (Extinct city) History--Early church, ca. 30-600. Thessalonik̄e (Greece)--Church history. Corinth (Greece)--Church history. Philippi (Extinct city)--Church history. Series: Dissertation series (Society of Biblical Literature); no. 168. LC Classification: BR868.T47 D48 1999 Dewey Class No.: 274.95/01 21

Deacy, Christopher. Screen christologies: redemption and the medium of film / Christopher Deacy. Published/Created: Cardiff: University of Wales Press, 2001. Related Authors: Deacy, Christopher, ed. Description: [viii], 212 p.; 22 cm. ISBN: 0708317138 070831712X (pbk.) Notes: "This book started out as a Ph.D. thesis"-- P. [viii]. Includes bibliographical references (p. [188]-200) and index. Filmography: p. [201]-204. Subjects: Motion pictures--Religious aspects-- Christianity. Redemption in motion pictures. Series: Religion, culture, and society LC Classification: PN1995.5 .D43 2001 Dewey Class No.: 791.43/6823 21

Dempsey, Corinne G. Kerala Christian sainthood: collisions of culture and worldview in South India / Corinne G. Dempsey. Published/Created: Oxford; New York: Oxford University Press, 2001. Description: xiii, 213 p.: ill.; 24 cm. ISBN: 0195130286 (alk. paper) Notes: Includes bibliographical references (p. 193-202) and index. Subjects: Alph¯onsa, Sister, 1910- 1946 --Cult--India--Kerala. Christians-- India--Kerala. Christian saints--Cult-- India--Kerala. Christianity and other religions--Hinduism. Hinduism--Relations- -Christianity. Kerala (India)--Religious life and customs. LC Classification: BR1156.K47 D45 2001 Dewey Class No.: 275.4/83 21

Dennis, Barbara, 1942- Charlotte Yonge (1823- 1901): novelist of the Oxford Movement: a literature of Victorian culture and society / Barbara Dennis. Published/Created: Lewiston: E. Mellen Press, c1992. Description: 176 p.: ill.; 24 cm. ISBN: 0773495444 Notes: Includes bibliographical references (p. [163]-168) and index. Subjects: Yonge, Charlotte Mary, 1823-1901. Church of England--In literature. Christianity and literature-- England--History--19th century. Literature and society--England--History--19th

century. Women and literature--England-- History--19th century. Women novelists, English--19th century--Biography. Anglo-Catholicism in literature. Oxford movement. LC Classification: PR5913 .D4 1992 Dewey Class No.: 823/.8 B 20

Dennis, Lane T. A reason for hope / Lane T. Dennis. Published/Created: Old Tappan, N.J.: F. H. Revell Co., c1976. Description: 189 p.; 21 cm. ISBN: 0800707729 : Notes: Includes bibliographical references. Subjects: Christian life. Christianity and culture. Country life--Michigan. LC Classification: BV4501.2 .D443 Dewey Class No.: 248/.4

DeParrie, Paul. Romanced to death: the sexual seduction of American culture / Paul deParrie. Edition Information: 1st ed. Published/Created: Brentwood, Tenn.: Wolgemuth & Hyatt, 1990. Description: ix, 273 p.; 22 cm. ISBN: 0943497906 Notes: Includes bibliographical references (p. 247-266) and index. Subjects: Sex-- Religious aspects--Christianity. Popular culture--United States. United States-- Moral conditions. LC Classification: BT708 .D46 1990 Dewey Class No.: 241/.66 20

Derrick, Christopher, 1921- Light of revelation and non-Christians. Published/Created: [Staten Island, N.Y., Alba House, 1965] Description: 141 p. 21 cm. Subjects: Catholic Church--Missions. Culture. Christianity and other religions. LC Classification: BR115.C8 D4 Dewey Class No.: 261.2

Desai, Ram. Christianity in Africa as seen by Africans. Edited, with an introd., by Ram Desai. Published/Created: Denver, A. Swallow [1962] Description: 135 p. 23 cm. Partial Contents: Christianity in danger: background. An historical perspective. Africans; the early missionary image. Motivations behind conversion. The role of the missionary in the conquest of Africa. Missionary contributions; real or apparent? Positive contributions of Christianity. Christianity and African nationalism. Islam; the cross and the crescent. By R.

Desai.--African life and ideals, by P. Nyabongo.--Religious life in Africa. Christianity in Africa. By M. Ojike.-- Imperialism and the spiritual freedom, by A. Adjei.--Christianity and clitoridectomy, by J. Kenyatta.--Christianity and the Bantu, by D.D.T. Jabavubu.--Christianity and Ashanti, by K.A. Busia. Subjects: Church and social problems--Africa. Christianity-- Influence--Africa. Christians--Africa. LC Classification: BR1360 .D42 Dewey Class No.: 261.83

Dhavamony, Mariasusai. Christian theology of inculturation / Mariasusai Dhavamony. Published/Created: Roma: Editrice pontificia università gregoriana, 1997. Description: 215 p.; 24 cm. ISBN: 8876527389 Notes: Includes bibliographical references (p. [211]-215). Subjects: Christianity and culture--History--20th century. Theology, Doctrinal--Asia. Series: Documenta missionalia; 24 LC Classification: BR115.C8 D45 1997 Dewey Class No.: 261 21

Dickson, Kwesi A. Uncompleted mission: Christianity and exclusivism / Kwesi A. Dickson. Published/Created: Maryknoll, N.Y.: Orbis Books, c1991. Description: x, 177 p.; 21 cm. ISBN: 0883447517 : Notes: Includes bibliographical references (p. 173-174) and index. Subjects: Missions. Christianity and culture. Religious tolerance--Christianity. Christianity and other religions. LC Classification: BV2063 .D48 1991 Dewey Class No.: 261 20

Diehl, Carl Gustav. Church and shrine; intermingling patterns of culture in the life of some Christian groups in South India. Published/Created: Uppsala, 1965. Description: 203 p. illus., map. 24 cm. Notes: Bibliography: p. [199]-203. Subjects: Christians in India. Christianity and other religions--Hinduism. Hinduism--Relations--Christianity. Series: Historia religionum; 2. LC Classification: BR1155 .D5

Discoveries, missionary expansion, and Asian cultures / edited by Teotonio R. de Souza; foreword by Gregory Naik.

Published/Created: New Delhi: Concept Pub. Co., 1994. Related Authors: De Souza, Teotonio R., 1947- Description: 215 p.; 23 cm. ISBN: 8170224977 : Summary: Contributed articles, most on Portuguese Missions in India. Notes: Includes bibliographical references and index. Subjects: Missions--India--History. Missions, Portuguese--India--History. Christianity and culture. LC Classification: BV3265.2 .D57 1994

Divine representations: postmodernism and spirituality / Ann W. Astell, editor. Published/Created: New York: Paulist Press, c1994. Related Authors: Astell, Ann W. Description: viii, 269 p.; 23 cm. ISBN: 0809135280 : Notes: Includes bibliographical references. Subjects: Mary, Blessed Virgin, Saint--Theology. Spirituality. Postmodernism--Religious aspects--Christianity. Religion and culture. LC Classification: BV4510.2 .D56 1994 Dewey Class No.: 248 20

Doing contextual theology: a festschrift in honour of Bruce John Nicholls / edited by Sunand Sumithra. Bangalore, India: Theological Book Trust, 1992. Related Authors: Nicholls, Bruce. Sumithra, Sunand. Description: vii, 172 p.; 23 cm. Notes: Cover Doing theology in context. "Published writings of Bruce J. Nicholls": p. 167-171. Includes bibliographical references. Subjects: Theology--Methodology. Christianity and culture. Series: Theological issues series; no. 2 LC Classification: BR118 .D623 1992

Doing theology in context: South African perspectives / edited by John W. de Gruchy and Charles Villa-Vicencio. Maryknoll, N.Y.: Orbis Books; Cape Town: D. Philip, 1994. Related Authors: De Gruchy, John W. Villa-Vicencio, Charles. Description: xi, 236 p.; 24 cm. ISBN: 0883449897 Notes: Includes bibliographical references and index. Subjects: Theology, Doctrinal--South Africa. Christianity and culture--South Africa. Series: Theology and praxis; v. 1 LC Classification: BT65 .D65 1994 Dewey Class No.: 230/.0968 20

Doing theology with cultures of Asia / [editor, Yeow Choo Lak]. Published/Created: Singapore: ATESEA, 1988. Related Authors: Yeow, Choo Lak. Association for Theological Education in South East Asia. Description: iv, 148 p.: ill.; 23 cm. ISBN: 9810003099 : Notes: Includes bibliographical references (p. 136-138). Subjects: Christianity and culture--Congresses. Theology, Doctrinal--Asia--Congresses. Series: ATESEA occasional papers; no. 6 LC Classification: BR115.C8 D65 1988 Dewey Class No.: 230/.095 20

DomNwachukwu, Peter Nlemadim, 1952- Authentic African Christianity: an inculturation model for the Igbo / Peter Nlemadim DomNwachukwu. Published/Created: New York: P. Lang, c2000. Description: xiv, 237 p.: map; 24 cm. ISBN: 0820444502 (acid-free paper) Notes: Includes bibliographical references (p. [213]-224) and index. Subjects: Christianity and culture--Nigeria--Imo State. Igbo (African people)--Religion. Series: American university studies. Series VII, Theology and religion, 0740-0446; vol. 210 LC Classification: BR1463.N5 D66 2000 Dewey Class No.: 276.69/4 21

Donaldson, Devlin, 1957- Pinocchio nation: embracing truth in a culture of lies / Devlin Donaldson and Steve Wamberg. Published/Created: Colorado Springs, CO: Piñon Press, c2001. Related Authors: Wamberg, Steve. Description: 174 p.; 23 cm. ISBN: 1576832244 (pbk.) Notes: "Includes a personal integrity workbook." Includes bibliographical references. Subjects: Truthfulness and falsehood--Religious aspects Christianity. LC Classification: BV4627.F3 D66 2001 Dewey Class No.: 241/.673 21

Dooyeweerd, H. (Herman), 1894-1977. Roots of Western culture: pagan, secular, and Christian options / Herman Dooyeweerd; John Kraay, translator; Mark Vander Vennen and Bernard Zylstra, editors. Published/Created: Toronto: Wedge Pub. Foundation, c1979. Related Authors: Vennen, Mark Vander. Zylstra, Bernard. Description: xii, 228 p.; 24 cm. ISBN:

0889061041 : Notes: Translation of Vernieuwing en bezinning. Includes bibliographical references and indexes. Subjects: Civilization, Christian. Christianity--Essence, genius, nature. Netherlands--Religion. LC Classification: BR115.C5 D613 Dewey Class No.: 261 19

Doran, Robert M., 1939- Psychic conversion and theological foundations: toward a reorientation of the human sciences / Robert M. Doran. Published/Created: Chico, Calif.: Scholars Press, c1981. Description: xiii, 231 p.; 23 cm. ISBN: 089130522X (pbk.) Notes: Includes bibliographical references. Subjects: Lonergan, Bernard J. F. History--Religious aspects--Christianity. Christianity and culture. Man (Christian theology) Series: AAR studies in religion; no. 25. LC Classification: BR115.H5 D65 Dewey Class No.: 230 19

Doran, Robert M., 1939- Theological foundations / Robert M. Doran. Published/Created: Milwaukee: Marquette University Press, c1995. Description: 2 v.; 22 cm. ISBN: 0874626323 (pbk.: v. 1) 0874626331 (pbk.: v. 2) Contents: v. 1. Intentionality and psyche -- v. 2. Theology and culture. Notes: Includes bibliographical references. Subjects: Catholic Church--Doctrines. Theology, Doctrinal. Christianity--Psychology. Man (Christian theology) Sociology, Christian (Catholic) Series: Marquette studies in theology; #8-9. LC Classification: BT78 .D56 1995 Dewey Class No.: 230/.01 20

Down to earth: studies in Christianity and culture: the papers of the Lausanne consultation on gospel and culture / edited by Robert T. Coote and John Stott. Published/Created: Grand Rapids, Mich.: Eerdmans, 1980. Related Authors: Coote, Robert T., 1932- Stott, John R. W. Description: x, 342 p.; 21 cm. ISBN: 0802818277 : Notes: Abridgement of Gospel & culture. Includes bibliographies. Subjects: Christianity and culture--Congresses. LC Classification: BR115.C8 G672 Dewey Class No.: 261 19

Drane, John William. The McDonaldization of the church: consumer culture and the church's future / by John Drane. Published/Created: Macon, Ga.: Smyth & Helwys Pub., 2002. Description: p. cm. ISBN: 1573123749 (pbk.) Notes: Originally published: London: Darton, Longman & Todd, 2000. Includes bibliographical references (p.) and index. Subjects: Church renewal. Spirituality--Christianity. LC Classification: BV600.2 .D67 2002 Dewey Class No.: 261 21

D'Souza, Jerome. The Church and civilization. Edition Information: [1st ed.] Garden City, N.Y., Doubleday, 1967. Description: 191 p. 22 cm. Notes: Bibliography: p. [189]-191. Subjects: Christianity and culture--History. LC Classification: BR148 .D68 Dewey Class No.: 270

DuCille, Frank O. (Frank Olivier) Indigenization: how to grow black churches in white denominations / Frank O. duCille, Sr. Published/Created: Pineville, N.C.: F.O. duCille, c1983. Description: 135 p.: ill.; 21 cm. Notes: Bibliography: p. 130-135. Subjects: Afro-American Presbyterians. Race relations--Religious aspects--Christianity. Race relations--Religious aspects--Presbyterian Church. Presbyterian Church--United States. Christianity and culture. LC Classification: BX8946.A35 D83 1983 Dewey Class No.: 285/.1/08996073 19

Dudley, Roger L. The world--love it or leave it? / Roger L. Dudley. Published/Created: Boise, Idaho: Pacific Press Pub. Assoc., c1986. Description: 77 p.; 21 cm. ISBN: 0816306656 (pbk.) Notes: Includes bibliographical references. Subjects: Christianity and culture. Seventh-Day Adventists. LC Classification: BR115.C8 D83 1986 Dewey Class No.: 261 19

Duffy, Regis A. An American Emmaus: faith and sacrament in the American culture / by Regis A. Duffy. New York: Crossroad, 1995. Description: 184 p.; 23 cm. ISBN: 0824515404 Notes: Includes bibliographical references (p. [154]-184). Subjects: Catholic Church--United States--Liturgy--Doctrines. Christianity and culture. Sacraments--Catholic Church. United States--Church history--20th century. LC Classification: BX1406.2 .D84 1995 Dewey Class No.: 282/.73 20

Dumais, Marcel, 1936- Cultural change and liberation in a Christian perspective / M. Dumais, R. Goldie, A. 'Swiecicki. Published/Created: Rome: Gregorian University Press, 1987. Related Authors: Goldie, R. M. (Rosemary M.) 'Swiecicki, Andrzej. Description: xi, 63 p.; 24 cm. Notes: Includes bibliographies. Subjects: Bible. N.T. Acts--Criticism, interpretation, etc. Sociology, Christian--History--Early church, ca. 30-600. Women--Religious life. Christianity and culture. Series: Inculturation; 10 LC Classification: BT738 .D767 1987 Dewey Class No.: 261 19

Durant, Will, 1885- The story of civilization. Published/Created: New York, Simon and Schuster, 1935- Related Authors: Durant, Ariel Description: v. illus., maps, ports. 26 cm. Notes: Vols. 7- by Will and Ariel Durant. Includes bibliographies. Subjects: Civilization--History. LC Classification: CB53 .D85 Dewey Class No.: 909

Dyrness, William A. How does America hear the gospel? / William A. Dyrness. Published/Created: Grand Rapids, Mich.: W.B. Eerdmans, c1989. Description: xi, 164 p.: ill.; 22 cm. ISBN: 0802804373 : Notes: Bibliography: p. 154-164. Subjects: Christianity and culture. United States--Religion--Church history--20th century. LC Classification: BR526 .D97 1989 Dewey Class No.: 261/.0973 20

Dyrness, William A. Invitation to cross-cultural theology: case studies in vernacular theologies / William A. Dyrness. Published/Created: Grand Rapids, Mich.: Zondervan, c1992. Description: 194 p.: ill.; 20 cm. ISBN: 0310535816 Notes: Includes bibliographical references (p. 188-193) and index. Subjects: Theology--Methodology--Christianity and culture--Case studies. LC Classification: BR118 .D97 1992 Dewey Class No.: 230/.09 20

Dyrness, William A. Learning about theology from the Third World / William A. Dyrness. Published/Created: Grand Rapids, MI: Academie Books, Zondervan Pub. House, c1990. Description: ix, 221 p.; 21 cm. ISBN: 0310209714 : Notes: Includes bibliographical references (p. 197-211) and index. Subjects: Theology, Doctrinal--Developing countries--History--20th century. Theology--Methodology. Christianity and culture. LC Classification: BT30.D44 D96 1990 Dewey Class No.: 230/.09172/4 20

Dyrness, William A. The earth is God's: a theology of American culture / William A. Dyrness. Published/Created: Maryknoll, N.Y.: Orbis Books, 1997. Description: xvi, 208 p.; 23 cm. ISBN: 157075151X (alk. paper) Notes: Includes bibliographical references (p. 165-198) and indexes. Subjects: Christianity and culture--Theology, Doctrinal--Evangelicalism--United States. Series: Faith and cultures series LC Classification: BR115.C8 D97 1997 Dewey Class No.: 261/.0973 21

Eagleton, Terence, 1943- The new left Church. London, Melbourne, Sheed & Ward, 1966. Description: x, 180 p. 18 cm. Subjects: Christianity and culture. LC Classification: BR115.C8 E3 1966a

Eagleton, Terry, 1943- The New Left church [essays] Published/Created: Baltimore, Helicon [1966] Description: x, 180 p. 18 cm. Notes: Bibliographical footnotes. Subjects: Christianity and culture. LC Classification: BR115.C8 E3 Dewey Class No.: 261

Eakin, Frank E., 1936- Religion in Western culture: selected issues / Frank E. Eakin, Jr. Published/Created: Washington: University Press of America, c1977. Description: xviii, 328 p.: ill.; 22 cm. ISBN: 0819102563 Notes: Includes indexes. Bibliography: p. 286-292. Subjects: Bible--Criticism, interpretation, etc. Religion. Christianity. Judaism. LC Classification: BL48 .E15 Dewey Class No.: 209/.182/1

Eckman, James P. Christian ethics in a postmodern world / by James P. Eckman. Wheaton, IL: Evangelical Training Association, 1999. Description: 96 p.; 22 cm. ISBN: 0910566798 Notes: Includes bibliographical references (p. 95-96). Subjects: Christian ethics. Postmodernism--Religious aspects--Christianity. Christianity and culture.

Edington, Carol, 1965- Court and culture in Renaissance Scotland: Sir David Lindsay of the Mount / Carol Edington. Amherst: University of Massachusetts Press, c1994. Description: x, 276 p.: ill.; 24 cm. ISBN: 0870239341 (alk. paper) Notes: Includes bibliographical references (p. 261-272) and index. Subjects: Lindsay, David, Sir, fl. 1490-1555. Politics and literature--Scotland--Christianity and literature--History--16th century. Authors, Scottish--To 1700-- Reformers--Renaissance--Scotland--Court and courtiers--Church history--16th century. Series: Massachusetts studies in early modern culture LC Classification: PR2296.L6 Z677 1994 Dewey Class No.: 821/.2 B 20

Edwards, D. Miall (David Miall), b. 1873. Crefydd a diwylliant, Published/Created: Wrecsam, Hughes a'i fab, 1934. Description: 4 p. l., xi-xiii, [15]-250 p. 22 cm. Subjects: Religion--Philosophy.Culture.Philosophy and religion.Christianity--20th century. LC Classification: PB1662 .E4

Edwards, David Lawrence. A reason to hope / [by] David L. Edwards. London; New York: Collins, 1978. Description: 252 p.; 22 cm. ISBN: 0529056208 : Notes: Includes index. Subjects: Civilization, Modern--1950- Christianity--20th century. Christianity and culture. LC Classification: CB430 .E34 1978 Dewey Class No.: 909

Effective inculturation and ethnic identity / Maria De La Cruz Aymes ... [et al.]. Rome: Centre "Cultures and Religions", Pontifical Gregorian University, 1987. Related Authors: Aymes, María de la Cruz. Description: xi, 127 p.; 24 cm. Notes: Includes bibliographies. Subjects:

Christianity and culture. Ethnicity. Series: Inculturation; 9 LC Classification: BR115.C8 E33 1987 Dewey Class No.: 261 19

Eich, David. Conquering the culture: the fight for our children's souls / by David Paul Eich. Published/Created: Lafayette, La.: Huntington House Publishers, c1996. Description: 223 p.; 22 cm. ISBN: 1563841010 Notes: Includes bibliographical references (p. 205-217). Subjects: Child rearing--Parenting--Religious aspects--Christianity. Imaginary letters. LC Classification: BV4529 .E53 1997 Dewey Class No.: 248.8/45 21

Ejizu, Christopher I. Dialogue at the depth-level: inculturation of prayer in the Nigerian Church / Christopher I. Ejizu. Port Harcourt: Regal Press, [1989] Description: 32 p.; 26 cm. Notes: Typescript. On cover: Theme: Issues in African traditional religion: prayer. "A paper presented at the Catholic Institute of West Africa, Port Harcourt, 1989 Aquinas lecture, Saturday 22nd April, 1989." Includes bibliographical references (p. 28-32). Subjects: Catholic Church--Nigeria--Church history. Christianity and culture. Prayer--Christianity. LC Classification: BX1682.N5 E55 1989 IN PROCESS

Elavathingal, Sebastian. Inculturation & Christian art: an Indian perspective / Sebastian Elavathingal. Rome: Urbaniana University Press, 1990. Description: 342 p.; 21 cm. ISBN: 8840180494 : Notes: Includes bibliographical references (p. 320-342). Subjects: Christian art and symbolism--India--Modern period, 1500-Art, Indic. Christianity and culture. LC Classification: N7976.A1 E44 1990

Eliot, T. S. (Thomas Stearns), 1888-1965 Christianity and culture: The idea of a Christian society and Notes towards the definition of culture. New York, Harcourt, Brace [1960,c1949] Description: 202 p. 21 cm. Subjects: Sociology, Christian. Culture. LC Classification: BT738 .E4 Dewey Class No.: 261.83

Eliot, T. S. (Thomas Stearns), 1888-1965. Points of view / by T. S. Eliot. Edition Information: Hyperion reprint ed. Published/Created: Westport, Ct.: Hyperion Press, 1979. Related Authors: Hayward, John, 1905-1965. Description: 158 p.; 22 cm. ISBN: 0883557886 : Notes: Reprint of the 1941 ed. published by Faber and Faber, London. "This selection of T. S. Eliot's critical writings has been made and edited ... by John Hayward." "Select bibliography of prose-writings": p. 6. Subjects: Literature--History and criticism. Criticism. Christianity and culture. LC Classification: PN37 .E4 1979 Dewey Class No.: 809

Elizondo, Virgilio P. Christianity and culture: an introduction to pastoral theology and ministry for the bicultural community / by Virgilio P. Elizondo. Published/Created: Huntington, Ind.: Our Sunday Visitor, inc., c1975. Description: 199 p.; 21 cm. ISBN: 0879738634 Notes: Bibliography: p. 197-199. Subjects: Mexican Americans--Missions. Mexican Americans. Pastoral theology--Catholic Church. LC Classification: BV2788.M4 E44 Dewey Class No.: 266/.022

Ellingsen, Mark, 1949- A common sense theology: the Bible, faith, and American society / by Mark Ellingsen. Published/Created: Macon, Ga., USA: Mercer, c1995. Description: xii, 251 p.; 23 cm. ISBN: 0865544573 (alk. paper) Notes: Includes bibliographical references (p. [231]-244) and index. Subjects: Bible--Hermeneutics. Theology, Doctrinal--United States. Christianity and culture. Storytelling--Religious aspects--Christianity. Common sense. United States--Civilization. United States--History--Religious aspects--Christianity. Postliberal biblical narrative model of theology Series: Studies in American biblical hermeneutics; 9 LC Classification: BT78 .E45 1995 Dewey Class No.: 230/.0973 20

Elliot, Elisabeth. The savage my kinsman / by Elisabeth Elliot; photographs by Elisabeth Elliot, Cornell Capa. Edition Information:

40th anniversary ed. Published/Created: Ann Arbor: Vine Books, Servant Publications, c1996. Description: 152 p.: ill.; 21 cm. ISBN: 1569550034 (acid-free) Notes: Originally published: Rev. ed. Ann Arbor, Mich.: Servants Books, 1981. With new epilogue. Subjects: Huao Indians--Missions --Social life and customs. Missionaries--Ecuador--United States--Biography. Christianity and culture. LC Classification: F3722.1.H83 E45 1996 Dewey Class No.: 266/.0089/98 20

Elliott, Michael C. Freedom, justice, and Christian counter-culture / Michael C. Elliott. Published/Created: London: SCM Press; Philadelphia: Trinity Press International, 1990. Description: xvii, 221 p.; 22 cm. ISBN: 0334024528 Notes: Includes bibliographical references (p. [213]-218) and indexes. Subjects: Elliott, Michael C. Christianity and culture. Christianity and justice. Christianity and politics. Christianity--20th century. LC Classification: BR115.C8 E44 1990 Dewey Class No.: 261 20

Ellul, Jacques. The subversion of Christianity / by Jacques Ellul; translated by Geoffrey W. Bromiley. Published/Created: Grand Rapids, Mich.: Eerdmans, c1986. Description: 212 p.; 22 cm. ISBN: 0802800491 Notes: Translation of: La subversion du christianisme. Includes bibliographical references. Subjects: Christianity and culture. LC Classification: BR115.C8 E4513 1986 Dewey Class No.: 270.8/2 19

Elmer, Duane, 1943- Cross-cultural connections: stepping out and fitting in around the world / Duane H. Elmer. Published/Created: Downers Grove, Ill.: InterVarsity Press, c2002. Description: p. cm. ISBN: 0830823093 (pbk.: alk. paper) Partial Contents: Monkeys, mission and us -- Your part of God's story -- Right, wrong and different -- Culture is everywhere and it sneaks up on you -- Culture shocks -- Identifying expectations -- Square heads and round heads -- Cultural adjustment map. Notes: Includes bibliographical references. Subjects: Intercultural communication--Religious aspects Christianity. Christianity and culture. Missions--Theory. LC Classification: BV2082.I57 E46 2002 Dewey Class No.: 261 21

Emerging voices in global Christian theology / William A. Dyrness, general editor. Published/Created: Grand Rapids, Mich.: Zondervan, 1994. Related Authors: Dyrness, William A. Description: 255 p.; 20 cm. ISBN: 0310463009 Notes: Includes bibliographical references. Subjects: Theology, Doctrinal--Developing countries. Theology, Doctrinal--Europe, Eastern. Evangelicalism--Developing countries. Evangelicalism--Europe, Eastern. Evangelicalism--United States. Christianity and culture. Missions--Theory. Christianity and other religions. Developing countries--Church history--20th century. Europe, Eastern--Church history--20th century. LC Classification: BT30.D44 E44 1994 Dewey Class No.: 230/.09172/4 20

Emilsen, William W. Violence and atonement: the missionary experiences of Mohandas Gandhi, Samuel Stokes and Verrier Elwin in India before 1935 / William W. Emilsen. Published/Created: Frankfurt am Main; New York: P. Lang, 1994. Description: x, 391 p.; 21 cm. ISBN: 3631470401 Notes: Includes bibliographical references (p. [360]-383) and index. Subjects: Stokes, Samuel, 1882-1946. Elwin, Verrier, 1902-1964. Gandhi, Mahatma, 1869-1948. Missions--India--History--20th century. Missions--Theory--History of doctrines--20th century. Christianity and culture. India--Church history. Series: Studien zur interkulturellen Geschichte des Christentums; Bd. 89. LC Classification: BV3265.2 .E45 1994 Dewey Class No.: 266/.00954/09041 20

Ernst, Eldon G. Without help or hindrance: religious identity in American culture / by Eldon G. Ernst. Philadelphia: Westminster Press, c1977. Description: 240 p.; 21 cm. ISBN: 066424128X Notes: Includes index. Bibliography: p. 225-231. Subjects: Christianity--Identification (Religion)

United States--Church history. LC Classification: BR515 .E76 Dewey Class No.: 209/.73

Ernst, Eldon G. Without help or hindrance: religious identity in American culture / Eldon G. Ernst. Edition Information: 2nd ed. Published/Created: Lanham, MD: University Press of America, c1987. Description: p. cm. ISBN: 0819155659 (pbk.: alk. paper) : Notes: Includes index. Bibliography: p. Subjects: Christianity--Identification (Religion) United States--Church history. LC Classification: BR515 .E76 1987 Dewey Class No.: 209/.73 19

Erskine, Thomas, 1788-1870. Remarks on the internal evidence for the truth of revealed religion. By T. Erskine. Published/Created: Philadelphia, A. Finley, 1821. Description: iv, 149 p. 15 cm. Notes: Microfiche (Negative). Louisville, Ky., Lost Cause Press, 1975. 3 fiches 10.5 x 15 cm. Subjects: Christianity--Evidence. Series: [British culture series; ser.7, no. 17] LC Classification: BT1101 .E75 1821

Eslinger, Ellen, 1956- Citizens of Zion: the social origins of camp meeting revivalism / Ellen Eslinger. Edition Information: 1st ed. Published/Created: Knoxville: University of Tennessee Press, c1999. Description: xxi, 306 p.: ill., maps; 24 cm. ISBN: 1572330333 (alk. paper) Contents: The revolutionary frontier in Kentucky -- The rural economy of the early National West -- A best poor man's country? -- Ordering a heterogeneous society -- A new political culture -- Western settlement and national policy -- Spiritual conditions on the eve of revival -- Spiritual awakening -- The social significance of camp meeting revivalism. Notes: Includes bibliographical references (p. [297]-301) and index. Subjects: Revivals--Camp meetings--Christianity and culture--Kentucky--History--18th century. Revivals--Camp meetings--Kentucky--Christianity and culture--Kentucky--History--19th century. LC Classification: BV3798 .E75 1999 Dewey Class No.: 269/.24/09769 21

Essays in order, by Jacques Maritain, Peter Wust [and] Christopher Dawson; with a general introduction by Christopher Dawson. General editors, Christopher Dawson [and] J. [!] F. Burns. Published/Created: New York, The Macmillan company, 1931. Related Authors: Maritain, Jacques, 1882-1973. Wust, Peter, 1884-1940. Dawson, Christopher, 1889-1970. Description: xxv, 243 p. 20 cm. Contents: Religion and culture, by Jacques Maritain.--Crisis in the west, by Peter Wust.--Christianity and the new age, by Christopher Dawson. Notes: Each essay is published seperately under its own title by Sheed and Ward, Lincoln, as no. 1-3 of the series Essays in order. Subjects: Catholic Church. LC Classification: BX1395 .E72 no. 1-3 Dewey Class No.: 204

Etchings in diversity: a book of brief stories commissioned by the Issues Committee of the Churchwide Coordinating Team of Presbyterian Women ... / [editor, Sarah Cunningham]. Published/Created: Harrisburg, PA (P.O. Box 1321, Harrisburg, 17105): Presbyterian Women, c1990. Related Authors: Cunningham, Sarah, 1925- Presbyterian Women (Presbyterian Church (U.S.A.)). Issues Committee. Description: 88 p.: ports.; 22 cm. Subjects: Presbyterian Church (U.S.A.)--Biography. Women in the Presbyterian Church--United States Biography. Presbyterian Church--United States--Biography. Christianity and culture. LC Classification: BX9220 .E88 1990 Dewey Class No.: 285/.137/082 20

Ethiopian review of cultures. Published/Created: Addis Ababa, Ethiopia: Theological and Philosophical Studies Centre, [1991- Related Authors: Theological and Philosophical Studies Centre (Addis Ababa, Ethiopia) St. Francis Institute (Addis Ababa, Ethiopia) Capuchin Franciscan Institute of Philosophy and Theology. Description: v.: ill.; 21-24 cm. Frequency given on issues as "bi-annual," despite less frequent publication pattern. Vol. 1 (1991)- Current Frequency: Biennial, 1994/95-<1996/97 Former

Frequency: Annual, 1991-1993 Notes: Chiefly English, some Amharic, French, and Italian. Issued by: Theological and Philosophical Studies Centre, v. 1 (1991); by: St. Francis Institute, v. 2-v. 3; by: Capuchin Franciscan Institute of Philosophy and Theology, v. 4/5 (1994/95)- Subjects: Catholic Church--Ethiopia--Periodicals. Christianity and culture--Periodicals. Christianity and culture--Ethiopia--Periodicals. LC Classification: IN PROCESS

Evangelization, culture, and Catholic identity: proceedings of a symposium for Catholic leaders / by William B. Friend ... [et al.]; D. Michael McCarron, Harold B. Bumpus, editors. Edition Information: 1st ed. Published/Created: Saint Leo, Fla.: Saint Leo College Press, 1996. Related Authors: Friend, William B., 1931- McCarron, D. Michael. Bumpus, Harold B. Symposium for Catholic Leaders on Evangelization, Culture, and Catholic Identity (1995: Altamonte Springs, Fla.) Description: 115 p.: ill.; 22 cm. ISBN: 094575907X Notes: Includes bibliographical references. Subjects: Catholic Church--Doctrines--Congresses. Evangelistic work--United States--Congresses. Christianity and culture--United States--Congresses. LC Classification: BX2347.4 .E89 1996 Dewey Class No.: 282/.73 21

Evangelizzazione e culture: atti del Congresso internazionale scientifico di missiologia, Roma, 5-12 ottobre 1975. Published/Created: Roma: Pontificia università urbaniana, 1976. Description: 3 v.: ill.; 22 cm. Notes: English, French, German, Italian, Portuguese, or Spanish. Includes bibliographical references and indexes. Subjects: Evangelistic work--Congresses. Christianity and culture--Congresses. Christianity and other religions--Congresses. LC Classification: BV3755 .C59 1975

Everett, William Johnson. God's federal republic: reconstructing our governing symbol / William Johnson Everett. Published/Created: New York: Paulist Press, c1988. Description: vi, 204 p.; 23

cm. ISBN: 0809129388 (pbk.) : Notes: Bibliography: p. 187-204. Subjects: Sociology, Christian. Christianity and politics. Series: Isaac Hecker studies in religion and American culture LC Classification: BT738 .E94 1988 Dewey Class No.: 261.7 19

Eversole, Finley, ed. Christian faith and the contemporary arts. New York, Abingdon Press [1962] Description: 255 p. illus. 25 cm. Partial Contents: Art and the renewal of human sensibility in mass society / Nathan A. Scott -- Literary tradition and the contemporary writer / Walter Sullivan -- Art tradition and the contemporary visual arts / Herbert Read -- The brave new world of the modern artist / Finley Eversole. Subjects: Art and religion. Art, Modern--20th century. Civilization, Christian. Music--Religious aspects. LC Classification: N72 .E9 Dewey Class No.: 704.92

Eyre, Stephen D., 1948- Defeating the dragons of the world: resisting the seduction of false values / Stephen D. Eyre. Published/Created: Downers Grove, Ill.: InterVarsity Press, c1987. Description: 154 p.; 21 cm. ISBN: 0877845182 (pbk.) : Notes: "With study questions for individuals or groups." Bibliography: p. [152]-154. Subjects: Christianity and culture. Christianity--20th century. Christian life. Series: The DragonSlayer series LC Classification: BR115.C8 E97 1987 Dewey Class No.: 248.4 19

Ezugwu, Tony Ifeanyi. Reconciliation: a community celebration: a case-study in inculturation for Igbo Catholics in Enugu State Nigeria / Tony Ifeanyi Ezugwu. xAltenberge: Oros Verlag, 1997. Description: xviii, 370 p.; 21 cm. ISBN: 3893751459 Notes: Includes bibliographical references (p. 347-370). Subjects: Catholic Church--Nigeria--Enugu State. Reconciliation--Religious aspects. Igbo (African people)--Religion. Christianity and culture. Series: Münsteraner theologische Abhandlungen; 46 LC Classification: IN PROCESS

Faith and culture in the Irish context / edited by Eoin G. Cassidy. Published/Created: Dublin: Veritas, 1996 Related Authors: Cassidy, Eoin G. Description: 175 p.: ill.; 21cm ISBN: 1853903310 Notes: Papers from a series of public lectures and a weekend symposium hosted by the Mater Dei Institute, Dublin. Includes bibliographical references. Subjects: Christianity and culture--Congresses. Ireland--Religion--Congresses LC Classification: BR792 .F35 1996 Dewey Class No.: 261/.09415 21

Faith and culture: issues for the Australian Church / edited by Neil Brown. Published/Created: Manly, N.S.W.: Catholic Institute of Sydney, 1982. Related Authors: Brown, Neil. Catholic Institute of Sydney. Description: 141 p.; 20 cm. ISBN: 0908224052 (pbk.) Notes: Includes bibliographies. Subjects: Catholic Church--Australia. Christianity and culture. LC Classification: BX1685 .F35 1982 Dewey Class No.: 282/.94 19

Faith and culture: the role of the Catholic university / Jean Ducruet ... [et al.]. Published/Created: Rome: Centre "Cultures and Religions," Pontifical Gregorian University; Paris: International Federation of Catholic Universities, 1989. Related Authors: Ducruet, Jean, 1922- International Federation of Catholic Universities. General Assembly (16th: 1988: Jakarta, Indonesia) Description: xi, 147 p.: ill.; 24 cm. ISBN: 8876526048 Notes: Proceedings of the 16th General Assembly of the International Federation of Catholic Universities held Jakarta, 1988. Includes bibliographical references. Subjects: Christianity and culture--Congresses. Catholic universities and colleges--Congresses. Series: Inculturation; 11 LC Classification: IN PROCESS (WBC)

Faith and fiction: interdisciplinary studies on the interplay between metaphor and religion: a selection of papers from the 25th LAUD-Symposium of the Gerhard Mercator University of Duisburg on "Metaphor and religion" / Benjamin

Biebuyck, René Dirven, John Ries (eds.). Published/Created: Frankfurt am Main; New York: P. Lang, c1998. Related Authors: Biebuyck, Benjamin. Dirven, René. Ries, John. Description: 253 p.; 21 cm. ISBN: 3631337604 (pbk.) 0820436240 (U.S.: pbk.) Notes: Symposium was held April 1-5, 1997. Subjects: Metaphor--Religious aspects--Congresses. Metaphor--Religious aspects--Christianity--Congresses. Series: Duisberger Arbeiten zur Sprach- und Kulturwissenschaft; Bd. 37. LC Classification: BL65.L2 I57 1997 Dewey Class No.: 210/.1/4 21

Faith in the centre: Christianity and culture / edited by Paul S. Fiddes. Published/Created: Oxford: Regent's Park College; Macon, Ga.: Smyth & Helwys Pub., 2001. Related Authors: Fiddes, Paul S. Description: p. cm. ISBN: 1573123633 (pbk.) Notes: Includes bibliographical references and index. Subjects: Christianity and culture. Series: Regent's study guides; 9 LC Classification: BR115.C8 F3 2001 Dewey Class No.: 261 21

Faith, culture, India today: perspectives / editor, Augustine Mulloor. Published/Created: Kalamassery, Kerala, India: Jyothir Dhara Publications, 1991. Related Authors: Mulloor, Augustine. Description: 208 p.; 23 cm. Notes: Contributed articles. Includes bibliographical references. Subjects: Jesus Christ--Person and offices. Bible. N.T. Epistles of Paul--Criticism, interpretation, etc. Christianity and culture. Christianity--India. Hope--Christianity. Church--Biblical teaching. India--Religion. Series: Religion and life series; 1 LC Classification: BR115.C8 F32 1991

Faith, scholarship, and culture in the 21st century / Alice Ramos and Marie I. George, editors; introduction by Robert Royal. Published/Created: [Mishawaka, Ind.]: American Maritain Association; Washington, DC: Distributed by the Catholic University of America Press, c2002. Related Authors: Ramos, Alice, 1948- George, Marie I. Description: x, 331 p.; 23 cm. ISBN: 0966922654 (alk. paper) Notes: Papers presented at a meeting held in Oct. 2000. Includes bibliographical references and index. Subjects: Catholic Church--Doctrines--Congresses. Faith and reason--Christianity--Congresses. Religion and science--Congresses. Church and college--Congresses. Sociology, Christian (Catholic)--Congresses. Series: American Maritain Association publications LC Classification: BT50 .F35 2002 Dewey Class No.: 261.5 21

Feeley-Harnik, Gillian, 1940- The Lord's Table: Eucharist and Passover in early Christianity / Gillian Feeley-Harnik. Published/Created: Philadelphia: University of Pennsylvania Press, 1981. Description: ix, 184 p.; 24 cm. ISBN: 0812277864 Notes: Includes index. Bibliography: p. 169-178. Subjects: Lord's Supper--History--Early church, ca. 30-600. Passover--History. Passover--Christian observance. Series: Symbol and culture LC Classification: BV823 .F4 Dewey Class No.: 264/.36 19

Fenn, Richard K. The secularization of sin: an investigation of the Daedalus complex / Richard K. Fenn. Edition Information: 1st ed. Published/Created: Louisville, Ky.: Westminster/John Knox Press, c1991. Description: 207 p.; 21 cm. ISBN: 0664251897 Notes: Includes bibliographical references (p. 193-199) and index. Subjects: Sociology, Christian-- United States. Guilt--Religious aspects-- Christianity. Guilt and culture--United States. Secularism--United States. Psychology, Religious. LC Classification: BR517 .F45 1991 Dewey Class No.: 261 20

Fernández-Armesto, Felipe. Reformations: a radical interpretation of Christianity and the world, 1500-2000 / Felipe Fernández-Armesto and Derek Wilson. Published/Created: New York: Scribner, [1997] Related Authors: Wilson, Derek A. Description: xi, 324 p., [32] p. of plates: ill.; 25 cm. ISBN: 068483104X (alk. paper) Notes: Originally published: Reformation. London: Transworld Publishers, 1996. Includes bibliographical references (p. [301]-316) and index.

Subjects: Reformation. Christianity and culture. Religious pluralism--Christianity. LC Classification: BR305.2 .F47 1997 Dewey Class No.: 270 21

Feuerbach, Ludwig, 1804-1872. The essence of Christianity. Translated from the German by George Eliot. Introductory essay by Karl Barth. Foreword by H. Richard Niebuhr. Published/Created: New York, Harper [1957] Description: xliv, 339 p. 21 cm. Notes: Harper torchbooks, TB11. Subjects: Religion--Philosophy. Christianity--Controversial literature. LC Classification: B2971.W4 E5 1957 Dewey Class No.: 201 19

Feuerbach, Ludwig, 1804-1872. The essence of faith according to Luther [by] Ludwig Feuerbach. Translated by Melvin Cherno. Edition Information: [1st American ed.] Published/Created: New York, Harper & Row [1967] Description: 127 p. 21 cm Notes: Translation of Das Wesen des Glaubens im Sinne Luthers. Subjects: Luther, Martin, 1483-1546. Faith. Christianity--Essence, genius, nature. LC Classification: B2971.W45 E5 Dewey Class No.: 234

Ficker, Victor B., comp. The revolution in religion. Edited by Victor B. Ficker [and] Herbert S. Graves. Published/Created: Columbus, Ohio, Merrill [1973] Related Authors: Graves, Herbert S., 1914- joint comp. Description: vi, 169 p. 23 cm. ISBN: 0675089328 Contents: Leary, J. P. The revolution in religion.--Harrington, M. Religion and revolution.--Gelpi, D. Religion in the age of Aquarius.--Berrigan, D. Conscience, the law, and civil disobedience.--Rose, S. C. The coming confrontation on the church's war investments.--Hadden, J. K. Clergy involvement in civil rights.--Groppi, J. E. The church and civil rights.--Newsweek. Verdict at First Baptist.--Bloy, M. B., Jr. The counter-culture: it just won't go away.--Forman, J. The Black manifesto.--McIntire, C. Christian manifesto.--Sandeen, E. R. Fundamentalism and American identity.--Kuhn, H. B. Obstacles to Evangelism in the world.--Zahn, G. C. A religious pacifist looks at abortion.--The Lutheran Church-Missouri Synod. Abortion: theological, legal, and medical aspects.--Bayer, C. H. Confessions of an abortion counselor.--Osborn, R. T. Religion on the campus.--Ficker, V. B. The search for meaning. Notes: Includes bibliographical references. Subjects: Theology. Church and social problems. Christianity--20th century. LC Classification: BR50 .F46 Dewey Class No.: 208

Fiddes, Paul S. The novel, spirituality and modern culture / edited by Paul S. Fiddes. Published/Created: Cardiff: University of Wales Press, 2000. Description: 192 p.; 22 cm. ISBN: 0708315984 0708315992 (pbk.) Subjects: Spirituality. Spirituality in literature. Authorship--Religious aspects--Christianity. Series: Religion, culture and society

Fiedler, Klaus, Dr. Christianity and African culture: conservative German Protestant missionaries in Tanzania, 1900-1940 / by Klaus Fiedler. Published/Created: Leiden; New York: E.J. Brill, 1996. Description: xiii, 239 p.; 25 cm. ISBN: 9004104976 (alk. paper) Notes: Includes bibliographical references (p. [215]-230) and index. Subjects: Missions--Tanzania--History--20th century. Missions, English--History--20th century. Christianity and culture--History--20th century. Series: Studies on religion in Africa; 14. LC Classification: BV3625.T4 F544 1996 Dewey Class No.: 266/.023430678 20

Fiedler, Klaus, Dr. Christianity and African culture: conservative German Protestant missionaries in Tanzania, 1900-1940 / Klaus Fiedler; with a text by Robin Lamburn. Published/Created: Blantyre, Malawi: Christian Literature Association in Malawi, 1999. Description: 248 p.; 21 cm. Notes: Includes bibliographical references (p. 221-240) and index. LC copy imperfect: p. 234-235 and 238-239 missing. Series: Kachere monograph; no. 9

Figgis, John Neville, 1866-1919. Hopes for English religion, by John Neville Figgis.

Published/Created: London, New York [etc.] Longmans, Green and co., 1919. Description: viii, 202 p., 1 l. 20 cm. Contents: Hopes for English religion.--Our Catholic inheritance.--University sermons; I. The Church and the future. II Freedom and authority. III. Christianity and culture. IV. The eternal refuge.--The need of God.--The Pharisee and the publican.--"Rejoice evermore."--Service.--'There was silence in heaven.'--Angelic ministry.--The ideal of a university life.--The ineluctable charm. Subjects: Church of England--Sermons. Great Britain--Religion. LC Classification: BX5131 .F5

Finney, Paul Corby. The invisible God: the earliest Christians on art / Paul Corby Finney. Published/Created: New York: Oxford University Press, 1994. Description: xxviii, 319 p.: ill., maps; 24 cm. ISBN: 0195082524 (acid-free paper) Notes: Includes bibliographical references (p. 299-307) and index. Subjects: Christian art and symbolism--To 500. Christianity and culture--History--Early church, ca. 30-600. God--Knowableness--History of doctrines--Early church, ca. 30-600. Art, Early Christian. Fathers of the church. LC Classification: BV150 .F56 1994 Dewey Class No.: 246/.2 20

Finucane, Ronald C. Miracles and pilgrims: popular beliefs in medieval England / Ronald C. Finucane. Edition Information: 1st paperback ed. Published/Created: New York: St. Martin's Press, 1995. Description: 248 p.: ill., maps; 21 cm. ISBN: 0312125283 (pbk.) Notes: Originally published: Totowa, N.J.: Rowman and Littlefield, 1977. Includes bibliographical references (p. [242]-244) and index. Subjects: Popular culture--England--Religious aspects--Christianity. Miracles--History of doctrines--Middle Ages, 600-1500. Christian pilgrims and pilgrimages--England. Christian saints--Cult--England. Christian shrines--England. Travel, Medieval. England--Church history--1066-1485. LC Classification: BR747 .F56 1995 Dewey Class No.: 274.2 20

Fischer, John, 1947- What on earth are we doing?: finding our place as Christians in the world / John Fischer. Published/Created: Ann Arbor, Mich.: Vine Books, c1996. Description: 194 p.; 21 cm. ISBN: 0892839767 Notes: Includes bibliographical references (p. [191]-194). Subjects: Christianity and culture. Church and the world. Christian life. LC Classification: BR115 .F57 1996 Dewey Class No.: 261 21

Fisher, James Terence. The Catholic counterculture in America, 1933-1962 / James Terence Fisher. Published/Created: Chapel Hill: University of North Carolina Press, c1989. Description: xv, 305 p.: ill., ports.; 24 cm. ISBN: 0807818631 (alk. paper) Notes: Includes bibliographical references: (p. [283]-298) and index. Subjects: Catholic Church--United States--History--20th century. Radicals--United States--History--20th century. Subculture--United States. Christianity and culture. United States--Intellectual life--20th century. Series: Studies in religion (Chapel Hill, N.C.) LC Classification: BX1407.I5 F57 1989 Dewey Class No.: 305.6/2/073 19

Fishwick, Marshall William. Great awakenings: popular religion and popular culture / Marshall W. Fishwick. Published/Created: New York: Haworth Press, c1995. Description: xiv, 284 p.: ill.; 22 cm. ISBN: 1560248645 (alk. paper) 1560238585 (pbk.) Notes: Includes bibliographical references (p. 237-245) and index. Subjects: Revivals--United States--History. Popular culture--United States. Popular culture--Religious aspects--Christianity. United States--Church history. Series: Haworth popular culture LC Classification: BR517 .F57 1995 Dewey Class No.: 277.3 20

Fitch, Robert Elliot, 1902- Odyssey of the self-centered self; or, Rake's progress in religion. Edition Information: [1st ed.] Published/Created: New York, Harcourt, Brace [1961] Description: 184 p. 21 cm. Notes: Includes bibliography. Subjects: Culture. Self. Christianity--Philosophy. LC Classification: BR115.C8 F5 Dewey Class No.: 179.8

Fitzpatrick, Joseph P. One church, many cultures: challenge of diversity / Joseph P. Fitzpatrick. Published/Created: Kansas City, MO: Sheed & Ward, c1987. Description: 205 p.; 22 cm. ISBN: 0934134634 (pbk.) Notes: Includes bibliographies. Subjects: Catholic Church--United States. Christianity and culture. Sociology, Christian (Catholic) Hispanic American Catholics. LC Classification: BR115.C8 F53 1987 Dewey Class No.: 261 19

Flake, Carol. Redemptorama: culture, politics, and the new evangelicalism / Carol Flake. Published/Created: New York, N.Y., U.S.A.: Penquin Books, 1985, c1984. Description: 301 p.; 20 cm. ISBN: 0140082654 (pbk.) : Notes: Includes index. Bibliography: p. [277]-291. Subjects: Evangelicalism--United States. Christianity and culture. Christianity and politics. LC Classification: BR1642.U5 F58 1985 Dewey Class No.: 280/.4 19

Flake, Carol. Redemptorama: culture, politics, and the new evangelicalism / Carol Flake. Edition Information: 1st ed. Published/Created: Garden City, N.Y.: Anchor Press, 1984. Description: viii, 300 p.; 22 cm. ISBN: 0385182414 : Notes: Includes index. Subjects: Evangelicalism--United States. Christianity and culture. Christianity and politics. LC Classification: BR1642.U5 F58 1984 Dewey Class No.: 280/.4 19

Flanagan, Kieran, 1944- The enchantment of sociology: a study of theology and culture / Kieran Flanagan. Published/Created: New York: St. Martin's Press, c1996. Description: xiv, 293 p.; 23 cm. ISBN: 0312129750 Notes: Includes bibliographical references (p. 262-281) and index. Subjects: Sociology, Christian (Catholic) Religion and sociology. Christianity and culture. LC Classification: BX1753 .F59 1996 Dewey Class No.: 306.6/3 20

Fleming, Bruce C. E., 1950- Contextualization of theology: an evangelical assessment / by Bruce C.E. Fleming. Published/Created: Pasadena, Calif.: William Carey Library, 1980. Description: xii, 147 p.: ill.; 22 cm. ISBN: 0878084312 (pbk.) Notes: Includes indexes. Bibliography: p. 139-143. Subjects: Theology--Methodology. Missions--Theory. Christianity and culture. LC Classification: BR118 .F6 Dewey Class No.: 230/.044

Florovsky, Georges, 1893-1979. Christianity and culture. Published/Created: Belmont, Mass., Nordland Pub. Co. [1974] Description: 245 p. 23 cm. Contents: Faith and culture.--The predicament of the Christian historian.--Antinomies of Christian history: empire and desert.--The iconoclastic controversy.--Christianity and civilization.--The social problem in the Eastern Orthodox Church.--Patriarch Jeremiah II and the Lutheran divines.--The Greek version of the Augsburg confession.--The Orthodox churches and the ecumenical movement prior to 1910. Notes: Includes bibliographical references. Subjects: Church history. Christianity and culture. LC Classification: BX260 .F55 vol. 2 BR155 Dewey Class No.: 230/.1/908 s 270

Florovsky, Georges, 1893-1979. Collected works of Georges Florovsky. Published/Created: Belmont, Mass., Nordland Pub. Co. [1972-<79 Description: v. <1-5; 23 cm. Subjects: Orthodox Eastern Church. Theology. LC Classification: BX260 .F55 Dewey Class No.: 230/.1/908

Fore, William F. Mythmakers: gospel, culture, and the media / William F. Fore. Published/Created: New York: Friendship Press, c1990. Description: 150 p.; 22 cm. ISBN: 0377002070 : Notes: Includes bibliographical references (p. 140-145) and index. Subjects: Communication--Mass media--Religious aspects--Christianity. Christianity and culture. Mass media--United States--Church history--20th century. LC Classification: BV4319 .F67 1990 Dewey Class No.: 261.5/2 20

Forell, George Wolfgang. The proclamation of the Gospel in a pluralistic world; essays on Christianity and culture [by] George W. Forell. Published/Created: Philadelphia, Fortress Press [1973] Description: vi, 138 p. 19 cm. ISBN: 0800610350 Contents: The proclamation of the Gospel in pluralistic world.--Varieties of religious commitment.--Christian freedom and religious liberty.--God is dead?--The illusion of neutrality.--The university's ethical crisis.--Some implications of the axioms of classical protestantism for the philosophy of education.--Work and vocation.--The development of an ecologic conscience.--Law and Gospel as a problem of politics.--The criminal justice system: a theological perspective.--Particularity, pluralism, and world community. Notes: Includes bibliographical references. Subjects: Christianity and culture. LC Classification: BR115.C8 F6 Dewey Class No.: 208

Forristal, Desmond. The Christian heritage / Desmond Forristal. Published/Created: Dublin: Veritas Publications, 1976. Description: 192 p., [4] leaves of plates: ill.; 25 cm. ISBN: 0905092201 : Subjects: Catholic Church--Christianity and culture--History. LC Classification: BR145.2 .F66 Dewey Class No.: 270

Fowler, Richard A., 1948- Civilization in crisis: a Christian response to homosexuality, feminism, euthanasia, and abortion / Richard A. Fowler and H. Wayne House. Edition Information: 2nd ed. Published/Created: Grand Rapids, Mich.: Baker Book House, c1988. Related Authors: House, H. Wayne. Fowler, Richard A., 1948- Christian confronts his culture. Description: x, 210 p.: ill.; 22 cm. ISBN: 0801035481 Notes: Rev. ed. of: The Christian confronts his culture. c1983. Includes bibliographical references (p. 201-202). Subjects: Feminism--Abortion--Homosexuality--Euthanasia--Religious aspects--Christianity. Church and social problems--Sociology, Christian--United States. LC Classification: HQ1221 .F68 1988 Dewey Class No.: 261.8/35 20

Fowler, Richard A., 1948- The Christian confronts his culture / by Richard A. Fowler and H. Wayne House. Published/Created: Chicago: Moody Press, c1983. Related Authors: House, H. Wayne. Description: xii, 218 p.: ill.; 22 cm. ISBN: 0802402321 (pbk.) Notes: Includes indexes. Bibliography: p. 209. Subjects: Feminism--Religious aspects--Christianity. Abortion--Religious aspects--Christianity. Homosexuality--Religious aspects--Christianity. Church and social problems--United States. Sociology, Christian--United States. LC Classification: HQ1221 .F68 1983 Dewey Class No.: 261.8/35 19

Fox, Matthew, 1940- Manifesto for a global civilization / by Matthew Fox & Brian Swimme. Published/Created: Santa Fe, NM: Bear, c1982. Related Authors: Swimme, Brian. Description: 54 p.; 22 cm. ISBN: 0939680068 (pbk.): 093968005X (pbk.) : Subjects: Christianity and culture. Spiritual life--Christianity. LC Classification: BR115.C8 F64 1982 Dewey Class No.: 261.1 19

Francis, Mark R. Liturgy in a multicultural community / Mark R. Francis. Published/Created: Collegeville, Minn.: Liturgical Press, c1991. Description: 78 p.; 21 cm. ISBN: 0814620469 Notes: Includes bibliographical references (p. 74-78). Subjects: Catholic Church--Liturgy. Catholic Church--United States--Liturgy. Christianity and culture. Series: American essays in liturgy (Collegeville, Minn.) LC Classification: BX1970 .F73 1991 Dewey Class No.: 264/.02/0089 20

Francis, Mark R. Shape a circle ever wider: liturgical inculturation in the United States / Mark R. Francis; foreword by Anscar J. Chupungco. Published/Created: Chicago: Liturgy Training Publications, c2000. Description: xv, 127 p.; 23 cm. ISBN: 1568542771 Notes: Includes bibliographical references. Subjects: Catholic Church--United States--Liturgy. Christianity and culture. LC Classification: BX1970 .F735 2000 Dewey Class No.: 264/.02/00973 21

Franklin, Simon. Byzantium-Rus-Russia: studies in the translation of Christian culture / Simon Franklin. Published/Created: Aldershot, Hants, England; Burlington, VT: Ashgate, 2002. Description: p. cm. ISBN: 0860788903 (alk. paper) Notes: Includes bibliographical references and index. Subjects: Christianity and culture--Kievan Rus. Christianity and culture--Russia. Kievan Rus--Civilization--Byzantine influences. Russia--Civilization. Series: Collected studies; CS754. LC Classification: DK71 .F69 2002 Dewey Class No.: 947 21

Friesen, Duane K. Artists, citizens, philosophers: seeking the peace of the city: an Anabaptist theology of culture / Duane K. Friesen; foreword by Glen Stassen. Published/Created: Scottdale, Pa.: Herald Press, c2000. Description: 349 p.: ill.; 23 cm. ISBN: 0836191390 (pbk.: alk. paper) Notes: Includes bibliographical references and indexes. Subjects: Christianity and culture. Anabaptists. Peace--Religious aspects--Christianity. LC Classification: BR115.C8 F68 2000 Dewey Class No.: 261/.088/243 21

From culture wars to common ground: religion and the American family debate / Don S. Browning ... [et al.]. Edition Information: 1st ed. Published/Created: Louisville, Ky.: Westminster John Knox Press, c1997. Related Authors: Browning, Don S. Description: xi, 399 p.; 23 cm. ISBN: 0664256511 (alk. paper) Notes: Includes bibliographical references (p. [335]-375) and index. Subjects: Family--Religious aspects--Christianity--History of doctrines--20th century. Family--United States. Christianity and culture--United States--History--20th century. United States--Church history--20th century. United States--Social life and customs--1971- Series: The family, religion, and culture LC Classification: BV4526.2 .F75 1997 Dewey Class No.: 261.8/3585/0973 21

From East to West: essays in honor of Donald G. Bloesch / edited by Daniel J. Adams. Published/Created: Lanham, Md.: University Press of America, 1997. Related

Authors: Bloesch, Donald G., 1928-
Adams, Daniel J. Description: p. cm.
ISBN: 0761808019 (alk. paper) Notes:
Includes bibliographical references.
Subjects: Theology, Doctrinal. Christianity
and culture. Evangelicalism. Missions--
Theory. East and West. LC Classification:
BR50 .F76 1997 Dewey Class No.:
230/.044 21

Fussell, Edwin S. The Catholic side of Henry
James / Edwin Sill Fussell.
Published/Created: Cambridge [England];
New York, NY, USA: Cambridge
University Press, 1993. Description: xvii,
166 p.; 24 cm. ISBN: 0521432022
(hardback) Notes: Includes bibliographical
references (p. 157-162) and index.
Subjects: James, Henry, 1843-1916 --
Religion. Catholic Church--In literature.
Catholic Church--Doctrine. Fiction--
Religious aspects--Christianity. Theology
in literature. Series: Cambridge studies in
American literature and culture LC
Classification: PS2127.R4 F8 1993 Dewey
Class No.: 813/.4 20

Gaede, S. D. When tolerance is no virtue:
political correctness, multiculturalism &
the future of truth & justice / S.D. Gaede;
foreword by James Davison Hunter.
Published/Created: Downers Grove, Ill.:
InterVarsity Press, c1993. Description: 119
p.; 21 cm. ISBN: 0830816992 (alk. paper)
Notes: Includes bibliographical references
(p. [113]-119). Subjects: Christianity--
United States. Christianity and culture.
Truth (Christian theology) Christianity and
justice--United States. Political
correctness--United States.
Multiculturalism--United States.
Toleration. United States--Church history--
20th century. United States--Politics and
government--1993-2001. LC
Classification: BR526 .G34 1993 Dewey
Class No.: 261/.0973 20

Gaggawala, Paul O. Fully Christian...fully
human: a model for the new evangelization
/ Paul O. Gaggawala, A. J.
Published/Created: Raton, Fl: Jeremiah
Press, 1999. Description: 193; 22 cm.
ISBN: 1883520177 Notes: Abridged

version of dissertation entitled: The drama
of inculturated evangelization at the center
of the Christian Bantu family in Africa:
toward a Christian Bantu culture and
identity. Includes bibliographical
references. Subjects: Catholic Church--
Africa. Christianity and culture--Africa.

Gaillardetz, Richard R., 1958- Transforming
our days: spirituality, community, and
liturgy in a technological culture / Richard
R. Gaillardetz. Published/Created: New
York: Crossroad Pub. Co., c2000.
Description: 158 p.: 21 cm. ISBN:
0824518446 (alk. paper) Contents: The
technological shape of daily life -- The life
of grace -- Toward a communal spirituality
-- Liturgy of the church, liturgy of the
world. Notes: Includes bibliographical
references (p. 147-158). Subjects:
Technology--Religious aspects--
Christianity. Christian life. LC
Classification: BR115.T42 G35 2000
Dewey Class No.: 248.4 21

Gallagher, Michael Paul. Clashing symbols: an
introduction to faith and culture / Michael
Paul Gallagher. Published/Created: New
York: Paulist Press, c1998. Description: vi,
170 p.: ill.; 22 cm. ISBN: 0809137844
(pbk.: alk. paper) Notes: Includes
bibliographical references (p. [167]-170).
Subjects: Catholic Church--History--20th
century. Christianity and culture. LC
Classification: BR115.C8 G27 1998
Dewey Class No.: 261 21

Gallagher, Michael Paul. Struggles of faith:
essays / by Michael Paul Gallagher.
Edition Information: 1st ed.
Published/Created: Dublin: Columba
Press; Mystic, CT: Twenty-third
Publications [distributor], 1990.
Description: 141 p.; 21 cm. ISBN:
0948183926 : Notes: Distributor statement
from label on p. [4] of cover. Includes
bibliographical references. Subjects:
Catholic Church--Ireland--Latin America.
Christianity and culture. Religion and
literature. Ireland--Latin America--Church
history. LC Classification: BX1505.2 .G35
1990 Dewey Class No.: 282/.09/045 20

Galloway, Allan Douglas, 1920- Faith in a
changing culture; Kerr lectures, delivered
at Glasgow University, 1966, by Allan D.
Galloway. Published/Created: London,
Allen & Unwin, 1967. Description: 3-122
p. 23 cm. Notes: Bibliographical footnotes.
Subjects: Christianity and culture. Series:
Kerr lectures, 1966 LC Classification:
BR115.C8 G3

García-Rivera, Alex. St. Martín de Porres: the
"little stories" and the semiotics of culture /
Alex García-Rivera; [foreword by Virgil
Elizondo; introduction by Robert J.
Schreiter]. Published/Created: Maryknoll,
N.Y.: Orbis Books, c1995. Description:
xvii, 142 p.; 23 cm. ISBN: 1570750335
(alk. paper) Notes: Includes bibliographical
references (p. 123-139) and index.
Subjects: Martín, de Porres, Saint, 1579-
1639. Catholic Church--Latin America.
Christianity and culture. Mestizaje. Latin
America--Religious life and customs.
Series: Faith and cultures series LC
Classification: BX4700.M397 G37 1995
Dewey Class No.: 282/.092 20

Garnett, Lucy Mary Jane, d. 1934. Turkey of
the Ottomans, by Lucy M. Garnett.
Published/Created: London, Sir I. Pitman
& sons, ltd., 1911. Description: 304 p.
front., plates, ports. 19 cm. Contents:
Moslem Ottomans.--Christian Ottomans.--
Hebrew Ottomans.--The Ottoman sultan.--
The Ottoman parliament.--Law courts,
police and army.--The religion of Islam.--
Christianity in Turkey.--Judaism in
Turkey.--Urban life.--Agrarian Turkey.--
Pastoral Turkey.--Ottoman homes and
home-life.--Education and culture.--Turkey
at play.--Index. Subjects: Turks. Turkey.
LC Classification: DR432 .G2

Garrison, Charles E. Two different worlds:
Christian absolutes and the relativism of
social science / Charles E. Garrison.
Published/Created: Newark: University of
Delaware Press; London: Associated
University Presses, c1988. Description:
174 p.; 25 cm. ISBN: 0874133300 (alk.
paper) Notes: Includes index.
Bibliography: p. 166-170. Subjects:
Christianity and the social sciences.

Christianity and culture. Cultural
relativism. LC Classification: BR115.S57
G37 1988 Dewey Class No.: 261.5 19

Garsoïan, Nina G., 1923- Church and culture in
early medieval Armenia / Nina G.
Garsoïan. Published/Created: Aldershot;
Brookfield, USA: Ashgate, c1999.
Description: 1 v. (various pagings); 24 cm.
ISBN: 0860787877 (hbk.) Notes: Includes
bibliographical references and index.
English and French. Subjects: Armenian
Church--History. Christianity--Armenia.
Armenia--Civilization. Armenia--History.
Series: Collected studies; CS648. LC
Classification: DS171 .G37 1999 Dewey
Class No.: 956.6/2 21

Gatta, John. American madonna: images of the
divine woman in literary culture / John
Gatta. Published/Created: New York:
Oxford University Press, 1997.
Description: xii, 179 p.: ill.; 24 cm. ISBN:
019511261X (cloth) 0195112628 (paper)
Notes: Includes bibliographical references
(p. 151-172) and index. Subjects: Mary,
Blessed Virgin, Saint--In literature. Mary,
Blessed Virgin, Saint--Cult--United States.
American literature--19th century--History
and criticism. American literature--
Protestant authors--History and criticism.
American literature--20th century--History
and criticism. Christianity and literature--
United States. Women in literature.
Femininity in literature. Christian saints in
literature. Series: Religion in America
series (Oxford University Press) LC
Classification: PS217.M35 G38 1997
Dewey Class No.: 810.9/351 21

Gay, Craig M. The way of the (modern) world,
or, Why it's tempting to live as if God
doesn't exist / Craig M. Gay.
Published/Created: Grand Rapids, Mich.:
W.B. Eerdmans Pub. Carlisle, Cumbria:
Paternoster Press, 1998. Description: xii,
338 p.; 23 cm. ISBN: 080284362X (pbk.:
alk. paper) Notes: Includes bibliographical
references (p. 315-334) and index.
Subjects: Christianity and culture.
Secularism. LC Classification: BR115.C8
G335 1998 Dewey Class No.: 261 21

Geering, Lloyd George. The world to come: from Christian past to global future / Lloyd Geering. Published/Created: Santa Rosa, Calif.: Polebridge Press, 1999. Description: 175 p.; 23 cm. ISBN: 0944344763 Notes: Includes bibliographical references (p. [169]-172) and index. Subjects: Christianity--Controversial literature. Religion and culture--Forecasting. LC Classification: BL2776 .G44 1999 Dewey Class No.: 200/.1/12 21

Gelpi, Donald L., 1934- Inculturating North American theology: an experiment in foundational method / Donald L. Gelpi. Published/Created: Atlanta, Ga.: Scholars Press, c1988. Description: ix, 176 p.; 24 cm. ISBN: 1555402100 (alk. paper) 1555402119 (pbk.: alk. paper) Notes: Includes bibliographical references. Subjects: Theology--Methodology. Theology, Doctrinal--North America. Christianity and culture. Series: AAR studies in religion; no. 54. LC Classification: BR118 .G43 1988 Dewey Class No.: 230/.01/8 19

Geoghegan, Arthur Turbitt. The attitude towards labor in early Christianity and ancient culture, by Arthur T. Geoghegan ... Published/Created: Washington, D.C., The Catholic university of America press, 1945. Description: xxviii p., 1 l., 250 p. vi pl. 23 cm. Notes: Added title-page: The Catholic university of America. Studies in Christian antiquity, ed. by Johannes Quasten ... No. 6 Thesis (S.T.D.) -- Catholic university of America, 1942. Bibliography: p. xvii-xxviii. Subjects: Labor and laboring classes--History. Church and labor. Sociology, Christian. LC Classification: HD4844 .G4 Dewey Class No.: 331.0901

Gerami, Shahin. Women and fundamentalism: Islam and Christianity / Shahin Gerami. Published/Created: New York: Garland Pub., 1996. Description: xiii, 178 p.; 23 cm. ISBN: 0815306636 (alk. paper) Notes: Includes bibliographical references (p. 159-171) and index. Subjects: Muslim women. Women in fundamentalist churches. Women in Islam. Islamic

fundamentalism. Religious fundamentalism. Series: Garland reference library of the humanities; vol. 1516 Women's history and culture; 9. LC Classification: HQ1170 .G45 1996 Dewey Class No.: 305.48/6971 20

Giffin, Michael, 1953- Jane Austen and religion: salvation and society in Georgian England / Michael Giffin. Published/Created: New York: Palgrave, 2002. Description: p. cm. ISBN: 0333948084 Notes: Includes bibliographical references and index. Subjects: Austen, Jane, 1775-1817 -- Religion. Christian fiction, English-- History and criticism. Christianity and literature--England--History. Literature and society--England--History. Religion in literature. Series: Cross-currents in religion and culture (Palgrave (Firm)) LC Classification: PR4038.R4 G54 2002 Dewey Class No.: 823/.7 21

Gilchrist, Roberta. Gender and material culture: the archaeology of religious women / Roberta Gilchrist. Published/Created: London; New York: Routledge, 1997. Description: xiii, 222 p.: ill., maps; 24 cm. ISBN: 0415156564 (pbk.) 0415089034 (hard) Notes: Originally published in 1994. Includes bibliographical references (p. 194-211) and index. Subjects: Monasticism and religious orders for women--Great Britain History--Middle Ages, 600-1500. Women--Great Britain--History--Middle Ages, 500-1500. Convents--Great Britain-- History. Christian antiquities--Great Britain. Excavations (Archaeology)--Great Britain. Sex role--Great Britain. Sex role-- Religious aspects--Christianity--History of doctrines--Middle Ages, 600-1500. Great Britain--Antiquities. Great Britain-- Religious life and customs. LC Classification: BX4220.G7 G55 1997 Dewey Class No.: 271/.90041 21

Gilchrist, Roberta. Gender and material culture: the archaeology of religious women / Roberta Gilchrist. Published/Created: London; New York: Routledge, 1994. Description: xiii, 222 p.: ill.; 25 cm. ISBN: 0415089034 Notes: Includes bibliographical references (p. 194-211) and index. Subjects: Monasticism and religious orders for women--Great Britain Middle Ages, 600-1500. Women--Great Britain--History--Middle Ages, 500-1500. Convents--Great Britain--History. Christian antiquities--Excavations (Archaeology)--Sex role--Great Britain. Sex role--Religious aspects--Christianity--History of doctrines--Middle Ages, 600-1500. Great Britain--Antiquities. Great Britain--Religious life and customs. LC Classification: BX4220.G7 G55 1994 Dewey Class No.: 271/.90041/0902 20

Giles, Paul. American Catholic arts and fictions: culture, ideology, aesthetics / Paul Giles. Published/Created: Cambridge; New York: Cambridge University Press, 1992. Description: ix, 547 p.: ill.; 24 cm. ISBN: 0521417775 Notes: Includes bibliographical references and index. Subjects: Catholic Church--In literature. American literature--Catholic authors--History and criticism. Christian literature, American--History and criticism. Catholics--United States--Intellectual life. Authors, American--Religious life. Christianity and literature. Catholics in literature. Arts, American--20th century. Christianity and the arts--United States. Series: Cambridge studies in American literature and culture; [58] LC Classification: PS153.C3 G55 1992 Dewey Class No.: 810.9/9222 20

Gilkey, Langdon Brown, 1919- Through the tempest: theological voyages in a pluralistic culture / Langdon Gilkey; selected and edited by Jeff B. Pool. Published/Created: Minneapolis: Fortress Press, c1991. Related Authors: Pool, Jeff B., 1951- Description: xx, 252 p.; 23 cm. ISBN: 080062484X : Notes: Includes bibliographical references and index. Subjects: Theology. Christianity--20th century. Christianity--United States. LC Classification: BR85 .G449 1991 Dewey Class No.: 230 20

Gill, Kenneth D., 1946- Toward a contextualized theology for the third world: the emergence and development of

Jesus' Name Pentecostalism in Mexico / by Kenneth D. Gill. Published/Created: Frankfurt am Main; New York: Peter Lang, c1994. Description: xi, 311 p.; 21 cm. ISBN: 3631470967 Notes: Thesis (Ph. D.)--University of Birmingham, 1989. Includes bibliography: (p. [279]-305) and index. Subjects: Iglesia Apostólica de la Fe en Cristo Jesús. Oneness Pentecostal churches--Mexico. Pentecostalism. Christianity and culture. Oneness doctrine (Pentecostalism) Trinity--History of doctrines. Series: Studien zur interkulturellen Geschichte des Christentums; Bd. 90. LC Classification: BX7990.I4 G55 1994 Dewey Class No.: 289.9/4/0972 20

Girard, René, 1923- Things hidden since the foundation of the world / René Girard; research undertaken in collaboration with Jean-Michel Oughourlian and Guy Lefort; translated by Stephen Bann (Books II & III) and Michael Metteer (Book I). Published/Created: Stanford, Calif.: Stanford University Press, 1987. Related Authors: Oughourlian, Jean-Michel. Lefort, Guy. Description: 469 p.; 24 cm. ISBN: 0804714037 Notes: Translation of: Des choses cachées depuis la fondation du monde. Includes index. Bibliography: p. [457]-463. Subjects: Sacrifice. Imitation. Violence--Religious aspects. Scapegoat. Christianity--Essence, genius, nature. Religion and culture. Psychology, Religious. LC Classification: BL570 .G56 1987 Dewey Class No.: 194 19

Gittins, Anthony J., 1943- Gifts and strangers: meeting the challenge of inculturation / Anthony J. Gittins. Published/Created: New York: Paulist Press, c1989. Description: xii, 144 p.; 23 cm. ISBN: 0809130882 : Notes: Includes bibliographical references. Subjects: Catholic Church--Missions. Missions--Theory. Christianity and culture. LC Classification: BV2180 .G58 1989 Dewey Class No.: 266/.001 20

Gladden, Washington, 1836-1918. Social facts and forces; the factory--the labor union--the corporation--the railway--the city--the church. Published/Created: Port Washington, N.Y., Kennikat Press [1971] Description: iv, 235 p. 21 cm. ISBN: 0804614806 Notes: Reprint of the 1897 ed. Lectures given in 1895-96 in Steinway Hall, Chicago, as the "Ryder lectures" and repeated the next year as the E. A. Rand course on applied Christianity, before the students of Iowa College. Includes bibliographical references. Subjects: Social problems. United States--Social conditions--1865-1918. LC Classification: HN64 .G6 1971 Dewey Class No.: 309.1/73

Goa, David J. Seasons of celebration: ritual in Eastern Christian culture = Temps de célébration: les rites dans la culture chrétienne d'Orient / David J. Goa; forward by Jaroslav Pelikan; essays by Heiko C. Schlieper, Nicolas Schidlovsky. Published/Created: Edmonton, Canada: Provincial Museum of Alberta, Alberta Culture, 1986. Related Authors: Schlieper, Heiko C. Schidlovsky, Nicolas. Provincial Museum of Alberta. Alberta. Alberta Culture. Description: vi, 57 p.: ill. (some col.); 26 x 31 cm. ISBN: 0919411444 Notes: English and French. Issued in conjunction with the exhibition, Seasons of celebration, at the Provincial Museum of Alberta. The exhibit was organized by David J. Goa to mark the millenia of Christianity in Russia. Includes bibliographical references (p. 56). Discography: p. 57. Subjects: Orthodox Eastern Church--Liturgy. Orthodox Eastern Church. LC Classification: MLCM 91/02386 (B)

God and culture: essays in honor of Carl F.H. Henry / edited by D.A. Carson and John D. Woodbridge. Published/Created: Grand Rapids, Mich.: Eerdmans; Carlisle,England: Paternoster Press, 1993. Related Authors: Henry, Carl Ferdinand Howard, 1913- Carson, D. A. Woodbridge, John D., 1941- Description: xii, 398 p.: port.; 23 cm. ISBN: 0802837093 Notes: Spine God & culture. "Chronological selected bibliography of the works of Carl F.H. Henry": p. 396-398. Includes bibliographical references. Subjects:

Christianity and culture. Christianity--20th century. LC Classification: BR115.C8 G63 1993 Dewey Class No.: 261 20

Goetz, William R. (William Ralph), 1933- When the empire strikes out: are we repeating the pattern of past civilizations? / William R. Goetz. Published/Created: Camp Hill, Pa.: Horizon Books, c2001. Description: xiii, 233 p.; 21 cm. ISBN: 0889651841 (pbk.) Notes: Includes bibliographical references (p. 215-219) and indexes. Subjects: Christianity and culture--United States. Conservatism--Religious aspects--Christianity. Culture conflict--United States--Civilization--20th century--Moral conditions. United States--Politics and government--20th century.

Gofwen, Rotgak I. Christain influence and culture change among the Ngas people: the Tuwan experience / Rotgak I. Gofwen. Published/Created: [S.l.: s.n.], 1994 (Jos: Printed by Plateau Publishing Ltd. Description: xii, 127 p.; 20 cm. ISBN: 9783216511 (pbk.) Notes: Cover title. Includes bibliographical references (p. 118-127). Subjects: Angas (African people)--Missions. Angas (African people)--Social life and customs. Missions--Nigeria. Christianity--Nigeria. Cross-cultural studies--Nigeria. Nigeria--Religion. LC Classification: BV3625.N5 G65 1994

González, Justo L. For the healing of the nations: the book of Revelation in an age of cultural conflict / Justo L. González. Published/Created: Maryknoll, N.Y.: Orbis Books, c1999. Description: ix, 117 p.; 21 cm. ISBN: 1570752737 Notes: Includes bibliographical references and index. Subjects: Bible. N.T. Revelation--Criticism, interpretation, etc. Hope--Religious aspects--Christianity--History of doctrines--Early church, ca. 30-600. Culture conflict--Religious aspects--Christianity--History of doctrines--Early church, ca. 30-600. LC Classification: BS2825.2.C84 G66 1999 Dewey Class No.: 228/.06 21

González, Justo L. Out of every tribe and nation: Christian theology at the ethnic Roundtable / Justo L. González. Nashville: Abingdon Press, c1992. Related Authors: United Methodist Roundtable of Ethnic Minority Theologians. Description: 128 p.; 23 cm. ISBN: 0687298601(pbk.) Notes: "Originated in the work of the Roundtable of Ethnic Minority Theologians"--Back cover. Includes bibliographical references (p. 121-128). Subjects: Theology, Doctrinal. Christianity and culture. LC Classification: BT78 .G637 1992 Dewey Class No.: 230/.089 20

Goodich, Michael, 1944- Violence and miracle in the fourteenth century: private grief and public salvation / Michael E. Goodich. Published/Created: Chicago: University of Chicago Press, 1995. Description: xi, 220 p.; 23 cm. ISBN: 0226302946 (cloth: alk. paper) 0226302954 (pbk.: alk. paper) Notes: Includes bibliographical references (p. 193-203) and index. Subjects: Saints--Europe--Legends. Popular culture--Religious aspects--Christianity--History. Miracles--History of doctrines--Middle Ages, 600-1500. Violence in literature. Hagiography. LC Classification: BX4662 .G65 1995 Dewey Class No.: 282/.4/09023

Goosen, Gideon. Australian theologies: themes and methodologies into the third millennium / Gideon Goosen. Published/Created: Strathfield, NSW.: St. Pauls Publications, 2000. Description: 330 p.; 22 cm. ISBN: 1876295260 Notes: Includes bibliographical references (p. [305]-321) and index. Subjects: Christianity and culture--Australia. Theology--Australia.

Gorospe, Vitaliano R., comp. The Filipino in the seventies; an ecumenical perspective. Editors: Vitaliano R. Gorospe and Richard L. Deats. Published/Created: Quezon City, New Day Publishers [1973] Related Authors: Deats, Richard L. Description: xxii, 425 p. map. 23 cm. Partial Contents: Bernad, M. A. Philippine culture and Filipino identity.--Costa, H. de la. The Philippine national tradition.--Ortiz, P. A. Our search for national identity.--Garcia, E. G. and Ledesma, A. J. Toward a Filipino social democracy.--Concepcion, M. B. Philippine population policy and program.--Poethig, R. P. Philippine cities.--Deats, R. L. Natural resources and environment.--Valdepeñas, V. B. The economy.--McCarthy, C. J. The Chinese in the Philippines.--Gomez, H. M. Muslim-Christian relations. Notes: Includes bibliographies. Subjects: Christianity--Philippines. Philippines. LC Classification: DS655 .G67 Dewey Class No.: 915.99/03/4

Gospel & culture: the papers of a consultation on the Gospel and culture / John Stott, and Robert T. Coote, editors; convened by the Lausanne Committee's Theology and Education Group. Published/Created: Pasadena, Calif.: William Carey Library, c1979. Related Authors: Stott, John R. W. Coote, Robert T. Description: xi, 464 p.: ill.; 22 cm. ISBN: 0878081666 Notes: "Sponsored by the Theology and Education Group and the Strategy Working Group of the Lausanne Committee for World Evangelization." Includes bibliographical references. Subjects: Christianity and culture--Congresses. LC Classification: BR115.C8 G67 Dewey Class No.: 261

Gospel in context. Published/Created: Abington, Pa.: Partnership in Mission, c1978- Related Authors: Partnership in Mission. Description: v.; 28 cm. Vol. 1, no. 1 (Jan. 1978) called also premiere issue. Vol. 1, no. 1 (Jan. 1978)-v. 2, no. 4 (Oct. 1979) Current Frequency: Quarterly ISSN: 0193-8320 Notes: Title from cover. SERBIB/SERLOC merged record Subjects: Missions--Periodicals. Christianity and culture--Periodicals. LC Classification: BV2350 .G724

Gostwick, Joseph. German culture and christianity... Published/Created: [n. p.] 1882. Description: 1 v. cm. LC Classification: BR852 .G6

Gottwald, Norman K. (Norman Karol), 1926- The church unbound; a human church in a human world, by Norman K. Gottwald. Edition Information: [1st ed.]

Published/Created: Philadelphia, Lippincott [c1967] Description: 188 p. 21 cm. Notes: Includes bibliographies. Subjects: Church and the world. Christianity and culture. LC Classification: BR115.W6 G68 Dewey Class No.: 260

Graggs, Charles Randall. Christianity and culture versus the negro, Published/Created: [Dallas, The Dallas express publishing company, 1917] Description: 16 p. 30 cm. Subjects: Afro-Americans.United States--Race relations. LC Classification: E185.61 .G73

Graham, Gael, 1958- Gender, culture, and Christianity: American Protestant mission schools in China, 1880-1930 / Gael Graham. Published/Created: New York: P. Lang, c1995. Description: 231 p.; 24 cm. ISBN: 0820427675 (hardcover: alk. paper) Notes: Includes bibliographical references (p. [203]-222) and index. Subjects: Protestant churches--Education--China--History--19th century. Protestant churches--Education--China--History--20th century. Missions--China--Educational work--History--19th century--20th century. Sex differences in education--China--History--19th century--20th century. Women missionaries--China. Series: Asian thought and culture, 0893-6870; vol. 25 LC Classification: LC626.C5 G73 1995 Dewey Class No.: 377/.84/0951 20

Grant, George, 1954- The changing of the guard: the vital role Christians must play in America's unfolding political and cultural drama / George Grant. Published/Created: Nashville, Tenn.: Broadman & Holman Publishers, c1995. Description: xix, 228 p.; 20 cm. ISBN: 0805462686 (pbk.) Notes: Includes bibliographical references (p. 215-227). Subjects: Christianity and politics. Christianity and culture. Conservatism--Religious aspects--Christianity. Church and state--United States--Church history--20th century. United States--Politics and government--1993-2001. LC Classification: BR526 .G74 1995 Dewey Class No.: 261.7/0973 20

Grant, Patrick, 1941- Breaking enmities: religion, literature, and culture in Northern Ireland, 1967-97 / Patrick Grant. Published/Created: New York: St. Martin's Press, 1999. Description: p. cm. ISBN: 0312221401 (cloth) Notes: Includes bibliographical references and index. Subjects: English literature--Irish authors--History and criticism. Christianity and literature--Northern Ireland--History 20th century. Literature and anthropology--Northern Ireland--History 20th century. Religion and literature--History--20th century. Social conflict in literature. Northern Ireland--Civilization. LC Classification: PR8891.N67 G73 1999 Dewey Class No.: 820.9/9416/09045 21

Graveson, Caroline Cassandra, 1874-1958. Religion and culture / By Caroline C. Graveson. Published/Created: London: George Allen & Unwin, 1937. Description: 54 p.; 19 cm. Subjects: Christianity--20th century. Culture Series: Swarthmore lecture, 1937 LC Classification: BR115.C8 G7

Gregory of Nazianzus, Saint. A Christian's guide to Greek culture: the pseudo-nonnus commentaries on sermons 4, 5, 39 and 43 / by Gregory of Nazainus; translated by Jennifer Nimmo-Smith. Published/Created: Liverpool: Liverpool University Press, 2001. Related Authors: Nimmo-Smith, Jennifer. Description: xlviii, 156 p.; 21 cm. ISBN: 0853239177 Notes: Translated from the Ancient Greek. Subjects: Gregory, of Nazianzus, Saint Sermons. Gregory, of Nazianzus, Saint--Allusions. Sermons, Early Christian. Christianity and culture--History--Early church, ca. 30-600. Series: Translated texts for historians 37 Dewey Class No.: 252.014 21

Grey, Mary C. Beyond the dark night: a way forward for the church? / Mary C. Grey. Published/Created: London; Herndon, VA: Cassell, 1997. Description: viii, 147 p.; 24 cm. ISBN: 0304337536 Notes: Includes bibliographical references and index. Subjects: Church--History of doctrines--20th century. Mission of the church. Christianity and culture--History--20th century. LC Classification: BV598 .G75 1997 Dewey Class No.: 262/.001/7 21

Griffith, Leonard, 1920- Illusions of our culture, by Leonard Griffith. Published/Created: London, Hodder & Stoughton, 1969. Description: 160 p. 23 cm. ISBN: 0340107138 Notes: Bibliographical footnotes. Subjects: Christianity--20th century. LC Classification: BR121.2 .G72 Dewey Class No.: 261

Griffiths, Michael, 1928- Shaking the sleeping beauty: arousing the church to its mission / Michael Griffiths. Leicester, England: Inter-Varsity Press, 1980. Description: 207 p.; 18 cm. ISBN: 0851104169 (pbk.) Notes: Includes bibliographical references. Subjects: Missions--Church growth--Christianity and culture--Church and the world--Addresses, essays, lectures. LC Classification: BV2070 .G743 1980 Dewey Class No.: 266 19

Griffiths, Michael, 1928- The church & world mission / Michael Griffiths. Published/Created: Grand Rapids, Mich.: Zondervan, 1982, c1980. Description: 207 p.: ill.; 21 cm. ISBN: 0310451116 Notes: Originally published: Shaking the sleeping beauty. 1980. Includes bibliographical references. Subjects: Missions. Church growth. Christianity and culture. Church and the world. LC Classification: BV2070 .G74 1982 Dewey Class No.: 266 19

Groothuis, Rebecca Merrill. Women caught in the conflict: the culture war between traditionalism and feminism / Rebecca Merrill Groothuis; foreword by Kenneth S. Kantzer. Published/Created: Grand Rapids, Mich.: Baker Books, c1994. Description: xiii, 249 p.; 23 cm. ISBN: 0801063043 Notes: Includes bibliographical references (p. 217-242) and indexes. Subjects: Women in Christianity. Feminism--Religious aspects--Christianity. Culture conflict. Evangelicalism. LC Classification: BV639.W7 G76 1994 Dewey Class No.: 208.2 20

Grunlan, Stephen A. Cultural anthropology: a Christian perspective / Stephen A. Grunlan and Marvin K. Mayers; with a foreword by Eugene A. Nida. Edition Information: 2nd ed. Published/Created: Grand Rapids, Mich.: Academie Books, 1988. Related Authors: Mayers, Marvin Keene, 1927- Description: 303 p.: ill.; 21 cm. ISBN: 0310363810 (pbk.) Notes: "A Zondervan publication." Includes indexes. Bibliography: p. 285-293. Subjects: Christianity and culture. Anthropology. LC Classification: BR115.C8 G76 1988 Dewey Class No.: 306 19

Grunlan, Stephen A. Cultural anthropology: a Christian perspective / Stephen A. Grunlan and Marvin K. Mayers; with a foreword by Eugene A. Nida. Published/Created: Grand Rapids: Zondervan, c1979. Related Authors: Mayers, Marvin Keene, 1927- joint author. Description: 309 p.; 21 cm. ISBN: 0310363217 Notes: Includes indexes. Bibliography: p. 287-294. Subjects: Christianity and culture. Anthropology. LC Classification: BR115.C8 G76 Dewey Class No.: 301.2

Guibbory, Achsah, 1945- Ceremony and community from Herbert to Milton: literature, religion, and cultural conflict in seventeenth-century England / Achsah Guibbory. Cambridge; New York: Cambridge University Press, 1998. Description: xiii, 275 p.: ill.; 24 cm. ISBN: 0521593557 (hardback) Notes: Includes bibliographical references (p. 228-268) and index. Subjects: Browne, Thomas, Sir, 1605-1682 --Religion. Herrick, Robert, 1591-1674. Hesperides. Herbert, George, 1593-1633 --Religion. Milton, John, 1608-1674 --Religion. English literature--Early modern, 1500-1700--History and criticism. Christianity and literature--Religion and literature----England--History--17th century. Rites and ceremonies in literature. Culture conflict in literature. Community in literature. Ritual in literature. England--Church history--17th century. LC Classification: PR438.R45 G85 1998 Dewey Class No.: 820.9/3823 21

Guinness, Os. Dining with the devil: the megachurch movement flirts with modernity / Os Guinness. Published/Created: Grand Rapids, Mich.: Baker Book House, c1993. Description: 113 p.; 22 cm. ISBN: 0801038553 Notes: "Hourglass books." Includes bibliographical references (p. 110-113). Subjects: Church growth--United States. Big churches. Christianity and culture. United States--Church history--20th century. LC Classification: BR526 .G85 1993 Dewey Class No.: 254/.5 20

Guinness, Os. The devil's gauntlet: the church and the challenge of society / Os Guinness. Published/Created: Downers Grove, Ill.: InterVarsity Press, c1989. Description: 30 p.; 18 cm. ISBN: 0830811087 Notes: Includes bibliographical references. Subjects: Christianity and culture. Fundamentalism. Series: Viewpoint pamphlets LC Classification: BR115.C8 G79 1989 Dewey Class No.: 261/.0973 19

Guinness, Os. The dust of death; a critique of the establishment and the counter culture, and the proposal for a third way. Published/Created: Downers Grove, Ill., InterVarsity Press [1972, c1973] Description: 419 p. 21 cm. ISBN: 0877849560 0877849110 (pbk) Notes: Includes bibliographical references. Subjects: Civilization, Modern--1950- Christianity--United States--20th century. United States--Civilization--1945- LC Classification: CB428 .G84 Dewey Class No.: 901.94

Gundry Volf, Judith M. A spacious heart: essays on identity and belonging / Judith M. Gundry-Volf, Miroslav Volf. Published/Created: Valley Forge, Pa.: Trinity Press International, c1997. Related Authors: Volf, Miroslav. Description: viii, 71 p.; 19 cm. ISBN: 1563382016 (pbk.: alk. paper) Notes: Includes bibliographical references (p. 67-71). Subjects: Jesus Christ--Political and social views. Syrophoenician woman (Biblical figure) Samaritan woman (Biblical figure) Multiculturalism--Religious aspects-- Christianity. Yugoslav War, 1991- --

Atrocities. Bosnia and Hercegovina-- Ethnic relations. Series: Christian mission and modern culture LC Classification: BR115.C8 G795 1997 Dewey Class No.: 261 21

Gunton, Colin E. The One, the Three, and the many: God, creation, and the culture of modernity / Colin E. Gunton. Published/Created: Cambridge; New York, NY, USA: Cambridge University Press, 1993. Description: xiv, 248 p.; 22 cm. ISBN: 052142030X 0521421845 (pbk.) Notes: "The Bampton lectures, 1992." Includes bibliographical references (p. 232-240) and index. Subjects: Theology. Christianity and culture. Trinity--History of doctrines--20th century. Modernism (Christian theology) LC Classification: BT28 .G86 1993 Dewey Class No.: 231/.044 20

Guroian, Vigen. Ethics after Christendom: toward an ecclesial Christian ethic / Vigen Guroian. Published/Created: Grand Rapids, Mich.: Eerdmans Pub. Co., c1994. Description: x, 206 p.; 23 cm. ISBN: 0802801285 (pbk.) Notes: Includes bibliographical references and indexes. Subjects: Christian ethics--Oriental Orthodox authors. Postmodernism-- Religious aspects--Christianity. Christianity and culture. LC Classification: BJ1250.5 .G85 1994 Dewey Class No.: 241 20

Hall, Douglas John, 1928- Confessing the faith: Christian theology in a North American context / Douglas John Hall. Published/Created: Minneapolis: Fortress Press, 1996. Description: xii, 534 p.; 24 cm. ISBN: 0800625471 (alk. paper) Notes: Includes bibliographical references and indexes. Subjects: Theology, Doctrinal-- North America. Christianity and culture. LC Classification: BT75.2 .H33 1996 Dewey Class No.: 230/.097 20

Hall, Douglas John, 1928- Lighten our darkness: toward an indigenous theology of the cross / by Douglas John Hall. Published/Created: Philadelphia: Westminster Press, c1976. Description:

253 p.; 24 cm. ISBN: 0664208088 Notes: Includes bibliographical references and index. Subjects: Christianity. Christianity and culture--North America. North America--Civilization. LC Classification: BR121.2 .H317 Dewey Class No.: 230

Hall, Douglas John, 1928- Lighten our darkness: toward an indigenous theology of the cross / Douglas John Hall; revised and with a foreword by David J. Monge. Edition Information: Rev. ed. Published/Created: Lima, Ohio: Academic Renewal Press, 2001. Description: p. cm. ISBN: 0788099000 (alk. paper) Notes: Includes bibliographical references and index. Subjects: Christianity and culture--North America. North America--Civilization. LC Classification: BR121.3 H35 2001 Dewey Class No.: 230 21

Hall, Douglas John, 1928- Professing the faith: Christian theology in a North American context / Douglas John Hall. Edition Information: First Fortress Press paperback ed. Published/Created: Minneapolis: Fortress Press, 1996. Description: x, 566 p.; 23 cm. ISBN: 080062548X (pbk.) Notes: Includes bibliographical references and indexes. Subjects: Theology, Doctrinal--North America. Christianity and culture. LC Classification: BT75.2 .H34 1996 Dewey Class No.: 230/.097 21

Hall, Douglas John, 1928- Professing the faith: Christian theology in a North American context / Douglas John Hall. Published/Created: Minneapolis: Fortress Press, c1993. Description: x, 566 p.; 24 cm. ISBN: 0800625463 (alk. paper) : Notes: Includes bibliographical references and indexes. Subjects: Theology, Doctrinal--North America. Christianity and culture. LC Classification: BT75.2 .H34 1993 Dewey Class No.: 230/.097 20

Hall, Douglas John, 1928- The end of Christendom and the future of Christianity / Douglas John Hall. Published/Created: Valley Forge, Pa.: Trinity Press International, 1996. Description: x, 69 p.; 19 cm. ISBN: 1563381931 (pbk.: alk. paper) 0852444214 (Gracewing) Notes:

Includes bibliographical references (p. 68-69). Subjects: Christianity--20th century. Church and the world. Series: Christian mission and modern culture LC Classification: BR121.2 .H315 1996 Dewey Class No.: 270.8/29 21

Hall, Douglas John, 1928- Thinking the faith: Christian theology in a North American context / Douglas John Hall. Published/Created: Minneapolis: Augsburg, c1989. Description: 456 p.; 24 cm. ISBN: 0806623888 (alk. paper) Notes: Includes bibliographical references and indexes. Subjects: Theology, Doctrinal--North America. Christianity and culture. LC Classification: BT30.N7 H35 1989 Dewey Class No.: 230/.097 19

Hambrick-Stowe, Charles E. The practice of piety: Puritan devotional disciplines in seventeenth-century New England / Charles E. Hambrick-Stowe. Published/Created: Chapel Hill: Published for the Institute of Early American History and Culture, Williamsburg, Virginia by the University of North Carolina Press, c1982. Related Authors: Institute of Early American History and Culture (Williamsburg, Va.) Description: xvi, 298 p.: ill.; 24 cm. ISBN: 0807815187 Notes: Includes bibliographical references and indexes. Subjects: Spiritual life--Christianity--History of doctrines--17th century. Puritans--New England. New England--Religious life and customs. LC Classification: BV4490 .H3 1982 Dewey Class No.: 248.4/0974 19

Hammond, Jeffrey. The American Puritan elegy: a literary and cultural study / Jeffrey A. Hammond. Published/Created: New York: Cambridge University Press, 2000. Description: xv, 264 p.; 24 cm. ISBN: 0521662451 Notes: Includes bibliographical references (p. 240-255) and index. Subjects: Elegiac poetry, American--History and criticism. American poetry--Colonial period, ca. 1600-1775--History and criticism. American poetry--Puritan authors--History and criticism. American poetry--New England--History and criticism. Literature and anthropology--

Christianity and literature--New England--History. Puritans--New England--Intellectual life. Death in literature. Grief in literature. Series: Cambridge studies in American literature and culture LC Classification: PS309.E4 H36 2000 Dewey Class No.: 811.009/3548 21

Hammond, Phillip E. The Protestant presence in twentieth-century America: religion and political culture / Phillip E. Hammond. Published/Created: Albany: State University of New York Press, c1992. Description: vii, 199 p.: ill.; 24 cm. ISBN: 0791411214 (alk. paper) 0791411222 (pbk.: alk. paper) Notes: Includes bibliographical references (p. 185-192) and index. Subjects: Protestant churches--United States--Christianity and politics--Christianity and culture--History--20th century. United States--Church history--20th century. Series: SUNY series in religion, culture, and society LC Classification: BR515 .H334 1992 Dewey Class No.: 280/.4/09730904 20

Handy, Robert T. A Christian America: Protestant hopes and historical realities / Robert T. Handy. Edition Information: 2nd ed., rev. and enl. Published/Created: Oxford; New York: Oxford University Press, 1984. Description: xii, 269 p.; 22 cm. ISBN: 0195033868 (U.S.): 0195033876 (U.S.: pbk.) : Notes: Includes index. Bibliography: p. 214-221. Subjects: Protestant churches--United States. Christianity and culture. United States--Church history. LC Classification: BR515 .H354 1984 Dewey Class No.: 280/.4/0973 19

Handy, Robert T. A Christian America; Protestant hopes and historical realities [by] Robert T. Handy. Published/Created: New York, Oxford University Press, 1971. Description: x, 282 p. 22 cm. ISBN: 0195014537 Notes: Bibliography: p. 227-236. Subjects: Protestant churches--United States. Christianity and culture. United States--Church history. LC Classification: BR515 .H354 Dewey Class No.: 280/.4/0973

Hangen, Tona J. Redeeming the dial: radio, religion, and popular culture in America / Tona J. Hangen. Published/Created: Chapel Hill: University of North Carolina Press, c2002. Description: p. cm. ISBN: 0807827525 0807854204 Notes: Includes bibliographical references (p.) and index. Subjects: Radio in religion--United States--History--20th century. Evangelicalism--United States--History--20th century. Religious broadcasting--Christianity--History--20th century. LC Classification: BV656 .H36 2002 Dewey Class No.: 269/.26/0973 21

Hankins, Barry, 1956- Uneasy in Babylon: Southern Baptist conservatives and American culture / Barry Hankins. Published/Created: Tuscaloosa, Ala.: University of Alabama Press, c2002. Description: p. cm. ISBN: 0817311424 (cloth: alk. paper) Contents: Moving off the plantation: Southern Baptist conservatives become American evangelicals -- "The war of the worlds": Southern Baptist conservatives as culture warriors -- From Christianity today to World magazine: Southern Baptist conservatives take their stand in Louisville -- The search for a useable past: religious liberty in a hostile culture -- Using a useable past: church-state positions -- No one has been shot yet: Southern Baptists and the abortion controversy -- Graciously submissive: Southern Baptist conservatives and women -- Conservatives can be progressive too: Southern Baptist conservatives and race. Notes: Includes bibliographical references and index. Subjects: Southern Baptist Convention--History--20th century. Conservatism--Religious aspects--Southern Baptist Convention--History--20th century. Series: Religion and American culture (Tuscaloosa, Ala.) LC Classification: BX6462.3 .H36 2002 Dewey Class No.: 286/.132 21

Hanley, Mark Y. Beyond a Christian commonwealth: the Protestant quarrel with the American Republic, 1830-1860 / Mark Y. Hanley. Published/Created: Chapel Hill: University of North Carolina Press, c1994.

Description: x, 210 p.; 24 cm. ISBN:
0807821217 (alk. paper) Notes: Includes
bibliographical references (p. [187]-203)
and index. Subjects: Protestant churches--
United States--History--19th century.
Christianity and culture--History of
doctrines--19th century. United States--
Church history--19th century. LC
Classification: BR525 .H324 1994 Dewey
Class No.: 280/.4/097309034 20

Hanratty, Gerald. Light from Paris: Cardinal
Lustiger on faith and contemporary culture
/ Gerald Hanratty. Published/Created:
Blackrock, Co., Dublin; Portland, OR:
Four Courts Press, c1995. Description: 32
p.; 24 cm. ISBN: 1851821848 Notes:
Includes bibliographical references (p. 32).
Subjects: Lustiger, Jean-Marie, 1926-
Christianity and culture--History--20th
century. LC Classification: BR115.C8 H37
1995

Happel, Stephen, 1944- Metaphors for God's
time in science and religion / Stephen
Happel. Published/Created: New York:
Palgrave, 2002. Description: p. cm. ISBN:
0333714105 Notes: Includes
bibliographical references and index.
Subjects: Religion and science. Time--
Religious aspects--Christianity. Metaphor--
Religious aspects--Christianity. Series:
Cross currents in religion and culture
(Palgrave (Firm)) LC Classification:
BL240.3 .H36 2002 Dewey Class No.:
261.5/5 21

Häring, Bernhard, 1912- Faith and morality in
the secular age, by Bernard Häring. Edition
Information: [1st ed.] Published/Created:
Garden City, N.Y., Doubleday, 1973.
Description: 237 p. 22 cm. ISBN:
0385038372 Subjects: Secularism.
Religion and culture. Faith. Prayer--
Christianity. LC Classification: BL2747.8
.H33 Dewey Class No.: 234/.2

Harnack, Adolf von, 1851-1930. What is
Christianity? Translated by Thomas Bailey
Saunders. Introd. by Rudolf Bultmann.
Edition Information: [1st Harper torchbook
ed.] Published/Created: New York, Harper
[1957] Description: 301 p. 21 cm. Notes:

Translation of Das Wesen des
Christentums. Subjects: Christianity--
Essence, genius, nature. LC Classification:
BT60 .H3713 1957 Dewey Class No.: 230

Hartt, Julian Norris. A Christian critique of
American culture; an essay in practical
theology [by] Julian N. Hartt. Edition
Information: [1st ed.] Published/Created:
New York, Harper & Row [1967]
Description: xix, 425 p. 22 cm. Subjects:
Christianity and culture. Church and the
world. LC Classification: BR115.C8 H38
Dewey Class No.: 230

Hartt, Julian Norris. The critique of modernity:
theological reflections on contemporary
culture / Julian N. Hartt, Ray L. Hart,
Robert P. Scharlemann. Published/Created:
Charlottesville: University Press of
Virginia, 1986. Related Authors: Hart, Ray
L. Scharlemann, Robert P. Description: xx,
92 p.; 24 cm. ISBN: 0813911184 Contents:
Introduction / Julian N. Hartt -- The pathos
of community in contemporary culture /
Julian N. Hartt -- The dialectic of home
and homelessness / Ray L. Hart -- The
forgotten self and the forgotten divine /
Robert P. Scharlemann. Notes: Papers,
presented at the Virginia lectures on
Individual and society, March 1984.
Includes bibliographies. Subjects:
Christianity and culture. Individuality. LC
Classification: BR115.C8 H385 1986
Dewey Class No.: 261 19

Hasman, Melvin, 1938- Spiritual life in the
Good Ol' USA: story-essays on popular
culture and Christianity / Melvin Hasman.
Published/Created: La Mesa, Calif.:
Potter's Books, c1994. Description: 234 p.:
ill.; 23 cm. ISBN: 0963824082 (alk.
paper): 0963824090 (pbk.: alk. paper) :
Notes: Includes bibliographical references
and index. Subjects: Popular culture--
Religious aspects--Christianity. Popular
culture--United States. Christian life. LC
Classification: BR115.C8 H387 1994
Dewey Class No.: 261/.0973 20

Hastings, Adrian. The Church in Africa: 1450-
1950 / Adrian Hastings. Published/Created:
Oxford: Clarendon Press; Oxford; New

York: Oxford University Press, 1994. Description: xiv, 706 p.: maps; 24 cm. ISBN: 0198269218 : Notes: Includes bibliographical references (p. [621]-685) and index. Subjects: Christianity--Church and state--Missions--Africa--History. Christianity and culture. Series: The Oxford history of the Christian Church LC Classification: BR1360 .H364 1994 Dewey Class No.: 276 20

Hatch, Edwin, 1835-1889. The influence of Greek ideas on Christianity. Foreword with new notes and a bibliography by Frederick C. Grant. Edition Information: [1st Harper torchbook ed.] Published/Created: New York, Harper [1957] Description: xxxv, 359 p. 21 cm. Notes: Harper torchbooks, TB18. First published in 1890 under The influence of Greek ideas and usages upon the Christian church. Subjects: Church history--Primitive and early church, ca. 30-600. Philosophy--History. Theology, Doctrinal. LC Classification: BR128.G8 H3 1957 Dewey Class No.: 270.1

Hauerwas, Stanley, 1940- After Christendom?: how the church is to behave if freedom, justice, and a Christian nation are bad ideas / Stanley Hauerwas. Published/Created: Nashville: Abingdon Press, c1991. Description: 192 p.; 22 cm. ISBN: 0687009294 (alk. paper) Notes: Includes bibliographical references (p. 163-189) and index. Subjects: Christianity and culture. Christian ethics--Methodist authors. Secularism. Christianity--20th century. LC Classification: BR115.W6 H38 1991 Dewey Class No.: 261 20

Hauerwas, Stanley, 1940- Resident aliens: life in the Christian colony / Stanley Hauerwas and William H. Willimon. Published/Created: Nashville: Abingdon Press, c1989. Related Authors: Willimon, William H. Description: 175 p.; 22 cm. ISBN: 0687361591 (alk. paper) Notes: "A provocative Christian assessment of culture and ministry for people who know that something is wrong." Subjects: Christianity and culture. Christian life--Methodist authors. Christianity--United States--Controversial literature. Christianity--20th

century--Controversial literature. Identification (Religion) Pastoral theology. LC Classification: BR115.C8 H393 1989 Dewey Class No.: 261.1 19

Hauerwas, Stanley, 1940- Where resident aliens live: exercises for Christian practice / Stanley Hauerwas, William H. Willimon. Published/Created: Nashville: Abingdon Press, c1996. Related Authors: Willimon, William H. Description: 124 p.: ill.; 22 cm. ISBN: 0687016053 (alk. paper) Notes: Includes bibliographical references (p. 119-121) and indexes. Subjects: Christian life--Methodist authors. Christianity and culture. Church and the world. LC Classification: BV4501.2 .H366 1996 Dewey Class No.: 261/.1 21

Healey, Joseph. Towards an African narrative theology / Joseph Healey, Donald Sybertz. Published/Created: Maryknoll, N.Y.: Orbis Books, c1996. Related Authors: Sybertz, Donald. Description: 400 p.: ill., map; 21 cm. ISBN: 1570751218 (alk. paper) Notes: Includes bibliographical references (p. 382-388) and index. Subjects: Catholic Church--Africa. Christianity and culture--Africa. Pastoral theology--Africa. Storytelling--Religious aspects--Christianity. Narrative theology--Africa. Series: Faith and cultures series LC Classification: BR1360 .H367 1996 Dewey Class No.: 230/.096 21

Healey, Joseph. Towards an African narrative theology / Joseph Healey, Donald Sybertz. Published/Created: Nairobi, Kenya: Paulines Publications Africa, 1996. Related Authors: Sybertz, Donald. Description: 397 p.: ill., map; 21 cm. ISBN: 996621187X Notes: Includes bibliographical references (p. 382-388) and index. Subjects: Catholic church--Africa. Christianity and culture--Africa. Pastoral theology--Africa. Storytelling--Religious aspects--Christianity. Narrative theology--Africa. LC Classification: BR1360 .H3672 1996 Dewey Class No.: 230/.096 21

Health, medicine, and empire: perspectives on colonial India / edited by Bisamoy Pati, Mark Harrison. Published/Created:

Hyderabad, India: Orient Longman, c2001. Related Authors: Pati, Biswamoy. Harrison, Mark. Description: x, 408 p.; 23 cm. ISBN: 8125020179 Contents: Medicine and orientalism: perspectives on Europe's encounter with Indian medical systems / Mark Harrison -- "Clinical Christianity": the emergence of medical work as a missionary strategy in colonial India, 1800-1914 / Rosemary Fitzgerald -- Colonial lunacy policies and the Madras lunatic asylum in the early nineteen century / Waltraud Ernst -- Indians into asylums: community use of the colonial medical institution in British India, 1857-1880 / James Mills -- Medical developments and patient unrest in the leprosy asylum, 1860 to 1940 / Sanjiv Kumar -- Re-devising jennerian vaccines?: European technologies, Indian innovation, and the control of smallpox in South Asia, 1850-1950 / Sanjoy Bhattacharya -- "Ordering" "Disorder" in a holy city: colonial health interventions in Puri during the nineteenth century / Biswamoy Pati -- "The Palkhi as plague carrier": the Pandharpur fair and the sanitary fixation of the colonial state; British India, 1908-1916 / Manjiri Kamat -- Politics, culture, and colonialism: Unani's debate with doctory / Neshat Quaiser -- The Indian drug industry under the raj, 1860-1920 / Anil Kumar. Notes: Includes bibliographical references (p. 383-385) and index. Subjects: Medicine--India. Public health--India. Series: New perspectives in South Asian history; 1 LC Classification: R606 .H43 2001

Hegland, Martin, 1880-1967. Christianity in education; an orientation in elements of Christian culture with suggestions for relating the subject-fields to Christianity. Published/Created: Minneapolis, Augsburg Pub. House [1954] Description: 110 p. 21 cm. Subjects: Church and education. LC Classification: LC368 .H4 Dewey Class No.: 377

Hellenization revisited: shaping a Christian response within the Greco-Roman world / edited by Wendy E. Helleman. Published/Created: Lanham: University

Press of America, c1994. Related Authors: Helleman, Wendy E. Description: 544 p.; 24 cm. ISBN: 081919543X (cloth: alk. paper) 0819195448 (paper: alk. paper) Notes: Proceedings of a conference held in summer 1991 in Toronto, Ont., sponsored by the Institute for Christian Studies. Includes bibliographical references (p. [513]-527) and index. Subjects: Gnosticism--Christianity--Early church, ca. 30-600--Judaism--History--Post-exilic period, 586 B.C.-210 A.D.--Christianity and other religions--Greek--Christianity and culture--Congresses. LC Classification: BT1390 .H45 1994 Dewey Class No.: 273/.1 20

Henderson, David W., 1959- Culture shift: communicating God's truth to our changing world / David W. Henderson; foreword by Haddon Robinson. Published/Created: Grand Rapids, Mich.: Baker Books, c1998. Description: 255 p.: ill.; 23 cm. ISBN: 0801090598 (pbk.) Notes: Includes bibliographical references (p. 236-246) and index. Subjects: Evangelistic work--Christianity and culture--United States. LC Classification: BV3793 .H46 1998 Dewey Class No.: 269/.2 21

Hendrix, Raymond F. America's other Jesus / Raymond F. Hendrix. Published/Created: Raleigh, N.C.: Pentland Press, c1999. Description: x, 206 p.; 22 cm. ISBN: 1571971661 Notes: Includes bibliographical references (p. [195]-199) and index. Subjects: Christianity and culture--United States. United States--Moral conditions. LC Classification: BR115.C8 .H45 1999 Dewey Class No.: 277.3 21

Henry, Carl Ferdinand Howard, 1913- Has democracy had its day? / by Carl F.H. Henry. Published/Created: Nashville, Tenn.: ERLC Publications, c1996. Description: viii, 63 p.; 23 cm. ISBN: 1888880007 Subjects: Democracy--Religious aspects--Christianity. Christianity and culture. LC Classification: BR115.P7 H466 1996 Dewey Class No.: 261.7/0973 20

Henry, Carl Ferdinand Howard, 1913- Twilight of a great civilization: the drift toward neo-paganism / Carl F.H. Henry. Published/Created: Westchester, Ill.: Crossway Books, c1988. Description: x, 192 p.; 23 cm. ISBN: 0891074910 Notes: Includes bibliographical references (p. 183-186) and indexes. Subjects: Christianity and culture. Evangelicalism--United States. Christianity--20th century. United States--Moral conditions. LC Classification: BR115.C8 H46 1988 Dewey Class No.: 277.3/0828 20

Henry, Rodney L. Filipino spirit world: a challenge to the church / Rodney L. Henry. Published/Created: Denver, CO: iAcademic Books, 2001. Description: p. cm. ISBN: 1588680843 (pbk.) Notes: Includes bibliographical references and index. Subjects: Christianity and culture--Philippines. Animism--Philippines. Philippines--Religious life and customs. LC Classification: BR1260 .H46 2001 Dewey Class No.: 261.5/13/09599 21

Hereford, Marie Judith. A new babel, a new pentecost: communicating the gospel in a mass mediated culture / Marie Judith Hereford, Corrine Thomas. Published/Created: Boston: Pauline Books & Media, c1997. Related Authors: Thomas, Corrine. Description: 90 p.: ill.; 28 cm. ISBN: 0819851345 Notes: Includes bibliographical references. Subjects: Communication--Religious aspects--Christianity. Mass media--Religious aspects--Christianity. Christianity and culture. LC Classification: IN PROCESS

Hesselgrave, David J. Contextualization: meanings, methods, and models / David J. Hesselgrave and Edward Rommen; foreword by George W. Peters. Published/Created: Pasadena, Calif.: William Carey Library, c2000. Related Authors: Rommen, Edward, 1947- Description: xii, 281p.: ill.; 23 cm. ISBN: 0878087753 (pbk.: alk. paper) Notes: Originally published: Grand Rapids, Mich.: Baker Book House, c1989. Includes bibliographical references (p. 259-268) and index. Subjects: Christianity and culture.

Missions--Theory. LC Classification: BR115.C8 H47 2000 Dewey Class No.: 261 21

Hesselgrave, David J. Contextualization: meanings, methods, and models / David J. Hesselgrave and Edward Rommen; foreword by George W. Peters. Published/Created: Grand Rapids, Mich.: Baker Book House, c1989. Related Authors: Rommen, Edward, 1947- Description: xii, 281 p.: ill.; 23 cm. ISBN: 0801043387 Notes: Includes index. Bibliography: p. 259-268. Subjects: Christianity and culture. Missions--Theory. LC Classification: BR115.C8 H47 1989 Dewey Class No.: 261 20

Hibbert, Giles. Man, culture, and Christianity; with a foreword by Lawrence Bright. Published/Created: London, Melbourne, Sheed & Ward, 1967. Description: xiv, 241 p. 21 cm. Notes: (SBN 722050516) Bibliography: p. 228-236. Subjects: Christianity and culture. LC Classification: BR115.C8 H5 Dewey Class No.: 201

Hiebert, Paul G., 1932- Anthropological insights for missionaries / Paul G. Hiebert. Published/Created: Grand Rapids, Mich.: Baker Book House, c1985. Description: 315 p.: ill.; 23 cm. ISBN: 0801042917 (pbk.) : Notes: Includes index. Bibliography: p. 299-305. Subjects: Missions--Anthropological aspects. Christianity and culture. Intercultural communication. LC Classification: BV2063 .H45 1985 Dewey Class No.: 266 19

Hiebert, Paul G., 1932- Anthropological reflections on missiological issues / Paul G. Hiebert. Published/Created: Grand Rapids, Mich.: Baker Books, c1994. Description: 272 p.: ill.; 23 cm. ISBN: 0801043948 Notes: Includes bibliographical references (p. 255-261) and index. Subjects: Missions--Theory. Missions--Anthropological aspects. Christianity and culture. LC Classification: BV2063 .H46 1994 Dewey Class No.: 266/.001 20

Hill, Jim, 1959- The Bible tells me so: uses and abuses of Holy Scripture / Jim Hill and Rand Cheadle. Edition Information: 1st ed. Published/Created: New York: Anchor Books/Doubleday, c1996. Related Authors: Cheadle, Rand. Description: 155 p.: ill.; 20 cm. ISBN: 0385476957 : Notes: Includes bibliographical references (p. 147). Subjects: Bible--Use. Bible--Influence. Christianity and politics--United States. Christianity and culture--United States. LC Classification: BS538.7 .H55 1996 Dewey Class No.: 220.6 20

Hillman, Eugene. Toward an African Christianity: inculturation applied / Eugene Hillman. Published/Created: New York: Paulist Press, c1993. Description: v, 101 p.; 22 cm. ISBN: 0809133814 (pbk.) : Notes: Includes bibliographical references (p. 86-98) and index. Subjects: Catholic Church--Africa, Sub-Saharan. Christianity and culture. Masai (African people)--Religion. Africa, Sub-Saharan--Church history. Kenya--Religion. Tanzania--Religion. LC Classification: BX1680.3 .H55 1993 Dewey Class No.: 261/.0967 20

Hirudayam, Ignatius, 1910- Christianity and Tamil culture / by Ignatius Hirudayam. Published/Created: [Madras]: Dr. S. Radhakrishnan Institute for Advanced Study in Philosophy, University of Madras, 1977. Description: vi, 85 p.; 25 cm. Notes: Includes quotations in Tamil. "A golden jubilee publication." Bibliography: p. [84]-85. Subjects: Christianity--Influence--India, South. Tamil (Indic people)--Religion. LC Classification: BR1170.S68 H57 Dewey Class No.: 261.2

History of Christianity in Oyo State of Nigeria: its influence in Yoruba culture/ Esther Feyisike. Published/Created: Orogun Ibadan: Freeman , 2000 .

Holland, J. G. (Josiah Gilbert), 1819-1881. Every-day topics; a book of briefs, by J. G. Holland. Edition Information: 1st ser. Published/Created: New York, C. Scribner's sons, 1882. Description: xi, 367 p. 18 cm. Partial Contents: Culture.--Literature and literary men.--Criticism.--

The popular lecture.--Personal dangers.--Personal development.--Preachers and preaching.--Christianity and science.--Revivals and reforms.--Christian practice.--The church of the future.--The common moralities.--Woman.--Woman and home. Subjects: Conduct of life. LC Classification: BJ1571 .H6 1882

Hollar, Barry Penn, 1953- On being the church in the United States: contemporary theological critiques of liberalism / Barry Penn Hollar. New York: P. Lang, c1994. Description: xii, 343 p.; 24 cm. ISBN: 0820423505 (alk. paper) Notes: Includes bibliographical references (p. [321]-337) and index. Subjects: Niebuhr, Reinhold, 1892-1971. Hauerwas, Stanley, 1940- Ruether, Rosemary Radford. Liberalism (Religion)--United States--Church and the world--History of doctrines--Christianity and culture--History--20th century. Series: American university studies. Series VII, Theology and religion, 0740-0446; vol. 170 LC Classification: BR517 .H553 1994 Dewey Class No.: 230/.046 20

Holmes, Barbara Ann, 1943- Race and the cosmos: an invitation to view the world differently / Barbara A. Holmes. Published/Created: Harrisburg, Pa.: Trinity Press International, c2002. Description: p. cm. ISBN: 1563383772 (pbk.: alk. paper) Notes: Includes bibliographical references and index. Subjects: African Americans--Religion. Race--Religious aspects--Christianity. Cosmology. LC Classification: BR563.N4 H654 2002 Dewey Class No.: 261.8/348 21

Holsinger, Bruce W. Music, body, and desire in medieval culture: Hildegard of Bingen to Chaucer / Bruce W. Holsinger. Published/Created: Stanford, Calif.: Stanford University Press, 2001. Description: xviii, 472 p.: ill.; 24 cm. ISBN: 0804732019 (cloth: acid-free paper) 0804740585 (paper: acid-free paper) Notes: Includes bibliographical references (p. [411]-450) and index. Subjects: Music--500-1400--Philosophy and aesthetics. Body, Human, in music. Body, Human, in literature. Body, Human--Religious aspects--Christianity--History of doctrines--Middle Ages, 600-1500. Series: Figurae (Stanford, Calif.) LC Classification: ML3845 .H64 2001 Dewey Class No.: 780/.9/02 21

Holsworth, Robert D. Let your life speak: a study of politics, religion, and antinuclear weapons activism / Robert D. Holsworth. Published/Created: Madison, Wis.: University of Wisconsin Press, c1989. Description: ix, 225 p.; 24 cm. ISBN: 0299120902: 0299120945 (pbk.) : Notes: Includes index. Bibliography: p. 217-220. Subjects: Nuclear warfare--Religious aspects--Christianity--Christianity and politics--Case studies. Antinuclear movement--Virginia--Richmond Region--History. Richmond (Va.)--Church history--20th century. Series: History of American thought and culture LC Classification: BR115.A85 H65 1989 Dewey Class No.: 261.8/73 19

Hood, Robert E. (Robert Earl), 1936- Must God remain Greek?: Afro cultures and God-talk / Robert E. Hood. Published/Created: Minneapolis: Fortress Press, c1990. Description: xiii, 273 p.; 22 cm. ISBN: 0800624491 (alk. paper) : Notes: Includes bibliographical references (p. 257-264) and index. Subjects: Black theology. Blacks--Caribbean Area--Religion. Liberation theology. Christianity and culture. Theology, Doctrinal. Africa, Sub-Saharan--Religion. LC Classification: BT82.7 .H65 1990 Dewey Class No.: 230/.089/96 20

Hoole, Charles R. A. Modern sannyasins: Protestant missionary contribution to Ceylon Tamil culture / Charles R.A. Hoole. Bern; New York: P. Lang, c1995. Description: 366 p.: map; 21 cm. ISBN: 3906755215 Notes: Includes bibliographical references (p. [331]-351) and index. Subjects: Sannyasi. Missions--Sri Lanka. Missions to Tamil (Indic people) Tamil (Indic people)--Religion. Sri Lanka--Civilization--Tamil influences. Series: Studien zur interkulturellen Geschichte des Christentums; Bd. 94. LC Classification: IN PROCESS

Hopler, Thom, 1936-1978. A world of difference, following Christ beyond your cultural walls / Thom Hopler. Published/Created: Downers Grove, Ill.: InterVarsity, c1981. Description: 223 p.: ill.; 21 cm. ISBN: 0877847479 : Notes: Bibliography: p. [221]-223. Subjects: Christianity and culture. Communication--Religious aspects--Christianity. Evangelistic work. LC Classification: BR115.C8 H66 1981 Dewey Class No.: 261 19

Hopler, Thom, 1936-1978. Reaching the world next door: how to spread the gospel in the midst of many cultures / Thom & Marcia Hopler; including a study guide for groups or individuals. Published/Created: Downers Grove, Ill.: InterVarsity Press, c1993. Related Authors: Hopler, Marcia, 1937- Hopler, Thom, 1936-1978. World of difference, following Christ beyond your cultural walls. Description: 245 p.; 21 cm. ISBN: 0830816615 (pbk.) Notes: Rev. ed. of: A world of difference, following Christ beyond your cultural walls. c1981. Includes bibliographical references (p. [237]-245). Subjects: Christianity and culture. Ethnicity--Religious aspects--Christianity. Reconciliation--Religious aspects--Christianity. Evangelistic work. LC Classification: BR115.C8 H66 1993

Hopper, Jeffery, 1930- Understanding modern theology / Jeffery Hopper. Published/Created: Philadelphia: Fortress Press, c1987- Description: v. <1: ill.; 23 cm. ISBN: 0800619293 (pbk.: v. 1) Notes: Includes bibliographies and indexes. Subjects: Theology, Doctrinal--History--Modern period, 1500- Christianity and culture--History. LC Classification: BT27 .H67 1987 Dewey Class No.: 230/.09/03 19

Horn, Thomas R. Spiritual warfare: the invisible invasion / by Thomas R. Horn. Published/Created: Lafayette, La.: Huntington House Publishers, c1998. Description: 207 p.; 22 cm. ISBN: 1563841290 Notes: Includes bibliographical references (p. 203-207). Subjects: Spiritual warfare. Christianity and culture--United States. LC Classification: BT975 .H67 1998 Dewey Class No.: 235/.4 21

Horton, Michael Scott. Beyond culture wars / Michael S. Horton. Published/Created: Chicago: Moody Press, c1994. Description: 288 p.; 24 cm. ISBN: 0802408931 Notes: Jacket sub-Is America a mission field or battlefield? Includes bibliographical references. Subjects: Christianity and culture. Christianity and politics. Evangelicalism. Fundamentalism. Mission of the church. LC Classification: BR115.C8 H67 1994

Horton, Michael Scott. Made in America: the shaping of modern American evangelicalism / Michael S. Horton. Published/Created: Grand Rapids, Mich.: Baker Book House, c1991. Description: 198 p.; 23 cm. ISBN: 0801043549 Notes: Includes bibliographical references (p. 189-198). Subjects: Evangelicalism--United States. Christianity and culture. LC Classification: BR1642.U5 H675 1991 Dewey Class No.: 270.8/29 20

Horton, Michael Scott. Where in the world is the church?: a Christian view of culture and your role in it / Michael S. Horton. Published/Created: Phillipsburg, NJ: P&R Pub., 2002. Description: p. cm. ISBN: 0875525652 (pbk.) Notes: Originally published: Chicago: Moody Press, c1995. With new index. Includes bibliographical references and index. Subjects: Christianity and culture. Church and the world. Christian life--Reformed authors. LC Classification: BR115.C8 H68 2002 Dewey Class No.: 261 21

Horton, Michael Scott. Where in the world is the church?: a Christian view of culture and your role in it / Michael S. Horton. Published/Created: Chicago [Ill.]: Moody Press, c1995. Description: 204 p.; 24 cm. ISBN: 0802492398 Notes: Includes bibliographical references. Subjects: Christianity and culture. Church and the world. LC Classification: BR115.C8 H68 1995 Dewey Class No.: 261 21

Hotchkiss, Valerie R., 1960- Clothes make the man: female cross dressing in medieval Europe / Valerie R. Hotchkiss. Published/Created: New York: Garland, 1996. Description: 201 p.; 23 cm. ISBN: 0815323697 (alk. paper) Notes: Includes bibliographical references (p. 177-192) and index. Subjects: Transvestism--Europe--History--Sources. Costume--History--Medieval, 500-1500. Women--Europe--History. Men's clothing--Europe--Psychological aspects. Costume--Europe--Religious aspects. Costume--Europe--Symbolic aspects. Christianity and culture--Europe--History--Middle Ages, 600-1500. Series: Garland reference library of the humanities; vol. 1991. Garland reference library of the humanities. New Middle Ages; vol. 1. LC Classification: HQ77 .H67 1996 Dewey Class No.: 305.3 20

How to run a Catholic foundation: increasing the impact of religious giving: proceedings of a symposium / sponsored by Foundations and Donors Interested in Catholic Activities, Inc. Published/Created: Washington, D.C. (1350 Connecticut Ave., N.W., Suite 303, Washington, 20036): FADICA, c1998. Related Authors: Foundations and Donors Interested in Catholic Activities, Inc. Description: 88 p.: ill.; 28 cm. Subjects: Catholic Church--United States--Charities--Congresses. Catholic Church--United States--Congresses. Christianity and culture--United States--Congresses. LC Classification: IN PROCESS

Huber, Carlo. Speaking of God / Carlo Huber. Published/Created: Washington, D.C.: Council for Research in Values and Philosophy, 2001. ISBN: 1565181697 Notes: Includes index. Subjects: God. Philosophical theology. Language and languages--Religious aspects--Christianity. Series: Cultural heritage and contemporary change. Series I, Culture and values; v. 24 Cultural heritage and contemporary change. Series IV, West Europe; v. 4 LC Classification: BT103 .H83 2001 Dewey Class No.: 231/.01/4 21

Huff, Peter A. Allen Tate and the Catholic revival: trace of the fugitive gods / Peter A. Huff. Published/Created: New York: Paulist Press, c1996. Description: xv, 159 p.; 23 cm. ISBN: 0809136619 (alk. paper) Notes: Includes bibliographical references and index. Subjects: Tate, Allen, 1899- --Knowledge--Literature. Tate, Allen, 1899- --Religion. American literature--20th century--History and criticism Theory, etc. Catholics--United States--Intellectual life--Christianity and literature--United States--Criticism--Southern States--History--20th century. Modernism (Literature)--Southern States. Man (Christian theology) in literature. Catholic converts--Southern States--Intellectual life--1865- Series: Isaac Hecker studies in religion and American culture LC Classification: PS3539.A74 Z68 1996 Dewey Class No.: 818/.5209 20

Huffstetter, Stephen, 1959- At this time [microform]: Lakota grieving, a pastoral response / Stephen Huffstetter. Published/Created: 1997. Description: ix, 181 leaves: ill.; 28 cm. Notes: Thesis (D. Min.)--Catholic Theological Union at Chicago, 1997. Includes bibliographical references (leaves 173-180). Microfiche. Portland, Or.: Theological Research Exchange Network, 1997. 1 microfiche: negative. Subjects: Teton Indians--South Dakota--Cheyenne River Indian Reservation--Funeral rites and practices. Grief--South Dakota--Cheyenne River Indian Reservation. Christianity and culture--South Dakota--Cheyenne River Indian Reservation. Pastoral counseling--South Dakota--Cheyenne River Indian Reservation. LC Classification: Microfiche 98/217 (B)

Hughson, D. Thomas. The believer as citizen: John Courtney Murray in a new context / Thomas Hughson. Published/Created: New York: Paulist Press, c1993. Description: vi, 185 p.; 23 cm. ISBN: 0809134128 (pbk.) : Notes: Includes bibliographical references (p. 150-185). Subjects: Murray, John Courtney. Catholic Church. National Conference of Catholic Bishops. Economic justice for all. Christianity and politics--Catholic Church--History--20th century.

Sociology, Christian (Catholic) United States--Religion--1960- Series: Isaac Hecker studies in religion and American culture LC Classification: BR516 .H775 1993 Dewey Class No.: 261.8/0973 20

Humanities. Published/Created: Mitaka, Japan: Institute for the Study of Christianity and Culture, International Christian University, 1975. Related Authors: Kokusai Kirisutokyō Daigaku. Kirisutokyō to Bunka Kenkyūjo. Description: 1 v.; 21 cm. 10. Continues: Jinbun kagaku kenkyū; Kirisutokyō to bunka (1968) (OCoLC)5931375 (DLC) 79648579 Continued by: Jinbun kagaku kenkyū: Kirisutokyō to bunka (1976) w (OCoLC)6080869 (DLC) 79648578 Notes: SERBIB/SERLOC merged record Subjects: Christianity and culture--Theology--Periodicals. Series: Kokusai Kirisutokyō Daigaku gakuhō; 4B LC Classification: BR9.J3 K57 Dewey Class No.: 261.5/05 19

Hunsberger, George R. Bearing the witness of the spirit: Lesslie Newbigin's theology of cultural plurality / George R. Hunsberger. Published/Created: Grand Rapids, Mich.: W.B. Eerdmans, c1998. Description: xii, 341 p.; 23 cm. ISBN: 0802843697 (pbk.: alk. paper) Notes: Includes bibliographical references (p. 283-332) and indexes. Subjects: Newbigin, Lesslie--Contributions in theology of multiculturalism. Multiculturalism--Religious aspects--Christianity. Series: The Gospel and our culture series LC Classification: BX7066.5.Z8 N494 1998 Dewey Class No.: 261/.092 21

Huxley, Thomas Henry, 1825-1895. Selections from the essays of Thomas Henry Huxley. Ed. by Alburey Castell. Published/Created: New York, F. S. Crofts, 1948. Related Authors: Castell, Alburey, 1904- ed. Description: vi, 119 p. 18 cm. Contents: On the advisableness of improving natural knowledge (1866)--A liberal education (1868)--On the physical basis of life (1868)--Administrative nihilism (1871)--Science and culture (1880)--The progress of science (1887)--The struggle for

existence in human society (1888)--
Agnosticism (1889)--Agnosticism and
Christianity (1889)--Prologue to
"controverted questions" (1892)--Evolution
and ethics (1893)--Prolegomena to
"Evolution and ethics" (1894) Notes:
Bibliography: p. 119 Subjects: Science. LC
Classification: Q171 .H973 Dewey Class
No.: 504

Identity and change: Nigerian philosophical
studies, I / edited by Theophilus Okere.
Published/Created: Washington, D.C.:
Council for Research in Values and
Philosophy, c1996. Related Authors:
Okere, Theophilus. Description: x, 221 p.;
23 cm. ISBN: 1565180712 (hard)
1565180720 (pbk.) Notes: "Published with
the support of CIPSH/UNESCO by Paideia
Publishers." Includes bibliographical
references and index. Subjects: Philosophy,
Nigerian. Identity (Psychology)--Nigeria.
National characteristics, Nigerian.
Urbanization--Moral education--Christian
ethics-- Social conditions--Nigeria.
Christianity and culture. Philosophical
anthropology. Series: Cultural heritage and
contemporary change. Series II, Africa;
vol. 3. LC Classification: B5619.N63 I34
1996 Dewey Class No.: 199/.669 20

Ilogu, Edmund. Christian ethics in an African
background: a study of the interaction of
Christianity and Ibo culture / door Edmund
Christopher Onyedum Ilogu.
Published/Created: Leiden: Brill, 1974.
Description: xi, 269 p.; 24 cm. Notes:
"Propositions": [3] p. inserted. Includes
index. Summary in Dutch. Thesis--Leiden.
Bibliography: p. [245]-255. Subjects: Igbo
(African people)--Religion. Igbo (African
people) Christian ethics--Nigeria.
Christianity--Nigeria. LC Classification:
BL2480.I2 I42 Dewey Class No.:
301.5/8/09669

Ilogu, Edmund. Christianity and Ibo culture /
by Edmund Ilogu. Published/Created:
Leiden: Brill, 1974. Description: xvi, 262
p.; 25 cm. ISBN: 9004040218 : Notes:
Originally presented as author's thesis,
Leiden, under the Christian ethics in an
African background. Includes index.

Bibliography: p. [245]-255. Subjects: Igbo
(African people)--Religion. Christianity--
Nigeria. LC Classification: BL2480.I2 I42
1974b Dewey Class No.: 301.5/8/09669

Ilogu, Edmund. Christianity and Igbo culture: a
study of the interaction of Christianity and
Igbo culture / by Edmund Ilogu; with a
foreword by M. A. C. Warren.
Published/Created: New York: NOK
Publishers, 1974. Description: xvi, 262 p.,
[2] leaves of plates: ill.; 25 cm. ISBN:
0883570300. 0883570319 Notes:
Originally presented as the author's thesis,
Leiden University, 1974, under Christian
ethics in an African background. Published
in 1974 by Brill, Leiden, under Christianity
and Ibo culture. Includes index.
Bibliography: p. [245]-255. Subjects: Igbo
(African people)--Religion. LC
Classification: BL2480.I2 I42 1974c
Dewey Class No.: 301.5/8

In all things: religious faith and American
culture: papers of the inaugural conference
of the Jesuit Institute at Boston College /
edited by Robert J. Daly.
Published/Created: Kansas City, MO:
Sheed & Ward, c1990. Related Authors:
Daly, Robert J., 1933- Boston College.
Jesuit Institute. Description: ix, 221 p.; 23
cm. ISBN: 1556123159 : Notes: Held
April 21-22, 1989 at Boston College.
Includes bibliographical references.
Subjects: Christianity and culture--
Congresses. United States--Civilization--
Congresses. LC Classification: BR115.C8
I45 1990 Dewey Class No.: 261/.0973 20

In old New Orleans / W. Kenneth Holditch,
editor. Published/Created: Jackson:
University Press of Mississippi, c1983.
Related Authors: Holditch, W. Kenneth.
Description: 188 p.: ill.; 23 cm. ISBN:
0878051864 (pbk.) : Contents: New
Orleans cemeteries / Peggy McDowell --
Minstrel dancing in New Orleans'
nineteenth century theaters / Kaye DeMetz
-- George David Coulon / Judith Hopkins
Bonner -- The Creole architecture of
nineteenth century New Orleans / Eugene
D. Cizek -- The singing heart / W. Kenneth
Holditch -- Christianity and Catholicism in

the fiction of Kate Chopin / Thomas Bonner, Jr. -- Love, death, and faith in the New Orleans poets of color / Alfred J. Guillaume, Jr. -- Alfred Mercier, French novelist of New Orleans / George Reinecke -- Nineteenth century New Orleans in books / Coleen Cole Salley. Notes: Includes bibliographies. Subjects: Arts, American--Louisiana--New Orleans--19th century. Popular culture--Louisiana--New Orleans. LC Classification: NX511.N39 I5 1983 Dewey Class No.: 700/.9763/35 19

Inch, Morris A., 1925- Doing theology across cultures / Morris A. Inch. Published/Created: Grand Rapids, Mich.: Baker Book House, c1982. Description: 110 p.: ill.; 22 cm. ISBN: 0801050324 (pbk.): 0801050359 (pbk.: cover) Notes: Includes indexes. Bibliography: p. 101-103. Subjects: Christianity and culture. Christianity and other religions. Missions--Theory. LC Classification: BR115.C8 I47 1982 Dewey Class No.: 261.2 19

Inch, Morris A., 1925- Making the good news relevant: keeping the Gospel distinctive in any culture / Morris A. Inch. Published/Created: Nashville: T. Nelson, c1986. Description: 111 p.; 21 cm. ISBN: 0840775407 (pbk.) : Notes: Bibliography: p. 109-111. Subjects: Christianity and culture. LC Classification: BR115.C8 I474 1986 Dewey Class No.: 266 19

Inculturation and liturgy: papers presented at Cardinal Parecatil memorial symposium / edited by Antony Nariculam. Published/Created: Alwaye: STAR Publications, 1992. Related Authors: Nariculam, Antony. Description: iv, 115 p.; 22 cm. Notes: Includes bibliographical references. Subjects: Catholic Church--India--Liturgy. Christianity and culture. LC Classification: BX1977.I4 I53 1992 Dewey Class No.: 264/.02/00954 20

Inculturation in seminary formation / edited by Peter Fernando. Published/Created: Pune: Ishvani Kendra; Indore: Satprakashan Sanchar Kendra, 1980. Related Authors: Fernando, Peter, 1939- Description: 149 p.; 23 cm. Notes: Includes bibliographical

references. Subjects: Theology--Study and teaching--India--Congresses. Theology--Study and teaching--Catholic Church--Congresses. Christianity and culture--Congresses. LC Classification: BX910.I4 I52 Dewey Class No.: 207/.54 19

Inculturation: abide by the otherness of Africa and the Africans: papers from a congress (October 21-22, 1993, Heerlen, the Netherlands) at the occasion of 100 years SMA-presence in the Netherlands / Peter Turkson, Frans Wijsen (eds.). Published/Created: Kampden, the Netherlands: J.H. Kok, 1994. Related Authors: Turkson, Peter, 1948- Wijsen, Frans Jozef Servaas, 1956- Society of African Missions. Description: x, 98 p.; 24 cm. ISBN: 9039005060 Notes: Includes bibliographical references. Subjects: Christianity and culture--Africa--Congresses. Africa--Church history--Congresses. Series: Kerk en theologie in context; nr. 26. LC Classification: BR115.C8 I476 1994 Dewey Class No.: 261/.096 21

Inculturation: its meaning and urgency / by J.M. Waliggo ... [et al.]. Published/Created: Kampala, Uganda: St. Paul Publications, 1986. Related Authors: Waliggo, John Mary, 1942- Description: 83 p.; 22 cm. Notes: Includes bibliographical references. Subjects: Christianity and culture. Christianity--Africa. Series: Christian leadership in Africa; ser. n. 1 LC Classification: BR115.C8 I48 1986 Dewey Class No.: 261 20

Inculturation: the faith that takes root in African cultures. Published/Created: Gweru, Zimbabwe: Mambo Press; Harare, Zimbabwe: IMBISA Secretariat, 1993. Related Authors: IMBISA Secretariat. Description: 67 p.: ill.; 24 cm. ISBN: 0869225669 Notes: "January 1993." Includes bibliographical references (p. 65-66). Subjects: Christianity and culture--Africa, Sub-Saharan. Series: IMBISA study document Mambo occasional papers. Missio-pastoral series; no. 24. LC Classification: BR115.C8 I483 1993

Inculturation: where do we stand? / edited by
Ugonna Igboaja & Obiora Ike.
Published/Created: Enugu: Lay Apostolate
Publishers, 1990. Related Authors:
Igboaja, Eugene Ugonna, 1944- Ike,
Obiora F., 1956- Description: 62 p.; 21 cm.
Notes: "Proceedings, lectures, discussion
and communique of a three-day seminar
organised at the Pastoral Centre. Ugwu-di-
Nso Eke, for Priests in the Catholic
Diocese of Enugu-March 13-15, 1989."
Subjects: Christianity and culture.
Christianity--Africa. LC Classification:
BR115.C8 I484 1990

Indigenous responses to western Christianity /
edited by Steven Kaplan.
Published/Created: New York: New York
University Press, c1995. Related Authors:
Kaplan, Steven. Description: x, 183 p.: ill.;
24 cm. ISBN: 0814746497 (hard: alk.
paper) Notes: Includes bibliographical
references and index. Subjects: Missions--
History. Christianity and culture. Asia--
Church history. LC Classification: BV2100
.I53 1995 Dewey Class No.: 270.8 20

Irarrázaval, Diego. Inculturation: new dawn of
the church in Latin America / Diego
Irarrázaval; translated by Phillip Berryman.
Published/Created: Maryknoll, N.Y.: Orbis
Books, c2000. Description: xi, 134 p.; 24
cm. ISBN: 1570752990 Notes: Includes
bibliographical references (p. 119-130) and
index. Subjects: Catholic Church--Latin
America. Christianity and culture--Latin
America. Evangelistic work--Latin
America. Series: Faith and cultures series
LC Classification: BX1426.2 .I7513 2000
Dewey Class No.: 282/.8/09051 21
282/.8/09051 21

Iroegbu, Pantaleon. Appropriate ecclesiology:
through narrative theology to an African
church / Pantaleon Osondu Iroegbu.
Published/Created: Owerri, Nigeria:
International Universities Press:
Obtainable at Seat of Wisdom [Seminary],
1996. Description: 268 p.: ill.; 21 cm.
ISBN: 9782047155 Notes: Includes
bibliographical references and index.
Subjects: Church. Christianity--Africa.
Theology, Doctrinal--Africa. Christianity

and culture--Africa. LC Classification:
BV600.2 .I76 1996

Is a culture of life still possible in the United
States?: proceedings from the twentieth
convention of the Fellowship of Catholic
Scholars, Washington, D.C., 1997 /
Anthony J. Mastroeni, editor.
Published/Created: South Bend, Ind.: St.
Augustine's Press, 1999. Related Authors:
Mastroeni, Anthony J. Description: vii, 177
p.; 22 cm. ISBN: 1890318272 Notes: Title
on spine: 1997 Fellowship of Catholic
Scholars. Includes bibliographical
references and index. Subjects: Abortion--
Religious aspects--Catholic Church--
Congresses. Pro-life movement--United
States--Congresses. Life--Religious
aspects--Christianity--Congresses. LC
Classification: HQ767.3 .F45 1997

Is a culture of life still possible in the United
States?: proceedings from the twentieth
convention of the Fellowship of Catholic
Scholars, Washington, D.C., 1997 /
Anthony J. Mastroeni, editor.
Published/Created: South Bend, Ind.: St.
Augustine's Press, 1999. Related Authors:
Mastroeni, Anthony J. Description: vii, 177
p.; 22 cm. ISBN: 1890318272 Partial
Partial Contents: Part I. Public philosophy
in the recent Catholic experi[e]nce / Dean
Hudson -- Response / Patrick Lee -- Part II.
Moral pluralism, public reason, and natural
law / Robert P. George -- Response:
Rawls, liberalism and the unity of reason /
David M. Gallagher -- Part III. Building
the culture of life in the city --
Introduction: The gospel of life in the city /
Stephen F. Brett -- Subjects: Life--
Religious aspects--Christianity.

Isasi-Díaz, Ada María. En la lucha = In the
struggle: a Hispanic women's liberation
theology / Ada María Isasi-Díaz.
Published/Created: Minneapolis: Fortress
Press, c1993. Description: xxi, 226 p.; 22
cm. ISBN: 0800626109 (pbk.: alk. paper) :
Notes: "Elaborating a mujerista theology."
English text with chapter summaries in
Spanish. Includes bibliographical
references (p. 205-222) and index.
Subjects: Hispanic American women--

Religious life. Mujerista theology. Christianity and culture. LC Classification: BR563.H57 I82 1993 Dewey Class No.: 230/.082 20

Isasi-Díaz, Ada María. Mujerista theology: a theology for the twenty-first century / Ada María Isasi-Díaz. Published/Created: Maryknoll, N.Y.: Orbis Books, 1996. Description: xi, 210 p.; 21 cm. ISBN: 1570750815 (alk. paper) Notes: Includes bibliographical references and index. Subjects: Feminist theology. Mujerista theology. Hispanic American women--Religious life. Christianity and culture. LC Classification: BT83.55 .I82 1996 Dewey Class No.: 230/.082 20

Iwe, Nwachukwuike S. S. (Nwachukwuike Sonde Sylvanus) Christianity and culture in Africa: organised religion and factors in a developing culture: a historical and cultural analysis / by Nwachukwuike S.S. Iwe. Published/Created: Onitsha [Nigeria]: University Publishing Co., [197-?] Description: viii, 100 p.: port.; 25 cm. Notes: Includes index. Bibliography: p. 90-96. Subjects: Christianity--Africa. Christianity and culture. LC Classification: BR1360 .I92 1970z Dewey Class No.: 276 19

Iwe, Nwachukwuike S. S. (Nwachukwuike Sonde Sylvanus) Christianity, culture, and colonialism in Africa: organised religion and factors in developing culture--an analysis / by Nwachukwuike S.S. Iwe. Published/Created: [S.l.: s.n., 1976?] (Port Harcourt: R.S.N.C.) Description: viii, 293 p.; 22 cm. Notes: Includes index. Bibliography: p. 278-286. Subjects: Christianity--Africa. Christianity and culture. Africa--Colonization. LC Classification: BR1360 .I93 1976 Dewey Class No.: 276 19

Jacobs, Alan, 1958- A visit to Vanity fair: moral essays on the present age / Alan Jacobs. Published/Created: Grand Rapids, Mich.: Brazos Press, c2001. Description: 173 p.; 24 cm. ISBN: 1587430142 (cloth) Notes: Includes bibliographical references. Subjects: Christianity and culture. LC

Classification: BR115.C8 J33 2001 Dewey Class No.: 261 21

Jahrbuch für kontextuelle Theologien = Yearbook of contextual theologies / Missionswissenschaftliches Institut Missio e.V. Published/Created: Frankfurt: IKO-Verlag für Interkulturelle Kommunikation, 1993- Description: v.; 21 cm. 93- Current Frequency: Annual Notes: In English, French, German, and Spanish. SERBIB/SERLOC merged record Subjects: Catholic Church--Doctrines x eriodicals Christianity and culture. LC Classification: BR115.C8 J34 Dewey Class No.: 230/.05 21

Janssen, Gretchen. Women on the move: a Christian perspective on cross-cultural adaptation / Gretchen Janssen. Yarmouth, ME: Intercultural Press, [1992], c1989. Description: xiii, 144 p.; 22 cm. ISBN: 1877864099 : Notes: Previously published as: Women overseas. c1989. Includes bibliographical references (p. 141-144). Subjects: Wives--Religious life. Cross-cultural orientation. Culture shock. Christianity and culture. LC Classification: BV4527 .J38 1992 Dewey Class No.: 248.8/435 20

Janssen, Gretchen. Women overseas: a Christian perspective on cross-cultural adaptation / Gretchen Janssen. Published/Created: [Yarmouth, Me.]: Intercultural Press, c1989. Description: xiii, 144 p.: ill.; 22 cm. ISBN: 0933662815 (pbk.) Notes: Includes bibliographical references (p. 135-144). Subjects: Janssen, Gretchen. Wives--Religious life. Cross-cultural orientation. Culture shock. Christianity and culture. LC Classification: BV4527 .J38 1989 Dewey Class No.: 248.8/435 20

Jeffrey, David L., 1941- People of the Book: Christian identity and literary culture / David Lyle Jeffrey. Published/Created: Grand Rapids, Mich.: Eerdmans; Cambridge, U.K.: Institute for Advanced Christian Studies, c1996. Description: xx, 396 p.: ill.; 23 cm. ISBN: 0802838170 (cloth: alk. paper) 0802841775 (pbk.: alk.

paper) Notes: Includes bibliographical references and indexes. Subjects: Bible--Criticism, interpretation, etc.--Influence--Western civilization. Bible as literature. Christianity and literature. Identification (Religion) LC Classification: BS511.2 .J44 1996 Dewey Class No.: 220/.09 20

Jelsma, Auke, 1933- Frontiers of the Reformation: dissidence and orthodoxy in sixteenth-century Europe / Auke Jelsma. Aldershot, Hants, England; Brookfield, Vt.: Ashgate, c1998. Description: xii, 192 p.; 25 cm. ISBN: 1840142804 (hb: alk. paper) Notes: Includes bibliographical references and index. Subjects: Reformation. Christianity and culture--Europe--History--16th century. Series: St. Andrews studies in Reformation history LC Classification: BR309 .J44 1998 Dewey Class No.: 274/.06 21

Jenson, Robert W. Essays in theology of culture / Robert W. Jenson. Published/Created: Grand Rapids, Mich.: Wm. B. Eerdmans Pub. Co., c1995. Description: xi, 224 p.; 23 cm. ISBN: 0802808883 (pbk.) Notes: Includes bibliographical references. Subjects: Christianity and culture. LC Classification: BR115.C8 J46 1995 Dewey Class No.: 261 20

Jerusalem in Russian culture / edited by Andrei Batalov and Aleksei Lidov Published/Created: New Rochelle, N.Y.: A.D. Caratzas, 1994. Related Authors: Batalov, A. L. (Andrei Leonidovich) Lidov, Aleksei. Description: p. cm. ISBN: 089241524X Subjects: Russkaia pravoslavnaia tserkov´. Orthodox Eastern Church. Jerusalem in Christianity. Christianity and culture. Arts, Russian--History. Russia (Federation)--Church history. LC Classification: BT93.5 .I4713 1994 Dewey Class No.: 263/.0425694/0947 20

Jewett, Robert. Paul the Apostle to America: cultural trends and Pauline scholarship / Robert Jewett. Edition Information: 1st ed. Published/Created: Louisville, KY: Westminster/John Knox Press, c1994. Description: xi, 178 p.; 23 cm. ISBN:

0664254837 (pbk.: alk. paper) Notes: Includes bibliographical references (p. 129-159) and indexes. Subjects: Bible. N.T. Epistles of Paul--Criticism, interpretation, etc.--United States. Christianity and culture. LC Classification: BS2652 .J477 1994 Dewey Class No.: 227/.06/0973 20

Jewett, Robert. Saint Paul at the movies: the apostle's dialogue with American culture / Robert Jewett. Edition Information: 1st ed. Published/Created: Louisville, Ky.: Westminster/John Knox Press, c1993. Description: 186 p.; 20 cm. ISBN: 0664254829 (pbk.: alk. paper) Notes: Includes bibliographical references (p. 162-180) and indexes. Subjects: Bible. N.T. Epistles of Paul--Theology. Motion pictures--Religious aspects--Christianity. LC Classification: BS2652 .J48 1993 Dewey Class No.: 225.9/2 20

Jing feng. Edition Information: [English ed.] Published/Created: Hong Kong: Christian Study Centre on Chinese Religion and Culture Description: v.; 22 cm. Began with vol. 8, winter 1964. Current Frequency: Quarterly Continues: Quarterly notes on Christianity and Chinese religion (DLC)sn 89028750 (OCoLC)3021413 ISSN: 0009-4668 Notes: "Quarterly notes on Christianity and Chinese religion and culture." Description based on: Vol. 21, no. 1. SERBIB/SERLOC merged record Chinese edition also exists. Cf. v. 8, no. 1. Indx'd selectively by: Religion index one. Periodicals 0149-8428 1978- Subjects: Christianity and other religions--Periodicals. Church and social problems--China--Periodicals. LC Classification: WMLC L 83/3796 Dewey Class No.: 291

Jo, Yung-hwan, 1932- comp. Korea's response to the West. Published/Created: Kalamazoo, Mich., Korea Research and Publications; [distributed by Cellar Book Shop, Detroit, 1971] Description: xi, 254 p. 28 cm. Partial Contents: The weight of tradition: preliminary observations on Korea's intellectual response, by H. D. Walker.--The acceptance of Western technology in early modern Korea, by

Young-ho Kim.--The acceptance of Western culture in Korea, by Hong-ryol Ryu. Notes: Includes bibliographical references. Subjects: Korea--Civilization--Western influences--Relations--Foreign countries. Series: Series on contemporary Korean problems, 6 LC Classification: DS904 .J57 Dewey Class No.: 327.519/018/21

Johnson, Eric, 1950- Say you want a revolution: we now find ourselves transported into a deceptive and deadly 90's culture / Eric Johnson. Published/Created: DeBary, FL.: Longwood Communications, c1994. Description: 372 p.; 23 cm. ISBN: 1883928036 Notes: Includes bibliographical references (p. 347-367). Subjects: Christianity--United States--20th century. Youth--Conduct of life. Popular culture--Religious aspects. Popular culture--United States--Moral conditions--Religion--1960- --Social conditions--1960-1980. LC Classification: BR481 .J58 1994 Dewey Class No.: 277.3/0829 20

Johnson, Robert Leon, 1930- Counter culture and the vision of God [by] Robert L. Johnson. Foreword by Tom Driver. Published/Created: Minneapolis, Augsburg Pub. House [1971] Description: 168 p. 21 cm. ISBN: 0806611251 Notes: Includes bibliographical references. Subjects: Christianity--20th century. Mysticism. Youth--Conduct of life. LC Classification: BR121.2 .J583 Dewey Class No.: 261.8/0973

Johnston, Jon. Will Evangelicalism survive its own popularity? / By Jon Johnston; [foreword by Ronald J. Sider; edited and designed by Mary J. Bombara. Published/Created: Grand Rapids, Mich.: Zondervan Pub. House, c1980. Description: 224 p.; 21 cm. ISBN: 0310425417 (pbk.) : Notes: Includes indexes. Bibliography: p. 223-224. Subjects: Evangelicalism--United States. Christianity and culture. LC Classification: BR1642.U5 J63 Dewey Class No.: 280/.4 19

Jorstad, Erling, 1930- Popular religion in America: the evangelical voice / Erling Jorstad. Published/Created: Westport, Conn.: Greenwood Press, 1993. Description: xiv, 217 p.; 24 cm. ISBN: 0313279691 (alk. paper) Notes: Includes bibliographical references (p. [205]-211) and index. Subjects: Evangelicalism--United States--History--20th century. Christianity and culture--History--20th century. United States--Religion--1960- United States--Religious life and customs. Series: Contributions to the study of religion, 0196-7053; no. 57 LC Classification: BR1642.U5 J684 1993 Dewey Class No.: 277.3/0825 20

Journal of inculturation theology. Published/Created: Port Harcourt, Nigeria: Faculty of Theology, Catholic Institute of West Africa, 1994- Related Authors: Catholic Institute of West Africa. Faculty of Theology. Description: v.; 22 cm. Vol. 1, no. 1 (Apr. 1994)- Current Frequency: Semiannual Notes: SERBIB/SERLOC merged record Subjects: Christianity and culture--Periodicals. Christianity--Africa--Periodicals. Theology, Doctrinal--Africa--Periodicals. Africa--Religion--Periodicals. LC Classification: BR115.C8 J65 Dewey Class No.: 230/.05 20

Judaeo-Christian intellectual culture in the seventeenth century: a celebration of the library of Narcissus Marsh (1638-1713) / edited by Allison P. Coudert ... [et al.]. Published/Created: Dordrecht; Boston: Kluwer Academic, 1999. Related Authors: Coudert, Allison, 1941- Description: xvii, 260 p.; 25 cm. ISBN: 0792357892 (hb: alk. paper) Notes: Includes index. Subjects: Bible--Criticism, interpretation, etc.--Congresses. Judaism--Relations--Christianity--Congresses. Christianity and other religions--Judaism--Congresses. Philosophy and religion--Congresses. Christians--Europe, Western--Intellectual life--17th century--Congresses. Series: Archives internationales d'histoire des idées; 163. LC Classification: BM535 .J75 1999 Dewey Class No.: 200 21

Jurjevich, Ratibor-Ray M., 1915- The contemporary faces of Satan / Ratibor-Ray M. Jurjevich. Published/Created: Denver, Colo.: Ichthys Books, 1985. Description: xxxix, 399 p.; 24 cm. Notes: Includes indexes. Bibliography: p. 379-388. Subjects: Devil. Civilization, Modern--20th century. Cults. Psychiatry and religion. Humanism. Secularism. Communism and Christianity. United States--Moral conditions. Series: Jurjevich, Ratibor-Ray M., 1915- Demonic maladies in the Western culture; v. 1. LC Classification: BT981 .J87 1985 Dewey Class No.: 235/.4 19

Kabasele Lumbala, François. Celebrating Jesus Christ in Africa: liturgy and inculturation / François Kabasele Lumbala. Published/Created: Maryknoll, N.Y.: Orbis Books, c1998. Description: xvi, 128 p.; 24 cm. ISBN: 0883449714 (pbk.) Notes: Includes bibliographical references (p. 124-128). Subjects: Catholic Church--Africa, Sub-Saharan--Liturgy--Texts History and criticism. Catholic Church--Liturgy, Experimental. Christianity and culture--Africa, Sub-Saharan. Liturgical adaptation. Series: Faith and cultures series LC Classification: BX1977.A357 K33 1998 Dewey Class No.: 264/.02/00967 21

Kallestad, Walther P., 1948- Entertainment evangelism: taking the church public / Walt Kallestad. Published/Created: Nashville: Abingdon Press, c1996. Description: 144 p.; 22 cm. ISBN: 0687054508 (hardcover: alk. paper) Notes: Includes bibliographical references (p. 141-144). Subjects: Evangelistic work--United States. Popular culture--United States. Popular culture--Religious aspects--Christianity. United States--Religion--1960- LC Classification: BV3773 .K35 1996 Dewey Class No.: 261.5 20

Kamensky, Jane. Governing the tongue: the politics of speech in early New England / Jane Kamensky. Published/Created: New York: Oxford University Press, 1997. Description: 291 p.: ill.; 24 cm. ISBN: 0195090802 (alk. paper) Notes: Includes bibliographical references (p. 203-280) and index. Subjects: English language--Political aspects--New England. English language--History. English language--Religious aspects--Christianity. English language--Spoken English--New England. Language and culture--New England--History. Oral communication--New England--History. English language--18th century--History. Americanisms--New England--History. Puritans--New England--Language. Women--New England--Language. Authorship--Sex differences. New England--History. LC Classification: PE2906 .K36 1997 Dewey Class No.: 420/.974 21

Kamu, Lalomilo, 1932- The Samoan culture and the Christian gospel / Lalomilo Kamu. Published/Created: Apia, Western Samoa: Donna Lou Kamu, [1996?] Description: vii, 196 p.; 22 cm. ISBN: 9823490015 Notes: Includes bibliographical references (p. 181-192). Subjects: Christianity and culture--Samoan Islands. Christianity--Samoan Islands. LC Classification: BR115.C8 K35 1996g

Kan, Sergei. Memory eternal: Tlingit culture and Russian Orthodox Christianity through two centuries / Sergei Kan. Published/Created: Seattle: University of Washington Press, c1999. Description: xxxi, 665 p.: ill., map; 24 cm. ISBN: 0295978066 (alk. paper) Notes: Includes bibliographical references and index. Subjects: Orthodox Eastern Church--Missions--Alaska--Sitka. Tlingit Indians--Missions--Alaska--Sitka. Tlingit Indians--Religion. Tlingit Indians--Rites and ceremonies. Sitka (Alaska)--Social life and customs. LC Classification: E99.T6 K339 1999 Dewey Class No.: 266/.19798 21

Kastfelt, Niels. Religion and politics in Nigeria: a study in Middle Belt Christianity / Niels Kastfelt. Published/Created: London; New York: British Academic Press, 1994. Description: xii, 204 p.; 23 cm. ISBN: 1850437882 Notes: Includes bibliographical references (p. [192]-200) and index. Subjects: Religion and politics--Nigeria--Middle Belt. Politics and culture--Nigeria--Middle Belt. Protestant churches--

Nigeria--Middle Belt--History. Nigeria--Politics and government--To 1960. Middle Belt (Nigeria)--Politics and government. Nigeria--History--1900-1960. Middle Belt (Nigeria)--Church history. LC Classification: DT515.75 .K37 1994 Dewey Class No.: 322/.1/0966988 20

Kaufman, Gordon D. God, mystery, diversity: Christian theology in a pluralistic world / Gordon D. Kaufman. Published/Created: Minneapolis, MN: Fortress Press, c1996. Description: xii, 233 p.; 23 cm. ISBN: 0800629590 (pbk.: alk. paper) Notes: Includes bibliographical references (p. 216-228) and indexes. Subjects: Theology, Doctrinal. Theology--Methodology. Christianity and culture. Christianity and other religions. Religious pluralism--Christianity. LC Classification: BT75.2 .K37 1996 Dewey Class No.: 230 20

Kay, William K., 1945- Drift from the Churches: attitude toward Christianity during childhood and adolescence / by William K. Kay and Leslie J. Francis. Published/Created: Cardiff: University of Wales Press, 1996. Related Authors: Francis, Leslie J. Description: 266 p.: ill.; 22 cm. ISBN: 0708313302 Notes: Includes bibliographical references (p. [250]-260) and index. Subjects: Youth--Religious life. Youth--Attitudes. Christianity. Religion Psychology Series: Religion, culture and society LC Classification: BV4531.2 .K39 1996 Dewey Class No.: 270.8/25/083 21

Keidel, Levi O. Conflict or connection: interpersonal relationships in cross-cultural settings / Levi Keidel. Published/Created: Wheaton, Ill.: Evangelical Missions Information Service, c1996. Description: 136, [5] p.; 22 cm. ISBN: 0961775122 (alk. paper) Notes: Includes bibliographical references (p. [137]-[138]) and index. Subjects: Intercultural communication--Religious aspects Christianity. Missions--Theory. Christianity and culture. Interpersonal relations and culture. LC Classification: BV2082.I57 K45 1996 Dewey Class No.: 266/.0023 20

Kelly, Joseph F. (Joseph Francis), 1945- The world of the early Christians / Joseph F. Kelly. Published/Created: Collegeville, Minn.: Liturgical Press, c1997. Description: xviii, 231 p.; 23 cm. ISBN: 0814653413 (case bound) 0814653138 (perfect bound) Notes: "A Michael Glazier book." Includes bibliographical references (p. 215-222) and index. Subjects: Church history--Primitive and early church, ca. 30-600. Sociology, Christian--History--Early church, ca. 30-600. Christianity and culture--History--Early church, ca. 30-600. Series: Message of the fathers of the church; v. 1 LC Classification: BR165 .K44 1997 Dewey Class No.: 270.1 21

Kenny, Mary, 1944- Why Christianity works / Mary Kenny. Published/Created: London: M. Joseph, c1981. Description: 220 p.; 23 cm. ISBN: 071811874X Notes: Includes index. Bibliography: p. [211]-216. Subjects: Christianity and culture. Civilization, Modern--1950- Christianity--20th century. LC Classification: BR115.C8 K46x 1981

Kessler, Aharon. Judaism as religion and culture / Aharon Kessler. Edition Information: 1st ed. New York: Vantage Press, c1997. Description: xxi, 936 p.; 24 cm. ISBN: 0533120802 Notes: Includes bibliographical references. Subjects: Bible. O.T. Psalms--Criticism, interpretation, etc. Judaism--Relations--Christianity. Christianity and other religions--Judaism. Christianity and antisemitism. Judaism--Liturgy--Study and teaching. LC Classification: BM45 .K47 1997 Dewey Class No.: 296 21

Kessler, Sanford, 1945- Tocqueville's civil religion: American Christianity and the prospects for freedom / Sanford Kessler. Albany: State University of New York Press, c1994. Description: xiv, 238 p.; 23 cm. ISBN: 0791419290 (CH: alk. paper) 0791419304 (PB: alk. paper) Notes: Includes bibliographical references (p. 209-222) and index. Subjects: Tocqueville, Alexis de, 1805-1859. De la démocratie en Amérique. Civil religion--United States--History--19th century. Christianity and

politics. Democracy--Religious aspects--
Christianity. United States--Church
history--19th century. Series: SUNY series
in religion, culture, and society LC
Classification: BR525 .K47 1994 Dewey
Class No.: 277.3/08/092 20

Khabela, M. Gideon The struggle of the Gods:
a study in Christianity and the African
culture / M. Gideon Khabela. ISBN:
0869861255

Kidwell, Clara Sue. A Native American
theology / Clara Sue Kidwell, Homer
Noley, George E. "Tink" Tinker.
Published/Created: Maryknoll, N.Y.: Orbis
Books c2001. Related Authors: Noley,
Homer, 1932- Tinker, George E.
Description: xii, 204 p.; 21 cm. ISBN:
157075361X (pbk.) Notes: Includes
bibliographical references (p. 181-196) and
index. Subjects: Indians of North America-
-Religion. Indian mythology--North
America. Christianity and culture--North
America. Christianity and other religions--
North America. LC Classification: E98.R3
K53 2001 Dewey Class No.: 230/.089/97
21

Kierkegaard, Søren, 1813-1855. The moment
and late writings / by Søren Kierkegaard;
edited and translated with introduction and
notes by Howard V. Hong and Edna H.
Hong. Published/Created: Princeton, N.J.:
Princeton University Press, 1998. Related
Authors: Hong, Howard Vincent, 1912-
Hong, Edna Hatlestad, 1913- Description:
xxxi, 678 p.; 22 cm. ISBN: 0691032262
(cloth: alk. paper) Notes: This book
comprises a series of articles (1854-1855)
from the newspaper, Fædrelandet;
followed by the pamphlet, The Moment
(all except no. 10) published during the last
ten months of Kierkegaarde's life; and a
number of separate division pieces.
Includes bibliographical references and
index. Subjects: Mynster, Jakob Peter,
1775-1854. Danske folkekirke--
Controversial literature. Christianity and
culture. Lutheran Church--Denmark--
Controversial literature. Christianity and
culture--Denmark--History--19th century.
Denmark--Church history--19th century.

Series: Kierkegaard, Søren, 1813-1855.
Works. English. 1978; 23. LC
Classification: BR115.C8 K544 1998
Dewey Class No.: 270.8/1 21

Killinger, John. Preaching to a church in crisis:
a homiletic for the last days of the mainline
church / John Killinger. Published/Created:
Lima, Ohio: CSS Pub., c1995. Description:
123 p.; 22 cm. ISBN: 0788003089 Notes:
Includes bibliographical references.
Subjects: Church renewal. Protestant
churches--United States--History--20th
century. Christianity and culture. United
States--Church history--20th century. LC
Classification: BV600.2 .K47 1995 Dewey
Class No.: 280/.4/097309049 20

Kim, Dong-Sun, 1956- The bread for today and
the bread for tomorrow: the ethical
significance of the Lord's Supper in the
Korean context / Dong-sun Kim.
Published/Created: New York: P. Lang,
c2001. Description: viii, 264 p.; 24 cm.
ISBN: 082045267X (alk. paper) Notes:
Includes bibliographical references (p.
[249]-264). Subjects: Lord's Supper--
Bread. Bread--Religious aspects--
Christianity. Food--Religious aspects.
Minjung theology. Theology, Doctrinal--
Korea (South)--20th century. Series: Asian
thought and culture; vol. 49 LC
Classification: BV825.52 .K56 2001
Dewey Class No.: 234/.163/09519 21

Kim, Heup Young, 1949- Wang Yang-ming
and Karl Barth: a Confucian-Christian
dialogue / Heup Young Kim.
Published/Created: Lanham, Md:
University Press of America, c1996.
Description: xii, 234 p.; 22 cm. ISBN:
0761802266 (cloth: alk. paper) Notes:
Includes bibliographical references (p.
[227]-234). Subjects: Wang, Yang-ming,
1472-1529. Barth, Karl, 1886-1968.
Confucianism--Relations--Christianity.
Christianity and other religions--
Confucianism. Neo-Confucianism.
Philosophy, Comparative. Christianity and
culture--Korea. LC Classification:
BR128.C43 K56 1996 Dewey Class No.:
299/.512/72 20

Kim, Jung Ha. Bridge-makers and cross-bearers: Korean-American women and the church / Jung Ha Kim. Published/Created: Atlanta, Ga.: Scholars Press, c1997. Description: viii, 168 p.: ill.; 23 cm. ISBN: 0788501658 (acid-free paper) 0788501666 (pbk.: acid-free paper) Notes: Includes bibliographical references (p. 145-168). Subjects: Korean American women--Religious life. Christianity and culture--United States. Religion and sociology--United States. Series: American Academy of Religion academy series; no. 92 LC Classification: BR563.K67 K52 1997 Dewey Class No.: 306.6/73 20

Kim, Kyong-jae. Christianity and the encounter of Asian religions: method of correlation, fusion of horizons, and paradigm shifts in the Korean grafting process / Kyoung Jae Kim. Published/Created: Zoetermeer: Uitgeverij Boekencentrum, c1994. Description: 215 p.; 24 cm. ISBN: 9023908317 Notes: Originally presented as author's thesis (doctoral)--Utrecht University, 1994. Abstract in Dutch and English. Includes bibliographical references (p. 189-197) and index. Subjects: Tillich, Paul, 1886-1965. Gadamer, Hans Georg, 1900- Kuhn, Thomas S. Missions--Theory. Christianity--Korea. Christianity and other religions--Asian. Christianity and culture-- Theology, Doctrinal--Korea. East Asia--Religion. Series: Serie MISSION; nr. 10 LC Classification: BV2063 .K56 1994 Dewey Class No.: 261.2/95 20

King, Arthur Henry. Arm the children: faith's response to a violent world / Arthur Henry King; with foreword by C. Terry Warner; edited by Daryl Hague. Published/Created: Provo, Utah: Brigham Young University, c1998. Related Authors: Hague, Daryl, 1963- King, Arthur Henry.Description: xxiii, 360 p.: port.; 23 cm. ISBN: 0842523588 Notes: Rev. ed. of: The abundance of the heart, c1986. Includes bibliographical references (p. 349-351) and index. Subjects: King, Arthur Henry. Church of Jesus Christ of Latter Day Saints--Doctrines. Spiritual warfare. Christianity and culture. Child rearing--Religious aspects--Mormon Church. Mormon Church--Doctrines. Series: BYU studies monographs LC Classification: BT975 .K55 1998 Dewey Class No.: 289.3/32 21

Kingdom, cross, and community: essays on Mennonite themes in honor of Guy F. Hershberger / edited by John Richard Burkholder and Calvin Redekop. Published/Created: Scottdale, Pa.: Herald Press, 1976. Related Authors: Hershberger, Guy F. (Guy Franklin), 1896- Burkholder, John Richard, 1928- Redekop, Calvin Wall, 1925- Description: 323 p.; 23 cm. ISBN: 0836111397 : Partial Contents: Schlabach, T. F. To focus a Mennonite vision.--Gross, L. History and community in the thought of Guy F. Hershberger.--Kreider, R. S. Discerning the times.--Lind, M. C. Reflections on Biblical hermeneutics.--Kraus, C. N. Toward a theology for the disciple community.--Bauman, H. E. Forms of covenant community.--Burkholder, J. L. Nonresistance, nonviolent resistance, and power.--Burkholder, L. J. Notes: Includes indexes. "A bibliography of the writings of Guy F. Hershberger, 1922-1976, Elizabeth H. Bauman": p. [286]-300. Bibliography: p. [307]-314. Subjects: Hershberger, Guy F. (Guy Franklin), 1896- Mennonites--Doctrines. Christianity and culture. LC Classification: BX8109 .K56 Dewey Class No.: 289.7

Kirby, John P., 1945- African parables: thoughts for Sunday readings (cycle B) / John P. Kirby. Published/Created: Tamale, Ghana: Tamale Institute of Cross Cultural Studies, 1988. Related Authors: Tamale Institute of Cross Cultural Studies. Description: iii, 73 p.; 22 cm. Notes: Cover title. Subjects: Parables. Homiletical illustrations. Preaching-- Storytelling--Africa. Storytelling--Religious aspects--Christianity. Series: Culture and ministry series; no. 2. Occasional paper (Tamale Institute of Cross Cultural Studies) LC Classification: ACQUISITION IN PROCESS (COPIED)

Knight, Frances. The nineteenth-century church and English society / Frances Knight. Published/Created: Cambridge [England]; New York: Cambridge University Press, 1995. Description: xiii, 230 p.: ill.; 24 cm. ISBN: 0521453356 (hbk.) Notes: Includes bibliographical references (p. 212-221) and index. Subjects: Church of England--History--19th century. Anglican Communion--England--History--19th century. England--Church history--19th century. Church and state--England--History--19th century. Christianity and culture--History--19th century. LC Classification: BX5055.2 .K55 1995 Dewey Class No.: 283/.42/09034 20

Kniss, Fred Lamar, 1956- Disquiet in the land: cultural conflict in American Mennonite communities / Fred Kniss. Published/Created: New Brunswick, N.J.: Rutgers University Press, c1997. Description: xiii, 257 p.: ill.; 24 cm. ISBN: 0813524229 (cloth: alk. paper) 0813524237 (pbk.: alk. paper) Notes: Originally presented as the author's thesis (doctoral)--University of Chicago. Includes bibliographical references (p. 243-250) and index. Subjects: Mennonites--United States--History. Mennonites--Parties and movements--United States. Social conflict--Religious aspects--Mennonites. Christianity and culture--United States. United States--Church history. LC Classification: BX8116 .K55 1997 Dewey Class No.: 289.7/73 21

Knox, John, 1900- ed. Religion and the present crisis, edited by John Knox. Published/Created: Chicago, Ill., The University of Chicago press [1942] Description: xi, 165 p. 21 cm. Partial Contents: Colwell, E. C. Christianity refinding itself.--Aubrey, E. E. Building a better democracy.--Knox, J. Re-examining pacifism.--Holman, C. T. Maintaining fellowship across lines of conflict.--Wieman, H. N. Notes: Bibliographical references included in preface. Subjects: Civilization, Christian. United States--Church history. LC Classification: BR516 .K63 Dewey Class No.: 261

Koester, Helmut, 1926- Introduction to the New Testament / Helmut Koester. Edition Information: 2nd ed. Published/Created: New York: Walter de Gruyter, c1995-c2000. Description: 2 v.: ill., maps; 24 cm. ISBN: 3110146932 (v. 1: alk. paper) 3110146924 (v. 1: pbk.: alk. paper) 3110149710 (v. 2) Contents: v. 1. History, culture, and religion of the Hellenistic age --v. 2. History and literature of early Christianity. Notes: Includes bibliographical references and indexes. Subjects: Bible. N.T.--History of contemporary events. Bible. N.T.--Introductions. LC Classification: BS2410 .K613 1995 Dewey Class No.: 225.9/5 20

Koester, Helmut, 1926- Introduction to the New Testament / Helmut Koester. Published/Created: Philadelphia: Fortress Press; Berlin [Germany]; New York: De Gruyter, c1982. Description: 2 v.: ill.; 25 cm. ISBN: 080062100X (v. 1) 0800621018 (v. 2) Contents: v. 1. History, culture, and religion of the Hellenistic Age -- v. 2. History and literature of early Christianity. Notes: Translation of: Einführung in das Neue Testament. Includes bibliographies and indexes. Subjects: Bible. N.T.--History of contemporary events. Series: Hermeneia--foundations and facets LC Classification: BS2410 .K613 1982 Dewey Class No.: 225.9/5

Korea and Christianity / edited by Chai-Shin Yu. Published/Created: Seoul; Berkeley: Korean Scholar Press, 1996. Related Authors: Yu, Chai-Shin, 1932- Description: 190, xiv p.; 23 cm. Notes: "A collection of relevant articles previously published in Korean ... "--Pref. Includes bibliographic references and index. Subjects: Korea--Church history. Series: Studies in Korean religions and culture; v. 8 LC Classification: BR1325 .K67 1996

Korea struggles for Christ; memorial symposium for the eightieth anniversary of Protestantism in Korea. Edited by Harold S. Hong, Won Yong Ji, and Chung Choon Kim. Published/Created: Seoul, Christian Literature Society of Korea [c1966] Related Authors: Hong, Harold S., 1911-

ed. Ji, Won Yong, 1924- ed. Kim, Chung Choon, 1914- ed. Description: 254 p. 22 cm. Partial Contents: Foreword by Won Yong Ji.--Introduction by H. S. Hong.--Past, present, and future of the Korean church: General picture of the Korean church; yesterday and today, by H. S. Hong. The present situation and future prospect of the Korean church, by Chai Choon Kim. Eighty year history of Korean christian social ethics, by Ha Eun Chung. The ecumenical movement and youth work, by Sang Jung Park. Development of christian education in Korea, by Tuk Yul Kim.--Studies on the Korean churches and their problems: The church and the problem of indigenization, by Chung Choon Kim. Notes: Bibliography: p. [252]-254. Subjects: Christianity--Korea. LC Classification: BR1320 .K67

Kraft, Charles H. Anthropology for Christian witness / Charles H. Kraft. Published/Created: Maryknoll, N.Y.: Orbis Books, c1996. Description: xvi, 493 p.; 26 cm. ISBN: 1570750858 (alk. paper) Notes: Includes bibliographical references (p. 475-483) and indexes. Subjects: Missions--Theory. Ethnology--Religious aspects--Christianity. Christianity and culture. Evangelistic work--Philosophy. LC Classification: BV2063 .K756 1996 Dewey Class No.: 266/.001 20

Kraft, Charles H. Christianity in culture: a study in dynamic Biblical theologizing in cross-cultural perspective / Charles H. Kraft. Published/Created: Maryknoll, N.Y.: Orbis Books, c1979. Description: xviii, 445 p.: ill.; 24 cm. ISBN: 088344075X (pbk.) Notes: Includes indexes. Bibliography: p. 405-426. Subjects: Christianity and culture. LC Classification: BR115.C8 K64 Dewey Class No.: 261

Kraft, Charles H. Culture, communication, and Christianity / Charles H. Kraft. Published/Created: Pasadena, Calif.: William Carey Library, 2001. Description: p. cm. ISBN: 0878087842 (alk. paper) Notes: Includes bibliographical references. Subjects: Missions--Theory. Christianity and culture. Intercultural communication--

Religious aspects Christianity. LC Classification: BV2063 .K7562 2001 Dewey Class No.: 261 21

Kraus, C. Norman (Clyde Norman), 1924- An intrusive Gospel?: Christian mission in the postmodern world / C. Norman Kraus. Published/Created: Downers Grove, Ill.: InterVarsity Press, c1998. Description: 141 p.: ill.; 21 cm. ISBN: 0830815465 (alk. paper) Notes: Includes bibliographical references (p. [139]-141). Subjects: Missions--Theory. Christianity and culture. Missions--History--20th century. LC Classification: BV2063 .K77 1998 Dewey Class No.: 266/.001 21

Krawchuk, Andrii. A finding aid for holdings in history at the Special and Rare Books Collection of the Ukrainian Catholic Seminary Library in Ottawa / Andrii Krawchuk. Published/Created: Ottawa: UCS Press, 1988. Description: 41 p.; 28 cm. Notes: On cover: Prepared on the occasion of the Symposium "Christianity in Ukrainian history and culture", University of Ottawa, October 7, 1988. Subjects: Ukrainian Catholic Seminary (Ottawa, Ont.). Library. Special and Rare Books Collection--Ukraine--Church history--Ukraine--History--Bibliography--Catalogs. LC Classification: Z7755 .K73 1988 BR937.U38

Kreeft, Peter. How to win the culture war: a Christian battle plan for a society in crisis / Peter Kreeft. Published/Created: Downers Grove, Ill.: InterVarsity Press, 2002. Description: p. cm. ISBN: 0830823166 (pbk.: alk. paper) Subjects: Christianity and culture. Social values--United States. Virtues. United States--Moral conditions--20th century. LC Classification: BR115.C8 .K65 2002 Dewey Class No.: 261 21

Kreider, Alan, 1941- The change of conversion and the origin of Christendom / Alan Kreider. Harrisburg, Pa.: Trinity Press International, c1999. Description: xviii, 126 p.; 19 cm. ISBN: 1563382989 (pbk.: alk. paper) Notes: Includes bibliographical references (p. 115-126). Subjects: Conversion--Christianity. Series: Christian

mission and modern culture LC
Classification: BV4916 .K74 1999 Dewey
Class No.: 248.2/4/09015 21

Kronenfeld, Judy. King Lear and the naked
truth: rethinking the language of religion
and resistance / Judy Kronenfeld. Durham:
Duke University Press, 1998. Description:
xi, 383 p.; 24 cm. ISBN: 082232038X
(pbk.: alk. paper) 0822320274 (alk. paper)
Notes: Includes bibliographical references
(p. [343]-365) and index. Subjects:
Shakespeare, William, 1564-1616. King
Lear. English language--Early modern,
1500-1700--Semantics. Lear, King
(Legendary character), in literature.
Christianity and literature--Literature and
history--Language and culture--England--
History. Dissenters, Religious, in literature.
Social ethics in literature. Costume in
literature. Nudity in literature. LC
Classification: PR2819 .K76 1998 Dewey
Class No.: 822.3/3 21

Kruithof, Bastian. Man in God's milieu.
Published/Created: Grand Rapids, Baker
Book House [1968] Description: 144 p. 20
cm. Notes: Includes bibliographies.
Subjects: Christianity and culture.
Christianity--20th century. LC
Classification: BR115.C8 K67 Dewey
Class No.: 260

Kuenning, Larry. Exiles in Babylon / Larry
Kuenning. Published/Created: Cambridge,
Mass.: Publishers of Truth, c1978.
Description: ix, 211 p.; 21 cm. ISBN:
0930682009 : Notes: Includes
bibliographical references. Subjects: Bible-
-Criticism, interpretation, etc. Christianity
and culture. LC Classification: BR115.C8
K78 Dewey Class No.: 261.1

Kuhns, William. Environmental man. Edition
Information: [1st ed.] Published/Created:
New York, Harper & Row [1969]
Description: 156 p. 22 cm. Notes: Includes
bibliographical references. Subjects:
Christianity and culture. Human beings--
Effect of environment on. Technology and
civilization. LC Classification: BR115.C8
K8 Dewey Class No.: 261.5

Kurewa, John Wesley Zwomunondiita. Biblical
proclamation for Africa today / John
Wesley Zwomunondiita Kurewa.
Published/Created: Nashville: Abingdon
Press, c1995. Description: 112 p.; 22 cm.
ISBN: 0687014441 (pbk.) Notes: Includes
bibliographical references (p. 105-108) and
indexes. Subjects: Bible--Evidences,
authority, etc. Bible--Homiletical use.
Christianity--Preaching--Africa, Sub-
Saharan. Christianity and culture. Africa,
Sub-Saharan--Religion--20th century. LC
Classification: BR1430 .K87 1995 Dewey
Class No.: 276.7/0825 20

Kurewa, John Wesley Zwomunondiita.
Preaching and cultural identity:
proclaiming the gospel in Africa / John
Wesley Zwomunondiita Kurewa.
Published/Created: Nashville: Abingdon
Press, c2000. Description: 232 p.; 23 cm.
ISBN: 0687090318 (alk. paper) Notes:
Includes bibliographical references (p.
225-232). Subjects: Preaching--Africa,
Sub-Saharan. Christianity and culture--
Africa, Sub-Saharan. LC Classification:
BV4208.A357 K87 2000 Dewey Class
No.: 251/.0096 21

Küster, Volker, 1962- The many faces of Jesus
Christ: intercultural christology / Volker
Küster. Published/Created: Maryknoll,
N.Y.: Orbis Books 2001. Description: xiii,
242 p.: ill.; 24 cm. ISBN: 1570753547
Notes: Includes bibliographical references
(p. [195]-237) and index. Subjects: Jesus
Christ--Person and offices. Christianity and
culture--Developing countries. LC
Classification: BT205 .K8413 2001 Dewey
Class No.: 232/.09 21

Kwa'ioloa, Michael. Living tradition: a
changing life in Solomon Islands / as told
by Michael Kwa'ioloa to Ben Burt.
Published/Created: Honolulu, Hawaii:
University of Hawai'i Press, c1997.
Related Authors: Burt, Ben. Description:
vi, 169, [1] p., [16] p. of plates: ill., maps;
22 cm. ISBN: 0824819608 (alk. paper)
Notes: Includes bibliographical references
(p. [170]). Subjects: Kwa'ioloa, Michael.
Kwara'ae (Solomon Islands people)--
Biography. Kwara'ae (Solomon Islands

people)--History. Kwara'ae (Solomon Islands people)--Social life and customs. Christianity and culture--Malaita (Solomon Islands)--Social life and customs. Honiara (Solomon Islands)--Social life and customs. LC Classification: DU850.K93 A3 1997 Dewey Class No.: 995.93 21

Kwawe, Daniel Badu. Culture and Christianity: a view / Daniel Badu Kwawe. Published/Created: Columbus, Ga.: Brentwood Christian Press, c1998. Description: 63 p.; 21 cm. ISBN: 1556305176 LC Classification: *

Kwok, Pui-lan. Discovering the Bible in the non-biblical world / Kwok Pui-lan. Published/Created: Maryknoll, N.Y.: Orbis Books, c1995. Description: xvi, 136 p.; 24 cm. ISBN: 0883449978 Notes: Includes bibliographical references (p. 121-132) and index. Subjects: Bible--Feminist criticism--Asia--Developing countries. Feminist theology--Asia. Christianity and culture. Series: Bible & liberation series LC Classification: BS521.4 .K96 1995 Dewey Class No.: 220.6/082 20

Kwong, Chungwah, 1958- The public role of religion in post-colonial Hong Kong: an historical overview of Confucianism, Taoism, Buddhism and Christianity / Chungwah Kwong. Published/Created: New York: Peter Lang, c2002. Description: ix, 207 p.; 24 cm. ISBN: 082045690X (alk. paper) Notes: Includes bibliographical references (p. [187]-203) and index. Subjects: Hong Kong (China)--Religion. Series: Asian thought and culture; 0893-6870 v. 53 LC Classification: BL1802 .K89 2002 Dewey Class No.: 200/.95125 21

Laistner, M. L. W. (Max Ludwig Wolfram), 1890-1959. Christianity and pagan culture in the later Roman Empire; together with an English translation of John Chrysostom's Address on vainglory and the right way for parents to bring up their children. Published/Created: Ithaca, Cornell University Press, [1951] Related Authors: John Chrysostom, Saint, d. 407. De inani gloria et de educandis liberis.

English. 1951. Description: vi, 145 p., 23 cm. Notes: Bibliographical references included in "Notes" (p. [123]-140). Subjects: Church history--Primitive and early church, ca. 30-600. Paganism. Pride and vanity. Religious education of children. Series: The James W. Richard lectures in history; 1950-1951 LC Classification: BR203 .L27 Dewey Class No.: 270.2

Lamle, Elias Nankap. Cultural revival and church planting: a Nigerian case study / Elias Nankap Lamle. Published/Created: Jos, Nigeria: CAPRO Media, c1995. Description: 196 p.: ill., maps; 21 cm. ISBN: 9782668508 Notes: Includes bibliographic references (180-191). Subjects: Christianity--Nigeria. Christianity and culture--Nigeria--Case studies. Church development, New. Church growth. Evangelistic work. LC Classification: IN PROCESS (COPIED) (lccopycat)

Lançon, Bertrand, 1952- Rome in late antiquity: AD 313-604 / Bertrand Lancon; translated by Antonia Nevill with an introduction and guide to further reading by Mark Humphries. Published/Created: Edinburgh: Edinburgh University Press, c2000. Related Authors: Nevill, Antonia. Description: 256 p.: ill., maps; 24 cm. ISBN: 0748612394 0748612408 (pbk.) Notes: Includes bibliographical references (p. 165-174) and index. Translated from the French. Subjects: Christianity and culture--History--Early church, ca. 30-600. Rome--History--Empire, 284-476. Rome--Civilization--Christian influences. LC Classification: DG311 .L3613 2000 Dewey Class No.: 937 21

Lange, Maurice de. Contemporary culture and Christianity / Maurice de Lange. Published/Created: Chicago: Franciscan Herald Press, c1979. Description: 76 p.; 18 cm. ISBN: 0819907413 : Notes: Bibliography: p. 75-76. Subjects: Christianity and culture--Addresses, essays, lectures. LC Classification: BR115.C8 L36 Dewey Class No.: 261

Langston, Richard L. A biblical perspective on bribery and extortion and its implications in the Philippine context from a missionary viewpoint [microform] / by Richard L. Langston. Published/Created: 1989. Description: vii, 173 leaves; 28 cm. Notes: Thesis (D. Miss.)--Trinity Evangelical Divinity School, 1989. Microfiche. Portland, Or.: Theological Research Exchange Network, 1989. 1 microfiche: negative. Subjects: Ethics in the Bible. Bribery--Biblical teaching. Extortion--Biblical teaching. Philippines--Moral conditions. Christianity and culture. Missions--Philippines. LC Classification: Microfiche 94/2794 (B)

Language, religion, culture: in memory of Professor Witold Tyloch / edited by Miroslaw Nowaczyk and Zbigniew Stachowski. Published/Created: Warsaw: Polish Society for the Study of Religions: International Association for the History of Religions, 1992. Related Authors: Tyloch, Witold. Nowaczyk, Miroslaw. Stachowski, Zbigniew. Description: 103, [1] p.: ill.; 23 cm. Partial Contents: Études Hébraiques et histoire des religions. Réflexions sur l'oeuvre de Witold Tyloch / André Caquot -- La situation de l'hébreu au temps de la Michna / Chaim Rabin -- An Asian starting point for the study of religion / Michael Pye -- And they ate and drank and rejoiced before the Lord / R.J. Zwi Werblowsky. Notes: Includes bibliographical references. "Essential bibliography of the publications of Witold Tyloch": p. 95-[104]. Subjects: Tyloch, Witold. Religion--Historiography. African poetry--History and criticism. LC Classification: BL43.T94 L36 1992 Dewey Class No.: 200/.7 21

Lapiz, Ed. Paano maging Pilipinong Kristiano = Becoming a Filipino Christian / Ed Lapiz. Published/Created: Makati City, Philippines: Kaloob, c1997. Description: xvi, 153 p.: ill.; 23 cm. ISBN: 9719187409 Notes: Includes bibliographical references (p. 153). English and Tagalog. Subjects: Christianity--Philippines. Christianity and culture--Philippines. Philippines--Civilization. LC Classification: BR1260

.L37 1997 Dewey Class No.: 275.99 21

Larkin, William J. Culture and biblical hermeneutics: interpreting and applying the authoritative Word in a relativistic age / William J. Larkin, Jr. Published/Created: Lanham, Md.: University Press of America, c1993. Description: 401 p.: ill.; 23 cm. ISBN: 0819192198 (paper: alk. paper) Notes: Originally published: Grand Rapids, Mich.: Baker Book House, c1988. Includes bibliographical references (p. 361-381) and index. Subjects: Bible--Evidences, authority, etc. Bible--Hermeneutics. Hermeneutics--Religious aspects--Christianity. LC Classification: BS480 .L35 1993

Larkin, William J. Culture and biblical hermeneutics: interpreting and applying the authoritative Word in a relativistic age / William J. Larkin, Jr. Published/Created: Grand Rapids, Mich.: Baker Book House, c1988. Description: 401 p.; 23 cm. ISBN: 0801056519 Notes: Includes indexes. Bibliography: p. 361-381. Subjects: Bible--Evidences, authority, etc. Bible--Hermeneutics. Hermeneutics--Religious aspects--Christianity. LC Classification: BS480 .L35 1988 Dewey Class No.: 220.6/01 19

Larousse, William. A local Church living for dialogue: Muslim-Christian relations in Mindanao-Sulu, Philippines: 1965-2000 / William Larousse. Published/Created: Roma: Pontificia università gregoriana, 2001. Related Authors: Pontificia Università gregoriana. Centre "Cultures and Religions." Description: xvii, 645 p.: ill., maps; 24 cm. ISBN: 8876528792 Notes: At head of Pontificia università gregoriana, Centro culture e religioni. Includes bibliographical references (p. 561-645). Subjects: Islam--Relations--Christianity. Christianity and other religions--Islam. Islam--Philippines. Christianity--Philippines. Series: Interreligious and intercultural investigations; 4 LC Classification: BP172 .L33 2001 Dewey Class No.: 261.2/7/095997 21

Larson, Duane H. (Duane Howard), 1952-
Times of the trinity: a proposal for theistic
cosmology / Duane H. Larson.
Published/Created: New York: P. Lang,
c1995. Description: 213 p.; 24 cm. ISBN:
0820427063 (alk. paper) Notes: Includes
bibliographical references(p. [187]-205 nd
index. Subjects: Trinity. Trinity--History of
doctrines. Time--Religious aspects--
Christianity. Religion and science. Series:
Worcester Polytechnic Institute studies in
science, technology, and culture; vol. 17
LC Classification: BT111.2 .L37 1995
Dewey Class No.: 231/.044 20

Law, Eric H. F. The bush was blazing but not
consumed: developing a multicultural
community through dialogue liturgy / by
Eric H.F. Law. Published/Created: St.
Louis, Mo.: Chalice Press, c1996.
Description: xiii, 161 p.: ill.; 23 cm. ISBN:
0827202229 Notes: Includes
bibliographical references. Subjects:
Christianity and culture--United States.
Multiculturalism--Religious aspects--
Christianity. Dialogue--Religious aspects--
Christianity. Reconciliation--Religious
aspects--Christianity. Liturgics. Worship
programs. Burning bush. Los Angeles
(Calif.)--Church history--20th century. LC
Classification: BR115.C8 L377 1996
Dewey Class No.: 261.8/34 20

Law, Eric H. F. The wolf shall dwell with the
lamb: a spirituality for leadership in a
multicultural community / by Eric H.F.
Law. Published/Created: St. Louis, Mo.:
Chalice Press, c1993. Description: xi, 131
p.; 22 cm. ISBN: 082724231X : Notes:
Includes bibliographical references.
Subjects: Christianity and culture. Peace--
Religious aspects--Christianity. Power--
Religious aspects--Christianity.
Intercultural communication. Multicultural
education. LC Classification: BR115.C8
L378 1993 Dewey Class No.: 261.8/73 20

Lawhead, Steve. Turn back the night / Stephen
R. Lawhead. Published/Created:
Westchester, Ill.: Crossway Books, c1985.
Description: 180 p.; 22 cm. ISBN:
089107340X (pbk.) : Notes: Bibliography:
p. 178-180. Subjects: Christianity and

culture. Mass media--Religious aspects--
Christianity. LC Classification: BR115.C8
L38 1985 Dewey Class No.: 260 19

Leahy, William P. Adapting to America:
Catholics, Jesuits, and higher education in
the twentieth century / William P. Leahy.
Published/Created: Washington, D.C.:
Georgetown University Press, c1991.
Description: xiv, 187 p.; 23 cm. ISBN:
0878405046 0878405054 (pbk.) Notes:
Includes bibliographical references (p.
[159]-180) and index. Subjects: Catholic
universities and colleges--United States--
History 20th century. Church and college--
United States--History--20th century.
Catholics--United States--Intellectual life--
20th century. Christianity and culture--
History--20th century. United States--
Intellectual life--20th century. LC
Classification: LC501 .L34 1991 Dewey
Class No.: 377 20

Lee, Jung Young. Marginality: the key to
multicultural theology / Jung Young Lee.
Published/Created: Minneapolis: Fortress
Press, c1995. Description: viii, 208 p.: ill.;
22 cm. ISBN: 0800628101 (alk. paper) :
Notes: Includes bibliographical references
(p. 175-201) and index. Subjects: Lee,
Jung Young. Christianity and culture.
Marginality, Social--Religious aspects--
Christianity. Multiculturalism--Religious
aspects--Christianity. LC Classification:
BR115.C8 L44 1995 Dewey Class No.:
230/.046 20

Lee, Jung Young. The Trinity in Asian
perspective / Jung Young Lee.
Published/Created: Nashville: Abingdon
Press, c1996. Description: 255 p.: ill.; 23
cm. ISBN: 0687426375 (pbk.: alk. paper)
Notes: Includes bibliographical references
(p. 246-251) and index. Subjects: Trinity.
Theology, Doctrinal--Asia. Christianity
and culture. East and West. Asia--Religion.
LC Classification: BT111.2 .L44 1996
Dewey Class No.: 231/.044/095 20

Lee, Robert. The clash of civilizations: an
intrusive gospel in Japanese civilization /
Robert Lee. Published/Created: Harrisburg,
Pa.: Trinity Press International, c1999.

Description: xv, 128 p.; 19 cm. ISBN: 1563383047 Notes: Includes bibliographical references (p.120-128). Subjects: Christianity and culture--Japan. Series: Christian mission and modern culture LC Classification: BR1305.5 .L44 1999 Dewey Class No.: 261/.0952 21

Leeuwen, Arend Theodoor van, 1918- Christianity in world history: the meeting of the faiths of East and West, by Arend Th. van Leeuwen. Foreword by Hendrik Kraemer. Translated by H. H. Hoskins. Published/Created: New York, Scribner [1966, c1964] Description: 487 p. 22 cm. Notes: Bibliography: p. 440-459. Subjects: Christianity and other religions. East and West. Christianity and culture. LC Classification: BR115.C5 L43 1966 Dewey Class No.: 261.2

Legrand, Lucien, 1927- Unity and plurality: mission in the Bible / Lucien Legrand; translated from the French by Robert R. Barr. Published/Created: Maryknoll, N.Y.: Orbis Books, c1990. Description: xv, 189 p.; 24 cm. ISBN: 0883446928 : Notes: Translation of: Le Dieu qui vient. Includes bibliographical references (p. 167-181) and index. Subjects: Catholic Church--Missions. Missions--Biblical teaching. Christianity and culture. Christianity and other religions. Missions--Theory. LC Classification: BV2073 .L4413 1990 Dewey Class No.: 266/.001 20

Lewy, Guenter, 1923- Why America needs religion: secular modernity and its discontents / Guenter Lewy. Published/Created: Grand Rapids, Mich.: W.B. Eerdmans, 1996. Description: xii, 160 p.; 23 cm. ISBN: 0802841627 (pbk.: alk. paper) Notes: Includes bibliographical references (p. 147-154) and index. Subjects: Christianity--United States. Secularism--United States. Religion and ethics. Christianity and culture. United States--Moral conditions. LC Classification: BR515 .L48 1996 Dewey Class No.: 277.3/0829 20

Liankhohau, T. Social, cultural, economic & religious life of a transformed community: a study of the Paite tribe / T. Liankhohau. Edition Information: 1st ed. Published/Created: New Delhi: Mittal Publications, 1994. Description: xi, 202 p.: ill., maps; 23 cm. ISBN: 8170995205 : Summary: Survey of the pre and post Christian culture of the Paite people of Manipur, India. Notes: Includes bibliographical references (p. [185]-196) and index. Subjects: Christianity--India--Manipur. Paite (Asian people)--India--Manipur--Religion. Manipur (India)--Religion. LC Classification: BR1156.M386 L5 1994 Dewey Class No.: 275.4/17 20

Life and death matters: the practice of inculturation in Africa / Anthony J. Gittins, ed. Published/Created: Nettetal: Steyler Verlag, c2000. Related Authors: Gittins, Anthony J., 1943- . Description: 175 p.; 24 cm. ISBN: 3805004435 Notes: Papers from a consultation held in Tamale, Ghana, at the Tamale Institute of Cross-Cultural Studies. "Distributor in the United States: Anthony J. Gittins, Catholic Theological Union, Chicago." (T.p.v.) Includes bibliographical references. Subjects: Catholic Church--Africa, Sub-Saharan--History--20th century. Christianity and culture--Africa, Sub-Saharan. Christianity and other religions--African. Africa, Sub-Saharan--Church history--20th century. Africa, Sub-Saharan--Religious life and customs. Series: Studia Instituti Missiologici Societatis Verbi Divini, 0562-2819; Nr. 72

Limberis, Vasiliki, 1954- Divine Heiress: the Virgin Mary and the creation of Christian Constantinople / Vasiliki Limberis. Published/Created: London; New York: Routledge, 1994. Related Authors: Orthodox Eastern Church. Akathistos hymnos. English. 1994. Description: x, 199 p.; 21 cm. ISBN: 0415096774 Notes: Includes bibliographical references (p. [187]-193) and index. Subjects: Mary, Blessed Virgin, Saint--Cult--Rome. Mary, Blessed Virgin, Saint--Cult--Turkey--Istanbul. Orthodox Eastern Church--Hymns--History and criticism. Christianity and culture--History--Early church, ca. 30-

600. Hymns, Greek--History and criticism. Istanbul (Turkey)--Church history. Byzantine Empire--Church history. LC Classification: BT652.R66 L56 1994 Dewey Class No.: 232.91/094961/8 20

Lindenauer, Leslie J. Piety and power: gender and religious culture in the American colonies, 1630-1700 / by Leslie J. Lindenauer. New York: Routledge, 2002. Description: p. cm. ISBN: 0415933927 Notes: Includes bibliographical references. Subjects: Women in Christianity--Protestant churches--United States--Church history--17th century. LC Classification: BR520 .L56 2002 Dewey Class No.: 277.3/06/082 21

Lindsell, Harold, 1913- The new paganism / Harold Lindsell. Edition Information: 1st ed. Published/Created: San Francisco: Harper & Row, c1987. Description: xv, 279 p.; 22 cm. ISBN: 0060652721 : Notes: Includes index. Bibliography: p. [264]-266. Subjects: Apologetics. Civilization, Christian. Christianity and culture. Neopaganism. Evangelicalism. Enlightenment. Civilization, Modern--20th century. LC Classification: BT1211 .L56 1987 Dewey Class No.: 261 19

Lingenfelter, Sherwood G. Agents of transformation: a guide for effective cross-cultural ministry / Sherwood G. Lingenfelter. Published/Created: Grand Rapids, Mich: Baker Books, c1996. Description: 282 p.: ill.; 23 cm. ISBN: 0801020689 (pbk.) Notes: Includes bibliographical references (p. 276-278) and index. Subjects: Missions--Anthropological aspects. Intercultural communication. Christianity and culture. Missions--Theory. Evangelistic work. LC Classification: BV2063 .L433 1996 Dewey Class No.: 266/.023/01 20

Lingenfelter, Sherwood G. Transforming culture: a challenge for Christian mission / Sherwood G. Lingenfelter. Published/Created: Grand Rapids, Mich.: Baker Book House, c1992. Description: 218 p.: ill.; 23 cm. ISBN: 0801056748 Notes: Includes bibliographical references

(p. 213-214) and indexes. Subjects: Missions--Anthropological aspects. Intercultural communication. Christianity and culture. LC Classification: BV2063 .L436 1992 Dewey Class No.: 266 20

Lingenfelter, Sherwood G. Transforming culture: a challenge for Christian mission / Sherwood Lingenfelter. Edition Information: 2nd ed. Published/Created: Grand Rapids, Mich.: Baker Books, c1998. Description: 190 p.: ill.; 22 cm. ISBN: 0801021782 (pbk.) Notes: Includes bibliographical references (p. 183-184) and indexes. Subjects: Missions--Anthropological aspects. Intercultural communication. Christianity and culture. LC Classification: BV2063 .L436 1998 Dewey Class No.: 266 21

Linn, Jan. Christians must choose: the lure of culture and the command of Christ / by Jan G. Linn. Published/Created: St. Louis, Mo.: CBP Press, c1985. Description: 104 p.; 22 cm. ISBN: 0827204485 Notes: Bibliography: p. 99-104. Subjects: Christianity and culture. Church renewal. United States--Church history--20th century. LC Classification: BR115.C8 L56 1985 Dewey Class No.: 277.3/0828 19

Lints, Richard. The fabric of theology: a prolegomenon to Evangelical theology / Richard Lints. Published/Created: Grand Rapids, Mich.: Eerdmans, c1993. Description: xii, 359 p.; 23 cm. ISBN: 0802806740 (pbk.) Notes: Includes bibliographical references (p. 337-356) and index. Subjects: Theology, Doctrinal. Evangelicalism. Christianity and culture. LC Classification: BT65 .L54 1993 Dewey Class No.: 230/.046 20

LiPuma, Edward, 1951- Encompassing others: the magic of modernity in Melanesia / Edward LiPuma. Published/Created: Ann Arbor: University of Michigan Press, c2000. Description: xvi, 342 p.: maps; 24 cm. ISBN: 0472110683 (cloth: alk. paper) Partial Contents: The flight of the cassowary: on subjectivity and encompassment -- In the fields of encompassment: colonialism and the

advent of modernity. Notes: Includes
bibliographical references (p. 325-336) and
index. Subjects: Maring (Papua New
Guinea people)--Social conditions. Maring
(Papua New Guinea people)--Missions.
Maring (Papua New Guinea people)--
Religion. Anglicans--Missions--Papua
New Guinea--Jimi River Valley.
Christianity and culture--Papua New
Guinea--Jimi River Valley. Jimi River
Valley (Papua New Guinea)--Religious life
and customs. Jimi River Valley (Papua
New Guinea)--Social life and customs. LC
Classification: DU740.42 .L566 2000
Dewey Class No.: 305.89/912 21

Little, David, 1933- Human rights and the
conflict of cultures: Western and Islamic
perspectives on religious liberty / by David
Little, John Kelsay, and Abdulaziz A.
Sachedina. Published/Created: Columbia,
S.C.: University of South Carolina Press,
c1988. Related Authors: Kelsay, John,
1953- Sachedina, Abdulaziz Abdulhussein,
1942- Description: x, 112 p.; 24 cm. ISBN:
0872495337 Notes: Spine Human rights
and the conflicts of culture. Includes
bibliographies and index. Subjects: Human
rights--Religious aspects--Comparative
studies. Human rights--Religious aspects--
Christianity. Human rights--Religious
aspects--Islam. Series: Studies in
comparative religion (Columbia, S.C.) LC
Classification: BL65.H78 L57 1988
Dewey Class No.: 291.1/772 19

Little, Joyce A. The church and the culture war:
secular anarchy or sacred order / Joyce A.
Little. Published/Created: San Francisco:
Ignatius Press, c1995. Description: 207 p.;
21 cm. Notes: Includes bibliographical
references and indexes. Subjects: Catholic
Church--Doctrines. Secularism. Feminism-
-Religious aspects--Catholic Church.
Christianity and culture. Culture conflict.
LC Classification: BX1751.2 .L535 1995
Dewey Class No.: 261 20

Little, Lawrence S. Disciples of liberty: the
African Methodist Episcopal Church in the
age of imperialism, 1884-1916 / Lawrence
S. Little. Edition Information: 1st ed.
Published/Created: Knoxville: University

of Tennessee Press, c2000. Description:
xvii, 246 p.: ill.; 24 cm. ISBN:
1572330856 (cl.: alk. paper) Contents: One
church indivisible: political structure and
ideology -- Rhetoric and the burden of
racial attitudes -- Redeem the world: the
influence of Black theology -- The paradox
of patriotism: the AME and American
imperialism -- Liberty and equality in the
American empire -- Ideology, culture, and
imperialism: Western Europe and Africa.
Notes: Includes bibliographical references
(p. [223]-237) and index. Subjects: African
Methodist Episcopal Church--History.
Christianity and politics--African
Methodist Episcopal Church--History.
Imperialism--History--19th century.
Imperialism--History--20th century. LC
Classification: BX8443 .L58 2000 Dewey
Class No.: 287/.83 21

Liturgical inculturation in the Anglican
Communion: including the York statement
"Down to earth worship" / edited by David
R. Holeton. Published/Created: Bramcote,
Nottingham: Grove Books, c1990. Related
Authors: Holeton, David. Description: 54
p.; 22 cm. ISBN: 1851741488 Notes:
Includes bibliographical references.
Subjects: Anglican Communion--Liturgy.
Christianity and culture. Series:
Alcuin/GROW liturgical study, 0951-2667;
15 Grove Liturgical Study; 62 LC
Classification: BX5141 .L57 1990 Dewey
Class No.: 264/.03 20

Liturgy and cultural religious traditions / edited
by Herman Schmidt and David Power.
Published/Created: New York: Seabury
Press, 1977. Related Authors: Schmidt,
Herman A. P., 1912- Power, David Noel.
Description: vi, 114 p.; 23 cm. ISBN:
0816421463 : Notes: "A Crossroad book."
Includes bibliographical references.
Subjects: Liturgics--Addresses, essays,
lectures. Christianity and culture--
Addresses, essays, lectures. Series:
Concilium (Glen Rock, N.J.); v. 102. LC
Classification: BV176 .L575 Dewey Class
No.: 261.2

Liturgy and spirituality in context: perspectives
on prayer and culture / Eleanor Bernstein,

editor. Published/Created: Collegeville, Minn.: Liturgical Press, c1990. Related Authors: Bernstein, Eleanor. Description: xiv, 170 p.; 23 cm. ISBN: 0814618421 Notes: Includes bibliographical references. Subjects: Catholic Church--Liturgy--Congresses. Catholic Church--Doctrines--Congresses. Christianity and culture--Congresses. Spirituality--Catholic Church--Congresses. Spirituality--Congresses. Liturgics--Congresses. LC Classification: BX1970.A1 L58 1990 Dewey Class No.: 261/.1 20

Llywelyn, Dorian. Sacred place, chosen people: land and national identity in Welsh spirituality / Dorian Llywelyn. Published/Created: Cardiff: University of Wales Press, 1999. Description: xii, 210 p.; 23 cm. ISBN: 0708315208 0708315194 (pbk.) Notes: Includes bibliographical references (p. [202]-205) and index. Subjects: Spirituality--Wales--History. Christian literature, Welsh--History and criticism. Sacred space--Wales--History. Nationalism--Religious aspects--Christianity--History of doctrines. Series: Religion, culture, and society LC Classification: BR773 .L59 1999 Dewey Class No.: 274.29 21

Lockerbie, D. Bruce. The cosmic center / by D. Bruce Lockerbie. Published/Created: Grand Rapids: Eerdmans, c1977. Description: 158 p.; 21 cm. ISBN: 0802816924 : Subjects: Jesus Christ--Person and offices. Christianity and culture. Secularism. LC Classification: BR115.C8 I.6 Dewey Class No.: 261 19

Lockerbie, D. Bruce. The cosmic center: the supremacy of Christ in a secular wasteland / D. Bruce Lockerbie. Edition Information: [Rev. ed.]. Portland, Ore.: Multnomah Press, c1986. Description: 194 p.; 22 cm. ISBN: 0880701323 Notes: Includes indexes. Subjects: Jesus Christ--Person and offices. Christianity and culture. Secularism. LC Classification: BR115.C8 L6 1986 Dewey Class No.: 261 19

Loewen, Jacob A. (Jacob Abram), 1922- Culture and human values: Christian

intervention in anthropological perspective: selections from the writings of Jacob A. Loewen. Published/Created: South Pasadena, Calif.: William Carey Library, [1975] Description: xviii, 443 p.; 23 cm. ISBN: 0878087222 Notes: Papers originally appeared in Practical anthropology, 1961-1970. Includes bibliographical references. Subjects: Missions. Communication--Religious aspects--Christianity. Indians of South America--Missions. LC Classification: BV2070 .L58 Dewey Class No.: 266

Loewen, Jacob A. (Jacob Abram), 1922- The Bible in cross-cultural perspective / Jacob A. Loewen. Published/Created: Pasadena, Calif.: W. Carey Library, c2000. Description: xv, 334 p.; 23 cm. ISBN: 0878082662 (alk. paper) Notes: Includes bibliographical references (p. 295-302) and indexes. Subjects: Loewen, Jacob A. (Jacob Abram), 1922- Bible--Hermeneutics--Cross-cultural studies. Ethnology in the Bible. Christianity and culture. Christianity and other religions. Ethnology--Religious aspects--Christianity. Missions--Theory. LC Classification: BS476 .L62 2000 Dewey Class No.: 220.6/7 20

Logan, Oliver. The Venetian upper clergy in the 16th and early 17th centuries: a study in religious culture / Oliver Logan. Published/Created: Lewiston, NY: Edwin Mellen Press, c1996. Description: x, 608 p.; 23 cm. ISBN: 0773489274 Notes: Originally published: The Venetian upper clergy in the sixteenth and early seventeenth centuries. Salzburg, Austria: Institut für Anglistik und Amerikanistik, Universität Salzburg, 1995. (Analecta Cartusiana; 35:18) Includes bibliographical references (p. [537]-600) and index. Subjects: Catholic Church--Italy--Venice--Clergy--History. Christianity and culture--History. Rhetoric--Italy--History and criticism. Venice (Italy)--Church history. Series: Texts and studies in religion; v. 68 LC Classification: BX1544 .L64 1996 Dewey Class No.: 262/.12 20

Logan, Oliver. The Venetian upper clergy in the sixteenth and early seventeenth centuries: a study in religious culture / Oliver Logan. Published/Created: Salzburg, Austria: Institut für Anglistik und Amerikanistik, Universität Salzburg, 1995. Description: 2 v. (x, 608 p.); 21 cm. ISBN: 3705204394 (v. 1) 3705204386 (v. 2) Notes: Includes bibliographical references (v. 2, p. 537-600) and index. Subjects: Catholic Church--Italy--Venice--Clergy--History. Christianity and culture--History. Rhetoric--Italy--History and criticism. Venice (Italy)--Church history. Series: Analecta Cartusiana; 35:18 Spiritualität heute und gestern; Bd. 18 LC Classification: BX3301.3 .S65 1984 vol. 18 BX1548.V4

Logos: a journal of Catholic thought and culture. Published/Created: St. Paul, MN: University of St. Thomas, c1997- Related Authors: University of St. Thomas (Saint Paul, Minn.) Description: v.: ill.; 23 cm. Issues for spring 1997- also designated 1:1- Vol. 1, no. 1 (spring 1997)- Current Frequency: Quarterly (irregular) ISSN: 1091-6687 Notes: Title from cover. Subjects: Catholic Church--Doctrines--Periodicals. Christianity and culture--Periodicals. LC Classification: BX1795.C85 L64 Dewey Class No.: 282 13

Long, D. Stephen, 1960- Living the discipline: United Methodist theological reflections on war, civilization, and holiness / D. Stephen Long. Published/Created: Grand Rapids, Mich.: W.B. Eerdmans, c1992. Description: x, 158 p.; 22 cm. ISBN: 0802806341 (pbk.) : Notes: Includes bibliographical references (p. 153-156) and index. Subjects: United Methodist Church (U.S.)--Doctrines--Membership. Pacifism--Religious aspects--United Methodist Church (U.S.) Christianity and culture. Holiness--United Methodist Church (U.S.) Methodist Church--Doctrines--Membership. LC Classification: BX8382.2.Z5 L66 1992 Dewey Class No.: 261.8/73 20

Long, Loretta M. (Loretta Marie), 1971- The life of Selina Campbell: a fellow soldier in the cause of restoration / Loretta M. Long. Published/Created: Tuscaloosa: University of Alabama Press, c2001. Description: 235 p.: ill.; 24 cm ISBN: 0817310592 (cloth.: alk. paper) Notes: Includes bibliographical references (p. [201]-229) and index. Subjects: Campbell, Selina Huntington, 1803?-1897. Christians (Disciples of Christ)--West Virginia Biography. Women in Christianity--United States--History--19th century. Series: Religion and American culture (Tuscaloosa, Ala.) LC Classification: BX7343.C2 .L6 2001 Dewey Class No.: 286.6/092 B 21

Lowber, James W. The highest culture and Christianity. Published/Created: [n.p.] (c1915) Description: 1 v. cm. LC Classification: BR121 .L66

Lowber, James William, 1847-1930. The highest culture and Christianity. Edition Information: [Rev. and enl. ed.] Published/Created: Cincinnati, Standard Pub. co. [c1915] Description: 2 l., 3-700 p. front. (port.) 20 cm. Subjects: Christianity--Philosophy. Apologetics--20th century. LC Classification: BT1105 .L6 1915

Lundin, Roger. The culture of interpretation: Christian faith and the postmodern world / Roger Lundin. Published/Created: Grand Rapids, Mich.: W.B. Eerdmans, c1993. Description: viii, 272 p.; 23 cm. ISBN: 0802806368 (pbk.) Notes: Includes bibliographical references and index. Subjects: Deconstruction. Postmodernism--Religious aspects--Christianity. Christianity and culture. United States--Civilization--1970- LC Classification: BT83.8 .L86 1993 Dewey Class No.: 261/.0973 20

Luzbetak, Louis J. The church and cultures: an applied anthropology for the religious worker / Louis J. Luzbetak. Published/Created: South Pasadena, Calif.: William Carey Library, 1975, c1970. Description: xiv, 429 p.; 22 cm. ISBN: 0878087257 : Notes: Includes bibliographies and index. Subjects:

Missions--Anthropological aspects. Christianity and culture. LC Classification: BV2063 .L886 1975 Dewey Class No.: 301.2

Luzbetak, Louis J. The church and cultures: new perspectives in missiological anthropology / Louis J. Luzbetak. Published/Created: Maryknoll, N.Y.: Orbis Books, c1988. Description: xx, 464 p.; 24 cm. ISBN: 0883446251 Notes: Includes index. Bibliography: p. 411-452. Subjects: Missions--Anthropological aspects. Christianity and culture. Series: American Society of Missiology series; no. 12 LC Classification: BV2063 .L89 1988 Dewey Class No.: 266/.001 19

Luzbetak, Louis J. The church and cultures; an applied anthropology for the religious worker [by] Louis J. Luzbetak. Published/Created: Techny, Ill., Divine Word Publications [1970] Description: xiv, 429 p. 22 cm. ISBN: 0872981207 Notes: Bibliography: p. 367-421. Subjects: Missions--Anthropological aspects. Christianity and culture. LC Classification: BV2063 .L886 1970 Dewey Class No.: 301.2/4

Lynch, Christopher Owen, 1954- Selling Catholicism: Bishop Sheen and the power of television / Christopher Owen Lynch. Published/Created: Lexington: University Press of Kentucky, c1998. Description: xii, 200 p.: ill.; 24 cm. ISBN: 0813120675 (alk. paper) Notes: Includes bibliographical references (p. [178]-194) and index. Subjects: Sheen, Fulton J. (Fulton John), 1895-1979. Life is worth living (Television program) Television in religion--United States--History. Christianity and culture--United States--History--20th century. Catholic Church--United States--History--20th century. LC Classification: BX4705.S612 L86 1998 Dewey Class No.: 282/.092 21

MacArthur, John, 1939- How to survive in a world of unbelievers: Jesus' words of encouragement on the night before his death / John MacArthur. Published/Created: Nashville, Tenn.: Word

Publishing, c2001. Description: x, 184 p.; 22 cm. ISBN: 0849955564 Subjects: Bible. N.T. John XIII-XVI--Criticism, interpretation, etc. Christianity and culture. Christian ethics. Series: MacArthur, John, 1939- Bible for life series. LC Classification: BS2615.52 M33 2001 Dewey Class No.: 226.5/06 21

Macchioro, Vittorio, b. 1880. From Orpheus to Paul; a history of Orphism, by Vittorio D. Macchioro. Published/Created: New York, H. Holt and Company [c1930] Description: 6 p. l., 3-262 p. front., plates (1 fold.) 23 cm. Notes: "Notes": p. 227-258. Subjects: Paul, the Apostle, Saint. Orpheus (Greek mythology) Mysteries, Religious. Christianity and other religions. LC Classification: BL795.O7 M3

Machin, G. I. T. Churches and social issues in twentieth-century Britain / G.I.T. Machin. Published/Created: Oxford: Clarendon Press; New York: Oxford University Press, 1998. Description: xi, 269 p.; 23 cm. ISBN: 0198217803 (hardcover) Notes: Includes bibliographical references (p. [232]-249) and index. Subjects: Church and social problems--Christianity and culture--Social change--Great Britain--History--20th century. Great Britain--Social conditions--Church history--20th century. Great Britain--Moral conditions. LC Classification: HN39.G7 M24 1998 Dewey Class No.: 261.8/3/09410704 21

Mack, Burton L. The Christian myth: origins, logic, and legacy / Burton L. Mack. Published/Created: New York: Continuum, 2001. Description: 237 p.; 23 cm. ISBN: 0826413552 (alk. paper) Notes: Includes bibliographical references(p/ 223-237). Subjects: Christianity--Origin. Christianity and culture. LC Classification: BR129 .M33 2001 Dewey Class No.: 270.1 21

MacKenzie, Charles Sherrard, 1924- The Trinity and culture / Charles Sherrard MacKenzie. Published/Created: New York: P. Lang, 1987. Description: ix, 150 p.; 24 cm. ISBN: 0820404926 : Notes: Bibliography: p. 147-150. Subjects: Trinity. Sociology, Christian. Christianity and culture. Civilization, Christian. Series: American university studies. Series VII, Theology and religion; vol. 34 LC Classification: BT111.2 .M2 1987 Dewey Class No.: 231/.044 19

MacMullen, Ramsay, 1928- Christianity and paganism in the fourth to eighth centuries / Ramsay MacMullen. Published/Created: New Haven, Conn.: Yale University Press, c1997. Description: vi, 282 p.: ill.; 24 cm. ISBN: 0300071485 (cloth: alk. paper) Notes: Includes bibliographical references (p. [247]-275) and index. Subjects: Church history--Primitive and early church, ca. 30-600. Paganism--Relations--Christianity. Christianity and culture--History--Early church, ca. 30-600. Evangelistic work--History--Early church, ca. 30-600. Christianity and other religions--Roman. Rome--Religion--Relations--Christianity. LC Classification: BR170 .M33 1997 Dewey Class No.: 270.2 21

Maddux, Bob. Fantasy explosion / Bob Maddux; foreword by Jack W. Hayford. Published/Created: Ventura, Calif., U.S.A.: Regal Books, c1986. Description: 153 p.; 21 cm. ISBN: 0830711635 (pbk.) : Notes: "How you & your family are being exploited by: pornography & teenage sex films, music videos, occult films, toys, soap operas & romantic novels, role-playing games, comic books." Bibliography: p. 148-153. Subjects: Fantasy in mass media. Mass media--Religious aspects--Christianity. Christianity--20th century. Popular culture--United States--History--20th century. Popular culture--Religious aspects--Christianity. LC Classification: P96.F362 U66 1986 Dewey Class No.: 302.2/34 19

Madigan, Patrick, 1945- The completion of the project of the West, and it romantic sequel: essays in the history of western culture / by Patrick Madigan. Published/Created: Scranton, PA: University of Scranton Press, 2002. Description: p. cm. ISBN: 1589660188 (hc) 1589660196 (pbk.) Notes: Includes bibliographical references and index. Subjects: Christianity--Philosophy--History. Philosophy and

religion--History. LC Classification: BR100 .M26 2002

Madison, James, 1749-1812. An address to the members of the Protestant Episcopal Church in Virginia / by Bishop Madison. Published/Created: Richmond: Printed by T. Nicolson ..., 1799. Related Authors: Episcopal Church. Diocese of Virginia. American Imprint Collection (Library of Congress) Description: 24 p.; 22 cm. (8vo) Notes: Signatures: [A]4 [B]8. References: Evans 35761 Subjects: Spiritual warfare--Early works to 1800. Christian life--Religion and culture--Spiritual life--Christianity--Early works to 1800. LC Classification: BV4509.5 BX5918.V8 A6 1799

Magliola, Robert R. On deconstructing life-worlds: Buddhism, Christianity, culture / by Robert Magliola. Atlanta, Ga.: Scholars Press, c1997. Description: xxii, 202 p.: ill.; 24 cm. ISBN: 0788502956 (cloth: acid-free paper) 0788502964 (paper: acid-free paper) Notes: Includes bibliographical references and index. Subjects: Magliola, Robert R. Derrida, Jacques. Philosophy and religion. Buddhism--Relations--Christianity. Christianity and other religions--Buddhism. Series: American Academy of Religion cultural criticism series; no. 3 LC Classification: BL51 .M247 1997 Dewey Class No.: 291.1/75 20

Mallard, William. The reflection of theology in literature: a case study in theology and culture / by William Mallard. Published/Created: San Antonio: Trinity University Press, c1977. Description: xi, 271 p.; 24 cm. ISBN: 0911536647 Notes: Includes bibliographical references and index. Subjects: Christianity and literature. Series: Trinity University monograph series in religion; v. 4. LC Classification: PN49 .M38 Dewey Class No.: 809/.933/1

Manathodath, Jacob. Culture, dialogue, and the Church: a study on the inculturation of the local churches according to the teaching of Pope Paul VI / Jacob Manathodath. Published/Created: New Delhi: Intercultural Publications, 1990.

Description: xxvi, 194 p.; 23 cm. Notes: Includes index. Includes bibliographical references (p. [186]-191). Subjects: Paul VI, Pope, 1897-1978 --Contributions in relationship of church and culture. Christianity and culture--Evangelistic work--History--20th century. LC Classification: BR115.C8 M227 1990 Dewey Class No.: 261 20

Mankind's search for God. Published/Created: Brooklyn, N.Y., U.S.A.: Watchtower Bible and Tract Society of New York: International Bible Students Association, c1990. Related Authors: Watchtower Bible and Tract Society of New York. International Bible Students Association. Description: 379 p.: ill. (some col.); 18 cm. Notes: Spine Search. Includes bibliographical references (p. [2]) and index. Subjects: Religions. Christianity and other religions. Religion and culture. Religion and civilization. LC Classification: BL80.2 .M2853 1990 Dewey Class No.: 291

Manus, Ukachukwu Chris, 1950- Christ, the African king: New Testament christology / Ukachukwu Chris Manus. Frankfurt am Main; New York: P. Lang, c1993. Description: 280 p.: ill.; 21 cm. ISBN: 363145211X (pbk.) Notes: Includes bibliographical references (p. 253-280). Subjects: Jesus Christ--Royal office. Kings and rulers--Religious aspects. Christianity and culture. Africa, Sub-Saharan--Kings and rulers--Religion. Series: Studien zur interkulturellen Geschichte des Christentums; Bd. 82. LC Classification: BT270 .M36 1993 Dewey Class No.: 232/.8 20

Many cultures, one nation: a festschrift for Beyers Naudé / edited by Charles Villa-Vicencio and Carl Niehaus. Edition Information: 1st ed. Published/Created: Cape Town: Human & Rousseau, 1995. Related Authors: Villa-Vicencio, Charles. Niehaus, Carl, 1959- Description: 183 p.; 22 cm. ISBN: 0798134127 Notes: Includes bibliographical references. Subjects: Naudé, Beyers. Christianity and culture. Anti-apartheid movements--South Africa--

Race relations. LC Classification: BR115.C8 M238 1995 Dewey Class No.: 261.8/34/0968 20

Markus, R. A. (Robert Austin), 1924- Christianity in the Roman world / R. A. Markus; with 74 illustrations and a map. Published/Created: London: Thames & Hudson, [1974] Description: 192 p.: ill.; 22 cm. ISBN: 0500830010 : Notes: Includes index. Bibliography: p. 187-189. Subjects: Church history--Primitive and early church, ca. 30-600. LC Classification: BR170 .M36 Dewey Class No.: 270.1

Marsden, George M., 1939- Fundamentalism and American culture: the shaping of twentieth century evangelicalism, 1870-1925 / George M. Marsden. Published/Created: New York: Oxford University Press, 1980. Description: xiv, 306 p.: ill.; 24 cm. ISBN: 0195027582 : Notes: Includes bibliographical references and indexes. Subjects: Fundamentalism--History. Christianity--United States. LC Classification: BT82.2 .M37 Dewey Class No.: 280/.4

Marsh, Joss. Word crimes: blasphemy, culture, and literature in nineteenth-century England / Joss Marsh. Published/Created: Chicago: University of Chicago Press, 1998. Description: xii, 431 p.: ill.; 24 cm. ISBN: 0226506908 (cloth: alk. paper) 0226506916 (pbk.: alk paper) Notes: Includes bibliographical references (p. 379-408) and index. Subjects: Foote, G. W. (George William), 1850-1915 --Trials, litigation, etc. Hone, William, 1780-1842 --Trials, litigation, etc. English literature--History and criticism. Blasphemy in literature. Christianity and literature--England--Trials (Blasphemy)--Great Britain--Language and culture--England--Freethinkers--Great Britain--Atheism--Great Britain--History--19th century. English language--19th century--Euphemism. LC Classification: PR468.B55 M37 1998 Dewey Class No.: 820.9/353 21

Martin, Lloyd, 1957- One faith, two peoples: communicating across cultures within the church / by Lloyd Martin. Published/Created: Paraparaumu Beach, N.Z.: Salt Co. Publishers, 1991. Description: 110 p.; 21 cm. ISBN: 0473014254 Notes: Includes bibliographical references (p. 109-110). Subjects: Christianity and culture. Intercultural communication--New Zealand. Maori (New Zealand people)--Religion. Maori (New Zealand people)--Missions. Sociology, Christian--New Zealand. LC Classification: BR115.C8 M244 1991 Dewey Class No.: 261.8/348994 20

Martung upah: black and white Australians seeking partnership / edited by Anne Pattel-Gray. Published/Created: Blackburn, Vic.: Harper Collins Religious, 1996. Related Authors: Pattel-Gray, Anne. Australian Council of Churches. Aboriginal & Islander Commission. Martung Upah Indigenous Conference: A Just and Proper Settlement (1993: University of Sydney) Description: ix, 340 p.; 21 cm. ISBN: 186371684X Notes: Papers, resolutions, and recommendations of the Martung Upah Indigenous Conference: A Just and Proper Settlement, held at the University of Sydney, Dec. 5-11, 1993, sponsored by the Aboriginal & Islander Commission of the Australian Council of Churches. Includes bibliographical references. Subjects: Australian aborigines--Social conditions--ivil rights--Congresses. Race--Religious aspects--Christianity--Christianity and culture--Australia--Race relations--Congresses. LC Classification: GN666 .M34 1996 Dewey Class No.: 305.89/915 21

Marvels, monsters, and miracles: studies in the medieval and early modern imaginations / edited by Timothy S. Jones and David A.. Sprunger. Published/Created: Kalamazoo, Mich.: Medieval Institute Publications, 2002. Related Authors: Jones, Timothy S. Sprunger, David A. Description: p. cm. ISBN: 1580440657 (casebound: alk. paper) 1580440665 (paperbound: alk. paper) Notes: Includes bibliographical references and index. Subjects: Popular culture--

Europe--Religious aspects--Christianity. Civilization, Medieval. Animals, Mythical. Miracles--History of doctrines--Middle Ages, 600-1500. Monsters. Series: Studies in medieval culture LC Classification: GR825 .M218 2002 Dewey Class No.: 809/.02 21

Masculinity and spirituality in Victorian culture / edited by Andrew Bradstock ... [et al.]. Published/Created: New York: St. Martin's Press, 2000. Related Authors: Bradstock, Andrew. Description: xi, 232 p.: ill.; 23 cm. ISBN: 0312235615 (hardcover) Notes: Includes bibliographical references and index. Subjects: English literature--19th century--History and criticism. Christianity and literature--Great Britain--History--19th century. Spirituality--Great Britain--History--19th century. Religion and literature--History--19th century. Men--Great Britain--Religious life. Spirituality in literature. Masculinity in literature. Men in literature. Great Britain--Religion--19th century. LC Classification: PR468.R44 M37 2000 Dewey Class No.: 820.9/352041 21

Massa, Mark Stephen. Catholics and American culture: Fulton Sheen, Dorothy Day, and the Notre Dame football team / Mark S. Massa. Published/Created: New York: Crossroad Pub. Co., c1999. Description: x, 278 p.; 24 cm. ISBN: 0824515374 (hardcover) Notes: Includes bibliographical references (p. 233-269) and index. Subjects: Catholic Church--United States--History--20th century. Catholics--United States--History--20th century. Christianity and culture--United States--History--20th century. LC Classification: BX1406.2 .M38 1999 Dewey Class No.: 305.6/2073 21

Massey, Lesly F., 1946- Women and the New Testament: an analysis of Scripture in light of New Testament era culture / by Lesly F. Massey. Published/Created: Jefferson, N.C.: McFarland & Co., c1989. Description: 152 p.; 24 cm. ISBN: 0899504388 (lib. bdg.: alk. paper) : Notes: Includes index. Bibliography: p. 137-150. Subjects: Jesus Christ--Views on women.

Bible. N.T.--Criticism, interpretation, etc. Women--Biblical teaching. Women in Christianity--History--Early church, ca. 30-600. LC Classification: BS2545.W65 M37 1989 Dewey Class No.: 225.8/3054 20

Maxwell, David (David James) Christians and chiefs in Zimbabwe: a social history of the Hwesa people / David Maxwell. Published/Created: Westport, Conn.: Praeger, 1999. Description: x, 291 p.: ill., maps; 24 cm. ISBN: 0275966267 (alk. paper) Notes: Includes bibliographical references (p. [267]-284) and index. Subjects: Hwesa (African people)--Religion. Christianity and culture--Zimbabwe--Hwesaland--History. Hwesaland (Zimbabwe)--Kings and rulers--Religious aspects. Hwesaland (Zimbabwe)--Church history. LC Classification: BR1367.H94 M39 1999 Dewey Class No.: 276.891 21

Mayers, Marvin Keene, 1927- Christianity confronts culture: a strategy for crosscultural evangelism / Marvin K. Mayers. Edition Information: Rev. and enl. ed. Published/Created: Grand Rapids, Mich.: Academie Books, c1987. Description: xiv, 418 p.: ill.; 21 cm. ISBN: 0310289017 (pbk.) Notes: "Zondervan publication"--Cover p. [4] Includes index. Bibliography: p. 399-411. Subjects: Missions--Theory. Intercultural communication. Christianity and culture. Evangelistic work. LC Classification: BV2063 .M38 1987 Dewey Class No.: 266 19

Mayers, Marvin Keene, 1927- Christianity confronts culture; a strategy for cross-cultural evangelism [by] Marvin K. Mayers. Published/Created: Grand Rapids, Zondervan Pub. House [1974] Description: 384 p. illus. 22 cm. Notes: Bibliography: p. 366-380. Subjects: Missions--Theory. Intercultural communication. Christianity and culture. Evangelistic work. LC Classification: BR115.C8 M25 Dewey Class No.: 301.1/02/42

Mbachu, Hilary. Inculturation theology of the Jerusalem Council in Acts 15: an inspiration for the Igbo Church today / Mbachu Hilary. Published/Created: Frankfurt am Main; New York: P. Lang, c1995. Description: 423 p.: maps; 22 cm. ISBN: 3631480059 Notes: Includes bibliographical references (p. 379-418). Subjects: Catholic Church--Missions--Nigeria--History. Council of Jerusalem (ca. 50) Bible. N.T. Acts XV--Criticism, interpretation, etc. Igbo (African people)--Religious life. Christianity and culture--History. Nigeria--Church history--20th century. Series: Europäische Hochschulschriften. Reihe XXIII, Theologie; Bd. 520. LC Classification: BS2625.2 .H55 1995 Dewey Class No.: 282/.089/96332 20

Mbanda, Laurent. Committed to conflict: the destruction of the church in Rwanda / Laurent Mbanda assisted by Steve Wamberg. Published/Created: London: SPCK, 1997. Description: x, 147 p.; 22 cm. ISBN: 0281050163 Notes: Includes bibliographical references and index. Subjects: Missions--Rwanda. Church--Credibility. Christianity and culture. Rwanda--Church history--19th century--20th century. Rwanda--Genocide--Ethnic relations. Local Call/Shelving: BR1443.R95 M32 1997

Mbefo, Luke Nnamdi. Theology and aspects of Igbo culture / Luke Nnamdi Mbefo. Published/Created: Onitsha, Nigeria: Spiritan Publications, c1997. Description: xiii, 86 p.; 23 cm. ISBN: 9782919578 Notes: Includes index. Subjects: Igbo (African people) Igbo (African people)--Religion. Christianity and culture--Nigeria.

Mbefo, Luke Nnamdi. Towards a mature African Christianity / Luke Nnamdi Mbefo. Published/Created: Enugu: Spiritan Publications, c1989. Description: 122 p.; 18 cm. Notes: Includes bibliographical references. Subjects: Catholic Church--Nigeria. Christianity--Africa, Sub-Saharan. Christianity and culture. Nigeria--Church history--20th century. LC Classification: BR1430 .M37 1989

McAlpine, Thomas H. By word, work, and wonder: cases in holistic mission / Thomas H. McAlpine. Published/Created: Monrovia, Calif.: MARC, c1995. Description: v, 151 p.: ill.; 23 cm. ISBN: 0912552921 (pbk.) Notes: Includes bibliographical references (p. 148-151). Subjects: Missions--Theory. Christianity and culture. Social structure--Religious aspects--Christianity. LC Classification: BV2061 .M34 1995 Dewey Class No.: 266/.001 21

McCullough, Donald W., 1949- Waking from the American dream: growing through your disappointments / Donald W. McCullough. Published/Created: Downers Grove, Ill.: InterVarsity Press, c1988. Description: 210 p.; 21 cm. ISBN: 0830817026 Notes: Bibliography: p. [205]-210. Subjects: Christian life. Christianity and culture. LC Classification: BV4501.2 .M43538 1988 Dewey Class No.: 261 19

McDannell, Colleen. Material Christianity: religion and popular culture in America / Colleen McDannell. Published/Created: New Haven: Yale University Press, 1995. Description: x, 312 p.: ill. (some col.); 27 cm. ISBN: 0300064403 Notes: Includes bibliographical references (p. [277]-305) and index. Subjects: Religious articles--United States. Christianity--United States. United States--Religious life and customs. LC Classification: BR515 .M35 1995 Dewey Class No.: 246/.0973 20

McDowell, Josh. The new tolerance: how a cultural movement threatens to destroy you, your faith, and your children / Josh McDowell and Bob Hostetler. Published/Created: Wheaton, Ill.: Tyndale House, c1998. Related Authors: Hostetler, Bob, 1958- Description: ix, 233 p.; 21 cm. ISBN: 0842370889 Notes: Includes bibliographical references (p. 225-226) and index. Subjects: Religious tolerance--Christianity. Relativity. Christianity and culture--United States. Child rearing--Religious aspects--Christianity. LC Classification: BR517 .M38 1998 Dewey Class No.: 261 21

McGavran, Donald Anderson, 1897- The clash between Christianity and cultures / Donald McGavran. Published/Created: Washington: Canon Press, [1974] Description: 84 p.; 22 cm. ISBN: 0913686123 Notes: Includes bibliographical references. Subjects: Christianity and culture. LC Classification: BR115.C8 M22 Dewey Class No.: 261.1

McGinness, Frederick J., 1944- Right thinking and sacred oratory in Counter-Reformation Rome / Frederick J. McGinness. Published/Created: Princeton, N.J.: Princeton University Press, c1995. Description: xii, 337 p.: ill.; 24 cm. ISBN: 0691034265 (alk. paper) Notes: Includes bibliographical references (p. [321]- 324) and index. Subjects: Preaching--Italy--Rome--History--16th century. Counter-Reformation--Italy--Rome. Rhetoric. Christianity and culture. Rome (Italy)--Church history--16th century. LC Classification: BV4208.I8 M35 1995 Dewey Class No.: 282/.45632/09031 20

McGregor, Donald E. The fish and the cross: a description and interpretation of a fish festival held at Teloute village, Papua New Guinea, through which the Wape participants of the Lumi area are discovered as people, with a discussion of problems met in bringing Christianity to these people / Donald E. McGregor. Edition Information: 2nd ed. / rev. by Oswald G. Fountain. Published/Created: Goroka, E.H.P., Papua New Guinea: Melanesian Institute, c1982. Related Authors: Fountain, Oswald G. Description: xi, 139 p.: ill.; 20 cm. Notes: Bibliography: p. 135-139. Subjects: Missions to Wape (Papua New Guinea people) Festivals--Papua New Guinea--Sandaun Province. Christianity and culture. Sandaun Province (Papua New Guinea)--Social life and customs. LC Classification: BV3680.N5 M34 1982

McIntosh, John A. Primary documents in Reformation theology for Batak theological students [microform]: a class syllabus / by John A. McIntosh. Published/Created: 1993. Description: xiii,

350 leaves; 28 cm. Notes: Thesis (D. Miss.)--Trinity Evangelical Divinity School, 1994. Microfiche. Portland, Or.: Theological Research Exchange Network, 1994. 1 microfiche: negative. High reduction. Subjects: Theology--Study and teaching--Sumatra (Indonesia) Reformation--Study and teaching. Batak (Indonesian people)--Religion. Christianity and culture. LC Classification: Microfiche 97/248 (B)

McKay, Stan. The first nations: a Canadian experience of the gospel-culture encounter / Stan McKay and Janet Silman. Published/Created: Geneva: WCC Publications, c1995. Description: x, 53 p.; 21 cm. ISBN: 2825411760 Subjects: Indians of North America--Canada-- Religion. Indians of North America-- Missions--Indians, Treatment of--Canada. Fur trade--Canada--History. Christianity and culture--Canada--Ethnic relations. Series: Gospel and cultures pamphlet; 2 LC Classification: E78.C2 M2145 1995 Dewey Class No.: 261/.089/97071 20

McKenzie, John L. The civilization of Christianity / John L. McKenzie. Published/Created: Chicago, Ill.: T. More Press, c1986. Description: 260 p.; 22 cm. ISBN: 0883471809 : Notes: Bibliography: p. 259-260. Subjects: Christianity and culture. LC Classification: BR115.C8 M265 1986 Dewey Class No.: 270.8/2 19

McLean, George F. Faith, reason, and philosophy: lectures at the al-azhar, Qum, Tehran, Lahore, and Beijing / George F. McLean. Published/Created: Washington, D.C.: Council for Research in Values and Philosophy, 2000. Description: 260 p.; 23 cm. ISBN: 1565181301 (alk. paper) Notes: "Appendix: the encyclical letter: Fides et ration."--P. [155]-244. Includes bibliographical references and index. Subjects: Faith and reason--Christianity-- Islam. Series: Cultural heritage and contemporary change. Series I, Culture and values; vol. 20 Cultural heritage and contemporary change. Series IIA, Islam; vol. 7 LC Classification: BT50 .M345

2000 Dewey Class No.: 210 21

McLean, George F. Religion and cooperation between civilizations: Islamic and Christian cultures in a global horizon / George F. McLean. Published/Created: Washington, D.C.: Council for Research in Values and Philosophy, c2000. Description: 198 p.; 23 cm. ISBN: 1565181522 (alk. paper) Notes: Includes bibliographical references and index. Subjects: Christianity and culture. Islamic countries--Civilization. Christianity and other religions--Islam--Relations-- Christianity. Series: Cultural heritage and contemporary change. Series I, Culture and values; vol. 21 Cultural heritage and contemporary change. Series IIA, Islam; vol. 12 LC Classification: BR115.C8 .M266 2000 Dewey Class No.: 291.1/7 21

McShane, Philip. Lonergan's challenge to the university and the economy / Philip McShane. Published/Created: Washington: University Press of America, c1980. Description: ix, 203 p.: ill.; 22 cm. ISBN: 0819109339: 0819109347 (pbk.) : Subjects: Lonergan, Bernard J. F. Humanities. Christianity and culture. LC Classification: BX4705.L7133 M32 Dewey Class No.: 909.82

McTighe, Michael J., 1948- A measure of success: Protestants and public culture in antebellum Cleveland / Michael J. McTighe. Published/Created: Albany: State University of New York Press, c1994. Description: xii, 283 p.: ill.; 24 cm. ISBN: 0791418251 (alk. paper) 079141826X (pbk.: alk. paper) Notes: Revision of thesis (Ph. D.--University of Chicago, 1983) originally presented under Embattled establishment. Includes bibliographical references (p. [233]-275) snd index. Subjects: Christianity and culture--History--19th century. Protestant churches--Ohio--History--19th century. Cleveland (Ohio)--Church history--19th century. Ohio--Church history--19th century. LC Classification: BR560.C57 M38 1994 Dewey Class No.: 280/.4/097713209034 20

Media, culture, and Catholicism / Paul A.
    Soukup, editor. Published/Created: Kansas
    City, MO: Sheed & Ward, c1996. Related
    Authors: Soukup, Paul A. Description:
    xviii, 220 p.: ill.; 24 cm. ISBN:
    1556127693 (alk. paper) Notes: Includes
    bibliographical references (p. 201-210) and
    index. Subjects: Catholic Church--United
    States. Mass media in religion--United
    States. Mass media--Religious aspects--
    Catholic Church. Christianity and culture--
    United States. Series: Communication,
    culture & theology LC Classification:
    BV652.97.U6 M43 1996 Dewey Class
    No.: 261.5/2/08822 20

Media, culture, and the religious right / Linda
    Kintz and Julia Lesage, editors.
    Published/Created: Minneapolis:
    University of Minnesota Press, c1998.
    Related Authors: Kintz, Linda, 1945-
    Lesage, Julia. Description: xviii, 380 p.; 24
    cm. ISBN: 0816630844 (hardcover: alk.
    paper) 0816630852 (pbk.: alk. paper)
    Notes: Includes bibliographical references
    and index. Subjects: Evangelicalism--
    United States. Christianity and culture--
    United States. Mass media--Religious
    aspects--Christianity. Conservatism--
    Religious aspects--Christianity. LC
    Classification: BR1642.U5 M43 1998
    Dewey Class No.: 261/.0973 21

Medieval encounters: Jewish, Christian, and
    Muslim culture in confluence and dialogue.
    Published/Created: Leiden; New York: E.J.
    Brill, c1995- Description: v.: ill.; 24 cm.
    Vol. 1, no. 1 (June 1995)- Current
    Frequency: Three times a year ISSN: 1380-
    7854 Notes: Title from cover. Chiefly
    English, with some French, German, and
    Latin; summaries in English.
    SERBIB/SERLOC merged record
    Subjects: Civilization, Medieval--
    Periodicals. Christianity and other
    religions--Periodicals. Islam--Relations--
    Periodicals. Judaism--Relations--
    Periodicals. LC Classification: CB351
    .M3923 CB351 .M43 Dewey Class No.:
    909.07/05 21

Meek, Donald E. The Scottish Highlands: the
    churches and Gaelic culture / Donald E.

Meek. Published/Created: Geneva,
    Switzerland: WCC Publications, c1996.
    Related Authors: World Council of
    Churches. Description: viii, 69 p.: map; 21
    cm. ISBN: 282541204X Notes: Booklet is
    based on a series of talks and articles
    written mostly since 1985. Includes
    bibliographical references (p. 68-69).
    Subjects: Christianity and culture.
    Christianity--Scotland--Highlands.
    Highlands (Scotland)--Church history.
    Series: Gospel and cultures pamphlet; 11
    LC Classification: BR782 .M66 1996
    Dewey Class No.: 274.11/5 21

Meilaender, Gilbert, 1946- Things that count:
    essays moral and theological / Gilbert
    Meilaender. Published/Created:
    Wilmington, Del.: ISI Books, 2000.
    Description: 393 p.; 24 cm. ISBN:
    1882926366 Notes: Includes
    bibliographical (p. [359]-371) and index.
    Subjects: Christianity and culture.
    Christian ethics. LC Classification:
    BR115.C8 M275 2000 Dewey Class No.:
    261 21

Melling, Philip H. Fundamentalism in America:
    millennialism, identity, and militant
    religion / Philip Melling.
    Published/Created: Edinburgh: Edinburgh
    University Press, c1999. Description: xiv,
    223 p.; 24 cm. ISBN: 0748609784 (pbk.)
    0748609776 Notes: Includes
    bibliographical references (p. [196]-208)
    and index. Subjects: Fundamentalism--
    United States. Religious fundamentalism--
    United States. Christianity and culture--
    United States. Religion in literature. United
    States--Church history. Series: Tendencies
    LC Classification: BT82.2 Dewey Class
    No.: 270.820973 21

Men's bodies, men's gods: male identities in a
    (post-) Christian culture / edited by Björn
    Krondorfer. Published/Created: New York:
    New York University Press, c1996.
    Related Authors: Krondorfer, Björn.
    Description: xviii, 324 p.: ill.; 24 cm.
    ISBN: 0814746683 (acid-free paper)
    0814746691 (pbk.: acid-free paper) Notes:
    Includes bibliographical references and
    index. Subjects: Men (Christian theology)

Body, Human--Religious aspects--
Christianity. Men (Christian theology)--
History of doctrines. Body, Human--
Religious aspects--Christianity--History of
doctrines. LC Classification: BT703.5
.M46 1996 Dewey Class No.: 233/.5/081
20

Mercado, Leonardo N. Christ in the Philippines
/ Leonardo N. Mercado.
Published/Created: Tacloban City,
Philippines: Divine Word University,
1982. Description: x, 118 p.; 23 cm. ISBN:
9711060175 Notes: Includes index.
Bibliography: p. [95]-105. Subjects: Jesus
Christ--History of doctrines--19th century.
Jesus Christ--History of doctrines--20th
century. Catholic Church--Doctrines.
Christian sects--Philippines. Christianity
and culture. Philippines--Church history--
19th century. Philippines--Church history--
20th century. LC Classification: BT198
.M417 1982 Dewey Class No.: 232/.09599
19

Mercado, Leonardo N. Inculturation and
Filipino theology / Leonardo N. Mercado.
Published/Created: Manila: Divine Word
Publications, c1992. Description: xi, 164
p.: ill.; 22 cm. ISBN: 9715100562 Notes:
Includes bibliographical references and
index. Subjects: Catholic Church--
Doctrines. Catholic Church--Philippines.
Christianity and culture. Philippines--
Religion. Series: Asia Pacific missiological
series; no. 2 LC Classification: BX1751.2
.M447 1992 Dewey Class No.: 230/.2599
20

Merrill, Dean. Sinners in the hands of an angry
church: finding a better way to influence
our culture / Dean Merrill.
Published/Created: Grand Rapids, Mich.:
Zondervan, c1997. Description: 183 p.: ill.;
20 cm. ISBN: 0310213088 (pbk.) Notes:
Includes bibliographical references (p.
177-183). Subjects: Christianity and
culture--United States--History--20th
century. Christianity and politics--United
States--History--20th century.
Communication--Religious aspects--
Christianity. Evangelicalism--United
States--History--20th century. United

States--Church history--20th century.
United States--Moral conditions. LC
Classification: BR526 .M47 1997 Dewey
Class No.: 261/.0973 21

Message of the Special Assembly of the Synod
of Bishops for Africa. Published/Created:
[S.l.: s.n., 1994 or 1995] Description: 26
p.; 23 cm. Notes: Cover title. Subjects:
Catholic Church--Missions--Africa--
Pastoral letters and charges--Bishops--
Relations. Christianity and culture.
Evangelistic work--Africa. Ministry and
Christian union. LC Classification: IN
PROCESS

Metuh, Emefie Ikenga. African inculturation
theology: Africanizing Christianity / E.
Ikenga-Metuh (ed.). Onitsha [Nigeria]:
Imico Books, 1996. Related Authors:
Uzukwu, E. Elochukwu. Description: xii,
187 p.; 21 cm. Notes: Written by Emefie
Ikenga Metuh, with 2 chapters by E.
Uzukwu. Includes bibliographical
references and index. Subjects: Christianity
and culture--Theology, Doctrinal--Africa.
Christianity and other religions--African.
LC Classification: BR115.C8 M295 1996
Dewey Class No.: 230/.096 21

Mielke, Arthur J. Christians, feminists, and the
culture of pornography / Arthur J. Mielke.
Published/Created: Lanham, MD:
University Press of America, c1995.
Description: xv, 137 p.; 23 cm. ISBN:
0819197645 (cloth: alk. paper)
0819197653 (pbk.) Notes: Includes
bibliographical references (p. 101-119) and
index. Subjects: Pornography--Social
aspects. Pornography--Religious aspects--
Christianity. Feminism. LC Classification:
HQ471 .M63 1995 Dewey Class No.:
363.4/7 20

Milbank, John. The word made strange:
theology, language, culture / John Milbank.
Published/Created: Cambridge, MA:
Blackwell Publishers, 1997 (1999 printing)
Description: viii, 298 p.; 23 cm. ISBN:
0631203354 (alk. paper) 0631203362
(pbk.: alk. paper) Notes: Includes index.
Subjects: Theology, Doctrinal. Language
and languages--Religious aspects--

Christianity. Christianity and culture. LC Classification: BT80 .M53 1997 Dewey Class No.: 230 20

Miles, Margaret Ruth. Image as insight: visual understanding in Western Christianity and secular culture / Margaret R. Miles. Published/Created: Boston: Beacon Press, c1985. Description: xiii, 200 p., [16] p. of plates: ill.; 26 cm. ISBN: 0807010065 : Notes: Includes index. Bibliography: p. 193-196. Subjects: Christian art and symbolism. Art--Language. Visual communication. Visual perception. LC Classification: BV150 .M47 1985 Dewey Class No.: 246 19

Miller, Haskell M., 1910- A Christian critique of culture. Published/Created: New York, Published for the Cooperative Association by Abingdon Press [1965] Description: 96 p. Subjects: Christianity--20th century. Culture. LC Classification: BR115.C8 M5

Mills, Kenneth (Kenneth R.) An evil lost to view?: an investigation of post-evangelisation Andean religion in mid-colonial Peru / Kenneth Mills. Published/Created: Liverpool: University of Liverpool, Institute of Latin American Studies, 1994. Related Authors: University of Liverpool. Institute of Latin American Studies. Description: 147 p.: map; 21 cm. ISBN: 0902806297 Notes: Includes bibliographical references (p. 131-147). Subjects: Jesuits--Missions--Peru--Cajatambo (Province)--History. Indians of South America--Peru--Cajatambo (Province) History--17th century--Government relations. Fasts and feasts--Peru--Cajatambo (Province)--History. Christianity and culture--Peru--Cajatambo (Province) Cajatambo (Peru: Province)--History--17th century. Series: Monograph series (University of Liverpool. Institute of Latin American Studies); no. 18. LC Classification: F3429.1.C344 M55 1994 Dewey Class No.: 985/.1500498 20

Mills, Kenneth (Kenneth R.) Idolatry and its enemies: colonial Andean religion and extirpation, 1640-1750 / Kenneth Mills. Published/Created: Princeton, N.J.:

Princeton University Press, c1997. Description: xiii, 337 p.: ill., map; 25 cm. ISBN: 0691029792 (cl: alk. paper) Notes: Includes bibliographical references (p. [295]-326) and index. Subjects: Catholic Church--Missions--Peru--Lima Region--History. Archdiocese of Lima (Peru)--History. Quechua Indians--Religion--Missions--Peru--Lima Region. Christianity and other religions--Christianity and culture--Peru--Lima Region. Spain--Colonies--America--Administration. LC Classification: F2230.2.K4 M56 1997 Dewey Class No.: 200/.985/09032 20

Minahane, John. The Christian druids: on the filid or philosopher-poets of Ireland / John Minahane. Published/Created: Dublin: Sanas Press, c1993. Description: 245 p.; 21 cm. ISBN: 095225820X Notes: Include bibliographical references (p. 232-245). Text in English with some Irish translations. Subjects: Christian poetry, Irish--History and criticism. Christianity and literature--Ireland. Civilization, Celtic, in literature. Language and culture--Ireland. Druids and druidism. Celts--Religion. LC Classification: PB1333 .M56 1993 Dewey Class No.: 891.6/21009382 21

Ministry and theology in global perspective: contemporary challenges for the church / edited by Don A. Pittman, Ruben L.F. Habito, and Terry C. Muck. Published/Created: Grand Rapids, Mich.: Eerdmans, c1996. Related Authors: Pittman, Don Alvin, 1948- Habito, Ruben L. F., 1947- Muck, Terry C., 1947- Description: xvii, 524 p.; 23 cm. ISBN: 0802808441 (pbk.: alk. paper) Notes: Includes bibliographical references and indexes. Subjects: Christianity and other religions. Missions--Theory. Religion and culture. LC Classification: BR127 .M56 1996 Dewey Class No.: 261 20

Minnery, Tom. Why you can't stay silent: a biblical mandate to shape our culture / by Tom Minnery. Published/Created: Wheaton, Ill.: Tyndale House, 2001. Description: p. cm. ISBN: 1561799254 Partial Contents: When you can't stay silent

-- Christians have always done something -- Shouldn't we keep away from controversy? -- There's more to Christianity than saving souls -- Why it's right to do what's right. Notes: Includes bibliographical references and index. Subjects: Church and the world. LC Classification: BR115.W6 M453 2001 Dewey Class No.: 261/.0973 21

Miranda-Feliciano, Evelyn. Filipino values and our Christian faith / Evelyn Miranda-Feliciano. Published/Created: Denver, Colo.: iAcademic Books, 2001. Description: p. cm. ISBN: 1588680851 (pbk.) Notes: Originally published: Manila: OMF Literature, 1990. Includes bibliographical references and indexes. Subjects: Christianity--Philippines. Christian life--Philippines. Christianity and culture--Philippines. Philippines--Religious life and customs. LC Classification: BR1260 .M57 2001 Dewey Class No.: 275.99 21

Miranda-Feliciano, Evelyn. Filipino values and our Christian faith / Evelyn Miranda-Feliciano. Published/Created: Manila: OMF Literature, 1990. Description: 126 p.: ill.; 21 cm. ISBN: 9715111726 Notes: Includes bibliographical references and indexes. Subjects: Christianity--Philippines. Christian life--Philippines. Christianity and culture--Philippines. Philippines--Religious life and customs. LC Classification: BR1260. .M56 1990

Missiology and the social sciences: contributions, cautions, and conclusions / Edward Rommen and Gary Corwin, editors. Published/Created: Pasadena, Calif.: William Carey Library, c1996. Related Authors: Rommen, Edward, 1947- Corwin, Gary, 1948- Description: 223 p.: ill.; 22 cm. ISBN: 0878083782 (alk. paper) Notes: Includes bibliographical references. Subjects: Missions--Theory. Christianity and culture. Religion and the social sciences. Series: Evangelical Missiological Society series; no. 4 LC Classification: BV2063 .M55 1996 Dewey Class No.: 266/.001/5 20

Mission in a pluralist world / Aasulv Lande, Werner Ustorf (eds.). Published/Created: New York: P. Lang, c1996. Related Authors: Lande, Aasulv. Ustorf, Werner, 1945- Description: 193 p.; 21 cm. ISBN: 0820429732 (US) Notes: Major contributions from a conference held June 18-23, 1994, at Selly Oak Colleges, Birmingham, England. Includes bibliographical references. Subjects: Missions--Theory--Congresses. Christianity and culture--Congresses. Christianity and other religions--Congresses. Pluralism (Social sciences)--Congresses. Religious pluralism--Christianity--Congresses. Series: Studien zur interkulturellen Geschichte des Christentums; Bd. 97. LC Classification: BV2063 .M5617 1996 Dewey Class No.: 266/.001 20

Mitchell, William, 1932- Building strong families: how your family can withstand the challenges of today's culture / William Mitchell and Michael A. Mitchell. Published/Created: Nashville, Tenn.: Broadman & Holman, c1997. Related Authors: Mitchell, Michael A. Description: vi, 230 p.: ill.; 23 cm. ISBN: 0805463704 (pbk.) Notes: Includes bibliographical references (p. 229-230). Subjects: Family--Religious life. Parenting--Religious aspects--Christianity. Child rearing--Religious aspects--Christianity. LC Classification: BV4526.2 .M49 1997 Dewey Class No.: 248.4 21

Molnar, Thomas Steven. The pagan temptation / by Thomas Molnar. Published/Created: Grand Rapids, Mich.: W.B. Eerdmans, c1987. Description: 201 p.; 22 cm. ISBN: 0802802621 (pbk.) Notes: Includes bibliographical references and index. Subjects: Christianity and culture. Civilization, Christian. Myth. Symbolism. Neopaganism. Occultism--Religious aspects--Christianity. Civilization, Modern--1950- LC Classification: BR115.C8 M64 1987 Dewey Class No.: 261.2 19

Moloney, Francis J. "A hard saying": the Gospel and culture / Francis J. Moloney.

Collegeville, Minn.: Liturgical Press, c2001. Description: xiv, 297 p.; 23 cm. ISBN: 0814659535 (alk. paper) Notes: " A Michael Glazier book." Includes bibliographical references and indexes. Subjects: Bible. N.T.--Bible. N.T. Gospels--Criticism, interpretation, etc. Christianity and culture. LC Classification: BS2361.3 .M65 2001 Dewey Class No.: 226/.06 21

Moltmann, Jürgen. On human dignity: political theology and ethics / Jürgen Moltmann; translated and with an introduction by M. Douglas Meeks. Published/Created: Philadelphia: Fortress Press, c1984. Description: xiv, 225 p.; 23 cm. ISBN: 0800607155 Notes: Includes bibliographical references and index. Subjects: Civil rights--Religious aspects--Christianity. Political theology. Religion and culture. Social ethics. Human rights--Religious aspects--Christianity. LC Classification: BT738.15 .M64 1984 Dewey Class No.: 261.7 19

Mommaers, Paul, 1935- Mysticism, Buddhist and Christian: encounters with Jan van Ruusbroec / Paul Mommaers & Jan van Bragt. Published/Created: New York: Crossroad, 1995. Related Authors: Bragt, Jan van. Description: v, 302 p.; 25 cm. ISBN: 0824514556 Notes: Includes bibliographical references and index. Subjects: Ruusbroec, Jan van, 1293-1381. Christianity and other religions--Buddhism. Mysticism--History--Middle Ages, 600-1500. Buddhism--Relations--Christianity. Mysticism--Buddhism. Series: Nanzan studies in religion and culture LC Classification: BV5095.J3 M63 1995 Dewey Class No.: 248.2/2 20

Montgomery-Fate, Tom. Beyond the white noise: mission in a multicultural world / Tom Montgomery-Fate. Published/Created: St. Louis, Mo.: Chalice Press, c1997. Description: xiii, 152 p.; 22 cm. ISBN: 0827202237 (pbk.) Notes: Includes bibliographical references. Subjects: Montgomery-Fate, Tom. Missionaries--Philippines--United States--Biography. Christianity and culture--Philippines. Multiculturalism--Religious

aspects--Christianity. Missions. LC Classification: BV3382.M66 A3 1997 Dewey Class No.: 266 21

Moore, Stephen D., 1954- God's gym: divine male bodies of the Bible / Stephen D. Moore. Published/Created: New York: Routledge, 1996. Description: xiii, 185 p.: ill.; 24 cm. ISBN: 0415917565 (hard) 0415917573 Notes: Includes bibliographical references (p. [141]-172) and index. Subjects: Jesus Christ--Crucifixion. Foucault, Michel--Influence. Bible. N.T.--Criticism, interpretation, etc.--Gay interpretations. Masculinity of God. Christianity and culture--History--20th century. Torture--Religious aspects--Christianity. Punishment--Body, Human--Bodybuilding--Religious aspects--Christianity. Atonement. LC Classification: BT153.F3 M66 1996 Dewey Class No.: 220.6 20

Moreland, James Porter, 1948- Love your God with all your mind: the role of reason in the life of the soul / J.P. Moreland; Dallas Willard, general editor. Published/Created: Colorado Springs, Colo.: NavPress, c1997. Related Authors: Willard, Dallas, 1935- Description: 249 p.; 22 cm. ISBN: 1576830160 (paper) Notes: Includes bibliographical references (p. 209-233). Subjects: Faith and reason--Christianity. Apologetics. Christianity and culture. Evangelicalism. United States--Intellectual life--20th century. LC Classification: BT50 .M62 1997 Dewey Class No.: 230/.01 21

Morgan, D. Densil. The span of the cross: Christian religion and society in Wales, 1914-2000 / D. Densil Morgan. Cardiff: University of Wales Press, 1999. Description: x, 310 p., [8] p. of plates; 23 cm. ISBN: 0708316166 0708315712 (pbk.) Notes: Includes bibliographical notes and index. Subjects: Christianity and culture--Wales--History--20th century--Church history--20th century. Wales--Religious life and customs--Social life and customs--20th century. LC Classification: BR776 .M59 1999 Dewey Class No.: 274.29/082 21

Morgan, Donn F. The making of sages: biblical wisdom and contemporary culture / Donn F. Morgan. Published/Created: Harrisburg, PA: Trinity Press International, 2002. Description: p. cm. ISBN: 1563383284 (alk. paper) Notes: Includes bibliographical references and index. Subjects: Wisdom literature--Criticism, interpretation, etc. Wisdom--Biblical teaching. Church and education. Wisdom--Religious aspects-- Christianity. LC Classification: BS1455 .M67 2002 Dewey Class No.: 223/.06 21

Morphologies of faith: essays in religion and culture in honor of Nathan A. Scott, Jr. / edited by Mary Gerhart, Anthony C. Yu. Published/Created: Atlanta, Ga.: Scholars Press, c1990. Related Authors: Scott, Nathan A. Gerhart, Mary. Yu, Anthony C., 1938- Description: xxix, 396 p.: ill.; 24 cm. ISBN: 1555405096 (alk. paper) 1555405347 (pbk.: alk. paper) Notes: Includes bibliographical references (p. [379]-388). Subjects: Theology. Christianity and literature. Series: AAR studies in religion; no. 59. LC Classification: BR50 .M657 1990 Dewey Class No.: 230 20

Mousalimas, S. A. The transition from Shamanism to Russian Orthodoxy in Alaska / by S.A. Mousalimas. Published/Created: Providence, RI: Berghahn Books, c1995. Description: viii, 254 p.: map; 23 cm. ISBN: 1571810064 Notes: Includes bibliographical references (p. [227]-249) and index. Subjects: Russkaia pravoslavnaia tserkov´-- Missions--Alaska. Orthodox Eastern Church--Missions--Alaska. Aleuts-- Missions. Aleuts--Religion. Pacific Gulf Yupik Eskimos--Missions--Religion. Indigenous peoples--Alaska--Religion. Christianity and other religions-- Shamanism. Shamanism--Relations-- Christianity. Shamanism--Alaska. Christianity and culture. Alaska--Church history. LC Classification: E99.A34 M68 1995 Dewey Class No.: 266/.19/089971 20

Mouw, Richard J. Consulting the faithful: what Christian intellectuals can learn from popular religion / Richard J. Mouw.

Published/Created: Grand Rapids, Mich.: Eerdmans, c1994. Description: vi, 84 p.; 23 cm. ISBN: 0802807380 (pbk.) Notes: Includes bibliographical references. Subjects: Popular culture--Religious aspects--Christianity. Christianity and culture. Laity. LC Classification: BR115.C8 M68 1994 Dewey Class No.: 270.82 20

Mouw, Richard J. When the kings come marching in: Isaiah and the new Jerusalem / Richard J. Mouw. Edition Information: Rev. ed. Published/Created: Grand Rapids, Mich.: W.B. Eerdmans Pub. Co., 2002. Description: p. cm. ISBN: 0802839967 (pbk.: alk. paper) Subjects: Bible. O.T. Isaiah LX--Criticism, interpretation, etc. Christianity and culture. LC Classification: BS1515.52 .M68 2002 Dewey Class No.: 224/.106 21

Mouw, Richard J. When the kings come marching in: Isaiah and the new Jerusalem / Richard J. Mouw. Published/Created: Grand Rapids, Mich: W.B. Eerdmans Pub. Co., c1983. Description: xvi, 77 p.; 21 cm. ISBN: 0802819354 (pbk.) 0802819672 (pbk.: cover) Subjects: Bible. O.T. Isaiah LX--Criticism, interpretation, etc. Christianity and culture. LC Classification: BS1515.2 .M68 1983 Dewey Class No.: 224/.106 19

Mueller, J. J. (John J.) Faith and appreciative awareness: the cultural theology of Bernard E. Meland / J.J. Mueller. Published/Created: Washington, D.C.: University Press of America, c1981. Description: xx, 146 p.; 22 cm. ISBN: 0819115606: 0819115614 (pbk.) : Notes: Bibliography: p. 139-146. Subjects: Meland, Bernard Eugene, 1899- Process theology--History--20th century. Christianity and culture--History--20th century. LC Classification: BT83.6 .M83 Dewey Class No.: 230/.044 19

Mueller, Walt, 1956- Understanding today's youth culture / Walt Mueller. Edition Information: Rev. & expanded Published/Created: Wheaton, Ill.: Tyndale House Publishers, c1999. Description: xiv,

461 p.; 23 cm. ISBN: 0842377395 (pbk.:
alk. paper) Notes: Includes bibliographical
references (p. 403-440) and index.
Subjects: Mass media and teenagers--
United States. Popular culture--Religious
aspects--Christianity. Parent and teenager--
Religious aspects. LC Classification:
HQ799.2.M35 M84 1999 Dewey Class
No.: 261.8/34235/0973 21

Mueller, Walt, 1956- Understanding today's
youth culture / Walt Mueller.
Published/Created: Wheaton, Ill.: Tyndale,
c1994. Description: xii, 392 p.; 23 cm.
ISBN: 0842377360 Notes: Includes
bibliographical references (p. 347-377) and
index. Subjects: Mass media and
teenagers--United States. Popular culture--
Religious aspects--Christianity. Parent and
teenager--Religious aspects. LC
Classification: HQ799.2.M35 M84 1994
Dewey Class No.: 261.8/34235/0973 20

Mugambi, J. N. Kanyua (Jesse Ndwiga
Kanyua) The biblical basis for
evangelization: theological reflections
based on an African experience / J.N.K.
Mugambi. Published/Created: Nairobi:
Oxford University Press, 1989.
Description: iv, 147 p.; 21 cm. ISBN:
0195727002 Notes: Includes
bibliographical references and index.
Subjects: Missions--Theory. Christianity
and culture. Missions--Africa, Sub-
Saharan. Missions--Biblical teaching.
Africa, Sub-Saharan--Church history. LC
Classification: BV2063 .M76 1989

Mughogho, Kelvin K. The impact of
Christianity on socio-cultural changes: a
case study on death and burial rituals
among the Tumbuka of Nkhamanga area /
Kelvin K. Mughogho. Published/Created:
Zomba [Malawi]: Chancellor College,
[1998] Description: 14 p.; 30 cm. Notes:
Caption title. "December 14, 1998." "A
dissertation presented to the Department of
Theology and Religious Studies in partial
fulfilment of the degree programme in
humanities (arts)." Includes bibliographical
references (p. 14). Subjects: Christianity
and culture--Malawi--Nankhwali.
Tumbuka (African people)--Funeral

customs and rites. Death--Religious
aspects. Nankhwali (Malawi)--Religious
life and customs. LC Classification:
BR115.C8 M76 1998

Mullins, Edgar Young, 1860-1928. Why is
Christianity true? Christian evidences, by
E. Y. Mullins. Published/Created: Chicago,
Christian culture press, 1905. Description:
xx,450 p. front. 20 cm. Notes:
Bibliography: p. 423-441. Subjects:
Christianity--Evidence. Apologetics. LC
Classification: BT1101 .M8

Mullins, Mark. Christianity made in Japan: a
study of indigenous movements / Mark R.
Mullins. Published/Created: Honolulu:
University of Hawai'i Press, c1998.
Description: x, 277 p.: ill.; 24 cm. ISBN:
0824821149 (alk. paper) 0824821327
(pbk.: alk. paper) Notes: Includes
bibliographical references (p. 261-265) and
index. Subjects: Christian sects--Japan.
Christianity and culture--Japan. Japan--
Church history. Series: Nanzan library of
Asian religion and culture LC
Classification: BR1307 .M85 1998 Dewey
Class No.: 275.2 21

Mulrain, George MacDonald, 1946- Theology
in folk culture: the theological significance
of Haitian folk religion / George
MacDonald Mulrain. Published/Created:
Frankfurt am Main; New York: P. Lang,
c1984. Description: 413 p.; 21 cm. ISBN:
3820474676 (pbk.) Notes: Bibliography: p.
391-407. Subjects: Haiti--Religion. Haiti--
Social life and customs. Series: Studien zur
interkulturellen Geschichte des
Christentums; Bd. 33. LC Classification:
BL2530.H3 M84 1984 Dewey Class No.:
299/.69 19

Murphy, J. Stanley (Joseph Stanley), ed.
Christianity and culture. With an introd. by
Donald McDonald. Published/Created:
Baltimore, Helicon Press, 1960 [i.e. 1961]
Description: 198 p. 23 cm. Notes: Includes
bibliography. Subjects: Christianity.
Culture. LC Classification: BR115.C8 M8
Dewey Class No.: 208.2

Muscular Christianity: embodying the Victorian Age / edited by Donald E. Hall. Published/Created: Cambridge [England]; New York: Cambridge University Press, 1994. Related Authors: Hall, Donald E. (Donald Eugene), 1960- Description: xiii, 244 p.; 24 cm. ISBN: 0521453186 Notes: Includes bibliographical references and index. Subjects: English prose literature--19th century--History and criticism. Masculinity in literature. Christianity and literature--Great Britain--History--19th century. Men in literature. Sex role in literature. Body, Human, in literature. Literature and society--Great Britain--History--19th century. Great Britain--Intellectual life--19th century. Series: Cambridge studies in nineteenth-century literature and culture; 2 LC Classification: PR788.M36 M87 1994 Dewey Class No.: 823/.809352041 20

Muzorewa, Gwinyai H. An African theology of mission / Gwinyai Henry Muzorewa. Published/Created: Lewiston, N.Y.: E. Mellen Press, c1990. Description: xvi, 204 p.: ill.; 24 cm. ISBN: 0889460736 Notes: Includes bibliographical references (p. 178-199) and index. Subjects: Missions--Africa, Sub-Saharan. Missions--Theory. Christianity and culture. Africa, Sub-Saharan--Church history. Series: Studies in the history of missions; v. 5. LC Classification: BV3520 .M89 1990 Dewey Class No.: 266/.00967 20

Myers, Ken. All God's children and blue suede shoes: Christians & popular culture / Kenneth A. Myers. Published/Created: Westchester, Ill.: Crossway Books, 1989. Description: 213 p.; 22 cm. ISBN: 0891075380 (pbk.) Subjects: Popular culture--Religious aspects--Christianity. Series: Turning point Christian worldview series LC Classification: BR115.C8 M93 1989 Dewey Class No.: 261 20

Nappa, Mike. Who moved my church?: a story about discovering purpose in a changing culture / by Mike Nappa; foreword by John C. Maxwell. Published/Created: Tulsa, Okla.: RiverOak Pub., c2001. Related Authors: Maxwell, John C., 1947-

Description: 125 p.: ill.; 22 cm. ISBN: 1589199901 Subjects: Christianity and culture. Christian life.

Nash, Kimberley. Joy / Kimberley Nash. Published/Created: Delano, Minn.: Resurrection Resources, c1996. Description: 104 p.; 21 cm. ISBN: 0965372308 Subjects: Halloween--United States. Christianity and culture--United States. Amusements--Religious aspects--Christianity. LC Classification: GT4965 .N37 1996 Dewey Class No.: 394.2646/0973 21

Ndiokwere, Nathaniel I. The African church, today and tomorrow / Nathaniel I. Ndiokwere. Published/Created: Onitsha, Nigeria: Effective Key Publishers, 1994. Description: 2 v.: ill., ports.; 22 cm. ISBN: 9782688096 (v. 1) 9782094897 (v. 2) Contents: v. 1. Prospects and challenges -- v. 2. Inculturation in practice. Notes: Vol. 2 has imprint: Enugu, Nigeria: Snaap Press. Includes bibliographical references and indexes. Subjects: Christianity--Africa. Religion and culture--Africa. Christianity and culture--Africa. LC Classification: BR1360 .N45 1994 Dewey Class No.: 276/.0829 20

Neckebrouck, V. Resistant peoples: the case of the pastoral Maasai of East Africa / Valeer Neckebrouck. Published/Created: Rome: Centre "Cultures and Religions"--Pontifical Gregorian University, 1993. Description: 85 p.; 24 cm. ISBN: 8876526633 Notes: Includes bibliographical references (p. 77-85). Subjects: Masai (African people)--Missions--Social conditions. Christianity and culture. Series: Inculturation; 14 LC Classification: DT433.545.M33 N43 1993

Neville, Gwen Kennedy, 1938- Kinship and pilgrimage: rituals of reunion in American Protestant culture / Gwen Kennedy Neville. Published/Created: New York: Oxford University Press, 1987. Description: vi, 162 p.: ill.; 22 cm. ISBN: 0195043383 (alk. paper) : Notes: Includes index. Bibliography: p. 149-156. Subjects: Reunions--Religious aspects--Christianity. Reunions--Christian pilgrims and pilgrimages--Southern States--Religious life and customs. LC Classification: BR517 .N48 1987 Dewey Class No.: 306/.6 19

New evangelization, human development, Christian culture: fourth General Conference of Latin American Bishops, October 12-28, 1992. Published/Created: London, UK: Catholic Fund for Overseas Development: Catholic Institute for International Relations, 1993. Related Authors: Catholic Church. Consejo Episcopal Latinoamericano. Description: 192 p.; 23 cm. ISBN: 1852871210 Notes: Cover Santo Domingo conclusions. Subjects: Evangelistic work--Congresses. Christianity and culture--Congresses. LC Classification: IN PROCESS (COPIED)

Newbigin, Lesslie. Foolishness to the Greeks: the Gospel and Western culture / by Lesslie Newbigin. Published/Created: Grand Rapids, Mich.: W.B. Eerdmans Pub. Co., c1986. Description: 156 p.; 21 cm. ISBN: 0802801765 (pbk.) : Notes: Expanded version of the Warfield Lectures given at Princeton Theological Seminary, March 1984. Includes index. Bibliography: p. 151-152. Subjects: Christianity and culture. Missions. LC Classification: BR115.C8 N467 1986 Dewey Class No.: 261 19

Newbigin, Lesslie. The Gospel in a pluralist society / Lesslie Newbigin. Published/Created: Grand Rapids, Mich.: W.B. Eerdmans; Geneva [SZ]: WCC Publications, 1989. Description: xi, 244 p.; 23 cm. ISBN: 0802804268 Subjects: Christianity and culture. Christianity--20th century. Apologetics. Missions--Theory. Evangelistic work--Philosophy. LC Classification: BR115.C8 N468 1989 Dewey Class No.: 261 20

Newbigin, Lesslie. The other side of 1984: questions for the churches / Lesslie Newbigin; with a postscript by S. Wesley Ariarajah. Published/Created: Geneva: World Council of Churches, c1983. Description: 75 p.; 21 cm. ISBN: 2825407844 (pbk.) Notes: Includes bibliographical references. Subjects:

Christianity and culture. Christianity--20th century. Series: The Risk book series; no. 18 LC Classification: BR115.C8 N47 1983 Dewey Class No.: 261.1 19

Newbigin, Lesslie. Truth and authority in modernity / Lesslie Newbigin. Published/Created: Valley Forge, Pa.: Trinity Press International, c1996. Description: ix, 85 p.; 19 cm. ISBN: 1563381680 (alk. paper) 0852443773 (Gracewing) Notes: "Revision and expansion of an essay published in Faith and modernity ... and in A word in season"--T.p. verso. Includes bibliographical references (p. 85). Subjects: Authority--Religious aspects-- Christianity. Truth (Christian theology) Mission of the church. Christianity and culture. Civilization, Modern--20th century. Postmodernism--Religious aspects--Christianity. Series: Christian mission and modern culture LC Classification: BT88 .N36 1996 Dewey Class No.: 231/.042 20

Nicholls, Kathleen D. Asian arts and Christian hope / Kathleen D. Nicholls. Published/Created: New Delhi: Select Books, 1983. Description: xviii, 189 p., [19] leaves of plates: ill.; 24 cm. Notes: Bibliography: p. [186]-189. Subjects: Arts, Indic. Christianity and culture. Arts, Indic-- Influence. LC Classification: NX576.A1 N52 1983 Dewey Class No.: 700/.954 19

Nichols, Aidan. Christendom awake: on re- energizing the church in culture / written by Aidan Nichols. Published/Created: Grand Rapids, Mich.: W.B. Eerdmans, 1999. Description: xiii, 255 p.; 24 cm. ISBN: 0802846904 (pbk.: alk. paper) Notes: Includes bibliographical references and index. Subjects: Catholic Church-- Doctrines. Christianity and culture. LC Classification: BR115.C8 N488 1999 Dewey Class No.: 230/.2 21

Nichols, Aidan. Scribe of the kingdom: essays on theology and culture / Aidan Nichols. Published/Created: London: Sheed & Ward, 1994- Description: v. <1; 23 cm. ISBN: 072207851X (v. 1): 0722078528 (v.

2) : Notes: Includes bibliographical references and index. Subjects: Catholic Church--Doctrines. Christianity and culture. LC Classification: BR115.C8 N49 1994

Niebuhr, H. Richard (Helmut Richard), 1894-1962. Christ and culture. Edition Information: [1st ed.] Published/Created: New York, Harper [1951] Description: x, 259 p. 22 cm. Notes: Bibliographical footnotes. Subjects: Culture. Christianity--20th century. LC Classification: BR115.C8 N5 Dewey Class No.: 261.6

Niebuhr, H. Richard (Helmut Richard), 1894-1962. Radical monotheism and western culture: with supplementary essays / H. Richard Niebuhr; foreword by James M. Gustafson. Published/Created: Louisville, Ky.: Westminster/John Knox Press, [1993] Description: 144 p.; 23 cm. ISBN: 0664253261 (alk. paper) Notes: Originally published: New York: Harper, 1960. Includes bibliographical references and index. Subjects: Theology, Doctrinal. Christian ethics--United Church of Christ authors. Monotheism. Civilization, Western. Christianity and culture. Religion and science. Series: Library of theological ethics LC Classification: BT78 .N495 1993 Dewey Class No.: 230 20

Nieman, James R., 1956- Preaching to every pew: cross-cultural strategies / James R. Nieman and Thomas G. Rogers. Published/Created: Minneapolis, MN: Fortress Press, c2001. Related Authors: Rogers, Thomas G., 1952- Description: ix, 159 p.; 23 cm. ISBN: 0800632435 (alk. paper) Notes: Includes bibliographical references (p. 158-159). Subjects: Preaching. Christianity and culture. LC Classification: BV4235.S6 N54 2001 Dewey Class No.: 251 21

Nigeria: people & culture / edited by 'Lai Olurode. Published/Created: Mushin, Lagos, Nigeria: Rebonik, 1999. Related Authors: Olurode, 'Lai. Description: 173 p.; 21 cm. Contents: Introduction / 'Lai Olurode -- The people of Nigeria / 'Lai Olurode -- Economic culture / Kehinde

Faluyi -- The impact of Christianity / Ayodeji Olukoju -- Influence of colonialism / O. Faseke -- Nigeria: elements of its political culture / Remi Anifowose -- Impact of military rule / O. Durowade -- Slum life in Nigeria (Lagos experience) / S.O. Kehinde. Notes: Includes bibliographical references and index. Subjects: Nigeria--Civilization. Nigeria--Social conditions. LC Classification: DT515.4 .N514 1999 Dewey Class No.: 966.9 21

Nigerian peoples and cultures / edited by Akinjide Osuntokun, Ayodeji Olukoju. Published/Created: Ibadan, Nigeria: Davidson Press, 1997. Related Authors: Osuntokun, Akinjide. Olukoju, Ayodeji. Description: ii, 365 p.; 22 cm. ISBN: 9783296434 Partial Contents: Nigeria: an ethno-historical survey / by Tunde Oduwobi and Obi Iwuagwu -- The evolution of Nigerian culture / by A.I. Asiwaju -- Political culture and urban development in Nigeria / by Akinjide Osuntokun -- Inter-group relations among Nigerian communities / by L.C. Dioka -- Forgotten aspects of Nigerian culture / by L.C. Dioka -- Islamic culture and Nigerian society / by T.G.O. Gbadamosi and M.O. Junaid -- Christianity and the development of the Nigerian state / by Ayodeji Olukoju -- Nigeria in the nineteenth century / by Kehinde Faluyi -- The economy and the state from the precolonial times to the present / by A.A. Lawal. Notes: Includes bibliographical references. Subjects: Ethnology--Nigeria. Nigeria--Civilization. Nigeria--History. LC Classification: DT515.42 .N53 1997

Nineham, D. E. (Dennis Eric), 1921- Christianity, mediaeval and modern: a study in religious change / Dennis Nineham. Published/Created: London: SCM Press Ltd., 1993. Description: x, 301 p., [8] p. of plates: ill.; 24 cm. ISBN: 033400182X Notes: Includes bibliographical references (p. [240]-248) and indexes. Subjects: Religion and culture--France--History--Medieval period, 987-1515. Religion and politics--France--History--Medieval period, 987-1515.

Franks--France--History. France--Church history--Middle Ages, 987-1515. Christianity History France LC Classification: IN PROCESS Dewey Class No.: 274.403 20

Nineteenth-century English religious traditions: retrospect and prospect / edited by D.G. Paz. Published/Created: Westport, Conn.: Greenwood Press, 1995. Related Authors: Paz, D. G. (Denis G.) Description: xiv, 232 p.; 25 cm. ISBN: 0313294763 (alk. paper) Notes: Includes bibliographical references (p. [221]-225) and index. Subjects: Christianity and culture--History--19th century. England--Church history--19th century. Series: Contributions to the study of religion, 0196-7053; no. 44 LC Classification: BR759 .N55 1995 Dewey Class No.: 274.1/081 20

Nobili, Roberto de', 1577-1656. Preaching wisdom to the wise: three treatises / by Roberto de Nobili, missionary and scholar in 17th century India. Published/Created: Saint Louis, MO: Institute of Jesuit Sources, c2000. Description: xxi, 345 p.; 23 cm. ISBN: 1880810379 Notes: Includes bibliographical references (p. 325-329) and index. Subjects: Nobili, Roberto de', 1577-1656. Jesuits--India--History--17th century. Catholic Church--India--History--17th century. Christianity and culture--India--History--17th century. Missions--India--History--17th century. India--Religious life and customs. India--Social life and customs. India--Church history--17th century. Series: Series I--Jesuit primary sources, in English translations; no. 19.

Nolan, Albert, 1934- God in South Africa: the challenge of the gospel / Albert Nolan. Published/Created: Cape Town: D. Philip; Grand Rapids, Mich.: W.B. Eerdmans, 1988. Description: xiii, 241 p.; 22 cm. ISBN: 0802804136 (U.S.) : Notes: Includes index. Bibliography: p. [230]-234. Subjects: Theology, Doctrinal--South Africa. Christianity and culture. LC Classification: BT30.S5 N65 1988 Dewey Class No.: 230/.0968 19

Noll, Mark A., 1946- The scandal of the evangelical mind / Mark A. Noll. Published/Created: Grand Rapids, Mich.: W.B. Eerdmans, 1994. Description: ix, 274 p.; 23 cm. ISBN: 0802837158 Notes: Includes bibliographical references and indexes. Subjects: Evangelicalism--United States. Christianity--United States--Forecasting. Christianity and culture. LC Classification: BR1642.U5 N65 1994 Dewey Class No.: 280/.4/0973 20

Noorbergen, Rene. The death cry of an eagle: the rise and fall of Christian values in the United States / Rene Noorbergen and Ralph W. Hood, Jr.; [ill. by Martha Bentley.] Published/Created: Grand Rapids, MI: Zondervan Pub. House, c1980. Related Authors: Hood, Ralph W., joint author. Description: 192 p.: ill.; 22 cm. ISBN: 0310304318 : Subjects: Christianity and culture. United States--Moral conditions. LC Classification: HN90.M6 N66 Dewey Class No.: 973 19

Norwegian contributions to American studies, dedicated to Sigmund Skard. Editor: Brita Seyersted. Editorial committee: Helge Normann Nilsen, Orm Øverland [and] Ingrid Semmingsen. Published/Created: Oslo, Universitetsforlaget [1973] Related Authors: Skard, Sigmund, 1903- Lindberg-Seyersted, Brita, ed. Description: xiii, 441 p. 24 cm. ISBN: 8200089363 Partial Contents: Tabula gratulatoria.--Haugen, E.L. and Semmingsen, I. Peder Anderson of Bergen and Lowell: artist and ambassador of culture.--Naess, H.S. Ygdrasil Literary Society, 1896-1971.--Elovson, H. August Strindberg and emigration to the United States, 1890-1912.--Bloch-Hoell, N. Norwegian ideas of American Christianity.--Smidt, K. T.S. Eliot, William Archer, and Henrik Ibsen.--Jacobsen, E. "Stationing" in Paradise lost and The scarlet letter.--Nilsen, H.N. Hawthorne's "My kinsman, Major Molineux": society and the individual.--Roppen, G. Melville's sea: shoreless, indefinite as God.--Reinert, O. Notes: Includes bibliographies. Subjects: Skard, Sigmund, 1903- American literature--History and criticism. United States--

Civilization. Series: Americana Norvegica, v. 4 Publications of the American Institute, University of Oslo LC Classification: PS121 .N64 Dewey Class No.: 810/.9/83982

Novalis, 1772-1801. Spiritual saturnalia; fragments of existence [by] Novalis. Translation and introd. by John N. Ritter. Edition Information: [1st ed.] Published/Created: New York, Exposition Press [1971] Description: 82 p. 21 cm. ISBN: 0682472468 Notes: Translation of the author's Die Christenheit oder Europa and translations of some of his notes. Subjects: Christianity and culture. LC Classification: BR115.C8 N6813 1971 Dewey Class No.: 261.1

Nwaigbo, Ferdinand. Mary--mother of the African Church: a theological inculturation of Mariology / Ferdinand Nwaigbo. Published/Created: Frankfurt am Main; New York: P. Lang, 2001. Description: 215 p. cm. ISBN: 0820453919 Notes: Includes bibliographical references. Subjects: Mary, Blessed Virgin, Saint--Theology. Catholic Church--Doctrines. Christianity and culture--Africa, Sub-Saharan. Series: Bamberger theologische Studien; Bd. 16 LC Classification: BT613 .N93 2001 Dewey Class No.: 232.91/096 21

Nygren, Anders, 1890- Agape and Eros. Translated by Philip S. Watson. New York, Harper & Row [1969] Description: 764 p. 21 cm. Contents: A study of the Christian idea of love.--The history of the Christian idea of love. Notes: Reprint of the 1953 ed. Translation of Den kristna kärlekstanken genom tiderna. Bibliographical footnotes. Subjects: Love--Religious aspects--Christianity. Agape. LC Classification: BV4639 .N813 1969 Dewey Class No.: 231/.6

Ó Murchú, Diarmuid. Our world in transition: making sense of a changing world / Diarmuid O'Murhcú. Published/Created: New York: Crossroad Pub. Co., 2000. Description: 160 p.; 21 cm. ISBN: 0824518624 Notes: Originally published:

Great Britain: Book Guild, 1992. Includes bibliographical references. Subjects: Christianity and culture. Social change. LC Classification: BR115.C8 O535 2000

Oates, Lynette Frances. Hidden people: how a remote New Guinea culture was brought back from the brink of extinction / Lynette Oates. Published/Created: Sutherland, NSW, Australia: Claremont CA, USA: Albatross Books, 1992 (1993 printing) Description: 352 p.: ill.; 20 cm. ISBN: 0732410142 Subjects: Bible--Translating. Binumarien (Papua New Guinea people)--Social conditions. Binumarien (Papua New Guinea people)--Religion. Christianity and culture--Papua New Guinea--Eastern Highlands Province--Social conditions. LC Classification: DU740.42 .O25 1992 Dewey Class No.: 306/.0899912 20

Obeng, J. Pashington. Asante Catholicism: religious and cultural reproduction among the Akan of Ghana / by Pashington Obeng. Published/Created: Leiden; New York: E.J. Brill, 1996. Description: xi, 243 p.: maps; 24 cm. ISBN: 9004106316 (alk. paper) Notes: Includes bibliographical references (p. [228]-233) and index. Subjects: Catholic Church--Ghana. Christianity and culture. Ashanti (African people)--Akan (African people)--Religion. Ghana--Church history. Series: Studies on religion in Africa, 0169-9814; 15 LC Classification: BX1682.G5 O24 1996 Dewey Class No.: 282/.089/963385 20

Obi, Obioma Des. Human suffering: a challenge to Christian faith in the Igbo/African Christian families (an anthropological and theological study) / Obioma Des. Obi. Published/Created: New York: P. Lang, c2001. Description: xvi, 235 p.: ill., maps; 23 cm. ISBN: 0820452327 (alk. paper) Notes: Includes bibliographical references (p. [227]-232) and index. Subjects: Suffering--Religious aspects--Christianity. Christianity and culture--Nigeria. Igbo (African people)--Religion. Series: Pastoral theology; vol. 2 LC Classification: BT732.7 .O64 2001 Dewey Class No.: 231/.8/08996332 21

O'Brien, Conor Cruise, 1917- On the eve of the millennium: the future of democracy through an age of unreason / Conor Cruise O'Brien. Edition Information: 1st. American ed. Published/Created: New York: Martin Kessler Books: Free Press, 1995. Description: 166 p.; 23 cm. ISBN: 002874098X (hard) 0028740947 (pbk.) Notes: Originally published: Don Mills, Ont.: House of Anansi, 1994, in Series: CBC Massey lecture series. Subjects: Catholic Church--Relations--Islam--Doctrines. Civilization, Modern--1950- Christianity and culture. Enlightenment. Democracy. Islam--Relations--Catholic Church. Sex--Religious aspects--Catholic Church. LC Classification: CB428 .O27 1995 Dewey Class No.: 303.49/09/05 20

O'Donnell, Michael (Michael Alan), 1956- The Oz syndrome: finding contentment in your family / Michael O'Donnell. Published/Created: Abilene, Tex.: HillCrest Publishing, c2001. Description: 222 p.; 22 cm. ISBN: 0891124802 Notes: Author uses Frank Baum's The wizard of Oz as a metaphor: "This marvelous odyssey of pop culture contains several deeply-rooted clues to help us learn how to fulfill our restless hearts and find contentment through trials like those Dorothy and her friends endured on their journey to the mythical land of Oz." -- Introduction. Subjects: Contentment--Religious aspects--Christianity. Family--Biblical teaching.

O'Donovan, Wilbur. Teaching theology from an African perspective [microform]: an evaluation of Introduction to biblical Christianity from an African perspective / by Wilbur O'Donovan, Jr. Published/Created: 1994. Related Authors: O'Donovan, Wilbur. Introduction to biblical Christianity from an African perspective. Description: x, 216 leaves; 28 cm. Notes: Thesis (D. Min.)--Columbia Biblical Seminary and Graduate School of Missions, 1994. Includes bibliographical references (leaves 213-216). Microfiche. Portland, Or.: Theological Research Exchange Network, 1994. 1 microfiche: negative. High reduction. Subjects:

Christianity and culture. Theology, Doctrinal--Africa--Study and teaching. LC Classification: Microfiche 98/116 (B)

Ogbajie, Chukwu. The impact of Christianity on the Igbo religion and culture / Chukwu Ogbajie. Published/Created: Umuahia, Abia State Nigeria: Ark Publishers, 1995. Description: xi, 84 p.: ill.; 21 cm. ISBN: 9782842109 Notes: Includes bibliographical references (p. 82) and index. Subjects: Igbo (African people)--Religion. Christianity and culture--Nigeria. Nigeria--Church history. LC Classification: BL2480.I2 O33 1995 Dewey Class No.: 276.69/0829/08996332 21

Okolo, Chukwudum Barnabas. African traditional religion and Christianity: the neglected dimensions / Chukwudum B. Okolo. Published/Created: Nsukka, Nigeria: Fulladu Pub. Co., c1995. Description: 38 p.; 18 cm. ISBN: 9783227092 Notes: Includes bibliographical references (p.34-38). Subjects: Christianity and other religions--African. Christianity and culture. Africa--Religion--20th century. Africa, Sub-Saharan--Religion. LC Classification: IN PROCESS

Okolo, Chukwudum Barnabas. Christian mothers, families, and new Nigeria: foundations of Christian culture / Chukwudum B. Okolo; foreword, Bishop A.K. Obiefuna. Published/Created: [Nsukka?]: C.B. Okolo, 1991 (Enugu SNAAP Press) Description: 48 p.; 19 cm. ISBN: 9782221317 Notes: Includes bibliographical references (p. 46-47). Subjects: Mothers--Nigeria--Religious life. Family--Nigeria--Religious life. Motherhood--Religious aspects--Christianity. LC Classification: BV4529 .O58 1991

Okolo, Chukwudum Barnabas. The African Synod: hope for the continent's liberation / Chukwudum B. Okolo. Published/Created: Eldoret, Kenya: AMECEA Gaba Publications, 1994. Related Authors: African Synod (1994: Rome, Italy) Description: x, 102 p.; 22 cm. ISBN:

9966836144 : Notes: Includes bibliographical references (p. [95]-102). Subjects: Catholic Church--Africa. African Synod (1994: Rome, Italy) Evangelistic work--Africa. Christianity and culture. Series: AMECEA Gaba Publications spearhead; 130-131. LC Classification: BX1675 .O46 1994 Dewey Class No.: 282/.6/09049 20

Oladipo, Caleb Oluremi, 1955- The development of the doctrine of the Holy Spirit in the Yoruba (African) indigenous Christian movement / Caleb Oluremi Oladipo. Published/Created: New York: P. Lang, c1996. Description: xiii, 192 p.; 23 cm. ISBN: 082042708X (alk. paper) Notes: Includes bibliographical references (p. [164]-188) and index. Subjects: Theology, Doctrinal--Africa, West--History--20th century. Holy Spirit--History of doctrines--20th century. Yoruba (African people)--Religion. Religious pluralism--Africa, West--Christianity. Christianity and culture. Series: American university studies. Series VII, Theology and religion; vol. 185 LC Classification: BT30.A358 O53 1996 Dewey Class No.: 231/.3/08996333 20

Olasky, Marvin N. Whirled views: tracking today's culture storms / Marvin Olasky, Joel Belz. Published/Created: Wheaton, Ill.: Crossway Books, c1997. Related Authors: Belz, Joel, 1941- Description: 224 p.; 22 cm. ISBN: 0891079386 (alk. paper) Notes: A collection of editorials which previously appeared in World magazine between 1987-1996. Subjects: Christianity and culture. Church and social problems. LC Classification: BR115.C8 O43 1997 Dewey Class No.: 261/.0973 21

O'Malley, John W. Religious culture in the sixteenth century: preaching, rhetoric, spirituality, and reform / John W. O'Malley. Published/Created: Aldershot, Great Britain; Brookfield, Vt., USA: Variorum, c1993. Description: 1 v. (various pagings): ill.; 23 cm. ISBN: 0860783693 (alk. paper) Notes: Includes bibliographical references and index. Subjects: Catholic Church--Christianity

and culture--Preaching--History--16th century. Series: Collected studies; CS404. LC Classification: BR115.C8 O53 1993 Dewey Class No.: 274/.06 20

One faith, many cultures: inculturation, indigenization, and contextualization / Ruy O. Costa, editor. Published/Created: Maryknoll, N.Y.: Orbis Books; Cambridge, Mass.: Boston Theological Institute, 1988. Related Authors: Costa, Ruy O. Description: xvii, 162 p.; 25 cm. ISBN: 0883445875 0883445867 (pbk.) Notes: Includes bibliographies. Subjects: Jesus Christ--Person and offices. Christianity and culture. Christianity--Developing countries--United States. Theology--Methodology. Series: Boston Theological Institute annual series; vol. 2. LC Classification: BR115.C8 O54 1988 Dewey Class No.: 261 19

Onuh, Charles Ok. Christianity and the Igbo rites of passage: the prospects of inculturation / Charles Ok. Onuh. Published/Created: Frankfurt am Main; New York: P. Lang, c1992. Description: xviii, 263 p.: maps; 21 cm. ISBN: 3631449747 Notes: Includes bibliographical references (p. 241-263). Subjects: Igbo (African people)--Religion--Social life and customs--Rites and ceremonies. Christianity and culture. Igbo (African people)--Cultural assimilation. Series: Europäische Hochschulschriften. Reihe XXIII, Theologie; Bd. 462. LC Classification: BL2480.I2 O58 1992 Dewey Class No.: 261.2/968332 20

Onwubiko, Oliver Alozie. Echoes from the African Synod: the future of the African church from present and past experiences / Oliver Alozie Onwubiko. Published/Created: Enugu: Snaap Press, 1994. Description: x, 158 p.; 21 cm. ISBN: 9782094579 Notes: Includes bibliographical references (p. 157-158). Subjects: Catholic Church--Africa. African Synod (1994: Rome, Italy) Evangelistic work--Africa. Christianity and culture--Africa. LC Classification: BX1675 .O58 1994 Dewey Class No.: 282/.6/09049 21

Onwubiko, Oliver Alozie. Facing the OSU issue in the African Synod: a personal response / Oliver A. Onwubiko. Published/Created: Enugu: O.A. Onwubiko, 1993. Description: vi, 96 p.: ill.; 21 cm. ISBN: 9782094420 Notes: Includes bibliographical references (p. 93-95). Subjects: Igbo (African people)--Religion. Igbo (African people)--Social conditions. Caste--Religious aspects--Christianity. Series: Christian mission and culture in Africa; vol. 3. LC Classification: BL2480.I2 O588 1993 Dewey Class No.: 261.8/345122/09669 20

Onwubiko, Oliver Alozie. Theory and practice of inculturation: an African perspective / by Oliver Alozie Onwubiko. Published/Created: Enugu: O.A. Onwubiko, 1992 (Enugu: SNAAP Press) Description: vi, 239 p.; 21 cm. ISBN: 9782221368 Notes: Includes bibliographical references (p. 205-225) and indexes. Subjects: Christianity and culture. Missions. Series: Christian mission and culture in Africa; vol. 2 LC Classification: BR115.C8 O543 1992 Dewey Class No.: 261 20

Onyeneke, Augustine O. African traditional institutions and the Christian church: a sociological prologue to Christian inculturation / by A. Onyeneke. Published/Created: Nsukka, Nigeria: Spiritan Publication, 1993. Description: 74 p.; 19 cm. ISBN: 9782094676 Notes: Includes bibliographical references (p. 73-74). Subjects: Christianity and culture--Africa. Christianity and culture--Nigeria. Igbo (African people)--Social life and customs. Igbo (African people)--Religion. LC Classification: BR115.C8 O544 1993 Dewey Class No.: 261/.09669 21

Opocenský, Milan, 1931- Faith challenged by history: reports, lectures, sermons, and Bible Studies / given by Milan Opocensky. Published/Created: Geneva: World Alliance of Reformed Churches, 2001. Related Authors: World Alliance of Reformed Churches. General Secretary. Description: 296 p.; 21 cm. ISBN: 9290750677 Notes: Includes bibliographical references. Subjects: Opocenský, Milan., 1931- --Sermons. Reformed Church--Doctrines--History. Theology, Doctrinal--History. Christianity and culture--History. Faith--Biblical teaching. Justice--Biblical teaching. Series: Studies from the World Alliance of Reformed Churches; 44

Ostrander, Richard, 1965- The life of prayer in a world of science: Protestants, prayer, and American culture, 1870-1930 / Rick Ostrander. Published/Created: Oxford; New York: Oxford University Press, 2000. Description: 232 p.; 25 cm. ISBN: 0195136101 (alk. paper) Notes: Includes bibliographical references (p. [203]-225) and index. Subjects: Prayer--Christianity--History--19th century. Protestant churches--United States--Doctrines--History 19th century. Prayer--Christianity--History--20th century. Protestant churches--United States--Doctrines--History 20th century. United States--Church history--19th century. United States--Church history--20th century. Series: Religion in America series (Oxford University Press) LC Classification: BV210.2 .O83 2000 Dewey Class No.: 248.3/2/097309034 21

O'Sullivan, Owen. Church and society in history / Owen O'Sullivan. Published/Created: Wellington: Tertiary Christian Studies Programme, 1977. Description: 83 p.; 20 cm. Notes: Includes bibliographical references. Subjects: Church history--Addresses, essays, lectures. Christianity and culture--Addresses, essays, lectures. Church and state--History--Addresses, essays, lectures. LC Classification: BR150 .O86 Dewey Class No.: 306/.6 19

Ott, Martin. African theology in images / Martin Ott. Published/Created: Blantyre, Malawi: Christian Literature Association in Malawi, 2000. Related Authors: Ott, Martin. Dialog der Bilder. Description: 604 p.: ill., maps; 24 cm. ISBN: 9990816301 Notes: Updated and rev. version of: Dialog der Bilder: die Begegnung von Evangelium und Kultur in afrikanischer Kunst. Freiburg: Herder, 1995. "Kachere series"--

Cover. Includes bibliographical references (p. [573]-604). Subjects: Theology--Africa, Sub-Saharan. Christianity and culture--Africa, Sub-Saharan. Christian art and symbolism--Africa, Sub-Saharan. Africa, Sub-Saharan--Religious life and customs. Series: Kachere monograph, 1025-0964; no. 12 LC Classification: BT30.A357 O88 2000 Dewey Class No.: 246/.096 21

Ottati, Douglas F. Reforming Protestantism: Christian commitment in today's world / Douglas F. Ottati. Edition Information: 1st ed. Published/Created: Louisville, Ky.: Westminster John Knox Press, c1995. Description: xiii, 174 p.; 23 cm. ISBN: 066425604X (pbk.) Notes: Includes bibliographical references (p. 151-172) and index. Subjects: Liberalism (Religion)--United States--History. Liberalism (Religion)--Protestant churches--History. Christianity and culture. United States--Church history. LC Classification: BR515 .O88 1995 Dewey Class No.: 280/.4/0973 20

Overman, Christian. Assumptions that affect our lives / Christian Overman. Published/Created: Chatsworth, Calif.: Micah 6:8, c1996. Description: 273 p.; 22 cm. ISBN: 1883035503 Notes: Includes bibliographical references (p. 263-268) and index. Subjects: Christianity--Philosophy. Christianity and culture. Secularism. LC Classification: BR100 .O92 1996 Dewey Class No.: 230 21

Overman, Christian. Different windows / Christian Overman. Published/Created: Wheaton, Ill.: Tyndale House Publishers, c1988. Description: 175 p.: ill.; 21 cm. ISBN: 084230553X : Notes: Includes index. Subjects: Christianity--Philosophy. Christianity and culture. Secularism. LC Classification: BR100 .O93 1988 Dewey Class No.: 200 20

Ovitt, George, 1948- The restoration of perfection: labor and technology in medieval culture / George Ovitt, Jr. New Brunswick: Rutgers University Press, c1987. Description: xiii, 272 p.; 24 cm. ISBN: 0813512352 : Notes: Includes

index. Bibliography: p. 241-266. Subjects: Technology--Religious aspects--Christianity--History. Work--Religious aspects--Christianity--History of doctrines--Middle Ages, 600-1500. LC Classification: BR115.T42 O95 1987 Dewey Class No.: 306/.36/0902 19

Owens, Virginia Stem. The total image: or, Selling Jesus in the modern age / Virginia Stem Owens. Published/Created: Grand Rapids, Mich.: W. B. Eerdmans Pub. Co., c1980. Description: v, 97 p.; 21 cm. ISBN: 0802818331 (pbk.) ; Subjects: Mass media in religion--United States. Christianity and culture. LC Classification: BV652.95 .O94 Dewey Class No.: 269/.2

Owoahene-Acheampong, Stephen, 1956- Inculturation and African religion: indigenous and Western approaches to medical practice / Stephen Owoahene-Acheampong. Published/Created: New York: Peter Lang, c1998. Description: xv, 225 p.; 24 cm. ISBN: 082043129X (alk. paper) Notes: Includes bibliographical references (p. [177]-194) and index. Subjects: Akan (African people)--Medicine--Religion. Traditional medicine--Medicine--Christianity and culture--Ghana--Social life and customs. Series: American university studies. Series XXI, Regional studies, 0895-0482; vol. 16 LC Classification: DT510.43.A53 O93 1998 Dewey Class No.: 306.4/61/09667 20

Pahl, Jon, 1958- Paradox lost: free will and political liberty in American culture, 1630-1760 / Jon Pahl. Published/Created: Baltimore: Johns Hopkins University Press, c1992. Description: xvi, 234 p.; 24 cm. ISBN: 0801843340 (alk. paper) Notes: Includes bibliographical references (p. [177]-223) and index. Subjects: Calvinism--Political culture--United States--History. Free will and determinism--History. Liberty--Religious aspects--Christianity. United States--Intellectual life--17th century--18th century. Series: New studies in American intellectual and cultural history LC Classification: E162 .P135 1992 Dewey Class No.: 973.2 20

Palma, Robert J. Karl Barth's theology of culture: the freedom of culture for the praise of God / by Robert J. Palma. Published/Created: Allison Park, Pa.: Pickwick Publications, 1983. Description: x, 122 p.; 22 cm. ISBN: 0915138549 (pbk.) Notes: Includes index. Bibliography: p. 111-115. Subjects: Barth, Karl, 1886-1968. Christianity and culture--History--20th century. Series: Pittsburgh theological monographs; new ser. 2 LC Classification: BR115.C8 P3 1983 Dewey Class No.: 261 19

Pamer, Nan. I will not bow / Nan M. Pamer. Published/Created: Hazelwood, MO: Word Aflame Press, c1997. Description: 56 p.: ill.; 21 cm. ISBN: 156722203X (pbk.) Subjects: Christianity and culture--United States. Christian life--Pentecostal authors. Mass media--United States--Influence. Clothing and dress--Religious aspects--Holiness--Christianity. LC Classification: BR115.C8 P32 1997 Dewey Class No.: 243 21

Parani, Maria G. Reconstructing the reality of images: Byzantine material culture and religious iconography, 11th-15th centuries / by Maria G. Parani. Published/Created: Leiden; Boston: Brill Academic Publishers, 2002. Description: p. cm. ISBN: 9004124624 Notes: Includes bibliographical references and index. Subjects: Material culture--Byzantine Empire. Material culture in art. Art, Byzantine. Christianity and art--Orthodox Eastern Church. Semiotics--Byzantine Empire. Series: Medieval Mediterranean, 0928-5520; v. 41 LC Classification: DF601 .P37 2002 Dewey Class No.: 391/.009495/9021 21

Pardini, David A. Chinese ancestor practices in light of the scriptures [microform] / by David A. Pardini. Published/Created: 1994. Description: viii, 194 leaves; 28 cm. Notes: Thesis (D. Miss.)--Trinity Evangelical Divinity School, 1994. Microfiche. Portland, Or.: Theological Research Exchange Network, 1994. 1 microfiche: negative. High reduction. Subjects: Ancestor worship--China. Christianity and other religions--Chinese. Christianity and culture. Parents--Death--Religious aspects. LC Classification: Microfiche 97/249 (B)

Parent, Mark, 1954- Spirit scapes: mapping the spiritual & scientific terrain at the dawn of the new millennium / Mark Parent. Published/Created: Kelowna, B.C., Canada: Northstone, c1998. Description: 256 p.; 23 cm. ISBN: 1896836119 : Notes: Includes bibliographical references (p. [235]-251) and index. Subjects: Christianity--20th century. Christianity--Forecasting. Christianity and culture. Church and the world. Science and religion. Christianisme et civilisation. Église et le monde. LC Classification: BR481 .P27 1998 Dewey Class No.: 261 21

Parshall, Janet, 1950- The light in the city: why Christians must advance and not retreat / Janet & Craig Parshall. Published/Created: Nashville: T. Nelson Publishers, c2000. Related Authors: Parshall, Craig, 1950- Description: xviii, 246 p.; 20 cm. ISBN: 0785268901 (pbk.) Notes: Includes bibliographical references (p. 239-245). Subjects: Christianity and culture--United States. Christian life--United States. United States--Religion--1960- LC Classification: BR526 .P36 2000 Dewey Class No.: 261/.1/0973 21

Parshall, Janet, 1950- Tough faith / Janet & Craig Parshall. Published/Created: Eugene, Or.: Harvest House Publishers, c1999. Related Authors: Parshall, Craig, 1950- Description: 263 p.; 22 cm.cm. ISBN: 1565079973 Notes: Includes bibliographical references (p. 259-263). Subjects: Christianity and culture--United States. Christian life--United States. United States--Religion--1960- LC Classification: BR526 .P37 1999 Dewey Class No.: 277.3/0829 21

Parshall, Phil. New paths in Muslim evangelism: evangelical approaches to contextualization / Phil Parshall; foreword by Warren W. Webster. Published/Created: Grand Rapids, Mich.: Baker Book House, c1980. Description: 280 p.; 22 cm. ISBN:

0801070562 (pbk.) : Notes: Includes indexes. Bibliography: p. 259-271. Subjects: Missions to Muslims. Christianity and culture. LC Classification: BV2625 .P37 Dewey Class No.: 266/.00917/671 19

Patterson, Philip D., 1954- Stay tuned: what every parent should know about media / Philip D. Patterson. Published/Created: Webb City, Mo.: Covenant Pub., c2002. Description: p. cm. ISBN: 1892435217 (pbk.) Contents: It's not what you watch, it's that you watch -- Parental discretion advised: abandoning protection for preparation -- Where have all the children gone? -- The three myths of television viewing -- Media literacy 101: a primer in how the media operate -- Caught in the world wide web: children and the internet -- TV land: the nation's most dangerous neighborhood -- Faith and culture: black and white in a technicolor world -- Taking every thought captive: biblical truths for a media age -- Anyone here got a few words of wisdom? Notes: Includes bibliographical references. Subjects: Mass media and children--Moral and ethical aspects--United States. Mass media--United States. Child rearing--Religious aspects--Christianity. LC Classification: HQ784.M3 P38 2002 Dewey Class No.: 302.23/083/0973 21

Pattison, George, 1950- Art, modernity, and faith: towards a theology of art / George Pattison. Published/Created: Houndmills, Basingstoke, Hampshire: Macmillan, 1991. Description: xii, 193 p.: ill.; 23 cm. ISBN: 0333529545 Notes: Title on spine: Art, modernity & faith. Includes bibliographical references (p. 188-[189]) and index. Subjects: Christian art and symbolism. Art and religion. Christianity and culture. LC Classification: BV150 .P37 1991b

Pattison, George, 1950- Art, modernity, and faith: towards a theology of art / George Pattison. Published/Created: New York: St. Martin's Press, 1991. Description: xii, 193 p.: ill.; 23 cm. ISBN: 0312057075 Notes: Includes bibliographical references (p. 188-[189])and index. Subjects: Christian

art and symbolism. Art and religion. Christianity and culture. LC Classification: BV150 .P37 1990 Dewey Class No.: 246 20

Pattison, George, 1950- Kierkegaard, religion, and the nineteenth-century crisis in culture / George Pattison. Published/Created: New York: Cambridge University Press, 2002. Description: p. cm. ISBN: 0521811708 052101042X (pbk.) Notes: Includes bibliographical references and index. Subjects: Kierkegaard, Søren, 1813-1855. Christianity and culture--History--19th century. LC Classification: B4378.C5 P38 2002 Dewey Class No.: 198/.9 21

Pattison, Robert. The great dissent: John Henry Newman and the liberal heresy / Robert Pattison. Published/Created: New York: Oxford University Press, 1991. Description: xiii, 231 p.; 22 cm. ISBN: 0195067304 (alk. paper) Notes: Includes bibliographical references and index. Subjects: Newman, John Henry, 1801-1890 --Contributions in criticism of liberalism in religion. Newman, John Henry, 1801-1890 --Contributions in criticism of modern civilization. Hampden, Renn Dickson, 1793-1868. Arius, d. ca. 336. Liberalism (Religion)--History of doctrines--Civilization, Modern--Christianity and culture--England--Intellectual life--Church history--19th century. LC Classification: BR1615 .P37 1991 Dewey Class No.: 230/.2/092 20

Pearce, Tariq Safina, b. 1888. Key to the door. With a foreword by S.A. Rahman. Published/Created: Lahore, Institute of Islamic Culture, 1961. Description: 158 p. 25 cm. Subjects: Muslim converts from Christianity. LC Classification: BP80.P4 A3

Peel, J. D. Y. (John David Yeadon), 1941- Religious encounter and the making of the Yoruba / J.D.Y. Peel. Published/Created: Bloomington, IN: Indiana University Press, c2000. Description: xi, 420 p.: ill.; 25 cm. ISBN: 0253337941 (alk. paper) Notes: Includes bibliographical references (p. 393-407) and index. Subjects: Missions--

Nigeria--History--19th century.
Christianity and culture--Nigeria--History--
19th century. Yoruba (African people)--
Religion. Nigeria--Church history--19th
century. Series: African systems of thought
LC Classification: BV3625.N5 P44 2000
Dewey Class No.: 266/.009669/09034 21

Peelman, Achiel, 1942- Christ is a Native
American / Achiel Peelman.
Published/Created: Ottawa: Novalis-Saint
Paul University; Maryknoll, N.Y.: Orbis
Books, 1995. Description: 253 p.: ill.; 23
cm. ISBN: 289088743X (Novalis)
1570750475 (Orbis) Notes: Includes
bibliographical references (p. [227]-253).
Subjects: Jesus Christ--Person and offices.
Indians of North America--Canada--
Religion. Christianity and culture. LC
Classification: BT205 .P3713 1995 Dewey
Class No.: 277/.0089/97 20

Pelikan, Jaroslav Jan, 1923- Christianity and
classical culture: the metamorphosis of
natural theology in the Christian encounter
with Hellenism / Jaroslav Pelikan.
Published/Created: New Haven: Yale
University Press, c1993. Description: xvi,
368 p.: maps; 25 cm. ISBN: 0300055544
(alk. paper) Notes: Includes bibliographical
references (p. 335-351) and indexes.
Subjects: Macrina, the Younger, Saint, ca.
330-379 or 80. Natural theology--History
of doctrines--Early church, ca. 30-600.
Cappadocian Fathers. Christianity and
culture--History--Early church, ca. 30-600.
Civilization, Classical. Series: Gifford
lectures; 1992-1993. LC Classification:
BL245 .P45 1993 Dewey Class No.:
210/.939/34 20

Pelikan, Jaroslav Jan, 1923- The Christian
intellectual, by Jaroslav Pelikan. Edition
Information: [1st ed.] Published/Created:
New York, Harper & Row [1965]
Description: 151 p. 22 cm. Notes:
Bibliographical references includes in
"Notes" (p. 131-148) Subjects: Christianity
and culture Faith and reason Religion and
science--1946- Series: Religious
perspectives, v. 14 LC Classification:
BR115.C8 P35 Dewey Class No.: 230.09

Pentecost, mission, and ecumenism: essays on
intercultural theology: festschrift in honour
of Professor Walter J. Hollenweger / Jan
A.B. Jongeneel, a.o. (eds.).
Published/Created: Frankfurt am Main;
New York: P. Lang, c1992. Related
Authors: Hollenweger, Walter J., 1927-
Jongeneel, J. A. B. Description: x, 376 p.:
port.; 21 cm. ISBN: 3631440103 Notes:
"Bibliography of Walter J. Hollenweger":
p. [311]-357. Includes bibliographical
references and index. Subjects:
Hollenweger, Walter J., 1927-
Pentecostalism. Missions. Missions--
Theory. Ecumenical movement.
Christianity and culture. Series: Studien
zur interkulturellen Geschichte des
Christentums; Bd. 75. LC Classification:
BX4827.H64 P46 1992 Dewey Class No.:
270.8/2 20

People on the way: Asian North Americans
discovering Christ, culture, and community
/ edited by David Ng. Published/Created:
Valley Forge, PA: Judson Press, c1996.
Related Authors: Ng, David. Description:
xxix, 300 p.; 22 cm. ISBN: 0817012427
(pbk.: alk. paper) Notes: Includes
bibliographical references. Subjects:
Asians--North America--Religion.
Christianity and other religions--Asian.
Christianity and culture. North America--
Religion--20th century. Asia--Religion--
20th century. LC Classification: BR510
.P46 1996 Dewey Class No.:
277/.0829/08995 20

Persaud, Winston D., 1950- The theology of the
cross and Marx's anthropology: a view
from the Caribbean / Winston D. Persaud.
Published/Created: New York: P. Lang,
c1991. Description: xi, 295 p.; 24 cm.
ISBN: 0820414093 Notes: Revised version
of thesis (doctoral)--University of St.
Andrew's, Scotland, 1980. Includes
bibliographical references (p. [267]-295)
and index. Subjects: Marx, Karl, 1818-
1883 --Contributions in philosophical
anthropology. Jesus Christ--Crucifixion.
Sociology, Christian. Theology, Doctrinal-
-Caribbean Area. Man (Christian theology)
Alienation (Philosophy) Reconciliation--
Religious aspects--Christianity.

Christianity and culture. Caribbean Area--Church history--20th century. Series: American university studies. Series VII, Theology and religion; vol. 84 LC Classification: BT738 .P459 1991 Dewey Class No.: 230/.09729 20

Perspectivas: Hispanic ministry / [edited by] Allan Figueroa Deck, Yolanda Tarango, Timothy M. Matovina. Kansas City, MO: Sheed & Ward,c 1995. Related Authors: Deck, Allan Figueroa, 1945- Tarango, Yolanda. Matovina, Timothy M., 1955- Description: vi, 152 p.; 22 cm. ISBN: 1556127707 (pbk.: alk. paper) Notes: Includes bibliographical references (p. 151-152). Subjects: Church work with Hispanic Americans. Hispanic American Catholics. Sociology, Christian (Catholic) Christianity and culture--United States. LC Classification: BV4468.2.H57 M56 1995 Dewey Class No.: 282/.73/08968 20

Perspectives on Christianity in Korea and Japan: the Gospel and culture in East Asia / edited by Mark R. Mullins and Richard Fox Young. Published/Created: Lewiston: E. Mellen Press, c1995. Related Authors: Mullins, Mark. Young, Richard Fox. Description: xxiii, 230 p.; 24 cm. ISBN: 0773488685 (hard) Notes: Includes bibliographical references (p. [211]-227). Subjects: Christianity--Korea--Japan. Christianity and culture. LC Classification: BR1325 .P47 1995 Dewey Class No.: 279.519 20

Peters, Ted, 1941- For the love of children: genetic technology and the future of the family / Ted Peters. Edition Information: 1st ed. Published/Created: Louisville, Ky.: Westminster John Knox Press, c1996. Description: xii, 227 p.; 23 cm. ISBN: 0664254683 (alk. paper) Notes: Includes bibliographical references (p. [183]-212) and indexes. Subjects: Human reproductive technology--Religious aspects Christianity. Human reproductive technology--Moral and ethical aspects. Family--Religious aspects--Christianity. Series: The family, religion, and culture LC Classification: RG133.5 .P485 1996 Dewey Class No.:

176 20

Phillips, Henry. Church and culture in seventeenth-century France / Henry Phillips. Published/Created: Cambridge; New York: Cambridge University Press, 1997. Description: ix, 334 p.; 23 cm. ISBN: 0521570239 Notes: Includes bibliographical references (p. 316-325) and index. Subjects: Catholic Church--Christianity and culture--France--History--17th century. France--Civilization--Church history--17th century. LC Classification: BR845 .P48 1997 Dewey Class No.: 261/.1 20

Pierce, Lorne Albert, 1890- Christianity and culture in our time. Published/Created: [Toronto, Ryerson Press, 1947] Description: 12 p. 24 cm. Subjects: Civilization, Christian. LC Classification: BR115.C8 P5

Pike, Kenneth Lee, 1912- With heart and mind: a personal synthesis of scholarship and devotion / Kenneth L. Pike. Published/Created: Duncanville, TX: Adult Learning Systems, c1996. Description: p. cm. ISBN: 1887493069 (paper) Notes: Includes bibliographical references and index. Subjects: Pike, Kenneth Lee, 1912- Bible--Translating. Religion and science. Language and languages--Religious aspects--Christianity. Christianity and culture. Evangelicalism. Apologetics. Christian life. LC Classification: BL241 .P54 1996 Dewey Class No.: 261.5/5 20

Pinto, Joseph Prasad. Inculturation through basic communities: an Indian perspective / Joseph Prasad Pinto. Published/Created: Bangalore: Asian Trading Corp., 1985. Description: xi, 273 p.; 22 cm. Notes: Includes index. Bibliography: p. 254-270. Subjects: Catholic Church--India--History--20th century. Christian communities--Catholic Church. Christian communities--India. Christianity and culture. Church relations. India--Church history. India--Religion. LC Classification: BX2347.72.I4 P56 1985 Dewey Class No.: 262 19

Pledges of jubilee: essays on the arts and culture, in honor of Calvin G. Seerveld / edited by Lambert Zuidervaart and Henry Luttikhuizen. Published/Created: Grand Rapids, Mich.: W.B. Eerdmans, c1995. Related Authors: Seerveld, Calvin. Zuidervaart, Lambert. Luttikhuizen, Henry, 1964- Description: xiv, 354 p.: ill.; 24 cm. ISBN: 0802837921 (alk. paper) Notes: "Writings and speeches by Calvin G. Seerveld, 1957-1994, compiled by Perry Recker": p. 328-349. Includes bibliographical references. Subjects: Seerveld, Calvin. Christianity and the arts. Christianity and culture. LC Classification: BR115.A8 P57 1995 Dewey Class No.: 261.5/7 20

Plou, Dafne Sabanes. Global communication: is there a place for human dignity? / Dafne Sabanes Plou. Published/Created: Geneva: WCC Publications, c1996. Description: xi, 74 p.; 22 cm. ISBN: 2825411868 Notes: Includes bibliographical references. Subjects: Communication--International cooperation. Communication--Religious aspects--Christianity. Communication and culture. Series: Risk book series; no. 71 LC Classification: P96.I5 P576 1996 Dewey Class No.: 302.2 21

Pluralism and oppression: theology in world perspective / R. Panikkar ... [et al.]; edited by Paul F. Knitter. Published/Created: Lanham, Md.: University Press of America, c1991. Related Authors: Panikkar, Raimundo, 1918- Knitter, Paul F. College Theology Society. Description: xii, 278 p.; 24 cm. ISBN: 0819179043 (alk. paper) 0819179051 (pbk.) Notes: Essays in this volume were given at the 1988 meeting of the College Theology Society at Loyola-Marymount University in Los Angeles. Inlcudes bibliographical references. Subjects: Theology--Christianity and culture--Religions--Suffering--Religious aspects--Christianity--Congresses. Series: Annual publication of the College Theology Society; v. 34. LC Classification: BR118 .P58 1990 Dewey Class No.: 230 20

Pobee, J. S. West Africa: Christ would be an African too / John Pobee. Published/Created: Geneva: WCC Publications, c1996. Related Authors: World Council of Churches. Description: xi, 52 p.; 21 cm. ISBN: 2825411981 Notes: Includes bibliographical references. Subjects: Christianity and culture. Christianity--Africa, West. Africa, West--Religious life and customs. Series: Gospel and cultures pamphlet; 9 LC Classification: IN PROCESS

Polish literature in the culture of Christian Europe / [editors, Edward Fiala, Bogumil Pietrasiewicz]. Published/Created: Lublin: Catholic University of Lublin, 1983. Related Authors: Fiala, Edward. Pietrasiewicz, Bogumil. Description: 81 p.; 21 cm. Notes: Translation of: Literature polska w kulturze chrze´scija´nskiej Europy. Includes bibliographical references. Subjects: Polish literature--European influences--Christian influences. Christianity and literature. Europe--Civilization. Series: University handbook series; 1 LC Classification: PG7019 .L4913 1983 Dewey Class No.: 891.8/5/09 19

Pope-Levison, Priscilla, 1958- Jesus in global contexts / Priscilla Pope-Levison, John R. Levison. Edition Information: 1st ed. Published/Created: Louisville, Ky.: Westminster/John Knox Press, c1992. Related Authors: Levison, John R. Description: 232 p.; 23 cm. ISBN: 066425165X (acid-free paper) Notes: Includes bibliographical references (p. 199-219) and indexes. Subjects: Jesus Christ--Person and offices. Christianity and culture. LC Classification: BT202 .P59 1992 Dewey Class No.: 232 20

Popular Catholicism in a world church: seven case studies in inculturation / edited by Thomas Bamat, Jean-Paul Wiest. Published/Created: Maryknoll, N.Y.: Orbis Books, c1999. Related Authors: Bamat, Tomás. Wiest, Jean-Paul. Description: xii, 315 p.: ill.; 23 cm. ISBN: 1570752524 (pbk.) Notes: Includes bibliographical references (p. 303-311). Subjects: Catholic

Church--Doctrines. Christianity and culture. Series: Faith and cultures series LC Classification: BX1795.C85 P67 1999 Dewey Class No.: 230/.2 21

Popular religion, liberation, and contextual theology: papers from a congress (January 3-7, 1990, Nijmegen, the Netherlands) dedicated to Arnulf Camps OFM / edited by Jacques Van Nieuwenhove and Berma Klein Goldewijk. Published/Created: Kampen: Kok, 1991. Related Authors: Nieuwenhove, Jacques van. Goldewijk, Berma Klein. Description: vii, 256 p.; 25 cm. ISBN: 9024234999 Notes: Selected bibliography of Arnulf Camps: p. 235-249. Includes bibliographical references. Subjects: Religion--Congresses. Christianity and culture--Congresses. Liberation theology--Congresses. Series: Kerk en theologie in context; nr. 8. LC Classification: BL21 .P67 1991

Porete, Marguerite, ca. 1250-1310. The mirror of simple souls / Margaret Porette; translated from the French with an introductory interpretative essay by Edmund Colledge, J.C. Marler, and Judith Grant; and a foreword by Kent Emery, Jr. Published/Created: Notre Dame, Ind.: University of Notre Dame Press, c1999. Related Authors: Colledge, Edmund. Grant, Judith. Marler, J. C. Description: lxxxvii, 209 p.; 24 cm. ISBN: 0268014353 (pbk.: alk. paper) Notes: Includes bibliographical references (p. 195-200) and indexes. Subjects: Contemplation--Early works to 1800. Spiritual life--Christianity--Early works to 1800. Series: Notre Dame texts in medieval culture; vol. 6 LC Classification: BV5091.C7 P6713 1999 Dewey Class No.: 248.2/2 21

Pounds, Norman John Greville. A history of the English parish: the culture of religion from Augustine to Victoria / N.J.G. Pounds. Published/Created: Cambridge, U.K.; New York: Cambridge University Press, 2000. Description: xxv, 593 p.: ill., maps; 26 cm. ISBN: 0521633486 0521633516 (pbk.) Notes: Includes bibliographical references (p. 511-578) and index. Subjects: Parishes--Christianity and culture--England--

History--Church history. LC Classification: BR744 .P58 2000 Dewey Class No.: 262/.22/0942 21

Poupard, Paul. The church and culture: challenge and confrontation: inculturation and evangelization / by Paul Cardinal Poupard; translated by John H. Miller. St. Louis, MO: Central Bureau, CCVA, c1994. Description: xii, 153 p.; 23 cm. ISBN: 0962625779 Notes: Includes bibliographical references (p. 151-153). Subjects: Catholic Church--Missions--Relations. Christianity and culture. LC Classification: BR115.C8 P65513 1994 Dewey Class No.: 261/.08/822 20

Power religion: the selling out of the evangelical church? / Charles Colson ... [et al.]; Michael Scott Horton, editor. Published/Created: Chicago: Moody Press, c1992. Related Authors: Colson, Charles W. Horton, Michael Scott. Description: 353 p.; 23 cm. ISBN: 0802467733 Notes: Includes bibliographical references. Subjects: Christianity--20th century. Mission of the church. Pentecostalism. Christianity and culture. Evangelicalism. LC Classification: BR481 .P68 1992 Dewey Class No.: 270.8/29 21

Power, David Noel. Culture and theology / David N. Power. Published/Created: Washington, DC: Pastoral Press, c1990. Description: xii, 283 p.; 23 cm. ISBN: 0912405775 Notes: Includes bibliographical references. Subjects: Christianity and culture. Liturgics. Worship. Series: Worship (Washington, D.C.) LC Classification: BR115.C8 P67 1990 Dewey Class No.: 264 20

Price, Maurice Thomas. The analysis of Christian propaganda in race contact: the reactions of "non-Christian" peoples to the Protestant missionary enterprise, from the standpoint of individual and group behavior; outline, materials, problems and tentative interpretations. Chicago, 1922. Description: p. cm. Subjects: Missions--Theory.Christianity and culture. LC Classification: BV2063 .P69

Price, Maurice Thomas. Christian missions and oriental civilizations, a study in culture contact; the reactions of non-Christian peoples to Protestant missions from the standpoint of individual and group behavior: outline, materials, problems, and tentative interpretations, by Maurice T. Price, with a foreword by Dr. Robert E. Park. Published/Created: Shanghai, China [Priv. print.] 1924. Description: xxvi, 578 p. 23 cm. Notes: Bibliography: p. [547]-578. "Bibliographical notes" at end of each chapter. Subjects: Missions. Christianity and other religions. Civilization, Christian. Civilization, Oriental. LC Classification: BV2063 .P7

Principe, Walter H. (Walter Henry) Faith, history, and cultures: stability and change in church teachings / by Walter H. Principe. Published/Created: Milwaukee, Wis.: Marquette University Press, c1991. Description: 63 p.; 19 cm. Notes: Includes bibliographical references (p. 55-63). Subjects: Catholic Church--Doctrines--History. History (Theology) Christianity and culture. Series: The Père Marquette lecture in theology; 1991 LC Classification: BX1747 .P75 1991 Dewey Class No.: 230/.2 20

Prior, Randall. Gospel and culture in Vanuatu: the founding missionary and a missionary for today / Randall Prior. Published/Created: Australia: Gospel Vanuatu Books, 1998. Description: viii, 87 p.: ill.; 22 cm. ISBN: 0646359177 Notes: Includes bibliographical references (p. 86-87). Subjects: Geddie, John, 1815-1872 --Diaries. Loughman, Graham, d. 1989. Jesus Christ--Art. Christianity and culture--Australia--Vanuatu. Missions--Australia--Vanuatu. Presbyterian Church--Missions--Australia--Vanuatu. Vanuatu--Church history. LC Classification: BR1483.V36 P75 1998 Dewey Class No.: 261/.099595 21

Problems and promises of Africa: towards and beyond the year 2000: a summary of the proceedings of the symposium convened by the AACC in Mombasa in November, 1991: a proposal for reflection / compiled by André Karamaga. Edition Information: 2nd ed. Published/Created: [Nairobi]: All Africa Conference of Churches, [1993] Related Authors: Karamaga, André. All Africa Conference of Churches. Symposium on the Problems and Promises of Africa (1991: Mombasa, Kenya) Description: 90 p.: ill., maps; 21 cm. ISBN: 9966987983 Notes: "August 1993"--T.p. verso. "The All Africa Conference of Churches organised a Symposium on the Problems and promises of Africa ..."--P. 7. Subjects: Christianity--Africa--Congresses. Church and social problems--Africa--Congresses. Christianity and culture--Africa--Congresses. Twenty-first century--Forecasts--Congresses. LC Classification: BR1360 .P76 1993 Dewey Class No.: 276/.0829 20

Proceedings of the Bishops' Study Session on inculturation held at Sacred Heart Pastoral Centre, Jos, November 9-10, 1988 / compiled, edited, and published by Catholic Secretariat of Nigeria. Published/Created: Nigeria: Catholic Secretariat of Nigeria, 1989. Related Authors: Catholic Secretariat of Nigeria. Description: 102 p.; 21 cm. Notes: Title on cover: Inculturation in Nigeria. Includes bibliographical references. Subjects: Christianity and culture--Congresses. LC Classification: BR115.C8 P74 1989

Profiles in Protestant witness: the first fifty years of evangelical Christianity in the Philippines, 1898-1948 / IRS Research Committee, Betty C. Abregana ... [et al.]. Published/Created: City of Muntinlupa, Philippines: Institute of Religion and Culture, Phils., 1999. Related Authors: Abregana, Betty C. Institute of Religion and Culture (Philippines) Description: 132 p.: ill.; 22 cm. ISBN: 9718710051 Notes: Includes bibliographical references (p. 123).

Project for Orthodox renewal: seven studies of key issues facing Orthodox Christians in America / Stephen J. Sfekas, George E. Matsoukas, editors. Published/Created: Chicago, Ill.: Orthodox Christian Laity, c1993. Related Authors: Matsoukas,

George. Sfekas, Stephen J. Description: xiv, 316, 11 p.; 22 cm. ISBN: 0937032956 Notes: Cover title. Includes bibliographical references (p. 309-316) and index. Subjects: Orthodox Eastern Church--United States--History--20th century Church renewal--Orthodox Eastern Church. Spiritual life--Orthodox Eastern Church. Christianity and culture. Language question in the church--United States. Women in the Orthodox Eastern Church--United States. LC Classification: BX735 .P76 1993 Dewey Class No.: 281.9/73 20

Puckett, Walter. Bringing the church off the slippery slope: recovery from culture wars / Walter Puckett. Published/Created: Columbus, GA: Brentwood Christian Press, c1992. Description: 333 p.; 21 cm. ISBN: 0916573508 Notes: Includes bibliographical references (p. 295-333). Subjects: Christianity and culture. Christianity--Forecasting. Church and the world. Culture conflict. LC Classification: BR115.C8 P75 1992 Dewey Class No.: 261 20

Pudaite, Lien Jacob. Developing a curriculum for the Northeast India Theological Seminary [microform] / by Lien Jacob Pudaite. Published/Created: 1994. Description: x, 205 leaves; 28 cm. Notes: Thesis (D. Min.)--Trinity Evangelical Divinity School, 1994. Microfiche. Portland, Or.: Theological Research Exchange Network, 1994. 1 microfiche: negative. High reduction. Subjects: Northeast India Theological Seminary (Manipur, India) Curricula. Theological seminaries--India--Curricula. Christianity and culture. LC Classification: Microfiche 97/263 (B)

Purves, Alan C., 1931- The web of text and the web of God: an essay on the third information transformation / Alan C. Purves. Published/Created: New York: Guilford Press, c1998. Description: xvi, 240 p.: ill.; 23 cm. ISBN: 1572302496 Notes: Includes bibliographical references (p. 227-235) and index. Subjects: Communication--Technological innovations. Hypertext systems.

Communication and culture. Communication--Religious aspects--Christianity. LC Classification: P96.T42 P87 1998 Dewey Class No.: 302.2 21

Pushing the faith: proselytism and civility in a pluralistic world / edited by Martin E. Marty and Frederick E. Greenspahn. Published/Created: New York: Crossroad, 1988. Related Authors: Marty, Martin E., 1928- Greenspahn, Frederick E., 1946- University of Denver. Center for Judaic Studies. Description: xiv, 190 p.; 24 cm. ISBN: 0824508718 Contents: Religions, worlds, and order / Charles H. Long -- Modernity and pluralism / Benton Johnson -- The place of other religions in ancient Jewish thought, with particular reference to early rabbinic Judaism / Robert Goldenberg -- Joining the Jewish people from Biblical to modern times / Robert M. Seltzer -- Proselytism and exclusivity in early Christianity / John G. Gager -- Christianity, culture, and complications / William R. Hutchison -- Changes in Roman Catholic attitudes toward proselytism and mission / Robert J. Schreiter -- Fundamentalists proselytizing Jews / Nancy T. Ammerman -- The psychology of proselytism / H. Newton Malony -- Proselytizing processes of the new religions / James T. Richardson -- Proselytism in a pluralistic world / Martin E. Marty. Notes: Papers from a symposium sponsored by the University of Denver Center for Judaic Studies. Bibliography: p. 164-188. Subjects: Proselytes and proselyting, Jewish--Congresses. Missions--Congresses. LC Classification: BM729.P7 P8 1988 Dewey Class No.: 291.7 19

Pyron, Bernard. The great rebellion / Bernard Pyron. Published/Created: Waco, Tex.: Rebound Publications, c1985. Description: vii, 291 p.; 22 cm. ISBN: 0961502401 (pbk.) : Notes: Includes bibliographies. Subjects: Christianity and culture--History--20th century. LC Classification: BR115.C8 P76 1985 Dewey Class No.: 261 19

Quest for reality: Christianity and the counter culture [by] Carl F. H. Henry and others.

Published/Created: Downers Grove, Ill., InterVarsity Press [1973] Related Authors: Henry, Carl Ferdinand Howard, 1913- Institute for Advanced Christian Studies. Description: 161 p. 21 cm. ISBN: 0877847614 Notes: Papers presented at a conference sponsored by the Institute for Advanced Christian Studies, held in Chicago, Oct., 1971. Includes bibliographical references. Subjects: Sociology, Christian--Addresses, essays, lectures. Civilization, Secular--Addresses, essays, lectures. LC Classification: BR115.W6 Q47 Dewey Class No.: 261.8/3

Raja, John Joshva. Facing the reality of communication: culture, church, and communication / by John Joshva Raja. Published/Created: Delhi: ISPCK, 2001. Related Authors: I.S.P.C.K. (Organization) Description: xiv, 339 p.; 23 cm. ISBN: 8172146051 Notes: Includes bibliographical references (p. [314]-337). "Webliography": (p. [338]-339). Subjects: Communication--Religious aspects--Christianity. Christian education. Mass media in religion. LC Classification: BV4319+

Rapisarda, Philip A. The Italian influence on Western law and culture; and, The Italian influence on the spread of Christianity / Philip A. Rapisarda. Edition Information: 1st revision. Published/Created: Baltimore, Md.: P.A. Rapisarda, 1993. Description: 2 v. in 1; 23 cm. ISBN: 0964251205 LC Classification: IN PROCESS

Raschke, Carl A. The bursting of new wineskins: reflections on religion and culture at the end of affluence / by Carl A. Raschke. Published/Created: Pittsburgh: Pickwick Press, 1978. Description: ix, 228 p.; 22 cm. ISBN: 0915138344 : Subjects: Sociology, Christian. Wealth--Religious aspects--Christianity. Liberalism (Religion)--United States. Series: Pittsburgh theological monograph series; 24 LC Classification: BT738 .R32 Dewey Class No.: 261.8

Readings in Christian humanism / edited by Joseph M. Shaw ... [et al.]; foreword by

Martin E. Marty. Published/Created: Minneapolis: Augsburg Pub. House, c1982. Related Authors: Shaw, Joseph M. Description: 685 p.; 22 cm. ISBN: 0806619384 (pbk.) Notes: Includes bibliographical references. Subjects: Christianity and culture. Civilization, Christian. Man (Christian theology) Humanism. LC Classification: BR115.C8 R33 1982 Dewey Class No.: 261.5 19

Readings on religion as news / edited by Judith M. Buddenbaum and Debra L. Mason. Edition Information: 1st ed. Published/Created: Ames: Iowa State University Press, 2000. Related Authors: Buddenbaum, Judith Mitchell, 1941- Mason, Debra L. Description: xx, 501 p.; 23 cm. ISBN: 0813829267 (alk. paper) Subjects: Mass media in religion--United States--Influence. Mass media in religion--United States. Christianity and culture--United States. LC Classification: BV652.97.U6 R43 2000 Dewey Class No.: 070.4/49200973 21

Reclaiming the sacred: the Bible in gay and lesbian culture / Raymond-Jean Frontain, editor. Published/Created: New York: Harrington Park Press, c1997. Related Authors: Frontain, Raymond-Jean. Description: 262 p.: ill.; 23 cm. ISBN: 1560230975 (acid-free paper) 1560231343 (pbk.) Notes: "Has also been published as Journal of homosexuality, volume 33, numbers 3/4, 1997"--T.p. verso. Includes bibliographical references and indexes. Subjects: Bible--In literature. Gays' writings, English--History and criticism. Homosexuality and literature--Great Britain. Christianity and literature--Great Britain. English literature--History and criticism. Holy, The, in literature. Religion and literature. Lesbians in literature. Gay men in literature. LC Classification: PR120.G39 R43 1997 Dewey Class No.: 820.9/920664 21

Reformed faith and politics: essays prepared for the Advisory Council on Church and Society of the United Presbyterian Church in the U.S.A. and the Council on Theology and Culture of the Presbyterian Church in the U.S. / Ronald H. Stone, editor. Published/Created: Washington, D.C.: University Press of America, c1983. Related Authors: Stone, Ronald H. United Presbyterian Church in the U.S.A. Advisory Council on Church and Society. Presbyterian Church in the U.S. Council on Theology and Culture. Description: viii, 201 p.; 23 cm. ISBN: 0819132950: 0819132969 (pbk.) : Notes: "Co-published by arrangement with the Council on Theology and Culture of the Presbyterian Church of the U.S., and the Advisory Council on Church and Society of the United Presbyterian Church of the USA"-- T.p. verso. Subjects: Christianity and politics--Presbyterian Church. Church and state--United States. Presbyterian Church-- Doctrines. LC Classification: BR115.P7 R4324 1983 Dewey Class No.: 261.7 19

Reid, David, 1927- New wine: the cultural shaping of Japanese Christianity / David Reid. Published/Created: Berkeley, Calif.: Asian Humanities Press, c1991. Description: ix, 199 p.: ill.; 24 cm. ISBN: 0895819317 (cloth) 0895819325 (pbk.) Notes: Includes bibliographical references (p. [169]-183) and index. Subjects: Christianity and culture--Japan. Ancestor worship--Christianity. Religion and state-- Japan. Japan--Church history. Japan-- Religion. Series: Nanzan studies in Asian religions; 2 LC Classification: BR1305 .R375 1991 Dewey Class No.: 275.2 20

Reisinger, Ernest C., 1919- The law and the gospel / Ernest C. Reisinger. Published/Created: Phillipsburg, N.J.: P&R Pub., c1997. Description: xxii, 196 p.; 22 cm. ISBN: 0875523870 (pbk.) Notes: Includes bibliographical references (p. 195-196). Subjects: Ten commandments-- Criticism, interpretation, etc. Law and gospel. Law (Theology) Christianity and culture. United States--Moral conditions. United States--Social conditions. LC Classification: BT79 .R45 1997 Dewey Class No.: 241/.2 21

Reist, Benjamin A. Processive revelation / Benjamin A. Reist. Edition Information: 1st ed. Published/Created: Louisville, Ky.:

Westminster/John Knox Press, c1992. Description: 205 p.; 24 cm. ISBN: 0664219551 (alk. paper) Notes: Includes bibliographical references (p. 195-201) and index. Subjects: Theology--Methodology. Revelation. Christianity and culture. Process theology. Theology, Doctrinal. LC Classification: BR118 .R44 1992 Dewey Class No.: 230/.046 20

Religion and culture in dialogue: a challenge for the next millenium / edited by Dermot A. Lane. Published/Created: Blackrock (Dublin): Columba Press, 1993. Related Authors: Lane, Dermot A., 1941- Description: 234 p.; 22 cm. ISBN: 185607076X (pbk) Subjects: Christianity and culture. LC Classification: BR115.C8 R37 1993 Dewey Class No.: 261 20

Religion and culture in Renaissance England / edited by Claire McEachern and Debora Shuger. Published/Created: Cambridge, U.K.; New York, NY, USA: Cambridge University Press, 1997. Related Authors: McEachern, Claire Elizabeth, 1963- Shuger, Debora K., 1953- Description: xii, 292 p.: ill.; 24 cm. ISBN: 0521584256 Notes: Includes bibliographic references and index. Subjects: Christianity and culture--History. English literature--Early modern, 1500-1700--History and criticism. England--Religious life and customs. LC Classification: BR756 .R444 1997 Dewey Class No.: 274.2/06 20

Religion and mass media: audiences and adaptations / [editors] Daniel A. Stout, Judith M. Buddenbaum. Published/Created: Thousand Oaks, Calif.: Sage Publications, c1996. Related Authors: Stout, Daniel A. Buddenbaum, Judith Mitchell, 1941- Description: 294 p.; 24 cm. ISBN: 0803971737 (cloth: alk. paper) 0803971745 (pbk.: alk. paper) Partial Contents: Introduction: toward a synthesis of mass communication research and the sociology of religion / Daniel A. Stout, Judith M. Buddenbaum -- Religion and mass media use: a review of the mass communication and sociology literature / Judith M. Buddenbaum, Daniel A. Stout -- Catholicism, conscience, and censorship /

Ted G. Jelen -- Mainline Protestants and the media / Judith M. Buddenbaum -- Evangelicals' uneasy alliance with the media / Quentin J. Schultze -- Fundamentalism and the media, 1930-1990 / Margaret Lamberts Bendroth -- Protecting the family: Mormon teachings about mass media / Daniel A. Stout -- Religion, mass media, and tolerance for civil liberties / Tony Rimmer -- The role of religion in newspaper trust, subscribing, and use for political information / Judith M. Buddenbaum. Notes: Includes bibliographical references. Subjects: Mass media--Religious aspects--Christianity. Mass media in religion. LC Classification: BV652.95 .R43 1996 Dewey Class No.: 291.1/75 20

Religion and political culture in Jefferson's Virginia / edited by Garrett Ward Sheldon and Daniel L. Dreisbach. Published/Created: Lanham, Md.: Rowman & Littlefield, c2000. Related Authors: Sheldon, Garrett Ward, 1954- Dreisbach, Daniel L. Description: xiii, 236 p.; 23 cm. ISBN: 0742507742 (alk. paper) 0742507750 (pbk.: alk. paper) Notes: Includes bibliographical references. Subjects: Jefferson, Thomas, 1743-1826. Madison, James, 1751-1836. Christianity and politics--Virginia--History--18th century. Church and state--Virginia--History--18th century. Virginia--Church history--18th century. LC Classification: BR555.V8 R45 2000 Dewey Class No.: 322/.1/0975509033 21

Religion and the arts: a journal from Boston College. Published/Created: Chestnut Hill, Mass.: Boston College, c1996- Related Authors: Boston College. Description: v.: ill.; 23 cm. Vol. 1, no. 1 (fall 1996)- Current Frequency: Quarterly ISSN: 1079-9265 Notes: Title from cover. SERBIB/SERLOC merged record Subjects: Religion and culture--Periodicals. Art and religion--Periodicals. Christianity and the arts--Periodicals. LC Classification: BL65.C8 R4453

Religion and the culture wars: dispatches from the front / John C. Green ... [et al.].

Published/Created: Lanham, Md.: Rowman & Littlefield, c1996. Related Authors: Green, John Clifford, 1953- Description: xxii, 368 p.: ill.; 23 cm. ISBN: 0847682676 (alk. paper) 0847682684 (pbk.: alk. paper) Notes: Includes bibliographical references and index. Subjects: Christianity and politics--Christianity and culture--United States--History--20th century. Culture conflict--United States. United States--Church history--20th century. United States--Politics and government--1945-1989. United States--Politics and government--1989-1993. United States--Politics and government--1993-2001. Series: Religious forces in the modern political world LC Classification: BR526 .R45 1996 Dewey Class No.: 320.5/5/0973 20

Religion in Europe: contemporary perspectives / Sean Gill, Gavin D'Costa, and Ursula King, eds. Published/Created: Kampen, Netherlands: Pharos, c1994. Related Authors: Gill, Sean. D'Costa, Gavin, 1958- King, Ursula. Description: ix, 213 p.; 23 cm. ISBN: 9039005087 Partial Contents: Judaism in Europe / Jonathan Gorsky -- Christianity in Europe / Duncan Forrester -- Islam in Europe / Peter Antes -- Hinduism and Hindus in Europe / Rohit Barot -- Buddhism and European culture in Europe / Stephen Batchelor -- Sikhs in Europe / Owen Cole. Notes: Includes bibiographical references. Subjects: Europe--Religion--20th century. LC Classification: BL695 .R434 1994 Dewey Class No.: 200/.94/0904 20

Religion, feminism, and the family / Anne Carr, Mary Stewart Van Leeuwen, editors. Edition Information: 1st ed. Published/Created: Louisville, Ky.: Westminster John Knox Press, c1996. Related Authors: Carr, Anne E. Van Leeuwen, Mary Stewart, 1943- Description: xiii, 398 p.; 23 cm. ISBN: 0664255124 (acid-free paper) Notes: Includes bibliographical references and index. Subjects: Family--Religious life--United States. Jewish families--Religious life--United States. Family--United States. Feminism--United States. Feminism--

Religious aspects--Christianity. Feminism--Religious aspects--Judaism. Judaism--Doctrines. Christianity--United States. United States--Religion--1960- United States--Social conditions--1980- Series: The family, religion, and culture LC Classification: BV4526.2 .R46 1996 Dewey Class No.: 249/.0973 20

Religion, politics, and the American experience: reflections on religion and American public life / edited by Edith L. Blumhofer; introduction by Martin E. Marty. Published/Created: Tuscaloosa: University of Alabama Press, c2001. Related Authors: Blumhofer, Edith Waldvogel. Description: p. cm. ISBN: 0817311165 (cloth: alk. paper) Partial Contents: Religion and American democracy / Jean Bethke Elshtain -- Toward a contextual appreciation of religion and politics / Laura R. Olson -- "A page of history is worth a volume of logic": charting the legal pilgrimage of public religion / John Witte, Jr. -- Politicians, religion, and civil discourse / Paul Simon -- Religion, politics, and the media / Stewart M. Hoover. Notes: Includes bibliographical references and index. Subjects: Christianity and politics--United States. Evangelicalism--United States. Series: Religion and American culture (Tuscaloosa, Ala.) LC Classification: BR526 .R46 2001 Dewey Class No.: 261.7/0973 21

Renan, Ernest, 1823-1892. Lectures on the influence of the institutions, thought and culture of Rome, on Christianity and the development of the Catholic church. By Ernest Renan ... Tr. by Charles Beard ... Published/Created: London, Edinburgh, Williams and Norgate, 1884. Related Authors: Beard, Charles, 1827-1888, tr. Description: vi, p., 2 l., [3]-213 p. 22 cm. Subjects: Catholic Church--History. Church history--Primitive and early church, ca. 30-600. Rome--Civilization. LC Classification: BR128.R7 R4 1884

Renan, Ernest, 1823-1892. Lectures on the influence of the institutions, thought, and culture of Rome, on Christianity and the

development of the Catholic Church / by Ernest Renan; translated by Charles Beard. Edition Information: 1st AMS ed. Published/Created: New York: AMS Press, 1979. Description: vi, 213 p.; 18 cm. ISBN: 0404604021 Notes: Reprint of the 4th ed. 1898, published by Williams and Norgate, London, in Series: The Hibbert lectures, 1880. Includes bibliographical references. Subjects: Catholic Church--History. Church history--Primitive and early church, ca. 30-600. Rome--Civilization. Series: Hibbert lectures (London, England); 1880. LC Classification: BR170 .R42 1979 Dewey Class No.: 281/.1

Renan, Ernest, 1823-1892. Lectures on the influence of the institutions, thought and culture of Rome, on Christianity and the development of the Catholic church. By Ernest Renan ... Translated by Charles Beard ... Published/Created: London, Edinburgh, Williams and Norgate, 1880. Related Authors: Beard, Charles, 1827-1888, tr. Description: vi p., 2 l., [3]-213 p. 23 cm. Notes: Series title also at head of t.-p. Subjects: Catholic Church--History. Christianity and other religions. Church history--Primitive and early church, ca. 30-600. Rome--Civilization. LC Classification: BL25 .H5 1880

Renck, G. L. Contextualization of Christianity and Christianization of language: a case study from the highlands of Papua New Guinea / Günther Renck. Published/Created: Erlangen: Verlag der Ev.-Luth. Mission, c1990. Description: xvi, 316 p.: 4 maps; 21 cm. ISBN: 3872143050 Notes: Originally presented as the author's thesis, Friedrich-Alexander University at Erlangen, Germany, 1987. Includes bibliographical references (p. 265-300). Subjects: Language and languages--Religious aspects--Christianity. Christianity and culture. Yagaria language. Missions--Papua New Guinea. Series: Erlanger Monographien aus Mission und Ökumene; Bd. 5 LC Classification: BR115.L25 R46 1990 Dewey Class No.: 230/.0899912 20

Research on culture and values: the intersection of universities, churches, and nations / edited by George F. McLean. Published/Created: Lanham: University Press of America; [Washington, D.C.]: Council for Research in Values and Philosophy, c1989. Related Authors: McLean, George F. Description: viii, 196 p.; 24 cm. ISBN: 0819173525 (alk. paper) 0819173533 (pbk.: alk. paper) Notes: Includes bibliographical references and index. Subjects: Christianity and culture--Research. Values--Research. Catholic learning and scholarship. Series: Cultural heritage and contemporary life. Series I, Culture and values; v. 1 LC Classification: BR115.C8 R45 1989 Dewey Class No.: 261/.072 19

Resistance or submission: snatches of a Christian conversation: Mary Beth Edelson, Alex Grey, Komar and Melamid, Owen Land, Tony Oursler, Michael Tracy = Résistance ou soumission: bribes d'une conversation chrétienne / curator, Manon Blanchette; Walter Phillips Gallery for the production, presentation & exhibition of contemporary art; [photo credits, Monty Greenshields; English translation, Jean-Pierre Le Grand]. Published/Created: Banff, Alta.: La Gallery, c1986. Related Authors: Blanchette, Manon, 1952- Le Grand, Jean-Pierre. Walter Phillips Gallery. Description: 51 p.: ill. (some col.); 25 cm. ISBN: 0920159265 Notes: Text in English and French. Exhibition held at the Walter Phillips Gallery, Banff, Alta., Aug. 19-Sept. 26, 1986 and other museums. Includes bibliographical references. Subjects: Art, American--20th century--Exhibitions. Christianity and culture--Exhibitions. LC Classification: N7880 .R47 1986 Dewey Class No.: 709/.73/074011233 19

Rethinking Luther's theology in the contexts of the Third World / Third World Lutheran Theological Educators Conference, São Leopoldo, Brazil, Sept. 5-11, 1988; edited by Nelson Kirst. Published/Created: Geneva: Lutheran World Federation, c1990. Related Authors: Kirst, Nelson. Lutheran World Federation. Description:

158 p.; 21 cm. ISBN: 3906706028 (English ed.) 3906706036 (Spanish ed.) Notes: Includes bibliographical references. Subjects: Luther, Martin, 1483-1546 -- Congresses. Lutheran Church--Doctrines--Congresses. Christianity and culture--Congresses. Developing countries--Religion--Congresses. LC Classification: BR323.7 .T48 1988

Return to Babel: global perspectives on the Bible / edited by Priscilla Pope-Levison and John R. Levison. Edition Information: 1st ed. Published/Created: Louisville, Ky.: Westminster John Knox Press, c1999. Related Authors: Pope-Levison, Priscilla, 1958- Levison, John R. Description: xiv, 234 p.; 23 cm. ISBN: 0664258239 (pbk.: alk. paper) Notes: Includes bibliographical references (p. [221]-223) and indexes. Subjects: Bible--Criticism, interpretation, etc. Christianity and culture. LC Classification: BS531 .R47 1999 Dewey Class No.: 220.6/09 21

Revolution of spirit: ecumenical theology in global context: essays in honor of Richard Shaull / edited by Nantawan Boonprasat Lewis. Published/Created: Grand Rapids, Mich.: W.B. Eerdmans, c1998. Related Authors: Shaull, Richard. Boonprasat-Lewis, Nantawan. Description: x, 303 p.: ill.; 23 cm. ISBN: 0802845916 Partial Contents: Introduction / Nantawan Boonprasat Lewis -- Disabilities and disorientations: resources for the struggle / T. Richard Snyder -- A journey of faith: a gay perspective from the late twentieth century / Andrew W. Conrad -- Latin American and Caribbean immigrants in the U.S.A.: the invisible and forgotten / María Marta Arís-Paúl -- Faith, belief, humbleness, and the hermeneutics of transformation / Joseph C. Nyce. Notes: "Selected bibliography of Richard Shaull": p. 292-300. Includes bibliographical references. Subjects: Christianity and culture. LC Classification: BR115.C8 R48 1998 Dewey Class No.: 261 21

Rewriting the Bible: the real issues: perspectives from within Biblical and religious studies in Zimbabwe / edited by

Isabel Mukonyora, James L. Cox, and Frans J. Verstraelen. Published/Created: Gweru, Zimbabwe: Mambo Press, 1993. Related Authors: Mukonyora, Isabel. Cox, James L. (James Leland) Verstraelen, F. J. Description: xiv, 309 p.; 22 cm. ISBN: 0869225383 Notes: Includes bibliographical references and indexes. Subjects: Bible--Criticism, interpretation, etc.--Congresses. Bible--Study and teaching--Zimbabwe--Congresses. Christianity and culture--Congresses. Series: Religious and theological studies series; 1 LC Classification: BS510 .R48 1993

Rhee, Jung Suck. Secularization and sanctification: a study of Karl Barth's doctrine of sanctification and its contextual application to the Korean Church / door Jung Suck Rhee. Published/Created: Amsterdam, The Netherlands: VU University Press, [1995] Description: xi, 324 p.; 24 cm. ISBN: 9053833803 Notes: "Academisch proefschrift ter verkrijging van de graad doctor aan de Vrije Universiteit te Amsterdam, op gezag van de rector magnificus prof. dr E Boeker, in het openbaar te verdedigen ten overstaan van de promtiecommissie van de faculteit der godgeleerdheid op maandag 20 februari 1995 te 15.45 uur jin het hoofdgebouw van de universiteit, De Boelelaan 1105"--T.p. At head of Vrije Universiteit. Includes bibliographical references (p. 306-320) and index. Subjects: Barth, Karl, 1886-1968 -- Contributions in doctrine of sanctification. Sanctification--History of doctrines--20th century. Secularization (Theology) Secularism. Christianity and culture--Korea. LC Classification: BT765 .R44 1995 Dewey Class No.: 234/.8 21

Rhodes, Stephen A. Where the nations meet: the church in a multicultural world / Stephen A. Rhodes. Published/Created: Downers Grove, Ill.: InterVarsity Press, c1998. Description: 240 p.; 21 cm. ISBN: 0830819363 (pbk.: alk. paper) Notes: Includes bibliographical references (p. [234]-237) and indexes. Subjects: Multiculturalism--Religious aspects--

Christianity. Christianity and culture. Christianity and the world. Church--Marks. Mission of the church--Biblical teaching. Christianity--20th century. LC Classification: BR115.C8 R56 1998 Dewey Class No.: 261.8/348 21

Riamela, Daniel Odafetite, 1951- The concept of life after death: African tradition and Christianity in dialogue (with special emphasis on the Urhobo culture) / Daniel Odafetite Riamela. Published/Created: [Ibadan: Claverianum Press, 199-?] Description: xiii, 103 p.: map; 22 cm. ISBN: 9783218425 Notes: Cover title. Includes bibliographical references (p. 77-103). Subjects: Sobo (African people)--Religion. Future life--Christianity. Future life--Comparative studies. LC Classification: BL2480.S63 R53 1990

Richardson, Tommy G. Paganism in the Church / by Tommy G. Richardson. Published/Created: Midwest City, Okla.: Love of God Fellowship, c1993. Description: v, 97 p.; 20 cm. Subjects: Church history--20th century. Christianity and culture. Secularism. LC Classification: BR477 .R53 1993 Dewey Class No.: 270.8/2 20

Ridings, Daniel. The attic Moses: the dependency theme in some early Christian writers / by Daniel Ridings. Published/Created: Göteborg, Sweden: Acta Universitatis Gothoburgensis, c1995. Description: 270 p.; 23 cm. ISBN: 9173462756 Notes: A revision of the author's thesis--Göteborg University. Includes bibliographical references (p. 239-250) and index. Subjects: Clement, of Alexandria, Saint, ca. 150-ca. 215. Eusebius, of Caesarea, Bishop of Caesarea, ca. 260-ca. 340. Theodoret, Bishop of Cyrrhus. Christianity and culture--History--Early church, ca. 30-600. Civilization, Classical. Series: Studia Graeca et Latina Gothoburgdensia, 0081-6450; 59 LC Classification: BR67 .R47 1995

Rightly teaching the word of your truth: studies in faith and culture, Church and Scriptures, Fathers and worship, Hellenism and the contemporary scene, in honor of his eminence Archbishop Iakovos / edited by Nomikos Michael Vaporis, with an introduction by bishop Methodios of Boston. Published/Created: Brookline, Mass.: Holy Cross Orthodox Press, c1995. Related Authors: Vaporis, N. M. (Nomikos Michael), 1926- Iakovos, Archbishop of the Greek Orthodox Archdiocese of North and South America. Symposium on Faith and Culture (1989: Brookline, Mass.) Description: xxxvi, 421 p.: ill. (some col.); 29 cm. ISBN: 1885652100 1885652119 (pbk.) Notes: Contains papers given at the Symposium on Faith and Culture, held August 1989, in Brookline, Mass., and papers written specially for various occasions honoring the archbishop. Includes bibliographical references. Subjects: Orthodox Eastern Church--Congresses. Orthodox Eastern Church--Doctrines--Congresses. Orthodox Eastern Church--Relations--Congresses. Christianity and culture--Congresses. LC Classification: BX323 .R54 1995 Dewey Class No.: 281.9 20

Risky business: brotherhood in American culture. Published/Created: Romeoville, Ill.: Christian Brothers National Office, c1986. Related Authors: Regional Conference of the Christian Brothers. Christian Brothers' Spirituality Seminar (1986) Description: 182 p.: ill.; 21 cm. Notes: Papers from the 1986 Christian Brothers' Spirituality Seminar sponsored by the Regional Conference of the Christian Brothers. Includes bibliographical references. Subjects: Christian Brothers--United States--Spiritual life--Christianity and culture--Congresses. LC Classification: BX2385 .R57 1986 Dewey Class No.: 255/.78 20

Robb, John D. Focus!: the power of people group thinking: a practical manual for planning effective strategies to reach the unreached / John D. Robb. Edition Information: New expanded ed. Published/Created: Monrovia, Calif.: MARC, c1994. Description: 167 p.: ill.; 21 cm. ISBN: 0912552662 Notes: Bibliography: p. [159]-164. Subjects:

Missions--Theory. Evangelistic work. Christianity and culture. LC Classification: BV2061 .R63 1994 Dewey Class No.: 266/.001 20

Roberts, J. Deotis (James Deotis), 1927- Black theology today: liberation and contextualization / James Deotis Roberts. Published/Created: New York: E. Mellen Press, c1983. Description: 217 p.; 24 cm. ISBN: 0889467552 : Notes: Includes bibliographical references. Subjects: Black theology. Christianity and culture. Series: Toronto studies in theology; v. 12 LC Classification: BT82.7 .R58 1983 Dewey Class No.: 230/.08996073 19

Roberts, Jon H. Darwinism and the divine in America: Protestant intellectuals and organic evolution, 1859-1900 / Jon H. Roberts. Published/Created: cNotre Dame, Ind.: University of Notre Dame Press, c2001. Description: xxii, 339 p.; 23 cm. ISBN: 0268025525 (pbk.: alk. paper) Notes: Originally published: Madison, Wis.: University of Wisconsin Press, 1988, in Series: History of American thought and culture. Includes bibliographical references (p. 245-327) and index. Subjects: Evolution--Religious aspects--Christianity--History of doctrines--19th century. Theology, Doctrinal--United States--History--19th century. Series: Erasmus Institute books LC Classification: BT712 .R63 2001 Dewey Class No.: 231.7/652/097309034 21

Roberts, Jon H. Darwinism and the divine in America: Protestant intellectuals and organic evolution, 1859-1900 / Jon H. Roberts. Published/Created: Madison, Wis.: University of Wisconsin Press, 1988. Description: xviii, 339 p.; 24 cm. ISBN: 0299115909 : Notes: Includes index. Bibliography: p. 245-327. Subjects: Evolution--Religious aspects--Christianity--History of doctrines--19th century. Theology, Doctrinal--United States--History--19th century. Series: History of American thought and culture LC Classification: BT712 .R63 1988 Dewey Class No.: 231.7/65 19

Robinson, Gnana, 1935- A voice in the wilderness / Gnana Robinson. Published/Created: Chennai: Christian Literature Society, 2000. Description: vi, 172 p.; 22 cm. Summary: On the issue relating to life both in the church and in society. Notes: Includes bibliographical references. Subjects: Sociology, Christian. Christianity and culture. LC Classification: BT738 .R615 2000

Roels, Shirley J. Organization man, organization woman: calling, leadership, and culture / Shirley J. Roels; with critical responses by Barbara Hilkert Andolsen and Paul F. Camenisch; introduction by Max L. Stackhouse. Nashville, Tenn.: Abingdon Press, c1997. Related Authors: Camenisch, Paul F. Andolsen, Barbara Hilkert. Stackhouse, Max L. Description: 134 p.; 23 cm. ISBN: 0687009642 (alk. paper) Notes: Includes bibliographical references. Subjects: Vocation--Christianity. Christians--Employment. Leadership--Management--Sex role--Religious aspects--Christianity. Sex discrimination in employment. Series: Abingdon Press studies in Christian ethics and economic life; #4. LC Classification: BV4740 .R64 1997 Dewey Class No.: 261.8/5 21

Roembke, Lianne. Building credible multicultural teams / Lianne Roembke. Published/Created: Pasadena, Calif.: William Carey Library, c2000. Description: x, 287 p.: ill.; 23 cm. ISBN: 0878083405 (pbk.: alk. paper) Notes: Includes bibliographical references (p. 265-273) and index. Subjects: Missions. Intercultural communication--Religious aspects Christianity. Christianity and culture. LC Classification: BV2063 .R5513 2000 Dewey Class No.: 266 21

Rohr, Richard. Hope against darkness: the transforming vision of Saint Francis in an age of anxiety / Richard Rohr; with John Bookser Feister. Published/Created: Cincinnati, Ohio: St. Anthony Messenger Press, 2001. Related Authors: Feister, John Bookser. Description: 182 p.; 24 cm. ISBN: 0867164409 Subjects: Francis, of Assisi, Saint, 1182-1226. Spiritual life--

Catholic authors. Christianity and culture--History--21st century.

Rohr, Richard. Love your enemy [sound recording]: the Gospel call to nonviolence / Richard Rohr. Published/Created: Cincinnati, OH: St. Anthony Messenger Press, [1997] Related Authors: Girard, René, 1923- Violence et le sacré. English. Bailie, Gil. Violence unveiled. Description: 1 sound cassette (1 hr., 23 min.): analog. Publisher Number: A6661 St. Anthony Messenger Press Summary: Richard Rohr explores the cultural expectations that contribute to the epidemic of violence in the modern world. Notes: Lecture based on the books, Violence and the sacred, by René Girard and Violence unveiled, by Gil Bailie. Subjects: Nonviolence--Religious aspects--Christianity. Violence--Religious aspects--Christianity. Culture conflict. Social conflict. LC Classification: RYG 5232

Romanowski, William D. Eyes wide open: looking for God in popular culture / William D. Romanowski. Published/Created: Grand Rapids, Mich.: Brazos Press, c2001. Description: 171 p.: ill.; 22 cm. ISBN: 1587430096 (pbk.) Subjects: Popular culture--Religious aspects--Christianity--United States. LC Classification: BR526 .R646 2001 Dewey Class No.: 261/.0973 21

Romanowski, William D. Pop culture wars: religion & the role of entertainment in American life / William D. Romanowski. Published/Created: Downers Grove, Ill.: InterVarsity Press, c1996. Description: 379 p.: ill.; 23 cm. ISBN: 0830819886 (pbk.: alk. paper) Notes: Includes bibliographical references (p. [339]-379). Subjects: Popular culture--Religious aspects--Christianity. Popular culture--Amusements--United States--History--20th century. Amusements--Religious aspects--Christianity. Christianity and culture--United States--History--20th century. Culture conflict--United States--Religion--1960- LC Classification: BR526 .R65 1996 Dewey Class No.: 261.5/7 20

Rosio, Bob. The culture war in America: a society in chaos / by Bob Rosio. Published/Created: Lafayette, La.: Huntington House Publishers, c1995. Description: 224 p.: ill.; 22 cm. ISBN: 1563840979 (pbk.) Notes: Includes bibliographical references (p. 215-222). Subjects: Christianity and culture--United States. Conservatism--Religious aspects--Christianity. Culture conflict--United States. United States--Civilization--20th century. United States--Moral conditions. United States--History--Religious aspects--Christianity. United States--Politics and government--20th century. LC Classification: BR526 .R665 1995 Dewey Class No.: 261/.0973 20

Rosman, Doreen M. Evangelicals and culture / Doreen M. Rosman. Published/Created: London: Croom Helm, c1984. Description: 262 p.; 23 cm. ISBN: 0709922531 : Notes: Includes index. Bibliography: p. 248-253. Subjects: Evangelicalism--England--History--18th century. Evangelicalism--England--History--19th century. Christianity and culture. England--Intellectual life--18th century. England--Intellectual life--19th century. LC Classification: BR1642.G7 R67 1984 Dewey Class No.: 280/.4 19

Ross, Kenneth R. The message of mainstream Christianity in Malawi: an analysis of contemporary preaching / K.R. Ross. Published/Created: [Zomba, Malawi: Dept. of Theology and Religious Studies, Chancellor College, University of Malawi, 1993] Description: 33 p.; 30 cm. Notes: Cover title. "July 1993"--P. 1. Includes bibliographical references (p. 33). Subjects: Preaching--Malawi. Christianity and culture. Independent churches--Malawi. Malawi--Church history--20th century. Series: Sources for the study of religion in Malawi; no. 17 LC Classification: BV4208.M3 R67 1993 Dewey Class No.: 251/.0096897 20

Rotholz, James M. Chronic fatigue syndrome, Christianity, and culture: between God and illness / James M. Rotholz. Published/Created: New York: Haworth Social Work Practice Press, 2002. Description: p. cm. ISBN: 0789014920 (alk. paper) 078901565X (pbk.: alk. paper) Notes: Includes bibliographical references and index. Subjects: Chronic fatigue syndrome--Patients--Religious life. Christianity and culture. LC Classification: BV4910.335 .R68 2002 Dewey Class No.: 261.8/321960478 21

Rouner, Leroy S. The discovery of humankind: an essay on the Christian understanding of community / by Leroy S. Rouner. Edition Information: 1st ed. Published/Created: New Delhi: Islam and the Modern Age Society, 1977. Description: x, 152 p.; 21 cm. Notes: Includes index. Subjects: Sociology, Christian. Christianity and culture. LC Classification: BT738 .R68 Dewey Class No.: 261.8/34

Rouner, Leroy S. To be at home: Christianity, civil religion, and world community / Leroy S. Rouner. Published/Created: Boston: Beacon Press, c1991. Description: viii, 151 p.; 23 cm. ISBN: 0807010162 : Notes: Includes bibliographical references (p. 133-146) and index. Subjects: Christianity and international affairs. Christianity and culture. Religious pluralism--Christianity. Christianity--20th century. Civil religion--United States. Christianity and other religions. Civil religion--India. United States--Religion--1965- India--Religion. LC Classification: BR115.I7 R68 1991 Dewey Class No.: 261/.1 20

Roxburgh, Alan J. Reaching a new generation: strategies for tomorrow's church / Alan J. Roxburgh. Published/Created: Downers Grove, Ill.: InterVarsity Press, c1993. Description: 140 p.; 21 cm. ISBN: 0830813403 (alk. paper) Notes: Includes bibliographical references (p. [137]-140). Subjects: Postmodernism--Religious aspects--Christianity and culture. Human ecology--Religious aspects--Christianity. Spirituality. Christianity--20th century. LC Classification: BT28 .R685 1993 Dewey Class No.: 261 20

Roxburgh, Alan J. The missionary congregation, leadership & liminality / Alan J. Roxburgh. Published/Created: Harrisburg, Pa.: Trinity Press International, c1997. Description: viii, 71 p.: ill.; 19 cm. ISBN: 1563381907 (pbk.: alk. paper) Notes: Includes bibliographical references (p. 70-71). Subjects: Missions--Theory--North America. Christianity and culture--North America--History--Religion--20th century. Series: Christian mission and modern culture LC Classification: BV2063 .R64 1997 Dewey Class No.: 266/.001 21

Ruckman, Peter S. The Christian's handbook of science and philosophy / by Peter S. Ruckman. Published/Created: Pensacola, Fla.: Bible Baptist Bookstore, c1985. Description: iv, 362 p.: ill.; 21 cm. Subjects: Religion and science. Philosophy and religion. Christianity and culture. Science. Philosophy. LC Classification: BL240.2 .R76 1985

Rudy, Gordon. The mystical language of sensation in the later Middle Ages / by Gordon Rudy. Published/Created: New York: Routledge, 2002. Description: p. cm. ISBN: 0415940702 Notes: Includes bibliographical references and index. Subjects: Bernard, of Clairvaux, Saint, 1090 or 91-1153. Hadewijch, 13th cent. Mystical union--History of doctrines--Middle Ages, 600-1500. Taste--Religious aspects--Christianity--History of doctrines--Middle Ages, 600-1500. Touch--Religious aspects--Christianity--History of doctrines--Middle Ages, 600-1500. Series: Studies in medieval history and culture; v. 14 LC Classification: BT767.7 .R83 2002 Dewey Class No.: 248.2/2/0902 21

Ruether, Rosemary Radford. Liberation theology: human hope confronts Christian history and American power. Published/Created: New York, Paulist Press [1972] Description: vi, 194 p. 21 cm. ISBN: 0809117444 Partial Contents: The foundations for a theology of liberation.--Christian origins and the counter-culture.--The vanishing religious order and the emerging human community.--Is celibacy eschatological? The suppression of

Christian radicalism.--Judaism and Christianity: a dialogue refused.--Christian anti-Semitism and the dilemma of Zionism.--Is Christianity misogynist? The failure of women's liberation in the church. Notes: Includes bibliographical references. Subjects: Liberation theology--Addresses, essays, lectures. Sociology, Christian--Addresses, essays, lectures. LC Classification: BT810.2 .R8 Dewey Class No.: 230

Ruether, Rosemary Radford. Radical social movement and the radical church tradition [by] Rosemary R. Ruether. Power and violence: a Biblical study [by] Graydon F. Snyder. Published/Created: Oak Brook, Ill., Bethany Theological Seminary [1971] Related Authors: Snyder, Graydon F. Power and violence: a Biblical study. 1971. Description: 59, [1] p. 23 cm. Notes: The first item was originally presented as the Hoff lectures at the seminary in Nov. 1970; the second was originally 4 lectures presented at the Burkhart Institute, held at La Verne College, Calif., in Apr. 1970. Bibliography: p. [60] Subjects: Church and state. Socialism. Christianity and culture. Power (Christian theology)--Biblical teaching. Series: Bethany Theological Seminary, Oak Brook, Ill. Colloquium no. 1 LC Classification: BV631 .R8 Dewey Class No.: 201/.1

Ruether, Rosemary Radford. To change the world: Christology and cultural criticism / Rosemary Radford Ruether. Published/Created: New York: Crossroad, 1981. Description: 85 p.; 22 cm. ISBN: 0824500849 : Notes: "First given as the Kuyper Lectures at the Free University in Amsterdam in September 1980"--P. 5. Includes bibliographical references and index. Subjects: Jesus Christ--Political and social views. Jesus Christ--Person and offices. Christianity and culture. Christianity and politics. LC Classification: BT202 .R73 1981 Dewey Class No.: 232 19

Rupp, George. Culture-protestantism: German liberal theology at the turn of the twentieth century / by George Rupp.

Published/Created: Missoula, Mont.: Published by Scholars Press for the American Academy of Religion, c1977. Description: 67 p.; 24 cm. ISBN: 0891301976 : Notes: Includes bibliographical references. Subjects: Protestant churches--Germany--Doctrines--History--20th century. Christianity and culture--History. Liberalism (Religion)--Germany--History--Protestant churches. Series: AAR studies in religion, 0084-6287; no. 15 LC Classification: BT30.G3 R86 Dewey Class No.: 230/.0943

Rushdoony, Rousas John. The one and the many; studies in the philosophy of order and ultimacy. Published/Created: [Nutley, N.J.] Craig Press, 1971. Description: viii, 388 p. 21 cm. Notes: Includes bibliographical references. Subjects: One (The One in philosophy) Many (Philosophy) Order (Philosophy) Christianity and culture. LC Classification: B105.O7 R8 Dewey Class No.: 190

Russian culture at the threshold of the third millenium of Christianity / compiled by Yuri B. Pishchik; translated by Lev N. Bobrov and Nikita N. Kuhmalin. Published/Created: Moscow: Disput magazine, c1993. Related Authors: Pishchik, Yuri B. Disput. Description: 126 p.; 20 cm. Subjects: Christianity--Russia (Federation)--20th century. Russia (Federation)--Church history--20th century. LC Classification: IN PROCESS (COPIED)

Russian culture in modern times / edited by Robert P. Hughes and Irina Paperno. Published/Created: Berkeley: University of California Press, c1994. Related Authors: Hughes, Robert P. Paperno, Irina. Description: viii, 334 p.; 24 cm. ISBN: 0520081757 (alk. paper) Notes: Based on papers delivered at two international conferences held in May 1988 at the University of California--Berkeley and the Kennan Institute for Advanced Russian Studies to commemorate the millennium of the Christianization of Kievan Rus. Includes bibliographical references and index. Subjects: Orthodox Eastern Church--Russia--History--Congresses. Russkaia pravoslavnaia tserkov´--History--Congresses. Russia--Intellectual life--1801-1917--Congresses. Russia--Intellectual life--18th century--Congresses. Russia--Religious life and customs--Congresses. Russia--Church history--Congresses. Series: Christianity and the Eastern Slavs; v. 2 California Slavic studies; vol. 17. LC Classification: DK4 .C33 vol. 17 DK189.2 Dewey Class No.: 947 s 306.6/0947 20

Russo, Steve, 1953- Halloween / Steve Russo. Published/Created: Eugene, Or.: Harvest House Publishers, c1998. Description: 140 p.: ill.; 21 cm. ISBN: 1565078519 Notes: Includes bibliographical references (p. 139-140). Subjects: Halloween. Amusements--Religious aspects--Christianity. Christianity and culture. LC Classification: GT4965 .R87 1998 Dewey Class No.: 394.2646 21

Rutler, George W. (George William) A crisis of saints: essays on people and principles / Geroge William Rutler. Published/Created: San Francisco: Ignatius Press, c1995. Description: 204 p.; 21 cm. ISBN: 0898705568 Notes: Includes bibliographical references and index. Subjects: Catholic Church--Apologetic works. Heroic virtue. Christianity and culture. LC Classification: BX1752 .R878 1995 Dewey Class No.: 282/.09/045 20

Rutler, George W. (George William) Beyond modernity: reflections of a post-modern Catholic / by George William Rutler. Published/Created: San Francisco: Ignatius Press, c1987. Description: 227 p.; 21 cm. ISBN: 089870135X (pbk.) Subjects: Catholic Church--Apologetic works. Postmodernism--Religious aspects--Catholic Church. Civilization, Modern--20th century. Civilization, Modern--19th century. Christianity and culture. LC Classification: BX1752 .R87 1987 Dewey Class No.: 282 19

Ryken, Leland. Culture in Christian perspective: a door to understanding & enjoying the arts / Leland Ryken.

Published/Created: Portland, Or.: Multnomah Press, c1986. Description: 283 p.; 22 cm. ISBN: 0880701153 : Notes: Includes bibliographies and indexes. Subjects: Christianity and the arts. LC Classification: BR115.A8 R95 1986 Dewey Class No.: 261.5/7 19

Ryken, Leland. The liberated imagination: thinking Christianly about the arts / Leland Ryken. Published/Created: Wheaton, Ill.: H. Shaw Publishers, c1989. Description: 283 p.: ill.; 21 cm. ISBN: 0877884951 : Notes: Reprint. Originally published: Culture in Christian perspective. Portland, Or.: Multnomah Press, c1986. Includes bibliographical references. Subjects: Christianity and the arts. Series: The Wheaton literary series LC Classification: BR115.A8 R96 1989 Dewey Class No.: 261.5/7 20

Ryken, Philip Graham, 1966- My Father's world: meditations on Christianity and culture / Philip Graham Ryken. Published/Created: Phillipsburg, NJ: P&R Pub., c2002. Description: p. cm. ISBN: 0875525601 (pbk.) Notes: Includes bibliographical references (p.) and indexes. LC Classification: BR115.C8 .R95 2002 Dewey Class No.: 261 21

Sabatier, Auguste, 1839-1901. Outlines of a philosophy of religion based on psychology and history. Published/Created: New York, Harper [1957] Description: 337 p. 21 cm. Subjects: Religion--Philosophy. Christianity--Philosophy. Dogma. LC Classification: BL51 .S3 1957

Sack, Daniel. Whitebread Protestants: food and religion in American culture / Daniel Sack. Edition Information: 1st ed. Published/Created: New York: St. Martin's Press, 2000. Description: x, 262 p.: ill.; 22cm. ISBN: 0312217315 Notes: Includes bibliographical references (p. [225]-248) and index. Subjects: Food--Religious aspects--Christianity--History of doctrines--19th century. Protestants--United States--History--19th century. Food--Religious aspects--Christianity--History of doctrines--20th century. Protestants--United States--

History--20th century. United States--Church history--19th century--20th century. LC Classification: BR115.N87 S23 2000 Dewey Class No.: 261 21

Sahay, Keshari N., 1935- Christianity and culture change in India / Keshari N. Sahay. Published/Created: New Delhi, India: Inter-India Publications, 1986. Description: 332 p.; 23 cm. ISBN: 8121001730 Summary: Study relates mainly to the Oraons of Chotanagpur in Bihar. Notes: Spine Christianity & culture change in India. Includes bibliographies and index. Subjects: Christianity--Tribes--India--Bihar. Oraon (Indic people)--Religion. Christianity and culture. LC Classification: BR1156.B54 S24 1986 Dewey Class No.: 275.4 20

Saints and sinners: the American Catholic experience through stories, memoirs, essays, and commentary / edited by Greg Tobin. Edition Information: 1st ed. Published/Created: New York: Doubleday, 1999. Related Authors: Tobin, Greg. Description: xvi, 347 p.; 25 cm. ISBN: 0385493312 Notes: Includes bibliographical references. Subjects: Catholic Church--Catholics--Christianity and culture--United States--History--20th century. Catholics--United States--Fiction. LC Classification: BX1406.2 .S25 1999 Dewey Class No.: 282/.73/0904 21

Sait⁻o, S⁻oichi, 1886- A study of the influence of Christianity upon Japanese culture, Published/Created: Tokyo, Japan Council of the Institute of Pacific Relations [cover 1931] Related Authors: Institute of Pacific Relations. 4th conference, Shanghai, 1931. Description: iii, 71 p. diagrs. 23 cm. Subjects: Christianity--Influence.Japan--Civilization. LC Classification: DS821 .S23

Samartha, S. J. (Stanley J.), 1920- One Christ, many religions: toward a revised Christology / S.J. Samartha. Published/Created: Maryknoll, N.Y.: Orbis Books, c1991. Description: xiv, 190 p.; 25 cm. ISBN: 0883447347: 0883447339 (pbk.) : Notes: Includes bibliographical

references (p. 179-185) and index.
Subjects: Jesus Christ--Person and offices.
Christianity and other religions. Religious
pluralism. Christianity--20th century.
Christianity and culture. Series: Faith
meets faith LC Classification: BT205 .S19
1991 Dewey Class No.: 261.2 20

Sambahaginan: an experience in community
development work. Published/Created:
Diliman, Quezon City, Philippines:
Institute for Studies in Asian Church and
Culture, c1992. Related Authors: Institute
for Studies in Asian Church & Culture.
Description: 126 p.: ill.; 22 cm. Subjects:
Rural development--Philippines--Wawa.
Rural development--Religious aspects--
Christianity. Wawa (Philippines)--Rural
conditions. LC Classification: HN720.Z9
C6764 1992 Dewey Class No.:
307.1/412/095991 20

Sample, Tex. Ministry in an oral culture: living
with Will Rogers, Uncle Remus, and
Minnie Pearl / Tex Sample. Edition
Information: 1st ed. Published/Created:
Louisville, Ky.: Westminster/John Knox
Press, c1994. Description: x, 100 p.; 20
cm. ISBN: 066425506X (pbk.) Notes:
Includes bibliographical references (p. 95-
100). Subjects: Pastoral theology--United
States. Popular culture--United States.
Popular culture--Religious aspects--
Christianity. United States--Church
history--20th century. LC Classification:
BR526 .S24 1994 Dewey Class No.: 253
20

Sample, Tex. The spectacle of worship in a
wired world: electronic culture and the
gathered people of God / Tex Sample.
Published/Created: Nashville, TN:
Abingdon Press, 1998. Description: 141 p.;
24 cm. ISBN: 0687083737 (pbk.: alk.
paper) Subjects: Church work with young
adults. Young adults--United States--
Religious life. Baby boom generation.
Generation X. Mass media--Religious
aspects--Christianity. Popular culture--
Religious aspects--Christianity. Liturgics.
LC Classification: BV4446 .S25 1998
Dewey Class No.: 261.5/2 21

Sánchez, Julio A. The Community of the Holy
Spirit: a movement of change in a convent
of nuns in Puerto Rico / Julio A. Sanchez.
Published/Created: Lanham: University
Press of America, c1983. Description: xii,
177 p.; 22 cm. ISBN: 0819133671 (alk.
paper): 081913368X (pbk.: alk. paper) :
Notes: Bibliography: p. 175-177. Subjects:
Monasticism and religious orders for
women--Puerto Rico. Christianity and
culture. Sociology, Christian--Puerto Rico.
Puerto Rico--Church history. LC
Classification: BX4220.P9 S36 1983
Dewey Class No.: 306/.6 19

Sanneh, Lamin O. Encountering the West:
Christianity and the global cultural
process: the African dimension / Lamin
Sanneh. Published/Created: Maryknoll,
N.Y.: Orbis Books, c1993. Description:
286 p.; 22 cm. ISBN: 0883449293 (cloth):
088344934X (paper) Notes: "First
published in Great Britain in 1993 by
Marshall Pickering"--T.p. verso. Includes
bibliographical references (p. 247-276) and
index. Subjects: Christianity and culture.
Missions. Missions--Africa. Christianity
and other religions. Christianity and other
religions--Islam. Islam--Relations--
Christianity. Religious pluralism--
Christianity. Africa--Civilization--Western
influences. Series: World Christian
theology series LC Classification:
BR115.C8 S26 1993 Dewey Class No.:
261 20

Sanneh, Lamin O. Religion and the variety of
culture: a study in origin and practice /
Lamin Sanneh. Published/Created: Valley
Forge, Pa.: Trinity Press International,
c1996. Description: viii, 87 p.; 19 cm.
ISBN: 1563381664 (alk. paper)
0852443781 (Gracewing) Notes: "Revised
and expanded version of chapter 1 of
Encountering the West"--T.p. verso.
Includes bibliographical references (p. 83-
87). Subjects: Religion and culture.
Christianity and culture. Series: Christian
mission and modern culture LC
Classification: BL65.C8 S26 1996 Dewey
Class No.: 291.1/7 20

Santo Domingo and after: the challenges for the Latin American Church / Gustavo Gutiérrez ... [et al.]. Published/Created: London, UK: Catholic Institute for International Relations, 1993. Related Authors: Gutiérrez, Gustavo, 1928- Description: 68 p.; 22 cm. ISBN: 1852871202 Contents: The Santo Domingo conference / Francis McDonagh -- The winds of Santo Domingo and the evangelisation of culture / Jon Sobrino -- An agenda / Gustavo Gutiérrez -- Reflections on collegiality: a letter to my brother bishops / Cándido Padin. Notes: Includes bibliographical references (p. 58-59). Subjects: Catholic Church--Latin America--Congresses. Catholic Church. Conferencia General del Episcopado Latinoamericano (4th: 1992: Santo Domingo, Dominican Republic) Councils and synods, Episcopal (Catholic)--Latin America. Evangelistic work--Latin America--Congresses. Christianity and culture--Congresses. Social change Role of Catholicism South America Central America LC Classification: IN PROCESS Dewey Class No.: 261.8098 20

Schaeffer, Francis A. (Francis August) A Christian view of philosophy and culture. Published/Created: Westchester, Ill.: Crossway Books, c1982, (1983 printing) Description: xx, 397 p.; 24 cm. ISBN: 0891072365 Contents: The God who is there -- Escape from reason -- He is there and He is not silent -- Back to freedom and dignity. Notes: Includes bibliographical references. Subjects: Apologetics. Christianity--20th century. Philosophy, Modern. Christianity--Philosophy. Knowledge, Theory of. Religion and science. Series: Schaeffer, Francis A. (Francis August). Works. 1982; v. 1. LC Classification: BR83 .S33 1982 vol. 1 BT1102 Dewey Class No.: 230 s 239 19

Schapera, Isaac, 1905- ed. Western civilization and the natives of South Africa; studies in culture contact; edited by I. Schapera ... Published/Created: London, G. Routledge and sons, limited, 1934. Description: xiv, 312 p. front. (port.) XI pl., double maps. 25 cm. Partial Contents: I. The old Bantu culture, by I. Schapera. (Bibliography: p. 35-36)--II. Present-day life in the native reserves, by M. I. Schapera.--III. Christianity and the religious life of the Bantu, by W. M. Einelen.--IV. The educated native in Bantu communal life, by W. G. A. Mears.--V. European influences upon the development of Bantu language and literature, by G. P. Lestrade.--VI. The effect of western civilization on Bantu music, by P. R. Kirby. Notes: "Select bibliography": p. 301-308. Subjects: Blacks--South Africa. Ethnology--South Africa. Indigenous peoples--South Africa. South Africa--Race relations. LC Classification: DT764.B2 S4 Dewey Class No.: 572.968

Scheinberg, Cynthia. Women's poetry and religion in Victorian England: Jewish identity and Christian culture / Cynthia Scheinberg. Published/Created: New York: Cambridge University Press, 2002. Description: p. cm. ISBN: 0521811120 Notes: Includes bibliographical references and index. Subjects: Rossetti, Christina Georgina, 1830-1894 --Religion. Browning, Elizabeth Barrett, 1806-1861 --Religion. Aguilar, Grace, 1816-1847 --Religion. Levy, Amy, 1861-1889 --Religion. Religious poetry, English--History and criticism. Christianity and literature--England--History--19th century. Judaism and literature--England--History--19th century. Women and literature--England--History--19th century. English poetry--Women authors--History and criticism. Christian poetry, English--Jewish poetry--History and criticism. Series: Cambridge studies in nineteenth-century literature and culture; 35 LC Classification: PR508.R4 S34 2002 Dewey Class No.: 821/.809382 21

Schenck, Paul C. The extermination of Christianity: a tyranny of consensus / by Paul C. Schenck with Robert Schenck. Published/Created: Lafayette, La.: Huntington House, c1993. Related Authors: Schenck, Robert L. Description: 239 p.; 22 cm. ISBN: 1563840510 Notes: Includes bibliographical references. Subjects: Popular culture--United States--

Religious aspects Christianity. Mass
Media--Religious aspects--Christianity.
United States--Religious life and customs--
1981- LC Classification: BR115.C8 S265
1993 Dewey Class No.: 277.3/0829 20

Schenck, Robert L. The ten words that will
change a nation: the Ten commandments /
Rob Schenck. Published/Created: Tulsa,
Okla.: Albury Pub., c1999. Description:
xxii, 262 p.: ill.; 24 cm. ISBN:
1577781287 Notes: Includes
bibliographical references. Subjects: Ten
commandments--Criticism, interpretation,
etc. Christianity and culture--Christianity
and politics--United States. Social ethics--
United States. LC Classification: BV4655
.S39 1999 Dewey Class No.: 241.5/2 21

Schilder, K. (Klaas), 1890-1952. Christ and
culture / K. Schilder; translated by G. van
Rongen and W. Helder. Published/Created:
Winnipeg: Premier, 1977. Description: 89
p.: port.; 24 cm. ISBN: 0887560083 Notes:
Translation of Christus en cultuur. Includes
bibliographical references. Subjects: Jesus
Christ--Person and offices. Christianity and
culture. LC Classification: BR115.C8
S2713 Dewey Class No.: 261.1

Schineller, Peter. A handbook on inculturation /
Peter Schineller. Published/Created: New
York: Paulist Press, c1990. Description: iv,
141 p.; 21 cm. ISBN: 0809131242 : Notes:
Includes bibliographical references (p.
124-141). Subjects: Christianity and
culture. LC Classification: BR115.C8 S275
1990 Dewey Class No.: 261 20

Schmidt, Alvin J. Veiled and silenced: how
culture shaped sexist theology / Alvin John
Schmidt. Published/Created: Macon, Ga.:
Mercer University Press, c1989.
Description: xvii, 238 p.; 24 cm. ISBN:
0865543291 (alk. paper) 0865543275
(pbk.: alk. paper) Notes: Includes
bibliographical references. Subjects:
Women--Religious aspects--Christianity--
History of doctrines. Women in
Christianity--History. Sexism--Religious
aspects--Christianity--History of doctrines.
LC Classification: BT704 .S36 1989

Dewey Class No.: 261.8/344 20

Schneider, John R. The good of affluence: a
theology for people seeking God in a
culture of modern capitalism / John R.
Schneider. Published/Created: Grand
Rapids, MI: W.B. Eerdmans, 2002.
Description: p. cm. ISBN: 0802847994
(pbk.: alk. paper) Notes: Includes
bibliographical references. Subjects:
Wealth--Religious aspects--Christianity--
Biblical teaching. Capitalism--Religious
aspects--Christianity. LC Classification:
BR115.W4 S37 2002 Dewey Class No.:
261.8/5 21

Schreiter, Robert J. The new catholicity:
theology between the global and the local /
Robert J. Schreiter. Published/Created:
Maryknoll, N.Y.: Orbis Books, c1997.
Description: xii, 140 p.; 24 cm. ISBN:
157075120X (alk. paper) Notes: "This
book is a revised edition of lectures given
at the University of Frankfurt in the
autumn of 1995"--Introd. Includes
bibliographical references and index.
Subjects: Catholic Church--History--1965-
Catholic Church--Doctrines. Christianity
and culture. Series: Faith and cultures
series LC Classification: BX1390 .S36
1997 Dewey Class No.: 230/.2 21

Schuller, David S. Power structures and and the
church [by] David S. Schuller.
Published/Created: Saint Louis, Concordia
Pub. House [1969] Description: 90 p. illus.
21 cm. Notes: Bibliographical references
included in "Notes" (p. 87-90) Subjects:
Church and the world. Christianity and
culture. LC Classification: BR115.W6 S33
Dewey Class No.: 261.8/3

Schultze, Quentin J. (Quentin James), 1952-
Televangelism and American culture: the
business of popular religion / Quentin J.
Schultze. Published/Created: Grand
Rapids, Mich.: Baker Book House, c1991.
Description: 264 p.; 24 cm. ISBN:
0801083192 Notes: Includes
bibliographical references (p. 249-259) and
index. Subjects: Television in religion--
United States. Religious broadcasting--
Christianity. Popular culture--United

States. United States--Church history--20th century. LC Classification: BV656.3 .S385 1991 Dewey Class No.: 269/.26/0973 20

Schwarz, John E. Word alive!: learning, loving, and living the Christian faith in the context of modern culture / [text by John Schwarz]. Published/Created: Minneapolis, MN (6913 Gleason Rd., Minneapolis 55439): Tabgha Foundation, c1993. Description: ix, 163 p.; 24 cm. Notes: Includes bibliographical references and index. Subjects: Christianity. LC Classification: BR121.2 .S387 1993 Dewey Class No.: 230 21

Scott, Steve, 1951- Like a house on fire: renewal of the arts in a postmodern culture / Steve Scott. Published/Created: Chicago: Cornerstone Press, c1997. Description: viii, 135 p.; 21 cm. ISBN: 0940895374 (pbk.) Notes: Includes bibliographical references (p. 129-131) and index. Subjects: Christianity and the arts. Postmodernism--Religious aspects--20th century. LC Classification: BR115.A8 S45 1997 Dewey Class No.: 261.5/7 21

Scoville, Gordon. Into the vacuum: being the church in the age of barbarism / Gordon Scoville. Published/Created: Harrisburg, Pa.: Trinity Press International, c1998. Description: x, 102 p.; 19 cm. ISBN: 1563382385 Notes: Includes bibliographical references (p. 83-102). Subjects: Mission of the church. Church and the world. Christianity and culture--United States--History--19th century. Christianity and culture--United States--History--20th century. United States--Civilization--19th century. United States--Civilization--20th century. Series: Christian mission and modern culture LC Classification: BV601.8 .S37 1998 Dewey Class No.: 277.3/0829 21

Scribner, Robert W. Religion and culture in Germany (1400-1800) / by R.W. Scribner; edited by Lyndal Roper; with a preface by Thomas A. Brady, Jr. Published/Created: Leiden; Boston: Brill, 2001. Related Authors: Roper, Lyndal. Description: xvi, 380 p.: ill.; 24 cm. ISBN: 9004114572

(hardcover: alk. paper) Notes: "Publications of R.W. 'Bob' Scribner": p. [xii]-xvi. Includes bibliographical references and indexes. Subjects: Christianity and culture--Germany--History. Germany--Church history. Series: Studies in medieval and Reformation thought, 0585-6914; v. 81 LC Classification: BR852 .S34 2001 Dewey Class No.: 274.3 21

Scriven, Charles. The transformation of culture: Christian social ethics after H. Richard Niebuhr / Charles Scriven; foreword by James W. McClendon, Jr. Published/Created: Scottdale, Pa.: Herald Press, c1988. Related Authors: Niebuhr, H. Richard (Helmut Richard), 1894-1962. Description: 224 p.: port.; 23 cm. ISBN: 0836131010 (pbk.) : Notes: Includes index. Bibliography: p. 217-220. Subjects: Niebuhr, H. Richard (Helmut Richard), 1894-1962. Christ and culture. Christianity and culture. Anabaptists. Social ethics--History--20th century. Christian ethics--History--20th century. LC Classification: BR115.C8 S37 1988 Dewey Class No.: 241 19

Sea of dreams / Israel Film Service; director and script, Etan Tal; producer, David Schütz; English version [script?], Reuven Morgan. Published/Created: United States: Embassy of Israel, [1990?] Related Authors: Israel. Shagrirut (U.S.) Embassy of Israel Collection (Library of Congress) Description: 1 videocassette of 1 (VHS) (28 min.): sd., col.; 1/2 in. viewing copy. Summary: This documentary focuses on the Sea of Galilee and its surroundings from historical, geographical and life-sustaining perspectives and concentrates on the area as the place where Judaism and Christianity flourished. Notes: Copyright: reg. unknown. Copyright notice on video: Israel Film Service; 1991. Israel Film Service produces films and television programs for all Israeli government ministries per Israel. Production Unit. Video catalogue, 1995, p. 14. Ministry of Foreign Affairs home page, government ministries, Ministry of Education, Culture and Sports, 9/23/97; Screen international

film & TV yearbook, 1987-88, p. 112.
Credits: Director of photography, Uri
Sharon; editor, Helen Hanna; music, Ilan
Harel; narration, Ohad Shachar, Danny
Ziv, Joe Jacobs. Subjects: Judaism--Israel--
Tiberias, Lake, Region--History. Tiberias,
Lake, Region (Israel)--Antiquities--Church
history. Genre/Form: Documentary--Short.
LC Classification: VAF 3552 (viewing
copy)

Seel, John. The Evangelical forfeit: can we
recover? / John Seel. Published/Created:
Grand Rapids, Mich.: Hourglass Books,
c1993. Description: 124 p.; 22 cm. ISBN:
0801083621 (pbk.) Notes: Includes
bibliographical references (p. 118-124).
Subjects: Evangelicalism--Christianity and
culture--United States--Church history--
20th century. LC Classification:
BR1642.U5 S44 1993 Dewey Class No.:
277.3/0829 20

Self-definition in early Christianity: protocol of
the thirty-seventh colloquy, 6 January 1980
/ the Center for Hermeneutical Studies in
Hellenistic and Modern Culture, the
Graduate Theological Union & the
University of California, Berkeley,
California; Ben F. Meyer; Irene Lawrence,
editor. Published/Created: Berkeley, CA:
The Center, c1980. Related Authors:
Meyer, Ben F., 1927- Lawrence, Irene,
1942- Description: 38 p.; 22 cm. ISBN:
0892420367 (pbk.) : Notes: Includes
bibliographical references. Subjects:
Christianity--Essence, genius, nature--
Congresses. Series: Colloquy (Center for
Hermeneutical Studies in Hellenistic and
Modern Culture); 37. LC Classification:
BT60 .C4 1980 Dewey Class No.: 270.1 19

Senior, John, 1923- The death of Christian
culture / John Senior. Published/Created:
New Rochelle, N.Y.: Arlington House,
c1978. Description: 185 p.; 24 cm. ISBN:
0870004166 : Notes: Includes
bibliographical references and index.
Subjects: Civilization, Christian.
Christianity--20th century. LC
Classification: BR115.C5 S46 Dewey
Class No.: 261.5

Senn, Frank C. Christian worship and its
cultural setting / Frank C. Senn.
Published/Created: Philadelphia: Fortress
Press, c1983. Description: xi, 148 p.; 22
cm. ISBN: 0800617002 (pbk.) Notes:
Includes bibliographical references and
indexes. Subjects: Liturgics. Public
worship. Christianity and culture. LC
Classification: BV176 .S45 1983 Dewey
Class No.: 264 19

Sernau, Scott. Please don't squeeze the
Christian into the world's mold / Scott
Sernau. Published/Created: Downers
Grove, Ill.: InterVarsity Press, c1987.
Description: 141 p.; 21 cm. ISBN:
0877845719 (pbk.) : Notes: Subtitle on
cover: How to find peace not hurriedness,
simplicity not clutter, quality not
superficiality, love not hype. Bibliography:
p. [139]-141. Subjects: Christianity and
culture. LC Classification: BR115.C8 S47
1987 Dewey Class No.: 261 19

Shairp, John Campbell, 1819-1885. Culture
and religion in some of their relations.
Published/Created: New York, Hurd and
Houghton, 1871. Description: 2 p. l., [vii]-
ix p., 1 l., [13]-197 p. 19 cm. Subjects:
Culture.Christianity.Religion. LC
Classification: BR115.C8 S5 1871

Shairp, John Campbell, 1819-1885. Culture
and religion in some of their relations.
Published/Created: Edinburgh, Edmonston
and Douglas, 1870. Description: ix, 147 p.
19 cm. Subjects: Culture.Christianity--19th
century.Religion. LC Classification:
BR115.C8 S5 1870 Microfilm 82/5760
(BR)

Shastri, Hermen P., 1953- Christ in tribal
culture: a study of the interaction between
Christianity and Semai society of
peninsular Malaysia in the context of the
history of the Methodist Mission (1930 -
1983) / by Hermen P. Shastri.
Published/Created: Heidelberg: Faculty of
Theology, Ruprecht-Karis-Universität of
Heidelberg, [1989] Description: 213
leaves; 30 cm. Notes: Thesis (doctoral)--
Universität Heidelberg, 1989. Includes
bibliographical references (leaves 191-

211). Subjects: Methodist Church--Missions--Malaysias--History--20th century. Senoi (Malaysian people) LC Classification: BV3320 .S53 1989 Dewey Class No.: 266/.75951 20

Shaw, Chandler. Seven centuries that rocked the world; a biographical history of ancient culture from the decline of the Greek city-state to the triumph of Christianity. Published/Created: [Bethany? W. Va., 1950] Description: vi, 270 p. illus., ports., map. 23 cm. Subjects: Civilization, Ancient.Civilization, Christian. LC Classification: CB311 .S48

Shaw, Charles Gray, 1871-1949. Christianity and modern culture; an essay in philosophy of religion [by] Charles Gray Shaw. Published/Created: Cincinnati, Jennings and Graham; New York, Eaton and Mains [c1906] Description: 310 p. 21 cm. Subjects: Christianity--Philosophy. LC Classification: BR100 .S4

Shaw, R. Daniel (Robert Daniel), 1943- Transculturation: the cultural factor in translation and other communication tasks / R. Daniel Shaw; [foreword by Mildred L. Larson]. Pasadena, Calif.: William Carey Library, c1988. Description: xii, 300 p.: ill.; 23 cm. ISBN: 0878082166 Notes: Includes indexes. Bibliography: p. 269-289. Subjects: Bible--Translating. Christianity and culture. Translating and interpreting. Culture. Cross-cultural studies. LC Classification: BR115.C8 S52 1988 Dewey Class No.: 261/.01 20

Sheen, Fulton J. (Fulton John), 1895-1979 The cross and the crisis [by] Fulton J. Sheen. Published/Created: Milwaukee, The Bruce publishing company [c1938] Description: xi, 219 p. 20 cm. Notes: "Catholicism...the salvation of civilization and culture."-Pref. Subjects: Catholic Church. Christianity--20th century. Civilization, Christian. Communism. LC Classification: BX1753 .S52 Dewey Class No.: 282 [226.8]

Sheets, Dutch. Praying for America / Dutch Sheets. Published/Created: Ventura, Calif.: Regal Books, c2001. Description: 142 p.;

22 cm. ISBN: 0830728953 Notes: Includes bibliographical references (p. [139]-142). Subjects: Christianity and culture--United States. Christian life--United States. United States--Religion--1960- LC Classification: BR526 .S53 2001 Dewey Class No.: 277.3/083 21

Shelley, Bruce L. (Bruce Leon), 1927- The Gospel and the American dream / Bruce L. Shelley. Published/Created: Portland, Or.: Multnomah Press, c1989. Description: 192 p.; 21 cm. ISBN: 0880703105 : Notes: Includes bibliographical references. Subjects: Christianity--United States. Christianity and culture. United States--Church history--20th century. United States--Moral conditions. United States--Civilization--20th century. LC Classification: BR526 .S57 1989 Dewey Class No.: 261/.0973 20

Shenk, David W., 1937- God's call to mission / David W. Shenk; foreword by Leighton Ford. Published/Created: Scottdale, Pa.: Herald Press, c1994. Description: 229 p.: ill.; 23 cm. ISBN: 0836136691 (alk. paper) : Notes: Includes bibliographical references (p. 222-227). Subjects: Missions--Theory. Christianity and culture. Christianity and other religions. Mennonites--Missions. LC Classification: BV2063 .S49 1994 Dewey Class No.: 266/.001 20

Shenk, Joseph C. Silver thread: the ups and downs of a Mennonite family in mission, 1895-1995 / Joseph C. Shenk. Published/Created: Intercourse, PA: Good Books, c1996. Description: 250 p.: ill., map; 22 cm. ISBN: 1561482072 Subjects: Shenk, Joseph C.--Family. Schenk family. Barge family. Landis family. Mennonites--Missions--Africa, East. Mennonites--Missions--Nicaragua. Mennonites--Biography. Missionaries--Biography. Christianity and culture. Missions--Theory. LC Classification: BV2545 .S44 1996 Dewey Class No.: 266/.97/0922 B 20

Short, Robert L. Something to believe in: Is Kurt Vonnegut the exorcist of Jesus Christ Superstar? / Robert Short. Edition Information: 1st ed. Published/Created:

San Francisco: Harper & Row, c1978. Description: ix, 321 p.: ill.; 21 cm. ISBN: 0060673818 Notes: Includes bibliographical references. Subjects: Vonnegut, Kurt--Religion. Blatty, William Peter. Exorcist. Jesus Christ superstar [Motion picture] Christianity and culture. Theology. Popular culture--United States. LC Classification: BR115.C8 S53 Dewey Class No.: 230/.09/04

Shorter, Aylward. African culture and the Christian church: an introduction to social and pastoral anthropology. Published/Created: London, G. Chapman, 1973. Description: xi, 229 p. illus. 22 cm. ISBN: 0225660288 Notes: Includes index. Bibliography: p. 221. Subjects: Christianity--Africa. Ethnology--Africa. LC Classification: BR1360 .S5 Dewey Class No.: 261.8/096

Shorter, Aylward. African culture and the Christian church; an introduction to social and pastoral anthropology. Published/Created: Maryknoll, N.Y., Orbis Books, 1974 [c1973] Description: xi, 229 p. 22 cm. ISBN: 0883440040 Notes: Includes bibliographies. Subjects: Christianity--Africa. Ethnology--Africa. LC Classification: BR1360 .S5 1974 Dewey Class No.: 261.8/096

Shorter, Aylward. Christianity and the African imagination: after the African Synod: resources for inculturation / Aylward Shorter. Published/Created: Nairobi, Kenya: Paulines Publications Africa, 1996. Related Authors: African Synod (1994: Rome, Italy) Description: 128 p.; 21 cm. Notes: Includes bibliographical references. Subjects: Christianity--Africa. Christianity and culture--Africa. LC Classification: BR1360 .S48 1996 Dewey Class No.: 261/.096 21

Shorter, Aylward. Religious poverty in Africa / Aylward Shorter. Published/Created: Nairobi, Kenya: Paulines Publications Africa, 1999. Related Authors: Shorter, Aylward. Celibacy and African culture. Description: 36 p.; 21 cm. ISBN: 996621447X Notes: "This booklet is a follow up of "Celibacy and African culture"--P. [4] of cover. Includes bibliographical references (p. 36). Subjects: Poverty--Religious aspects--Christianity. Poverty--Africa. Africa--Religious life and customs. Africa--Economic conditions. LC Classification: BV4647.P6 S56 1999

Shorter, Aylward. Toward a theology of inculturation / Aylward Shorter. Published/Created: Maryknoll, N.Y.: Orbis Books, c1989. Description: xii, 291 p.; 22 cm. ISBN: 0883445360 (pbk.) Notes: Includes index. Bibliography: p. 272-279. Subjects: Catholic Church--Doctrines. Catholic Church--Missions. Catholic Church--Relations. Christianity and culture. Missions--Theory. LC Classification: BR115.C8 S55 1989 Dewey Class No.: 261 19

Siddiqui, Abdul Hameed. Main springs of Western civilisation / by Abdul Hameed Siddiqui. Published/Created: Lahore: Islamic Book Centre: stockists Sh. Muhammad Ashraf, [1975] Description: xxi, 159 p.; 22 cm. Notes: Includes bibliographies and index. Subjects: Civilization, Western. Christianity and culture. Civilization, Western--Islamic influences. LC Classification: CB245 .S5 Dewey Class No.: 940

Sih, Paul K. T. (Kwang Tsien), 1910- Chinese culture and Christianity; selected works of Paul K. T. Sih. Pref. by Chang Chi-yun. Compiled and published by China Culture Pub. Foundation. Published/Created: Taipei, Taiwan, 1957. Description: 194 p. 21 cm. Notes: Title also in Chinese. Subjects: Catholic Church--China. China--Civilization. East Asia--Politics and government. LC Classification: DS703.5 .S523

Simons, Gerald. Barbarian Europe, by Gerald Simons and the editors of Time-Life Books. Published/Created: New York, Time-Life Books [1968] Related Authors: Time-Life Books. Description: 192 p. illus. (part col.), col. maps. 28 cm. Summary: A six-hundred-year history of medieval

Europe, covering the spread of Christianity to barbaric tribes; the rise of parliamentary government and the stabilization of nation states; the development of court and jury justice; the revival and expansion of trade; the growth of towns, feudal life, and education; and the new trends in art and architecture. Notes: Bibliography: p. 186. Subjects: Middle Ages--History. Middle Ages--History. Series: Great ages of man. LC Classification: D117 .S55 Dewey Class No.: 940.1

Sindima, Harvey J. The gospel according to the marginalized / Harvey J. Sindima. Published/Created: New York: P. Lang, 1998. Description: p. cm. ISBN: 0820426857 Notes: Includes bibliographical references and index. Subjects: Liberation theology. Christianity and culture. Church work with the poor. Series: Martin Luther King, Jr. memorial studies in religion, culture, and social development; vol. 6 LC Classification: BT83.57 .S625 1995 Dewey Class No.: 230/.046 20

Sine, Tom. Cease fire: searching for sanity in America's culture wars / Tom Sine. Published/Created: Grand Rapids, Mich.: W.B. Eerdmans Pub. Co., c1995. Description: x, 302 p.; 24 cm. ISBN: 0802837999 (alk. paper) Notes: Includes bibliographical references and index. Subjects: Christianity and culture--History--20th century. Christianity and politics--History--20th century. Culture conflict--United States--History--20th century. Evangelicalism--United States--History--20th century. United States--Church history--20th century. United States--Civilization--1970- LC Classification: BR526 .S577 1995 Dewey Class No.: 261/.0973 20

Sire, James W. Discipleship of the mind: learning to love God in the ways we think / James W. Sire. Published/Created: Downers Grove, Ill.: InterVarsity Press, c1990. Description: 248 p.; 21 cm. ISBN: 0877849854 (alk. paper) Notes: Includes bibliographical references (p. [201]-243). Subjects: Christianity--Philosophy.

Christianity and culture. Education (Christian theology) Evangelicalism. Best books. Civilization, Modern--20th century. LC Classification: BR100 .S517 1990 Dewey Class No.: 201 20

Sittler, Joseph. Essays on nature and grace. Published/Created: Philadelphia, Fortress Press [1972] Description: 134 p. 21 cm. ISBN: 0800600703 Contents: The emergence of a theme.--Grace in the Scriptures.--Some crucial moments in ecumenical Christology.--Grace in post-Reformation culture.--Grace and a sense for the world.--Christian theology and the environment. Notes: Includes bibliographical references. Subjects: Grace. Nature--Religious aspects--Christianity. LC Classification: BT761.2 .S58 Dewey Class No.: 234/.1

Slosser, Bob. Changing the way America thinks / Bob Slosser with Cynthia Ellenwood. Published/Created: Dallas: Word Pub., c1989. Related Authors: Ellenwood, Cynthia, 1944- Description: xii, 221 p.; 24 cm. ISBN: 0849906571 : Notes: Includes bibliographical references. Subjects: Christianity and culture. Evangelicalism--United States. Fundamentalism. United States--Moral conditions. LC Classification: BR115.C8 S57 1989 Dewey Class No.: 277.3/0828 20

Slusser, Gerald H. A Christian look at secular society, by Gerald H. Slusser. Published/Created: Philadelphia, Published for the Cooperative Publication Association by the Westminster Press [1968, c1969] Description: 112 p. 22 cm. ISBN: 0664212824 Notes: Bibliographical references included in "Notes" (p. [109]-112) Subjects: Christianity and culture. LC Classification: BR115.C8 S58 Dewey Class No.: 261

Small arms, big impact: a challenge to the churches: a report of the Consultation on Microdisarmament / organized by the World Council of Churches Programme to Overcome Violence, Rio de Janeiro, May 1998; edited by Salpy Eskidjian, [with the assistance of Sarah Woodside].

Published/Created: Geneva, Switzerland; New York, N.Y., USA: Commission of the Churches on International Affairs, 1998. Related Authors: Eskidjian, Salpy. Woodside, Sarah. World Council of Churches. Programme to Overcome Violence. Commission of the Churches on International Affairs. Consultation on Microdisarmament (1998: Rio de Janeiro, Brazil) Description: 155 p.: ill.; 21 cm. Partial Contents: Final document of the Consultation -- Small arms and light weapons proliferation: Latin America: Rio de Janeiro, Brazil / Rubem César Fernandes -- Small arms and light weapons proliferation: Africa: the Great Lakes region / Josephine Ajema Odera -- Local and grassroots campaigns towards the ban of small arms and light weapons: transforming the culture of violence: lessons learned: Scotland / Maxwell Craig -- Local and grassroots campaigns towards the ban of small arms and light weapons: transforming the culture of violence: lessons learned: Australia / Rebecca Peters -- Local and grassroots campaigns towards the ban of small arms and light weapons: transforming the culture of violence: lessons learned: South Africa / Adele Kirsten. Notes: Includes bibliographical references. Subjects: Disarmament--Religious aspects--Christianity--Congresses. Firearms--Religious aspects--Christianity--Congresses. Series: Background information; 1998/2 LC Classification: IN PROCESS (COPIED) (lccopycat)

Smalley, William Allen, ed. Readings in missionary anthropology. Published/Created: Tarrytown, N.Y., Practical Anthropology [c1967] Description: 368 p. 23 cm. Partial Contents: Anthropological study and missionary scholarship / William A. Smalley -- Mariology in Latin America / Eugene A. Nida -- The transformation of God and the conversion of man / William D. Reyburn -- The Roman Catholic, communist, and Protestant approach to social structure: The relationship of social structure to the problems of evangelism in Latin America / Eugene A. Nida --

Mushroom ritual versus Christianity / Eunice Pike, Florence Cowan -- Gbeya prescientific attitudes and Christianity / William J. Samarin -- Vocabulary and the preaching of the Gospel / William A. Smalley -- Polygamy, economy, and Christianity in the eastern Cameroun: Kaka kinship, sex, and adultery / William D. Reyburn -- A Franco-african cross-cultural clash / Robert C. Blaschke -- Drunkenness in indigenous religious rites / Eugene A. Nida -- Planting the church in a disintegrating society / Lois Sorensen, William A. Smalley -- The moral implications of social structure / Paul Abrecht, William A. Smalley -- Conversion and culture change / Dale W. Kietzman -- A culturally relevant witness / John Beekman . Notes: Consists of articles reprinted from Practical anthropology, 1953-1960. Bibliographical footnotes. Includes bibliographical references. Subjects: Missions--Theory. LC Classification: BV2063 .S58

Smith, Christian (Christian Stephen), 1960- Christian America?: what evangelicals really want / Christian Smith. Published/Created: Berkeley: University of California Press, c2000. Description: x, 257 p.: ill., map; 24 cm. ISBN: 0520220412 (cloth: alk. paper) Notes: Includes bibliographical references (p. 243-251) and index. Subjects: Evangelicalism--United States--History--20th century. Christianity and culture--United States--History--20th century. Christianity and politics--United States--History--20th century. LC Classification: BR1642.U5 S623 2000 Dewey Class No.: 277.3/0829 21

Smith, Debbie, 1962- Israel: the culture / Debbie Smith. Published/Created: New York: Crabtree Pub. Co., c1999. Description: 32 p.: col. ill.; 28 cm. ISBN: 0865053111 (paper) 086505231X (rlb.) Summary: Surveys the practice of various religions--Judaism, Islam, Christianity, and others--in Israel and the different customs that are part of the religious holidays and festivals. Notes: Includes index. Subjects: Israel--Civilization--Religion--Juvenile literature. Israel--Religion--Social life and customs. LC Classification: DS112 .S64 1999 Dewey Class No.: 956.94 21

Smith, Oran P., 1963- The rise of Baptist republicanism / Oran P. Smith. Published/Created: New York: New York University Press, c1997. Description: xii, 320 p.: ill.; 24 cm. ISBN: 0814780733 (acid-free paper) Partial Contents: Introduction: Baptist republicanism's cultural antecedents -- Backlash: Baptist republicanism as fundamentalist reaction -- Culture war: Baptist republicanism as cultural defense -- Fundamental differences: Baptist republicanism's political partners -- Bible Belt: Baptist republicanism in the Palmetto State. Notes: Includes bibliographical references (p. 281-311) and index. Subjects: Southern Baptist Convention--Political activity. Southern Baptist Convention--History--20th century. Republican Party (U.S.: 1854-) Baptists--United States--Political activity. Christianity and politics--Baptists--Christianity and politics--United States--History--20th century. Conservatism--Religious aspects--Baptists--20th century. United States--History--1969- United States--Church history--20th century. LC Classification: BX6462.3 .S65 1997 Dewey Class No.: 286/.132 21

Smith, Theophus Harold. Conjuring culture: biblical formations of black America / Theophus H. Smith. Published/Created: New York: Oxford University Press, 1994. Description: xvi, 287 p.; 24 cm. ISBN: 0195067401 (alk. paper) Notes: Includes bibliographical references (p. 257.272) and index. Subjects: Bible--Influence--Western civilization. Bible--Criticism, interpretation, etc.--United States History. Afro-Americans--Religion. Religion and culture--United States. Typology (Theology)--History of doctrines. Magic--Religious aspects--Christianity--History of doctrines. Series: Religion in America series (Oxford University Press) LC Classification: BR563.N4 S574 1994 Dewey Class No.: 277.3/08/08996073 21

Snyder, Graydon F. Inculturation of the Jesus tradition: the impact of Jesus on Jewish and Roman cultures / Graydon F. Snyder. Published/Created: Harrisburg, Pa.: Trinity Press International, c1999. Description: x, 247 p.: ill.; 23 cm. ISBN: 1563382954 (alk. paper) Notes: Includes bibliographical references (p. 215-230) and indexes. Subjects: Christianity and culture--History--Early church, ca. 30-600. Jews--Civilization--Christian influences. Rome--Civilization--Christian influences. LC Classification: BR166 .S58 1999 Dewey Class No.: 232.9/04 21

Society and culture in North-East India: a Christian perspective / edited by Saral K. Chatterji. Published/Created: Delhi: Published for the Christian Institute for the Study of Religion and Society, Bangalore by ISPCK, 1996. Related Authors: Chatterji, Saral Kumar, 1932- Christian Institute for the Study of Religion and Society, Bangalore. Description: 154 p.; 22 cm. Notes: Contributed papers of a seminar held at Shillong, 1992. Includes bibliographical references. Subjects: Christianity--India, Northeastern. India, Northeastern--Social life and customs. LC Classification: DS483.4 .S6 1996 Dewey Class No.: 306/.09541 21

Sockman, Ralph W. (Ralph Washington), 1889-1970. Date with destiny, a preamble to Christian culture, by Ralph W. Sockman ... Published/Created: New York, Nashville, Abingdon-Cokesbury press [1944] Description: 157 p. 20 cm. Notes: Bibliographical foot-notes. Subjects: Christianity and culture. Church and social problems--United States. Reconstruction (1939-1951) LC Classification: BR115.C8 S6 Dewey Class No.: 261

Song, Choan-Seng, 1929- Jesus in the power of the spirit / C.S. Song. Minneapolis: Fortress Press, c1994. Description: xiv, 335 p.; 23 cm. ISBN: 0800627903 (alk. paper) : Notes: Includes bibliographical references and indexes. Subjects: Jesus Christ--Person and offices. Christianity and culture. Theology, Doctrinal--East Asia. Series: Song, Choan-Seng, 1929- Cross in the lotus world; v. 3. LC Classification: BT75.2 .S638 1990 vol. 3 BT205 Dewey Class No.: 230/.095 s 232 20

Spae, Joseph John, 1913- Buddhist-Christian empathy / by Joseph J. Spae. Published/Created: Chicago: Chicago Institute of Theology and Culture; Tokyo: Oriens Institute for Religious Research, 1980. Description: 269 p.; 27 cm. ISBN: 0936078022 : Notes: Includes index. Bibliography: p. [245]-252. Subjects: Christianity and other religions--Buddhism. Buddhism--Relations--Christianity. LC Classification: BR128.B8 S64 Dewey Class No.: 261.2/943 19

Spae, Joseph John, 1913- Church and China, towards reconciliation? / Joseph J. Spae. Published/Created: Chicago: Chicago Institute of Theology and Culture, 1980. Description: 167 p.; 21 cm. ISBN: 0936078014 (pbk.) : Notes: Includes index. Bibliography: p. 158-159. Subjects: Catholic Church--China. Christianity--China. Communism and Christianity--China. LC Classification: BR1288 .S63 Dewey Class No.: 275.1 19

Spae, Joseph John, 1913- East challenges West: towards a convergence of spiritualities / by Joseph J. Spae. Published/Created: South Yarra, Australia: Charles Strong Memorial Trust; Chicago: distribution by Chicago Institute of Theology and Culture, 1979. Description: 81 p.; 26 cm. Notes: Includes bibliographical references. Subjects: Christianity and other religions--Buddhism--Buddhism--Relations--Christianity--East and West--Japan--Religion--Addresses, essays, lectures. Series: Charles Strong Memorial Trust. Charles Strong Memorial Trust lecture; 1979. LC Classification: BL2210 .S62 Dewey Class No.: 261.2

Spinka, Matthew, 1890- A history of Christianity in the Balkans; a study in the spread of Byzantine culture among the Slavs. Published/Created: [Hamden, Conn.] Archon Books, 1968 [c1933] Description: 202 p. 23 cm. Notes: Bibliography: p. 189-191. Subjects:

Orthodox Eastern Church--History. Slavs, Southern--Church history. LC Classification: BR737.S6 S6 1968 Dewey Class No.: 209/.496

Spinka, Matthew, 1890-1972. A history of Christianity in the Balkans; a study in the spread of Byzantine culture among the Slavs, by Matthew Spinka ... Published/Created: Chicago, Ill., The American Society of Church History [c1933] Description: 3 p. l., 202 p. 25 cm. Notes: "Selected bibliography": p. 189-191. Subjects: Orthodox Eastern Church--History. Slavs--Church history. Series: Studies in church history, v. 1 LC Classification: BR737.S6 S6 Dewey Class No.: 274.96

Spirit at work: discovering the spirituality in leadership / [contributions by] Jay A. Conger and associates. Edition Information: 1st ed. Published/Created: San Francisco: Jossey-Bass, c1994. Related Authors: Conger, Jay Alden. Description: xxxi, 222 p.: ill.; 22 cm. ISBN: 1555426395 Notes: Includes bibliographical references and index. Subjects: Leadership--Moral and ethical aspects. Corporate culture. Quality of work life. Leadership--Religious aspects--Christianity. Spiritual life. Series: The Jossey-Bass management series LC Classification: HD57.7 .S695 1994 Dewey Class No.: 658.4/092 20

Spiritual encounters: interactions between Christianity and native religions in colonial America / edited by Nicholas Griffiths and Fernando Cervantes. Lincoln: University of Nebraska Press, c1999. Related Authors: Griffiths, Nicholas, 1962- Cervantes, Fernando. Description: xi, 304 p.; 22 cm. ISBN: 080327081X Notes: Includes bibliographical references and index. Subjects: Indians--Religion. Indians--Missions. Christianity and culture--America--History. LC Classification: E59.R38 S69 1999 Dewey Class No.: 261.2/97 21

Sproul, R. C. (Robert Charles), 1939- Lifeviews: understanding the ideas that shape society today / R.C. Sproul. Published/Created: Old Tappan, N.J.: F.H. Revell, c1986. Description: 220 p.: ill.; 24 cm. ISBN: 0800714695 Notes: Includes index. Subjects: Apologetics. Christianity and culture. Ideology. LC Classification: BT1102 .S588 1986 Dewey Class No.: 261 19

Squire, Aelred. Summer in the seed / Aelred Squire. Published/Created: New York: Paulist Press, c1980. Description: xv, 240 p.; 22 cm. ISBN: 0809122375 Notes: Includes bibliographical references. Subjects: Christianity and culture. Spiritual life--Christianity. LC Classification: BR115.C8 S68 Dewey Class No.: 261

St. James, Rebecca. Wait for me: rediscovering the joy of purity in romance / Rebecca St. James with Dale Reeves. Nashville, Tenn.: Thomas Nelson Publishers, c2002. Related Authors: Reeves, Dale. Description: p. cm. ISBN: 0785271279 Contents: Dream again: recovering the dream of true romance -- Mind matters: guarding your thoughts to make wise decisions -- The ecstasy (or agony) of sex: why waiting is best -- Protecting purity: practical ways to wait in a culture that screams, "just do it!" -- Love and marriage: what it is we're waiting for -- A second chance: forgiveness and hope for the guilt-ridden and hurting -- I'm glad you asked!: Q & A on sexual purity. Subjects: Chastity. Youth--Religious life. Marriage--Sexual abstinence--Religious aspects-- Christianity. LC Classification: BV4647.C5 S7 2002 Dewey Class No.: 241/.66 21

St. Kilda, Martin. Near the far bamboo: an insightful look at cross-cultural clashes through the eyes of a tentmaking missionary / Martin St. Kilda. Camp Hill, Pa.: Christian Publications, c1993. Description: 248 p.; 21 cm. ISBN: 0875095100 Subjects: St. Kilda, Martin. Missions--Christianity and culture-- Miscellanea. LC Classification: BV2063 .S79 1993 Dewey Class No.: 266/.02373 20

Stackhouse, Max L. Apologia: contextualization, globalization, and mission in theological education / by Max L. Stackhouse with Nantawan Boonprasat-Lewis ... [et al.]; foreword by Donald Shriver. Published/Created: Grand Rapids, Mich.: Eerdmans, c1988. Description: xvi, 237 p.; 22 cm. ISBN: 0802802850 (pbk.) Notes: Includes bibliographical references. Subjects: Theology. Theology--Study and teaching. Missions--Theory. Christianity and culture. Internationalism. LC Classification: BR118 .S69 1988 Dewey Class No.: 230/.01 19

Stackhouse, Max L. Covenant and commitments: faith, family, and economic life / Max L. Stackhouse. Edition Information: 1st ed. Published/Created: Louisville, Ky.: Westminster John Knox Press, c1997. Description: viii, 195 p.; 23 cm. ISBN: 0664254675 (acid-free paper) Notes: Includes bibliographical references (p. [161]-189) and index. Subjects: Family--Religious aspects--Christianity. Covenants--Religious aspects-- Christianity. Sociology, Christian. Series: The family, religion, and culture LC Classification: BV4526.2 .S67 1997 Dewey Class No.: 306.85/088/204 21

Stassen, Glen Harold, 1936- Authentic transformation: a new vision of Christ and culture / Glen H. Stassen, D.M. Yeager, and John Howard Yoder; with a previously unpublished essay by H. Richard Niebuhr. Published/Created: Nashville: Abingdon Press, c1996. Related Authors: Yeager, Diane M. Yoder, John Howard. Niebuhr, H. Richard (Helmut Richard), 1894-1962. Types of Christian ethics. Description: 299 p.; 23 cm. ISBN: 0687022738 (alk. paper) Notes: Includes bibliographical references (p. 271-299). Subjects: Niebuhr, H. Richard (Helmut Richard), 1894-1962. Christ and culture. Christianity and culture. Christianity and culture--United States. Sociology, Christian. Christian ethics. LC Classification: BR115.C8 S72 1996 Dewey Class No.: 261 20

Staunton, Michael. The illustrated story of Christian Ireland: from St Patrick to the peace process / [by] Michael Staunton. Published/Created: Dublin: Emerald Press, 2001. Description: vi, 204 p.: ill.; 26cm. ISBN: 1903582059 Notes: Includes bibliographical references and index. Subjects: Patrick, Saint, 373?-463? Brigid, of Ireland, Saint, ca. 453-ca. 524. Brendan, Saint, the Voyager, ca. 483-577. Columba, Saint, 521-597. Columban, Saint, 543-615. Malachy, Saint, 1094?-1148. Reformation--Ireland--History. Penal laws in Ireland. Christianity--Ireland. Christianity and culture--Ireland. Christianity--Northern Ireland. Christianity and culture--Northern Ireland. Ireland--Church history. Ireland--Religion. Ireland--Church history. Dewey Class No.: 274.15 21

Steinmetz, Paul B. The sacred pipe: an archetypal theology / Paul B. Steinmetz. Edition Information: 1st ed. Published/Created: Syracuse, N.Y.: Syracuse University Press, 1998. Description: 219 p.: ill.; 22 cm. ISBN: 0815605447 (cloth: alk. paper) Notes: Includes bibliographical references (p. 199-213) and index. Subjects: Catholic Church--Missions--United States--History. Oglala Indians--Rites and ceremonies--Religion. Oglala mythology. Calumets--Religious aspects. Christianity and culture--United States. Popular culture--Religious aspects--Catholic Church. LC Classification: E99.O8 S74 1998 Dewey Class No.: 299/.74 21

Sterner, Douglas W., 1945- Priests of culture: a study of Matthew Arnold & Henry James / Douglas W. Sterner. Published/Created: New York: Peter Lang, c1999. Description: xiv, 282 p.: ill.; 24 cm. ISBN: 0820441813 (alk. paper) Notes: Includes bibliographical references (p. [269]-277) and index. Subjects: Arnold, Matthew, 1822-1888 --Criticism and interpretation. James, Henry, 1843-1916 --Criticism and interpretation. Christianity and literature--England--History--19th century. Culture--Social aspects--England--History--19th century. Culture--Social aspects--England--History--20th century. Culture--Social aspects--United States--History. Literature, Comparative--English and American.

Literature, Comparative--American and English. Modernism (Literature)--History--19th century. United States--Civilization. Series: Sociocriticism (New York, N.Y.); vol. 9. LC Classification: PR4024 .S824 1999 Dewey Class No.: 821/.8 21

Stewart, James Livingstone. Chinese culture and Christianity; a review of China's religions and related systems from the Christian standpoint, by James Livingstone Stewart. Published/Created: New York, F.H. Revell [c1926] Description: 316 p. illus. 21 cm. Notes: Bibliography: p. 309-311. Subjects: Christianity and other religions. Philosophy, Chinese. Folklore, Chinese. China--Religion. LC Classification: BL1801 .S8

Stone, Charles J. Christianity before Christ, or Prototypes of our faith and culture. Published/Created: 1885. Description: 1 v. cm. LC Classification: BR127 .S8

Storck, Thomas. The Catholic milieu / by Thomas Storck. Published/Created: Front Royal, VA: Christendom College Press, c1987. Description: 79 p.; 22 cm. ISBN: 0931888255 (pbk.) Notes: Bibliography: p. 78-79. Subjects: Sociology, Christian (Catholic) Christianity and culture. LC Classification: BX1753 .S84 1987 Dewey Class No.: 261 19

Streit, Jakob. Sun and cross: the development from Megalithic culture to early Christianity in Ireland / Jakob Streit; [translated by Hugh Latham]. Edition Information: 2nd ed. Edinburgh: Floris Books, 1993. Description: 223 p. ISBN: 0863151574 Subjects: Christian antiquities--Megalithic monuments--Crosses--Ireland. Missions--Europe. Ireland--Church history--To 1172. Ireland--Civilization. Ireland--Antiquities. LC Classification: IN PROCESS (COPIED)

Streit, Jakob. Sun and cross: the development from Megalithic culture to early Christianity in Ireland / Jakob Streit; [translated by Hugh Latham]. Published/Created: Edinburgh: Floris Books, 1984. Description: 223 p.: ill.; 25

cm. ISBN: 0863150101 : Notes: Translation of: Sonne und Kreuz. Includes index. Bibliography: p. 215-219. Subjects: Christian antiquities--Megalithic monuments--Crosses--Ireland. Missions--Europe. Ireland--Church history--To 1172. Ireland--Civilization. Ireland--Antiquities. LC Classification: BR794 .S8513 1984 Dewey Class No.: 274.15/01 19

Studies in world Christianity. Published/Created: Edinburgh, Scotland: Edinburgh University Press, 1995- Description: v.; 24 cm. Vol. 1, pt. 1 (1995)- Current Frequency: Semiannual ISSN: 1354-9901 Notes: Issued in pts. SERBIB/SERLOC merged record Subjects: Christianity and culture--Periodicals. LC Classification: BR115.C8 S75 Dewey Class No.: 270/.05 21

Stürzenhofecker, G. (Gabriele) Times enmeshed: gender, space, and history among the Duna of Papua New Guinea / Gabriele Stürzenhofecker. Published/Created: Stanford, Calif.: Stanford University Press, 1998. Description: xii, 242 p.: ill.; 24 cm. ISBN: 0804728992 (cloth: alk. paper) Notes: Includes bibliographical references (p. 225-235) and index. Subjects: Duna (Papua New Guinea people)--Social conditions. Duna (Papua New Guinea people)--Religion. Philosophy, Duna--Papua New Guinea--Aluni. Sex role--Papua New Guinea--Aluni. Christianity and culture--Witchcraft--Papua New Guinea--Aluni--Social conditions. LC Classification: DU740.42 .S79 1998 Dewey Class No.: 305.89/912 21

Sullivan, Timothy. Repetition and the visions of secular culture / Timothy Sullivan. Published/Created: [S.l.]: Gurteen Press, c1984. Description: 189 p.; 22 cm. Subjects: Christianity. Capitalism. Socialism. Repetition (Philosophy) LC Classification: BR121.2 .S788 1984 Dewey Class No.: 261.2/1 19

Suttles, Virgil. Developing cross-cultural fellowship within a multiethnic group of Christians in Cayenne, French Guiana

[microform] / by Virgil Suttles. Published/Created: 1994. Description: 1 v. (various pagings): ill.; 28 cm. Notes: Thesis (D. Min.)--Southwestern Baptist Theological Seminary, 1994. Microfiche. Portland, Or.: Theological Research Exchange Network, 1995. 1 microfiche: negative. High reduction. Subjects: Christianity and culture. Missions--Cayenne (French Guiana) Cultural relations. Cross-cultural studies. LC Classification: Microfiche 97/260 (B)

Sweet, Leonard I. FaithQuakes / Leonard Sweet. Published/Created: Nashville: Abingdon Press, c1994. Description: 237 p.; 24 cm. ISBN: 0687126479 (alk. paper) Notes: "For Christians with the shakes, who know that the church is the last hope for saving our families, our cities, our businesses, and the earth." Includes bibliographical references (p. 213-237). Subjects: Christianity and culture--United States. Twenty-first century--Forecasts. Christianity--Forecasting. Church renewal. LC Classification: BR526 .S94 1994 Dewey Class No.: 277.3/0829 20

Sweet, Leonard I. Post-modern pilgrims: first century passion for the 21st century world / Leonard Sweet. Published/Created: Nashville, Tenn.: Broadman & Holman, c2000. Description: xxiii, 194 p.; 24 cm. ISBN: 0805421378 (hb) Notes: Includes bibliographical references (p. 161-194). Subjects: Christianity and culture. Postmodernism--Religious aspects--Christianity. Civilization, Modern--1950- LC Classification: BR115.C8 S94 2000 Dewey Class No.: 261 21

Sweet, Leonard I. SoulTsunami [sound recording]: sink or swim in new millennium culture / Leonard Sweet. Published/Created: Grand Rapids, Mich.: Zondervan, p1999. Description: 2 sound cassettes: analog, Dolby processed. ISBN: 0310227127 Summary: A Drew University theology professor discusses cultural and technological changes that threaten organized religion. He recommends embracing the opportunities the future presents, and using technological advances not only to predict but also shape the future of religion. Notes: Subtitle from original container. Subjects: Christianity and culture--United States. Twenty-first century--Forecasts. Christianity--Forecasting. Church renewal. LC Classification: RYI 4849, etc.

Sweet, Leonard I. SoulTsunami: sink or swim in new millennium culture / Leonard Sweet. Published/Created: Grand Rapids, Mich.: Zondervan, c1999. Description: 446 p.; 24 cm. ISBN: 0310227623 (hardcover: alk. paper) Notes: Includes bibliographical references. Subjects: Christianity and culture--United States. Twenty-first century--Forecasts. Christianity--Forecasting. Church renewal. LC Classification: BR526 .S943 1999 Dewey Class No.: 261 21

Syrjänen, Seppo, 1939- In search of meaning and identity: conversion to Christianity in Pakistani Muslim culture / Seppo Syrjänen. Published/Created: Helsinki: Finnish Society for Missiology and Ecumenics, 1984. Description: 246 p.: ill.; 21 cm. ISBN: 9519520708 (pbk.) Notes: Bibliography: p. [232]-246. Subjects: Christian converts from Islam--Pakistan. Conversion--Christianity. Series: Missiologian ja Ekumeniikan Seuran julkaisuja; 45. LC Classification: BV2625 .S97 1984 Dewey Class No.: 248.2/46/095491 19

Taber, Charles R. The world is too much with us: "culture" in modern Protestant missions / by Charles R. Taber. Published/Created: Macon, Ga.: Mercer University Press, c1991. Description: xxiv, 208 p.; 24 cm. ISBN: 0865543887 (alk. paper) Notes: Includes bibliographical references (p. [189]-203) and index. Subjects: Missions--Theory. Christianity and culture--History--19th century--20th century. Protestant churches--Missions--History--19th century--20th century. Missions--Anthropological aspects. Series: The Modern mission era, 1792-1992 LC Classification: BV2063 .T28 1991 Dewey Class No.: 266/.001 20

Taber, Charles R. To understand the world, to save the world: the interface between missiology and the social sciences / Charles R. Taber. Published/Created: Harrisburg, Pa.: Trinity Press International, c2000. Description: xiii, 146 p.; 19 cm. ISBN: 1563383160 Notes: Includes bibliographical references (p.139-146). Subjects: Missions--Theory. Christianity and the social sciences. Series: Christian mission and modern culture LC Classification: BV2063 .T27 2000 Dewey Class No.: 266/.001 21

Takatemjen. Studies on theology and Naga culture / by Takatemjen. Delhi: Published by Indian Society for Promoting Christian Knowledge for Clark Theological College, Mokokchung, 1998. Related Authors: I.S.P.C.K. (Organization) Description: x, 154 p.; 23 cm. ISBN: 8172144369 Summary: Collection of various seminar papers presented by the author during the last fifteen years. Notes: Includes bibliographical references (p. [149]-154). Subjects: Theology, Doctrinal--India--Christianity and culture. N¯ag¯aland (India)--Religion. LC Classification: BT30.N35 T35 1998 Dewey Class No.: 230/.0954/165 21

Takenaka, Masao. God is rice: Asian culture and Christian faith / Masao Takenaka. Published/Created: Geneva: World Council of Churches, c1986. Description: 82 p.: ill.; 21 cm. ISBN: 2825408549 (pbk.) Contents: God is rice -- Christ and culture in Asia -- The ethics of betweenness -- Christ of wabi. Notes: "The first three were the Earl lectures ... January 1985, at the invitation of the Pacific School of Religion. The last lecture was given at Diana Pura in Bali, Indonesia, at a consultation on "Theology and Culture" sponsored by the Reformed Church in Indonesia in March 1985"--P. 1. Includes bibliographical references. Subjects: Christianity and culture. Christianity--Japan. Christianity--Asia. Series: The Risk book series; no. 30 LC Classification: BR115.C8 T35 1986 Dewey Class No.: 261/.0952 19

Talitha, qumi!: proceedings of the Convocation of African Women Theologians, Trinity College, Legon-Accra, September 24-October 2, 1989 / story told by Mercy Amba Oduyoye and Musimbi Kanyoro. Published/Created: Ibadan: Daystar Press, 1990. Related Authors: Oduyoye, Mercy Amba. Kanyoro, Rachel Angogo, 1953- Description: 241 p.: ill.; 23 cm. ISBN: 9781222182 Subjects: Institute of African Women in Religion and Culture Congresses. Women in Christianity--Congresses. Women--Africa--Congresses. LC Classification: BV639.W7 C59 1989 Dewey Class No.: 276/.082/082 20

Talking back to civilization: Indian voices from the Progressive Era / edited with an introduction by Frederick E. Hoxie. Published/Created: Boston: Bedford/St. Martins, c2001. Related Authors: Hoxie, Frederick E., 1947- Description: xv, 190 p.: ill., ports.; 21 cm. ISBN: 0312103859 (paperback) 0312128088 (hardback) Partial Contents: Introduction: American Indian activism in the Progressive Era -- Speaking out at the World's Columbian Exposition, 1893 -- Critics of Indian education -- Discussing Christianity and religion. Notes: Includes bibliographical references (p. 182-184) and index. Subjects: Indians of North America--Government relations--1869-1934. Progressivism (United States politics)--History. Indians, Treatment of--United States--History. United States--Politics and government--1865-1933. United States--Race relations. United States--Social conditions--1865-1918. Series: The Bedford series in history and culture LC Classification: E93 .T215 2001 Dewey Class No.: 970.004/97 21

Tamney, Joseph B. The resilience of Christianity in the modern world / Joseph B. Tamney. Published/Created: Albany: State University of New York Press, c1992. Description: x, 178 p.; 24 cm. ISBN: 0791408213 (alk. paper) 0791408221 (pbk.: alk. paper) Notes: Includes bibliographical references (p. [155]-173) and index. Subjects: Sociology, Christian. Christianity--20th century.

Series: SUNY series in religion, culture, and society LC Classification: BT738 .T25 1992 Dewey Class No.: 306.6/3 20

Tang, Yijie. Confucianism, Buddhism, Daoism, Christianity, and Chinese culture / Tang Yi-Jie. Published/Created: [Peking]: University of Peking; Washington, D.C.: Council for Research in Values and Philosophy, c1991. Description: viii, 186 p.: ill.; 23 cm. ISBN: 1565180356 1565180348 (pbk.) Notes: Translated from the Chinese. Includes bibliographical references and index. Subjects: Philosophy, Chinese. China--Religion. China--Civilization. Series: Cultural heritage and contemporary change. Series III, Asia; vol. 3 LC Classification: B5231 .T36 1991 Dewey Class No.: 181 20

Tanner, Kathryn, 1957- Theories of culture: a new agenda for theology / Kathryn Tanner. Published/Created: Minneapolis: Fortress Press, c1997. Description: xi, 196 p.; 21 cm. ISBN: 0800630971 (pbk.: alk. paper) Notes: Includes bibliographical references (p. 176-193) and index. Subjects: Christianity and culture. Theology--Methodology. Series: Guides to theological inquiry LC Classification: BR115.C8 T36 1997 Dewey Class No.: 261/.01 21

Tano, Rodrigo D. Theology in the Philippine setting: a case study in the contextualization of theology / Rodrigo D. Tano. Published/Created: Quezon City, Philippines: New Day Publishers, 1981. Description: viii, 176 p.; 22 cm. Notes: Originally presented as the author's thesis (doctoral--Baylor University, Waco, Tex., 1979) Bibliography: p. [158]-176. Subjects: Theology, Doctrinal--Philippines--History. Christianity and culture. Philippines--History. LC Classification: BT30.P6 T36 1981 Dewey Class No.: 230/.09599 19

Tao, reception in East and West = Tao, Rezeption in Ost und West = Tao, réception est et ouest = [Tao tsai tung fang chi hsi fang chih chieh shou] / edited by Adrian Hsia. Published/Created: Bern; New York: P. Lang, c1994. Related

Authors: Hsia, Adrian. Lao-tzu. Tao te ching. Description: vii, 288, 22 p.: ill.; 22 cm. ISBN: 3906752526 Notes: Parallel title also in Chinese character. Includes the full Chinese text of Tao Te Ching, by Lao-Tzu. Includes bibliographical references. English, Chinese, German and French. Subjects: Lao-tzu. Tao te ching. Christianity and culture--China. Christianity and other religions--Taoism. Taoism in literature. Taoism. Series: Euro-sinica; Bd. 5 LC Classification: BL1900.L35 T3285 1994 Dewey Class No.: 181/.114 21

Tarr, Delbert Howard. Double image: biblical insights from African parables / by Del Tarr; illustrated by John L. Weidman. Published/Created: New York: Paulist Press, c1994. Description: ix, 209 p.: ill.; 22 cm. ISBN: 0809134691 (pbk.) : Notes: Includes bibliographical references and indexes. Subjects: Jesus Christ--Parables. Bible--Criticism, Narrative. Christianity and culture. Folk literature, African. Storytelling--Religious aspects--Christianity. Africa, West--Civilization--Philosophy. LC Classification: BS521.7 .T37 1994 Dewey Class No.: 220.6/1 20

Tate, Allen, 1899- Christ and the unicorn: an address delivered on June the 23d, 1954, at the Third International Congress for Peace and Christian Civilization held in Florence, Italy, under the auspices of the Mayor / by Allen Tate. Published/Created: West Branch, Iowa: Cummington Press, 1966, c1955. Description: 10, [1] p.; 23 cm. Notes: Reprinted from the Sewanee review, v. 63, no. 2. "One hundred and twenty-five copies printed"--Colophon. Subjects: Civilization, Christian. Christianity and politics. Christianity and culture. LC Classification: BR115.C5 T38 1966 Dewey Class No.: 261.1 19

Taylor, Mark L. (Mark Lewis), 1951- Remembering Esperanza: a cultural-political theology for North American praxis / Mark Kline Taylor. Published/Created: Maryknoll, N.Y.: Orbis Books, c1990. Description: xii, 292 p.; 24 cm. ISBN: 0883446421 Notes: Includes

bibliographical references and index. Subjects: Jesus Christ--Person and offices. Theology--Methodology. Postmodernism--Religious aspects--Catholic Church. Political theology--North America. Christianity and culture. Christianity and justice. Theology--North America. LC Classification: BR118 .T39 1989 Dewey Class No.: 261.8/097 20

Taylor, Richard Shelley, 1912- The disciplined life-style / Richard S. Taylor. Published/Created: Minneapolis, Minn.: Bethany Fellowship, [1980?] c1973. Description: 95 p.; 18 cm. ISBN: 0871231107 (pbk.) : Notes: First published in 1973 under A return to Christian culture. Bibliography: p. 95. Subjects: Christianity and culture. LC Classification: BR115.C8 T39 1980 Dewey Class No.: 248.4 19

Tending the flock: congregations and family ministry / K. Brynolf Lyon, Archie Smith, Jr., editors. Edition Information: 1st ed. Published/Created: Louisville, Ky.: Westminster John Knox Press, c1998. Related Authors: Lyon, K. Brynolf, 1953- Smith, Archie, 1939- Description: x, 219 p.; 23 cm. ISBN: 0664256279 (pbk.: alk. paper) Notes: Includes bibliographical references. Subjects: Family--Religious aspects--Christianity--Case studies. Church work with families--United States--Religion--1960---Case studies. Series: The family, religion, and culture LC Classification: BL2525 .T46 1998 Dewey Class No.: 259/.1/0973 21

Terrell, Richard. Resurrecting the Third Reich: are we ready for America's modern fascism? / by Richard Terrell. Published/Created: Lafayette, La.: Huntington House, c1994. Description: 224 p.; 22 cm. ISBN: 1563840197 Notes: Includes bibliographical references (p. 217-220). Subjects: Christianity--United States--20th century. Fascism--United States. Fascism and culture. LC Classification: BR526 .T47 1994 Dewey Class No.: 277.3/0829 20

Terry, Randall A. Accessory to murder: the enemies, allies, and accomplices to the death of our culture / written from a prison work camp, Randall A. Terry. Edition Information: 1st ed. Published/Created: Brentwood, Tenn.: Wolgemuth & Hyatt, c1990. Description: xiv, 281 p.; 23 cm. ISBN: 0943497787 Notes: Includes bibliographical references (p. 265-280). Subjects: Pro-life movement--United States. Abortion--Religious aspects--Christianity. LC Classification: HQ767.5.U5 T48 1990 Dewey Class No.: 363.4/6 20

Text & experience: towards a cultural exegesis of the Bible / edited by Daniel Smith-Christopher. Published/Created: Sheffield, England: Sheffield Academic Press, c1995. Related Authors: Smith-Christopher, Daniel L. Description: 354 p.; 24 cm. ISBN: 1850757402 (pbk. :alk. paper) Notes: Includes bibliographical references and indexes. Subjects: Bible--Hermeneutics--Congresses. Bible--Criticism, interpretation, etc.--Congresses. Christianity and culture--Congresses. Ethnology in the Bible--Congresses. Series: The biblical seminar; 35 LC Classification: BS476 .T43 1995 Dewey Class No.: 220.6/01 21

Teyegaga, B. D. Dipo custom and the Christian faith: the nature of a people is in their traditions, culture, religion, and customs. Published/Created: [S.l.: s.n., 1985?] (Accra: J'piter Print. Press) Description: 66 p.: ill.; 19 cm. Notes: Includes bibliographical references. Subjects: Krobo (African people)--Rites and ceremonies. Krobo (African people)--Religion. Puberty rites--Ghana. Christianity--Ghana. LC Classification: DT510.43.K76 T49 1985

The Aquinas review of Thomas Aquinas College. Published/Created: Santa Paula, CA: Office of the Dean, Thomas Aquinas College, c1994- Related Authors: Thomas Aquinas College. Office of the Dean. Description: v.; 22 cm. Vol. 1, no. 1- Current Frequency: Two no. a year ISSN: 1076-8319 Notes: Title from cover. SERBIB/SERLOC merged record Subjects: Catholic Church--Doctrines--Periodicals. Catholic Church--Apologetic

works--Periodicals. Religion and science--Periodicals. Christianity and culture--Periodicals. LC Classification: BX1751.2 .A867 Dewey Class No.: 378 12

The Catholic church and American culture: reciprocity and challenge / edited by Cassian Yuhaus; preface by Donald S. Nesti. Published/Created: New York: Paulist Press, c1990. Related Authors: Yuhaus, Cassian J. Description: xvi, 115 p.; 21 cm. ISBN: 0809131536 : Notes: Includes bibliographical references. Subjects: Catholic Church--United States--Membership. Christianity and culture. United States--Civilization. United States--Church history. LC Classification: BX1406.2 .C356 1990 Dewey Class No.: 282/.73 20

The changing face of the church / edited by Timothy Fitzgerald and Martin Connell. Published/Created: Chicago, IL: Liturgy Training Publications, c1998. Related Authors: Fitzgerald, Timothy, 1950- Connell, Martin F. Description: 244 p.; 23 cm. ISBN: 1568542593 Notes: Includes bibliographical references. Subjects: Catholic Church--History--1965---Congresses. Multiculturalism--Religious aspects--Catholic Church Congresses. Christianity and culture--Congresses. Church renewal--Catholic Church--Congresses. Change--Religious aspects--Catholic Church--Congresses. LC Classification: BX1390 .C27 1998 Dewey Class No.: 282/.73/089 21

The Christian tradition / [compiled by] World Religions Curriculum Development Center; project co-directors, Lee Smith and Wes Bodin, project assistants, Joan Voigt and Pat Noyes. Published/Created: Niles, Ill.: Argus Communications, c1978. Related Authors: World Religions Curriculum Development Center. Description: vi, 186 p.: ill.; 23 cm. ISBN: 0895050137 Subjects: Christianity--Addresses, essays, lectures. Series: Religion in human culture LC Classification: BR123 .C614 Dewey Class No.: 201

The Church and culture since Vatican II: the experience of North and Latin America / edited by Joseph Gremillion. Published/Created: Notre Dame, Ind.: University of Notre Dame Press, c1985. Related Authors: Gremillion, Joseph. Conference on the Church and Culture since Vatican II (1983: University of Notre Dame). Description: xvii, 330 p.; 23 cm. ISBN: 0268007535 (pbk.) : Contents: pt. 1. The Papers and discussions, convergences and perspectives -- pt. 2. Documents of the Church on culture. Notes: Based on the papers and discussions of the Conference on the Church and Culture since Vatican II, held at the University of Notre Dame, Nov. 1983. Includes bibliographies and index. Subjects: Catholic Church--America--Congresses. Catholic Church--Doctrines--Congresses. Christianity and culture--Congresses. LC Classification: BX1753 .C427 1985 Dewey Class No.: 261 19

The Church and homosexuality: a preliminary study. Published/Created: Atlanta: Office of the Stated Clerk, Presbyterian Church in the United States, c1977. Description: 37 p.; 26 cm. Notes: Bibliography: p. 33-34. Subjects: Homosexuality--Religious aspects--Christianity. LC Classification: BR115.H6 P73 1977 Dewey Class No.: 261.8/34/157

The church and the future of Africa: problems and promises / edited by J.N.K. Mugambi. Published/Created: Nairobi: All Africa Conference of Churches, 1997. Related Authors: Mugambi, J. N. Kanyua (Jesse Ndwiga Kanyua) All Africa Conference of Churches. Description: iii, 216 p.; 21 cm. ISBN: 9966886028 Notes: Includes bibliographical references. Subjects: Christianity and culture--Africa--Congresses. Christianity--20th century--Congresses. Christianity--Africa--Forecasting--Congresses. LC Classification: BR1360 .C485 1997 Dewey Class No.: 276/.0829 21

The church and the new world mind, by William E. Hocking [and others] Published/Created: St. Louis, The Bethany press [1944] Related Authors: Hocking,

William Ernest, 1873-1966. Description: 256 p. 21 cm. Contents: Faith and world order, by E. W. Hocking.--Culture and peace, by W. E. Hocking.--Statesmanship and Christianity, by W. E. Hocking.--The church, the press, and world opinion, by Willmott Lewis.--Toward peace in the Orient, by M. S. Bates.--A christian view of inter-American relationships, by G. Baez-Camargo.--Peace begins at home, by C. W. Blackburn.--The racial issue and the Christian church, by Georgia Harkness.--How can the churches in America work for peace? By W. W. Van Kirk.--The church and the new world mind, by R. M. Jones. Subjects: Christianity and politics. LC Classification: BR115.P7 D7 Dewey Class No.: 261

The church and the new world mind, by William E. Hocking [and others] Published/Created: Freeport, N.Y., Books for Libraries Press [1968, c1944] Related Authors: Hocking, William Ernest, 1873-1966. Description: 256 p. 23 cm. Contents: Faith and world order, by W. E. Hocking.--Culture and peace, by W. E. Hocking.--Statesmanship and Christianity, by W. E. Hocking.--The church, the press, and world opinion, by W. Lewis.--Toward peace in the Orient, by M. S. Bates.--A Christian view of inter-American relationships, by G. Baez-Camargo.--Peace begins at home, by C. W. Blackburn.--The racial issue and the Christian church, by G. Harkness.--How can the churches in America work for peace? By W. W. Van Kirk.--The church and the new world mind, by R. M. Jones. Notes: Bibliographical footnotes. Subjects: Christianity and politics. Series: Drake Conference, Drake University, 1944. Drake lectures. LC Classification: BR115.P7 D7 1944aab Dewey Class No.: 261.8

The church as counterculture / Michael L. Budde and Robert W. Brimlow, editors. Published/Created: Albany: State University of New York Press, 2000. Related Authors: Budde, Michael L. Brimlow, Robert W., 1954- Description: viii, 233 p.; 24 cm. ISBN: 0791446077 (alk. paper) 0791446085 (pbk.: alk. paper)

Notes: Includes bibliographical references and index. Subjects: Christianity and culture--United States. Series: SUNY series in popular culture and political change LC Classification: BR115.C8 C49 2000 Dewey Class No.: 261/.0973 21

The church between Gospel and culture: the emerging mission in North America / edited by George R. Hunsberger, Craig Van Gelder. Published/Created: Grand Rapids, Mich.: W.B. Eerdmans Pub. Co., c1996. Related Authors: Hunsberger, George R. Van Gelder, Craig. Description: xix, 369 p.: ill.; 23 cm. ISBN: 0802841090 Notes: Includes bibliographical references. Subjects: Missions--North America. Christianity and culture. Missions--Theory. Evangelistic work--North America. North America--Religion--20th century. LC Classification: BV2760 .C48 1996 Dewey Class No.: 261/.097 20

The Church in Africa and her evangelising mission towards the year 2000: "You shall be my witnesses" (Acts 1:8). Published/Created: Nairobi: St. Paul Publications-Africa, [1990 or 1991] Related Authors: Catholic Church. Synodus Episcoporum. African Synod (1994: Rome, Italy) Description: ix, 93 p.; 21 cm. Notes: Cover Towards the African Synod. At head of Synod of Bishops. Special Assembly for Africa. "Lineamenta." Includes bibliographical references. Subjects: Catholic Church--Africa. Catholic Church--Relations. Catholic Church--Missions--Africa. Christianity and culture. Evangelistic work--Africa. Church and social problems--Africa. Church and social problems--Catholic Church. Africa--Church history--20th century. LC Classification: BX1675 .C49 1990

The Church in Africa and her evangelising mission towards the year 2000: "You shall be my witnesses" (Acts 1:8): instrumentum laboris. Published/Created: Vatican City: General Secretariat of the Synod of Bishops: Libreria Editrice Vaticana, 1993. Related Authors: Catholic Church. Synodus Episcoporum. African Synod

(1994: Rome, Italy) Description: 118 p.; 25 cm. Notes: At head of Synod of Bishops, Special Assembly for Africa. Includes bibliographical references. Subjects: Catholic Church--Africa. Catholic Church--Relations. Catholic Church--Missions--Africa. Christianity and culture. Evangelistic work--Africa. Church and social problems--Africa. Church and social problems--Catholic Church. Africa--Church history--20th century. LC Classification: IN PROCESS

The Church in response to human need / edited by Vinay Samuel and Christopher Sugden. Published/Created: Grand Rapids, Mich.: W.B. Eerdmans Pub. Co.; Oxford, U.K.: Regnum Books, c1987. Related Authors: Samuel, Vinay. Sugden, Chris, 1948- World Evangelical Fellowship. Consultation on the Church in Response to Human Need (1983: Wheaton, Ill.) Description: xii, 268 p.; 23 cm. ISBN: 0802802869 (pbk.) : Notes: Papers from the Consultation on the Church in Response to Human Need, held in Wheaton, Ill., in June 1983 and sponsored by the World Evangelical Fellowship. Bibliography: p. 266-267. Subjects: Church work with the poor--Congresses. Economic development--Religious aspects--Christianity Congresses. Christianity and culture--Congresses. Social change--Congresses. LC Classification: BV639.P6 C49 1987 Dewey Class No.: 261 19

The Ciskei--a Bantu homeland: a general survey. Published/Created: Fort Hare: Fort Hare University Press, 1971. Related Authors: Sabra Study Group of Fort Hare. Suid-Afrikaanse Akademie vir Wetenskap en Kuns. Fort Hare Branch. University of Fort Hare. Description: iv, 215 p.: ill., maps.; 30 cm. Partial Contents: The physical character of the Ciskei and some notes on its potential, by W. C. Els.--Tribal history of the Bantu of the Ciskei, by E. J. de Jager.--The Ciskei: historical background, by C. G. Coetzee. Notes: "A publication of the Sabra Study Group of Fort Hare in co-operation with the Fort Hare branch of the South African Academy of Arts and Science." "'Festschrift' on the occasion of the attainment of University status by the University College of Fort Hare." Subjects: Xhosa (African people) Ciskei (South Africa) Ciskei (South Africa)--Social conditions. LC Classification: DT2400.C58 C57 1971 Dewey Class No.: 968.75/5 21

The compromised church: the present evangelical crisis / John H. Armstrong, general editor. Published/Created: Wheaton, Ill.: Crossway Books, c1998. Related Authors: Armstrong, John H. (John Harper), 1949- Description: 330 p.; 23 cm. ISBN: 1581340060 (tpb: alk. paper) Notes: Includes bibliographical references and index. Subjects: Evangelicalism--United States. Christianity and culture--United States. LC Classification: BR1642.U5 C644 1998 Dewey Class No.: 277.3/0829 21

The consuming passion: Christianity & the consumer culture / edited by Rodney Clapp. Published/Created: Downers Grove, Ill.: InterVarsity Press, c1998. Related Authors: Clapp, Rodney. Description: 223 p.; 22 cm. ISBN: 0830818979 (pbk.: alk. paper) Notes: Includes bibliographical references (p. [205]-223). Subjects: Consumption (Economics)--Religious aspects--Christianity. Christianity and culture. LC Classification: BR115.C67 C66 1998 Dewey Class No.: 241/.68 21

The death of truth / [edited by] Dennis McCallum. Published/Created: Minneapolis, Minn.: Bethany House Publishers, c1996. Related Authors: McCallum, Dennis. Description: 288 p.; 21 cm. ISBN: 1556617240 Notes: Includes bibliographical references and index. Subjects: Christianity and culture. Christianity--20th century. Postmodernism--Religious aspects--Christianity. Postmodernism. Multiculturalism--Religious aspects--Christianity. Multiculturalism. Evangelicalism. LC Classification: BR115.C8 D34 1996 Dewey Class No.: 261 20

The Dynamic character of Christian culture: essays on Dawsonian themes / edited by Peter J. Cataldo. Published/Created: Lanham, MD: University Press of America; [Saint Louis, Mo.: Society for Christian Culture], c1984. Related Authors: Cataldo, Peter J., 1956- Society for Christian Culture (U.S.) Description: xii, 229 p.; 24 cm. ISBN: 0819139599 (alk. paper): 0819139602 (pbk.: alk. paper) : Notes: "Originally delivered at the second and third annual conferences (1982-1983) of the Society for Christain Culture (SCC) held in Saint Louis, Missouri"--Pref. Includes bibliographies and index. Subjects: Dawson, Christopher, 1889-1970 --Congresses. Christianity and culture--Congresses. LC Classification: BR115.C8 D96 1984 Dewey Class No.: 209 19

The emancipation of Russian Christianity / edited by Natalia A. Pecherskaya, with the assistance of Ruth Coates. Published/Created: Lewiston: E. Mellen Press, c1995. Related Authors: Pecherskaya, Natalia A., 1951- Coates, R. (Ruth) Description: xiii, 119 p.; 24 cm. ISBN: 0773488715 088946975X (ser.) Notes: Includes bibliographical references. Subjects: Russkaia pravoslavnaia tserkov'--Doctrines. Orthodox Eastern Church--Russia (Federation)--Doctrines. Christianity and culture. Theology. Philosophy. Russia (Federation)--Religion. Series: Toronto studies in theology; v. 33 LC Classification: BX493 .E43 1995 Dewey Class No.: 230/.1947 20

The encyclopedia of apocalypticism. Published/Created: New York: Continuum, 1998. Related Authors: Collins, John Joseph, 1946- McGinn, Bernard, 1937- Stein, Stephen J., 1940- Description: 3 v.: ill.; 25 cm. ISBN: 0826410715 (v. 1: hardcover) Contents: v. 1. The origins of apocalypticism in Judaism and Christianity / edited by John J. Collins -- v. 2. Apocalypticism in Western history and culture / edited by Bernard McGinn -- v. 3. Apocalypticism in the modern period and the contemporary age / edited by Stephen J. Stein. Notes: Includes bibliographical references and indexes. Subjects:

Apocalyptic literature--Comparative studies. End of the world--Comparative studies. LC Classification: BL501 .E53 1998 Dewey Class No.: 291.2/3 21

The Failure of the American Baptist culture: a symposium / edited by James B. Jordan. Published/Created: Tyler, Tex.: Geneva Divinity School, c1982. Related Authors: Jordan, James B., 1949- Description: xv, 299 p.; 22 cm. ISBN: 0939404044 (pbk.) : Notes: Includes bibliographical references. Subjects: Christianity--United States-- Congresses. Baptists--United States-- Congresses. Baptism--Congresses. Reformed Church--Congresses. Christianity and culture--Congresses. United States--Church history-- Congresses. Series: Christianity and civilization; no. 1. LC Classification: BR517 .F34 1982 Dewey Class No.: 286/.0973 19

The formulation of Christianity by conflict through the ages / edited by Katharine B. Free. Published/Created: Lewiston, N.Y.: E. Mellen Press, c1995. Related Authors: Free, Katharine B. Description: viii, 278 p.; 24 cm. ISBN: 0773489266 088946989X (series) Notes: Collection of papers delivered at the conference Crisis of Cultures and the Birth of Faith, held at Loyola Marymount University, Los Angeles, on Sept. 25-26, 1993. Includes bibliographical references and index. Subjects: Christianity and culture-- Congresses. Identification (Religion)-- Congresses. Church history--Primitive and early church, ca. 30-600 Congresses. Church and state--Europe, Eastern-- History--20th century Congresses. Europe, Eastern--Church history--20th century-- Congresses. Series: Symposium series (Edwin Mellen Press); v. 34. LC Classification: BR115.C8 F63 1995 Dewey Class No.: 261/.09 20

The Globalization of theological education / Alice Frazer Evans, Robert A. Evans, David A. Roozen, editors. Published/Created: Maryknoll, N.Y.: Orbis Books, c1993. Related Authors: Evans, Alice F., 1939- Evans, Robert A., 1937-

Roozen, David A. Description: xvii, 366 p.: ill.; 24 cm. ISBN: 0883449188 (pbk.) : Notes: Includes bibliographical references. Subjects: Theology--Study and teaching. Christianity and culture. Missions--Theory. Christian union. LC Classification: BV4022 .G57 1993 Dewey Class No.: 207 20

The Gospel as good news for African cultures: a symposium on the dialogue between faith and culture / G.M. Tonucci ... [et al.]. Published/Created: [Nairobi]: Catholic University of Eastern Africa, 1999. Related Authors: Tonucci, G. M. (Giovanni Mwenda) Catholic University of Eastern Africa. Description: iii, 180 p.: ill. (some col.); 23 cm. Notes: Includes bibliographical references. Subjects: Christianity--Africa--Congresses. Christianity and culture--Africa-- Congresses. Series: CUEA publications LC Classification: BR1360 .G66 1999 Dewey Class No.: 261/.096 21

The Human person and philosophy in the contemporary world: proceedings of the meeting of the World Union of Catholic Philosophical Societies, Cracow, 23-25 August 1978 / edited by J.M. Zyci´nski. Published/Created: Kraków: Pontifical Faculty of Theology, 1980. Related Authors: Zyci´nski, Józef. World Union of Catholic Philosophical Societies. Description: 2 v. (iii, 508 p.); 21 cm. Notes: English, French, German, Italian, and Spanish. Includes bibliographical references. Subjects: Philosophical anthropology--Congresses. Christianity-- Philosophy--Congresses. Culture-- Philosophy--Congresses. LC Classification: BD450 .H86 1980 Dewey Class No.: 190 19

The Impact of the church upon its culture; reappraisals of the history of Christianity, by Quirinus Breen [and others] Edited by Jerald C. Brauer. Published/Created: Chicago, University of Chicago Press [1968] Related Authors: Brauer, Jerald C., ed. Breen, Quirinus, 1896- University of Chicago. Divinity School. Description: x, 396 p. 24 cm. Notes: Most of the papers

were presented at the Alumni Conference
of the Field of History of Christianity, Oct.
6-8, 1966, celebrating the 75th anniversary
of the University of Chicago and the 100th
anniversary of its Divinity School.
Bibliographical footnotes. Subjects:
Church history--Addresses, essays,
lectures. Series: Essays in divinity, v. 2 LC
Classification: BR155 .I5 Dewey Class
No.: 270

The Jesuits: cultures, sciences, and the arts,
1540-1773 / edited by John W. O'Malley ...
[et al.]. Published/Created: Toronto:
University of Toronto Press, c1999.
Related Authors: O'Malley, John W.
Description: xx, 772 p.: ill.; 24 cm. ISBN:
0802042872 (alk. paper) Notes: Papers
from an international conference organized
at Boston College in late May 1997..
Includes bibliographical references and
index. Subjects: Jesuits--History--16th
century--17th century--18th century--
Congresses. Jésuites--Histoire--16e siècle--
17e siècle--18e siècle--Congrès.
Christianity and culture--History--16th
century--17th century--18th century
Congresses. Christianisme et civilisation--
Histoire--16e siècle--17e siècle--18e siècle
Congrès. LC Classification: BX3706.2
.J464 1999 Dewey Class No.: 271/.53 21

The Labor of God: an Ignatian view of church
and culture / edited by William J. O'Brien.
Published/Created: Washington, D.C.:
Georgetown University Press, c1991.
Related Authors: O'Brien, William James.
Description: xv, 104 p.; 23 cm. ISBN:
0878405275 Notes: Includes
bibliographical references. Subjects:
Ignatius, of Loyola, Saint, 1491-1556.
Latin America--History. Christianity and
culture. Journalism, Religious. LC
Classification: BX4700.L7 L29 1991
Dewey Class No.: 261 20

The limits of ancient Christianity: essays on
late antique thought and culture in honor of
R.A. Markus / edited by William E.
Klingshirn and Mark Vessey.
Published/Created: Ann Arbor: University
of Michigan Press, c1999. Related
Authors: Markus, R. A. (Robert Austin),

1924- Klingshirn, William E. Vessey,
Mark. Description: xxv, 348 p.; 24 cm.
ISBN: 0472109979 (alk. paper) Notes:
Includes bibliographical references and
indexes. Subjects: Church history--
Primitive and early church, ca. 30-600.
Christianity--Origin. Christianity--Essence,
genius, nature. Series: Recentiores LC
Classification: BR219 .L55 1999 Dewey
Class No.: 270.2 21

The Nigerian church: evangelisation through
inculturation: pastoral letter / by the
Catholic Bishops' Conference of Nigeria.
Published/Created: [Lagos]: Catholic
Secretariat of Nigeria, 1991. Related
Authors: Catholic Secretariat of Nigeria.
Description: 27 p.; 18 cm. Notes: Cover
title. Subjects: Catholic Church--Nigeria.
Christianity and culture. Evangelistic work.
Nigeria--Church history. LC Classification:
BX1682.N5 C34 1991

The novel, spirituality and modern culture /
edited by Paul S. Fiddes.
Published/Created: Cardiff: University of
Wales Press, 2000. Related Authors:
Fiddes, Paul S. Description: x, 161 p.; 23
cm. ISBN: 0708315984 0708315992 (pbk.)
Notes: Includes bibliographical references
and index. Subjects: Fiction--Religious
aspects--Christianity. Spirituality in
literature. Authorship--Religious aspects--
Christianity. Series: Religion, culture, and
society. LC Classification: PN3351 .N68
2000 Dewey Class No.: 809.3/93823 21

The Peacemaking struggle: militarism and
resistance: essays prepared for the
Advisory Council on Church and Society
of the Presbyterian Church (U.S.A.) /
Ronald H. Stone and Dana W. Wilbanks,
editors. Published/Created: Lanham, MD:
University Press of America, c1985.
Related Authors: Stone, Ronald H.
Wilbanks, Dana W. Presbyterian Church
(U.S.A.). Advisory Council on Church and
Society. Description: vii, 294 p.; 22 cm.
ISBN: 0819147729 (alk. paper):
0819147737 (pbk.: alk. paper) : Notes:
"Copublished by arrangement with the
Council on Theology and Culture and the
Advisory Council on Church and Society

of the Presbyterian Church (U.S.A.)--T.p. verso. Includes bibliographies. Subjects: Presbyterian Church (U.S.A.)--Doctrines. War--Religious aspects--Christianity. Peace--Religious aspects--Christianity. Government, Resistance to--Religious aspects Christianity. Presbyterian Church--United States--Doctrines. LC Classification: BT736.2 .P335 1985 Dewey Class No.: 261.8/73 19

The scandal of a crucified world: perspectives on the Cross and suffering / edited by Yacob Tesfai. Published/Created: Maryknoll, N.Y.: Orbis Books, c1994. Related Authors: Tesfai, Yacob. Description: ix, 155 p.: ill.; 24 cm. ISBN: 0883449765 (pbk.) : Notes: Includes bibliographical references and index. Subjects: Suffering--Religious aspects--Christianity. Holy Cross. Christianity and culture. Christianity--Developing countries. LC Classification: BT732.7 .S338 1994 Dewey Class No.: 231/.8 20

The strange new word of the Gospel: re-evangelizing in the postmodern world / edited by Carl E. Braaten and Robert W. Jenson. Published/Created: Grand Rapids, MI: W.B. Eerdmans, 2002. Related Authors: Braaten, Carl E., 1929- Jenson, Robert W. Description: p. cm. ISBN: 0802839479 (alk. paper) Partial Contents: The gospel of affinity / John Milbank -- What is a post-Christian? / Robert W. Jenson -- Religion and secularity in a culture of abstraction: on the integrity of space, time, matter, and motion / David Schindler -- Postmodern irony and Petronian humanism / R.R. Reno. Notes: Includes bibliographical references. Subjects: Evangelistic work. Postmodernism--Religious aspects--Christianity. LC Classification: BV3793 .S6775 2002 Dewey Class No.: 269/.2 21

The Theology of Christian resistance: a symposium / edited by Gary North. Published/Created: Tyler, Tex.: Geneva Divinity School Press, 1983. Related Authors: North, Gary. Description: xxx, 357 p.; 22 cm. ISBN: 0939404052 (pbk.) : Notes: Includes bibliographical references.

Subjects: Violence--Religious aspects--Christianity--Congresses. War--Religious aspects--Christianity--Congresses. Christianity and culture--Congresses. Christianity and politics--Congresses. Sociology, Christian (Reformed Church)--Congresses. Series: Christianity and civilization, 0278-8187; no. 2 (winter 1983) LC Classification: BT736.15 .T48 1983 Dewey Class No.: 261.7 19

The Third World and Bernard Lonergan: a tribute to a concerned thinker / edited by Walter L. Ysaac. Published/Created: Manila, Philippines: Lonergan Centre, 1986. Related Authors: Lonergan, Bernard J. F. Ysaac, Walter L. Description: vi, 68 p.: ill.; 22 cm. Notes: Includes bibliographical references. Subjects: Lonergan, Bernard J. F. Christianity and culture--History--20th century. Developing countries. LC Classification: BX4705.L7133 Y78 1986

The Trinity in a pluralistic age: theological essays on culture and religion / edited by Kevin J. Vanhoozer. Published/Created: Grand Rapids, Mich.: W.B. Eerdmans Pub., c1997. Related Authors: Vanhoozer, Kevin J. Edinburgh Conference in Christian Dogmatics (5th: 1993: Edinburgh) Description: x, 166 p.; 23 cm. ISBN: 0802841171 (pbk.: alk. paper) Notes: Papers of the Fifth Edinburgh Dogmatics Conference held in Edinburgh, Aug. 31-Sept. 3, 1993. Includes bibliographical references. Subjects: Trinity--Congresses. Religious pluralism--Congresses. Religious pluralism--Christianity--Congresses. Multiculturalism--Congresses. Christianity and culture--Congresses. LC Classification: BT111.2 .T76 1997 Dewey Class No.: 231/.044 20

The West and Islam: towards a dialogue / [speaker] Ekmeleddin Ihsanoglu and guest speakers at IRCICA, Hillary R. Clinton ... [et al.]; edited by Zeynep Durukal Abuhusayn, Muhammad Isa Waley. Published/Created: Istanbul: Organisation of the Islamic Conference Research Centre for Islamic History, Art and Culture, 1999.

Related Authors: Ihsanoglu, Ekmeleddin.
Clinton, Hillary Rodham. Abuhusayn,
Zeynep Durukal. Waley, Muhammad Isa.
Description: vi, 125 p.: col. ill.; 24 cm.
ISBN: 9290630809 Notes: Includes
bibliographical references. Subjects: Islam-
-Europe. Islam--Relations--Christianity.
Christianity and other religions--Islam.
Islamic countries--Relations--Europe.
Europe--Relations--Islamic countries. LC
Classification: BP65.A1 W47 1999 Dewey
Class No.: 297.2/8/094 21

The Word among us: contextualizing theology
for mission today / Dean S. Gilliland,
editor. Published/Created: Dallas: Word
Pub., c1989. Related Authors: Gilliland,
Dean S. Description: viii, 344 p.: ill.; 23
cm. ISBN: 0849931541 Notes:
Bibliography: p. [318]-336. Subjects:
Missions--Theory. Christianity and culture.
Word of God (Theology) LC
Classification: BV2063 .W59 1989 Dewey
Class No.: 266/.001 20

Theology and lived Christianity / David M.
Hammond, editor. Published/Created:
Mystic, CT: Twenty-Third
Publications/Bayard, c2000. Related
Authors: Hammond, David M.
Description: xvii, 324 p.: ill.; 22 cm. ISBN:
1585950203 Notes: Includes
bibliographical references. Subjects:
Theology, Practical. Christianity and
culture. Series: Annual publication of the
College Theology Society; v. 45. LC
Classification: BV3 .T446 2000 Dewey
Class No.: 230/.2 21

Third World theologies: commonalities and
divergences: papers and reflections from
the Second General Assembly of the
Ecumenical Association of Third World
Theologians, December 1986, Oaxtepec,
Mexico / edited by K.C. Abraham for the
Executive Committee of the Ecumenical
Association of Third World Theologians;
[Tissa Balasuriya ... et al.].
Published/Created: Maryknoll, N.Y.: Orbis
Books, c1990. Related Authors: Abraham,
K. C. Balasuriya, Tissa. Ecumenical
Association of Third World Theologians.
Executive Committee. Description: xix,

216 p.; 24 cm. ISBN: 0883446812 Notes:
Includes bibliographical references.
Subjects: Theology, Doctrinal--Developing
countries--Theology--Developing
countries--Church history--20th century--
Liberation theology--Congresses.
Christianity and culture. LC Classification:
BT30.D44 E28 1986 Dewey Class No.:
230/.09172/4 20

Thomas, George Finger, 1899- ed. The vitality
of the Christian tradition. Edited by George
F. Thomas. Published/Created: Freeport,
N.Y., Books for Libraries Press [1971,
c1944] Description: xi, 367 p. 24 cm.
ISBN: 0836923782 Partial Contents: The
faith of ancient Israel, by J. Muilenburg.--
The beginnings of Christianity, by J.
Knox.--The early centuries of the church,
by V. Corwin.--The significance of
medieval Christianity, by L. D. [i.e. T.]
White. Subjects: Christianity--Essence,
genius, nature. Christianity--Philosophy.
Civilization, Christian. LC Classification:
BR121 .T49 1971 Dewey Class No.: 201

Thomas, George Finger, 1899- ed. The vitality
of the Christian tradition, edited by George
F. Thomas. Published/Created: New York,
London, Harper & brothers [1944]
Description: xi p., 1 l., 358 p. 23 cm.
Partial Contents: The faith of ancient
Israel, by James Mullenburg.--The
beginnings of Christianity, by John Knox.-
-The early centuries of the church, by
Virginia Corwin.--The significance of
medieval Christianity, by L. D. [i.e. T.]
White. Notes: "First edition." Subjects:
Christianity--Essence, genius, nature.
Christianity--Philosophy. Civilization,
Christian. LC Classification: BR121 .T49
Dewey Class No.: 270

Thomas, George M. Revivalism and cultural
change: Christianity, nation building, and
the market in the nineteenth-century
United States / George M. Thomas.
Published/Created: Chicago: University of
Chicago Press, 1989. Description: xii, 238
p.: 24 cm. ISBN: 0226795853 (alk. paper)
Notes: Bibliography: p. 217-230. Subjects:
Republican Party (U.S.: 1854-) Revivals--
Sociology, Christian--United States--

Christianity and culture--History--19th century. United States--Politics and government--19th century. United States--Economic conditions--1865-1918. United States--Church history--19th century. LC Classification: BV3773 .T49 1989 Dewey Class No.: 306/.6 19

Thomas, T. Jacob (Thannikapurathoot Jacob) Human freedom an Indian culture: Christian ethical reflections / T. Jacob Thomas. Published/Created: Calcutta: Punthi Pustak, 1995. Description: xi, 330 p.; 22 cm. ISBN: 818509487X Summary: Comparative study of theology of freedom based on classical and some contemporary Christian and Hindu doctrines; includes both religion cultural review in Kerala, Bengal, and Northeast India. Notes: Includes bibliographical references (p. [309]-322) and index. Subjects: Liberty--Religious aspects--Comparative studies. Christianity--Doctrines. Hinduism--Doctrines. India--Religion. LC Classification: BT810 .T47 1995 Dewey Class No.: 233 20

Thompson, James, 1942- The Church in exile: God's counter culture in a non-Christian world / James Thompson. Published/Created: Abilene, Tex.: ACU Press, c1990. Description: viii, 140 p.; 23 cm. ISBN: 0891120955 Notes: Includes bibliographical references. Subjects: Bible. N.T. Peter, 1st--Criticism, interpretation, etc. Christianity--20th century. LC Classification: BR121.2 .T524 1990 Dewey Class No.: 270.8/25 20

Thompson, T. Jack. Christianity in northern Mala^wi: Donald Fraser's missionary methods and Ngoni culture / by T. Jack Thompson. Published/Created: Leiden; New York: E.J. Brill, 1995. Description: x, 292 p., [12] p. of plates: ill., map; 25 cm. ISBN: 9004102086 (cloth: alk. paper) Notes: Includes bibliographical references (p. [275]-284) and index. Subjects: Fraser, Donald, 1870-1933. Ngoni (African people)--Missions--History. Missions--Missions, Scottish--Malawi--Church history. Series: Studies in Christian mission, 0924-9389; v. 15 LC

Classification: BV3625.N8 T46 1995 Dewey Class No.: 266/.02341106897 20

Thornhill, John, 1929- Modernity: Christianity's estranged child reconstructed / John Thornhill. Published/Created: Grand Rapids, Mich.: W.B. Eerdmans Pub. Co., c2000. Description: x, 240 p.; 23 cm. ISBN: 0802846947 (pbk.) Notes: Includes bibliographical references and index. Subjects: Modernism (Christian theology) Christianity and culture. LC Classification: BT82 .T46 2000 Dewey Class No.: 261 21

Tigner, Hugh Stevenson, 1907- Our prodigal son, culture; a critical comment on modern culture from the standpoint of the Christian religion, by Hugh Stevenson Tigner. Published/Created: Chicago, New York, Willett, Clark,& co., 1940. Description: 162 p. 21 cm. Notes: "Notes" (bibliographical) at end of each chapter. Subjects: Civilization. Christianity--20th century. LC Classification: BR115.C5 T5

Tillich, Paul, 1886-1965. The irrelevance and relevance of the Christian message / Paul Tillich; edited by Durwood Foster. Published/Created: Cleveland, Ohio: Pilgrim Press, c1996. Related Authors: Foster, Durwood. Description: xxix, 74 p.; 21 cm. ISBN: 0829810811 (alk. paper) Notes: Includes bibliographical references (p. 65-68) and index. Subjects: Theology, Doctrinal. Christianity--20th century. Christianity and culture. LC Classification: BT80 .T49 1996 Dewey Class No.: 230 21

Tillich, Paul, 1886-1965. Theology of culture, edited by Robert C. Kimball. New York, Oxford University Press, 1959. Related Authors: Kimball, Robert C., ed. Description: ix, 213 p. 20 cm. Subjects: Christianity--Philosophy. Culture. LC Classification: BT40 .T5 Dewey Class No.: 201

Tillich, Paul, 1886-1965. Visionary science: a translation of Tillich's "On the idea of a theology of culture," with an interpretive essay / Victor Nuovo. Published/Created: Detroit: Wayne State University Press, 1987. Related Authors: Nuovo, Victor,

1931- Description: 194 p.; 24 cm. ISBN: 0814319408 (alk. paper) Notes: Translation of: Über die Idee einer Theologic der Kultur. Includes index. Bibliography: p. 179-188. Subjects: Christianity and culture. LC Classification: BR115.C8 T4813 1987 Dewey Class No.: 261 19

Tillich, Paul, 1886-1965. Writings in the philosophy of culture / Paul Tillich; edited by Michael Palmer = Kulturphilosophische Schriften / Paul Tillich; herausgegeben von Michael Palmer. Published/Created: Berlin; New York: De Gruyter; Berlin: Evangelisches Verlagswerk, 1990. Related Authors: Palmer, Michael F., 1945- Description: xiv, 382 p.; 24 cm. ISBN: 0899256066 (N.Y.: alk. paper): 3110115360 (Berlin: alk. paper) Notes: In the original English and German. Subjects: Christianity and culture. Civilization, Modern. Civilization--Philosophy. Series: Tillich, Paul, 1886-1965. Selections. 1987; v. 2. LC Classification: BR45 .T54 1987 vol. 2 Dewey Class No.: 261 20

Tippit, Sammy. The choice: America at the crossroads of ruin and revival / Sammy Tippit. Published/Created: Chicago: Moody Press, c1998. Description: 186 p.; 23 cm. ISBN: 0802452477 Notes: Includes bibliographical references (p. [181]-186). Subjects: Christianity and culture--United States. Revivals--United States. Commitment to the church. United States--Social conditions--1980- LC Classification: BR115.C8 T57 1998 Dewey Class No.: 277.3/0829 21

Torrance, Thomas Forsyth, 1913- Christian theology and scientific culture / by Thomas F. Torrance. Published/Created: New York: Oxford University Press, 1981. Description: 152 p.; 22 cm. ISBN: 0195202724 Contents: Christianity in scientific change -- The priority of belief -- The theology of light -- Word and number. Notes: Includes bibliographical references and index. Subjects: Religion and science. LC Classification: BL241 .T67 1981 Dewey Class No.: 261.5/5 19

Torrance, Thomas Forsyth, 1913- The Christian frame of mind / Thomas F. Torrance. Published/Created: Edinburgh: Handsel Press, 1985. Description: 62 p.; 21 cm. ISBN: 0905312430 (pbk.) Notes: Includes bibliographies and index. Subjects: Christianity and culture. Religion and science. LC Classification: BR115.C8 T67 1985 Dewey Class No.: 261.5 19

Torwesten, Hans, 1944- Ramakrishna and Christ, or, The paradox of the incarnation / Hans Torwesten. Edition Information: 1st ed. Published/Created: Calcutta: The Ramakrishna Mission Institute of Culture, 1999. Description: xii, 228 p.; 22 cm. ISBN: 818584397X Notes: Translated by John Phillips from the German original "Ramakrishna und Christus oder das paradox der inkarnation"--Cover. Includes bibliographical references. Subjects: Jesus Christ--Hindu interpretations. Ramakrishna, 1836-1886. Christianity and other religions--Hinduism. LC Classification: BT304.94 .T67 1999 Dewey Class No.: 294.5/55/092 21

Tovey, Phillip. Inculturation: the Eucharist in Africa / by Phillip Tovey. Published/Created: Bramcote, Nottingham: Grove Books, c1988. Description: 45 p.; 21 cm. ISBN: 1851740910 : Notes: Includes bibliographical references. Subjects: Lord's Supper. Christianity and culture. Africa, Sub-Saharan--Religious life and customs. Series: Alcuin/GROW liturgical study, 0951-2667; 7 Grove liturgical study; 55 LC Classification: BV825.2 .T68 1988 Dewey Class No.: 264/.36/096 19

Towards an indigenous African church: a post-synodal theological review of the Africa Synod in the context of Nigeria: lectures and resolutions at the 7th Enugu Diocesan Priests' Annual Seminar (EDPAS), held at Ugwu-Di-Nso, Eke, on 20, 21, 22 February, 1995 / editors, Obiora Ike, Ugonna Igboaja, Ikechukwu Ani. Published/Created: Uwani Enugu, Enugu State, Nigeria: EDPAS Secretariat, Catholic Institute for Development, Justice & Peace, 1996. Related Authors: Ike,

Obiora, 1956- Igboaja, Eugene Ugonna, 1944- Ani, Ikechukwu. Description: 107 p.; 25 cm. ISBN: 9783313851 Partial Contents: The Synod documents -- An address to the priest-participants / Michael U. Eneja -- Evangelization and proclamation / Obiakoizu A. Iloanusi Notes: Includes bibliographical references. Subjects: African Synod (1994: Rome, Italy)--Evangelistic work--Nigeria--Christianity and culture--Nigeria--Congresses. LC Classification: IN PROCESS (COPIED: lccopycat)

Towns, Elmer L. Putting an end to worship wars / Elmer Towns. Published/Created: Nashville, Tenn.: Broadman & Holman Publishers, c1997. Description: vii, 193 p.: ill.; 23 cm. ISBN: 0805430172 (pbk.) Notes: "Understanding: Why people disagree over worship, the six basic worship styles, how to find balance and make peace." Includes bibliographical references (p. 189-193). Subjects: Public worship. Church attendance. Church membership. Choice of church. Evangelistic work. Popular culture--Religious aspects--Christianity. Christianity and culture. LC Classification: BV15 .T68 1997 Dewey Class No.: 264/.001 20

Trace, Arther S. Christianity and the intellectuals / Arther Trace. Edition Information: 1st ed. Published/Created: La Salle, Ill.: Sherwood Sugden, c1983. Description: 205 p.; 21 cm. ISBN: 0893850187 (pbk.) : Notes: Includes index. Subjects: Christianity and culture. Secularism. Humanism. LC Classification: BR115.C8 T73 1983 Dewey Class No.: 270 19

Transition and permanence, Chinese history and culture: a festschrift in honor of Dr. Hsiao Kung-ch`üan / edited by David C. Buxbaum and Frederick W. Mote. Published/Created: [s.l.: s.n.], 1972 (Hong Kong: Cathay Press) Related Authors: Hsiao, Kung-ch`üan, 1897- Buxbaum, David C. Mote, Frederick W., 1922- Description: xxvi, 433 p.; 24 cm. Partial Contents: Mote, F. W. The cosmological

gulf between China and the West.--Mann, A. B. Cheng Ch`iao.--Fincher, J. China as a race, culture, and nation.--Huang, P. Liang Ch`i-ch`ao.--Gasster, M. Intellectuals, revolution, modernization.--Treadgold, D. W. Sun Yat-sen and modern Christianity.--Franke, W. Some remarks on Chinese historical sources in Southeast Asia.--Wong, Y. Notes: Includes bibliographical references and index. Subjects: Hsiao, Kung-ch`üan, 1897-China--Civilization. LC Classification: DS721 .T69 Dewey Class No.: 951

Troeger, Thomas H., 1945- Ten strategies for preaching in a multimedia culture / Thomas H. Troeger. Published/Created: Nashville: Abingdon Press, c1996. Description: 125 p.; 22 cm. ISBN: 0687007011 (pbk.: acid-free paper) Notes: Includes bibliographical references (p. 122-125). Subjects: Preaching. Mass media--Religious aspects--Christianity. LC Classification: BV4211.2 .T7655 1996 Dewey Class No.: 251/.07 20

Trueblood, Elton, 1900- The teacher / D. Elton Trueblood. Published/Created: Nashville, Tenn.: Broadman Press, c1980. Description: 131 p.; 22 cm. ISBN: 0805469338 Subjects: Trueblood, Elton, 1900- Church and college. Christianity and culture. Christian life--Friends authors. LC Classification: LC383 .T85 Dewey Class No.: 207 19

Tuttle, Robert G., 1941- Can we talk?: sharing your faith in a pre-Christian world / Robert G. Tuttle, Jr. Published/Created: Nashville, TN: Abingdon Press, c1999. Description: 110 p.; 23 cm. ISBN: 0687084164 (alk. paper) Notes: Includes bibliographical references. Subjects: Evangelistic work--Philosophy. Christianity and culture. LC Classification: BV3793 .T88 1999 Dewey Class No.: 266 21

Twiss, Richard, 1954- One church, many tribes / Richard Twiss. Published/Created: Ventura, Calif.: Regal, c2000. Description: 219 p.; 21 cm. ISBN: 0830725458 (trade paper) Notes: Includes bibliographical references (p. [217]-219). Subjects: Indians of North America--Religion. Christianity and culture--North America. Indigenous peoples--Religion. LC Classification: E98.R3 T85 2000 Dewey Class No.: 277/.0089/97 21

Udeafor, Ndubisi Innocent, 1953- Inculturation: path to African Christianity / by Ndubisi Innocent Udeafor. Published/Created: Lustenau, Austria: N.I. Udeafor, 1994. Description: 171 p.; 22 cm. ISBN: 978209434X (pbk.) Notes: Includes bibliographical references (p. [148]-163) and index. Subjects: Christianity and culture--Africa. Christianity and culture. Religion and culture--Africa. Africa-- Church history. Africa--Religion. LC Classification: BR1360 .U34 1994 Dewey Class No.: 261/.096 21

Udoidem, S. Iniobong, 1951- Pope John Paul II on inculturation: theory and practice / S. Iniobong Udoidem. Published/Created: Lanham, Md.: University Press of America, c1996. Description: 141 p.; 22 cm. ISBN: 0761805028 (cloth: alk. paper) Notes: Includes bibliographical references (p. [131]-134) and index. Subjects: John Paul II, Pope, 1920- --Contributions in doctrine of inculturation. Catholic Church- -Doctrines--History--20th century. Christianity and culture--History--20th century. LC Classification: BR115.C8 U36 1996 Dewey Class No.: 261/.08/822 20

Ugolnik, Anthony, 1944- The illuminating icon / by Anthony Ugolnik. Published/Created: Grand Rapids, Mich.: Eerdmans, c1989. Description: xxiv, 276 p.; 22 cm. ISBN: 0802836526 : Notes: Includes bibliographical references. Subjects: Russkaia pravoslavnaia tserkov´. Orthodox Eastern Church--Soviet Union. Orthodox Eastern Church--United States. Christianity and culture. Civil religion--United States. Soviet Union--Church history. United States--Church history. Soviet Union-- Relations--United States. United States-- Relations--Soviet Union. LC Classification: BX510 .U36 1989 Dewey Class No.: 281.9/47 19

Uzukwu, E. Elochukwu. The church and inculturation: a century of Roman Catholicism in Eastern Nigeria / by E. Elochukwu Uzukwu. Published/Created: Uruowulu, Obosi: Pacific College Press, 1985. Description: ix, 37 p.; 18 cm. ISBN: 9782347175 (pbk.) Notes: Bibliography: p. 35-37. Subjects: Catholic Church--Nigeria. Igbo (African people)--Religion. Christianity and culture. Nigeria--Church history. Series: Spiritan booklets; no. 1 LC Classification: BX1682.N5 U96 1985

Van der Peet, G. 20 essays on inculturation / by G. van der Peet. Published/Created: Iperu-Remo, Ogun State, Nigeria: Ambassador Publications, 1992. Description: iii, 45 p.; 22 cm. ISBN: 9782107174 Subjects: Catholic Church--Africa. Christianity and culture--Africa. LC Classification: BX1675 .V36 1992

Van der Walt, B. J. Afrocentric or eurocentric?: our task in a multicultural South Africa / B.J. van der Walt. Published/Created: [Potchefstroom, South Africa?]: Potchefstroomse Universiteit vir Christelike Hoër Onderwys, 1997. Related Authors: Van der Walt, B. J. Hand in eie boesem. Description: ii, 190 p.; 21 cm. ISBN: 186822256X Notes: Book is a follow-up of author's previous publication Die hand in eie boesem, 1995. Includes bibliographical references (p. 183-190). Subjects: Christianity and culture-- Pluralism (Social sciences)--Multicultural education--South Africa--Cultural policy. Series: Wetenskaplike bydraes van die PU vir CHO. Reeks F2, Brosjures van die Instituut vir Reformatoriese Studie; nr. 67. LC Classification: BR115.C8 V28 1997 Dewey Class No.: 306/.0968 21

Van Dyke, Henry, 1852-1933. Ideals and applications, by Henry Van Dyke. Published/Created: New York, C. Scribner's sons, 1921. Description: ix, 277 p. front. 22 cm. Contents: On politics and politethics: Is the world growing better? Ruling classes in a democracy. The people responsible. The Americanism of Washington and the men who stood with him. The chivalry of Lafayette. Humane culture or German kultur? Honour to France.-- On religion: Christianity and current literature. The church in the city, Property and theft.-- On education and conduct: The flood of books. Books, literature, and the people. Creative education. Theaching English in schools. The school of life. To-morrow's message to to-day. LC Classification: PS3115 .A2 1920 vol. 13

Van Rheenen, Gailyn, 1946- Missions: biblical foundations & contemporary strategies / Gailyn Van Rheenen. Published/Created: Grand Rapids, Mich: Zondervan Pub. House, c1996. Description: 251 p.: ill.; 25 cm. ISBN: 0310208092 (hbk.: acid-free paper) Notes: Includes bibliographical references (p. 229-235) and indexes. Subjects: Missions--Theory. Christianity and culture. LC Classification: BV2063 .V35 1996 Dewey Class No.: 266/.001 20

Varacalli, Joseph A. Bright promise, failed community: Catholics and the American public order / Joseph A. Varacalli. Published/Created: Lanham, Md.: Lexington Books, c2000. Description: xv, 133 p.; 24 cm. ISBN: 0739100866 (cloth: alk. paper) Notes: Includes bibliographical references (p. 115-123) and index. Subjects: Catholic Church--United States. Christianity and culture--United States. Sociology, Christian (Catholic)--United States. LC Classification: BX1406.2 .V365 2000 Dewey Class No.: 282/.73/0904 21

Vecsey, Christopher. The paths of Kateri's kin / Christopher Vecsey. Published/Created: Notre Dame, Ind.: University of Notre Dame Press, c1997. Description: xvi, 392 p., [7] p. of plates: ill., maps; 24 cm. ISBN: 0268038201 (alk. paper) Notes: Includes bibliographical references (p. 353-374) and index. Subjects: Catholic Church--Missions--North America--History. Catholic Church--Missions--New France--History. Indians of North America--Religion. Indians of North America--Missions. Indian Catholics--North America--History. Christianity and culture--North America--History. America--Discovery and exploration--Religious

aspects Catholic Church. Series: Vecsey, Christopher. American Indian Catholics; v. 2. LC Classification: E98.R3 V444 1997 Dewey Class No.: 282/.7/08997 21

Veith, Gene Edward, 1951- Postmodern times: a Christian guide to contemporary thought and culture / Gene Edward Veith, Jr. Published/Created: Wheaton, Ill.: Crossway Books, c1994. Description: 256 p.; 22 cm. ISBN: 0891077685 : Notes: Includes bibliographical references (p. [235]-248) and index. Subjects: Christianity and culture. Postmodernism--Religious aspects--Christianity. Contemporary, The. Sociology, Christian. Series: Turning point Christian worldview series LC Classification: BR115.C8 V37 1994 Dewey Class No.: 261 20

Vernacular Christianity: essays in the social anthropology of religion presented to Godfrey Lienhardt / edited by Wendy James and Douglas H. Johnson. Published/Created: New York: Lilian Barber Press, 1988. Related Authors: James, Wendy. Johnson, Douglas Hamilton, 1949- Description: xiv, 196 p.: ill.; 25 cm. ISBN: 093650823X Notes: Includes index. Bibliography: p. [183]-184. Subjects: Lienhardt, R. G. (R. Godfrey) Christianity and culture. Sociology, Christian. Christianity--Africa. LC Classification: BR115.C8 V43 1988 Dewey Class No.: 270 19

Voices from the margin: interpreting the Bible in the Third World / edited by R.S. Sugirtharajah. Edition Information: New ed. Published/Created: Maryknoll, NY: Orbis/SPCK, 1995. Related Authors: Sugirtharajah, R. S. (Rasiah S.) Description: ix, 484 p.; 22 cm. ISBN: 1570750467 Notes: Includes bibliographical references (p. 474-475) and indexes. Subjects: Bible--Hermeneutics--Comparative studies. Bible. O.T. Exodus--Hermeneutics--Comparative studies. Christianity--Developing countries. Christianity and culture. LC Classification: BS476 .V65 1995 Dewey Class No.: 220.6/01 20

Voices from the margin: interpreting the Bible in the Third World / edited by R.S. Sugirtharajah. Published/Created: Maryknoll, N.Y.: Orbis Books, c1991. Related Authors: Sugirtharajah, R. S. (Rasiah S.) Description: ix, 454 p.; 22 cm. ISBN: 0883447703 (pbk.) : Notes: Includes bibliographical references and indexes. Subjects: Bible--Hermeneutics--Comparative studies. Bible. O.T. Exodus--Hermeneutics--Comparative studies. Christianity--Developing countries. Christianity and culture. LC Classification: BS476 .V65 1991 Dewey Class No.: 220.6/01 20

Voices in the Holy Land / [Israel Film Service]. Published/Created: United States: Embassy of Israel, [1994?] Related Authors: Tizmoret ha-kamerit ha-kibutsit. Israel. Shagrirut (U.S.) Embassy of Israel Collection (Library of Congress) Description: 1 videocassette of 1 (VHS) (ca. 11 min.): sd., [col.]; 1/2 in. viewing copy. Summary: This video surveys the ancient sites in Israel which are appropriate for concerts. The historical and archaeological sites featured hold religious significance for both Christianity and Judaism. The video includes performances by the Kibbutz Chamber Orchestra. Notes: Copyright: reg. unknown. Title taken from videocassette label and confirmed in sources cited below. Israel Film Service produces films and television programs for all Israeli government ministries per Israel. Production Unit. Video catalogue no. A2173. Sources used: Israel. Ministry of Foreign Affairs. Production Unit. Video catalogue, 1995, p. 32; Embassy of Israel home page, films catalog, 9/17/97; videocassette label; Israel. Ministry of Foreign Affairs home page, government ministries, Ministry of Education, Culture and Sports, 9/23/97; Screen international film & TV yearbook, 1987-88, p. 112. Cast: Performers: Kibbutz Chamber Orchestra. Subjects: Music facilities--Israel. Historic sites--Israel. Excavations (Archaeology)--Israel. Genre/Form: Documentary--Short. LC Classification: VAF 3572 (viewing copy)

Vööbus, Arthur. Studies in the history of the Estonian people: with reference to aspects of social conditions, in particular, the religious and spiritual life and the educational pursuit / by Arthur Vööbus. Published/Created: Stockholm: ETSE, 1969-<1984 Description: v. <1-10; 26 cm. Notes: Includes bibliographical references and indexes. Subjects: Christianity--Estonia. Christianity and culture. Estonia--Civilization. Series: Papers of the Estonian Theological Society in Exile; 18, etc. LC Classification: DK511.E53 V63 Dewey Class No.: 947/.41

Voshaar, Jan. Maasai: between the Oreteti-tree and the tree of the cross / Jan Voshaar. Published/Created: Kampen: Kok, 1998. Description: 262 p.: ill., maps; 24 cm. ISBN: 9024293707 Notes: Includes bibliographical references (p. 254-262). Subjects: Masai (African people)--History. Masai (African people)--Religion. Masai (African people)--Social conditions. Mythology, Masai. Christianity and culture--Kenya. Series: Kerk en theologie in context; nr. 34. LC Classification: DT433.545.M33 V65 1998 Dewey Class No.: 305.8965 21

Waldecker, Gary. The contextualization of the gospel in Chile [microform] / by Gary Waldecker. Published/Created: 1997. Description: iii, 266 leaves. Notes: Thesis (D. Min.)--Westminister Theological Seminary, 1997. Includes bibliographical references (leaves 262-266). Microfiche. Portland, Or.: Theological Research Exchange Network, 1997. 1 microfiche: negative. High reduction. Subjects: Christianity and culture. Missions--Chile. LC Classification: Microfiche 98/141 (B)

Walker, Keith, 1933- Images or idols?: the place of sacred art in churches today / Keith Walker. Published/Created: Norwich, Norfolk: Canterbury Press, 1996. Description: vii, 184 p., [8] p. of plates: col. ill.; 22 cm. ISBN: 1853111341 Notes: Includes bibliographical references (p. 181-182) and index. Subjects: Christian art and symbolism--Great Britain--Modern period, 1500- Church decoration and ornament--Great Britain. Christianity and culture--Great Britain. Churches Interiors Decoration Great Britain LC Classification: IN PROCESS (COPIED) (lccopycat)

Walls, Andrew F. (Andrew Finlay) The cross-cultural process in Christian history: studies in the transmission and appropriation of faith / Andrew F. Walls. Published/Created: Maryknoll, N.Y.: Orbis Books, c2002. Description: x, 284 p.; 24 cm. ISBN: 1570753733 (pbk.) Notes: Includes bibliographical references and index. Subjects: Missions--History. Christianity and culture. LC Classification: BV2100 .W257 2002 Dewey Class No.: 270 21

Walls, Andrew F. (Andrew Finlay) The missionary movement in Christian history: studies in the transmission of faith / Andrew F. Walls. Published/Created: Maryknoll, N.Y.: Orbis Books; Edinburgh: T&T Clark, c1996. Description: xix, 266 p.; 24 cm. ISBN: 1570750599 (alk. paper) Notes: Includes bibliographical references and index. Subjects: Missions--History. Missions--Africa--History--19th century. Missions--Africa--History--20th century. Missions--Theory--History of doctrines. Christianity and culture. LC Classification: BV2100 .W26 1996 Dewey Class No.: 266/.009 20

Walsh, Andrew D., 1965- Religion, economics, and public policy: ironies, tragedies, and absurdities of the contemporary culture wars / Andrew D. Walsh. Published/Created: Westport, Conn.: Praeger, 2000. Description: xi, 156 p.; 24 cm. ISBN: 0275966119 (alk. paper) Notes: Includes bibliographical references (p. [141]-150) and index. Subjects: Economics--Religious aspects--Christianity--History--20th century. United States--Economic policy. LC Classification: BR115.E3 W33 2000 Dewey Class No.: 261.8/5 21

Walsh, Brian J., 1953- The transforming vision: shaping a Christian world view / Brian J. Walsh, J. Richard Middleton; foreword by

Nicholas Wolterstorff. Published/Created: Downers Grove, Ill.: InterVarsity Press, c1984. Related Authors: Middleton, J. Richard. Description: 214 p.; 21 cm. ISBN: 0877849730 (pbk.) : Notes: Bibliography: p. [203]-214. Subjects: Christianity--Philosophy. Christianity and culture. Identification (Religion) Civilization, Modern--20th century. LC Classification: BR100 .W35 1984 Dewey Class No.: 201 19

Wang, Xiaochao. Christianity and imperial culture: Chinese Christian apologetics in the seventeenth century and their Latin patristic equivalent / by Xiaochao Wang. Published/Created: Leiden; Boston: Brill, 1998. Description: xvii, 259 p.; 25 cm. ISBN: 9004109277 (alk. paper) Notes: Includes bibliographical references (p. [250]-259) and index. Subjects: Apologetics--China--History--17th century. Christianity and culture--China--History--17th century. Apologetics--History--Early church, ca. 30-600. Christianity and culture--History--Early church, ca. 30-600. China--Church history--17th century. Series: Studies in Christian mission, 0924-9389; v. 20 LC Classification: BR1286 .W36 1998 Dewey Class No.: 239/.0951/09032 21

Ward, Lionel O. Teaching moral values. Published/Created: [Oxford, Religious Education Press, 1969] Description: 66 p. 18 cm. ISBN: 0080063764 Notes: Includes bibliographies. Subjects: Moral education. LC Classification: LC268 .W37 Dewey Class No.: 370.11/4

Ward, Merrill, 1901- Gay threads in the fabric of Western culture: dramatized biographies of famous gay men / by Merrill Ward. Published/Created: San Leandro, CA: Community Pub., c1985. Description: 148 p.; 21 cm. ISBN: 0961504307 (pbk.) : Subjects: Gay men--Drama. Gay men--Biography. Homosexuality, Male--Religious aspects--Christianity. LC Classification: PS3573.A7336 G39 1985 Dewey Class No.: 812/.54 19

Warhola, James W. (James Walter), 1953-
Russian Orthodoxy and political culture
transformation / James W. Warhola.
Published/Created: Pittsburgh, Pa.: Center
for Russian & East European Studies,
University of Pittsburgh, c1993.
Description: 53 p.; 22 cm. Notes:
"September 1993"--T.p. verso. Includes
bibliographical references (p. 41-53).
Subjects: Russkaia pravoslavnaia tserkov´-
-Influence. Orthodox Eastern Church--
Russia--Influence. Church and state--
Russia. Christianity and culture. Russia
(Federation)--Politics and government.
Russia--Politics and government. Russia
(Federation)--Church history. Russia--
Church history. Series: Carl Beck papers in
Russian and East European studies; no.
1006. LC Classification: BX493 .W37
1993 Dewey Class No.: 261.7/0947 20

Wariboko, Waibinte E. (Waibinte Elekima),
1956- Planting church-culture at New
Calabar: some neglected aspects of
missionary enterprise in the eastern Niger
Delta, 1865-1918 / Waibinte E. Wariboko.
San Francisco: International Scholars
Publications, 1998. Description: p. cm.
ISBN: 1573093157 (alk. paper) Notes:
Includes bibliographical references and
index. Subjects: Church Missionary
Society--Missions--Nigeria--New Calabar-
-History 19th century. Christianity and
culture--Nigeria--New Calabar--History
19th century. New Calabar (Nigeria)--
Church history--19th century. LC
Classification: BV3625.N5 W35 1998
Dewey Class No.: 266/.366944 21

Warren, Michael, 1935- Faith, culture, and the
worshiping community / Michael Warren.
Published/Created: New York: Paulist
Press, c1989. Description: xvi, 214 p.; 21
cm. ISBN: 0809130491 : Notes: Includes
bibliographies. Subjects: Catholic Church--
Education--United States. Catholic
Church--Liturgy. Christian education--
Philosophy. Christianity and justice--
Catholic Church. Christianity and culture.
LC Classification: BX932 .W37 1989
Dewey Class No.: 268/.82 19

Warren, Michael, 1935- Faith, culture, and the
worshiping community: shaping the
practice of the local church / Michael
Warren. Edition Information: Rev. ed.
Published/Created: Washington, DC:
Pastoral Press, c1993. Description: xv, 194
p.; 21 cm. ISBN: 1569290024 Notes:
Includes bibliographical references.
Subjects: Catholic Church--Education--
United States. Catholic Church--Liturgy.
Christian education--Philosophy.
Christianity and justice--Catholic Church.
Christianity and culture. LC Classification:
BX932 .W37 1993 Dewey Class No.:
268/.8273 20

Watson, David Lowes. God does not foreclose:
the universal promise of salvation / David
Lowes Watson. Published/Created:
Nashville: Abingdon Press, c1990.
Description: 160 p.; 23 cm. ISBN:
0687149649 (alk. paper) Notes: Includes
bibliographical references (p. 147-157) and
index. Subjects: Church renewal--United
States. Christianity and culture. Mission of
the church. LC Classification: BR526
.W32 1990 Dewey Class No.: 262/.001/7
20

We dare to dream: doing theology as Asian
women / edited by Virginia Fabella and
Sun Ai Lee Park. Edition Information: U.S.
ed. Published/Created: Maryknoll, N.Y.:
Orbis Books, 1990, c1989. Related
Authors: Fabella, Virginia. Park, Sun Ai
Lee. Asian Women's Resource Centre for
Culture and Theology. Ecumenical
Association of Third World Theologians.
Women's Commission. Description: x, 156
p.; 24 cm. ISBN: 0883446731 Partial
Contents: Christology from an Asian
woman's perspective / Virginia Fabella --
Christology and women / Monica
Melanchton -- Ecclesiology and women /
Lily Kuo Wang -- New ways of being
church. I. A Catholic perspective /
Christine Tse. II. A Protestant perspective /
Yong Ting Jin -- Woman and the Holy
Spirit / Crescy John Notes: "First
published by the Asian Women's Resource
Centre for Culture and Theology and the
Asian Office of the Women's Commission
of the Ecumenical Association of Third

World Theologians (EATWOT)"-- T.p. verso. Includes bibliographical references. Subjects: Women in Christianity--Asia. Theology, Doctrinal--Asia. LC Classification: BV639.W7 W43 1990 Dewey Class No.: 230.095

Weakland, Rembert. Seeking God in contemporary culture / Rembert G. Weakland. Published/Created: Milwaukee, Wis.: Marquette University Press, c1994. Description: vi, 45 p.; 19 cm. ISBN: 0874625491 Notes: Includes bibliographical references (p. 40-45). Subjects: Catholic Church--United States--History--20th century. Christianity and culture. Desire for God. Series: The Père Marquette lecture in theology; 1994 LC Classification: BR115.C8 W39 1994 Dewey Class No.: 231.7 20

Weaver, Rufus W. (Rufus Washington), 1870-1947. The revolt against God; the conflict between culture and Christianity. Published/Created: New York, Fleming H. Revell [1944] Description: 243 p. 21 cm. Notes: "References": p. 237-239. Subjects: Culture. Religious thought--History. Civilization, Christian. Apologetics--20th century. LC Classification: BR115.C8 W4 Dewey Class No.: 100

Webb, William J. Slaves, women & homosexuals: exploring the hermeneutics of cultural analysis / William J. Webb. Published/Created: Downers Grove, Ill.: InterVarsity Press, c2001. Description: 301 p.: ill.; 23 cm. ISBN: 0830815619 (pbk.: alk. paper) Notes: Includes bibliographical references (p. [279]-292) and index. Subjects: Bible--Hermeneutics. Slavery in the Bible. Women in the Bible. Homosexuality in the Bible. Christianity and culture. LC Classification: BS476 .W38 2001 Dewey Class No.: 220.6/01 21

Webber, Robert. People of the truth: a christian challenge to contemporary culture / Robert E. Webber, Rodney Clapp. Published/Created: Harrisburg, PA: Morehouse Pub., c1993. Related Authors: Clapp, Rodney. Description: 144 p.; 22 cm. ISBN: 0819215988 (pbk.) Notes:

Originally published: San Francisco: Harper & Row, 1988. Includes bibliographical references (p. [133]-142) and index. Subjects: Christianity and politics. Church and social problems. Church. Public worship. LC Classification: BR115.P7 W36 1993 Dewey Class No.: 261.7 20

Webber, Robert. The secular saint: a case for evangelical social responsibility / Robert E. Webber. Published/Created: Grand Rapids, Mich.: Zondervan Pub. House, c1979. Description: 219 p.; 23 cm. ISBN: 0310366402 Notes: Includes bibliographical references and indexes. Subjects: Sociology, Christian. Christianity and culture. LC Classification: BT738 .W344 Dewey Class No.: 261

Webster, A. C. (Alan C.) What difference does it make?: values and faith in a shifting culture: dialogue between social scientists and the churches on the second New Zealand study of values / by Alan C. Webster and Paul E. Perry; with responses from the churches; edited by Norman E. Brookes and Margaret Reid Martin; foreword by Penelope Jamieson. Published/Created: Palmerston North [N.Z.]: Alpha Publications: Research Directorate of the New Zealand Study of Values, Massey University, c1992. Related Authors: Perry, Paul E. Brookes, Norman E. Martin, Margaret Reid. Description: x, 188 p.; 21 cm. ISBN: 0959793356 Notes: Includes bibliographical references (p. 184-185) and index. Subjects: Christianity--Christian ethics--Social sciences and ethics--Social ethics--Christianity and culture--New Zealand--Religion. LC Classification: BR1480 .W43 1992

Webster, Douglas D. Christian living in a pagan culture / Douglas D. Webster. Wheaton, Ill.: Tyndale House Publishers, c1980. Description: 165 p.; 21 cm. ISBN: 0842302417 (pbk.) : Notes: Includes bibliographical references. Subjects: Christianity and culture. Christianity--20th century. LC Classification: BR115.C8 W42 Dewey Class No.: 261.1 19

Wegh, Shagbaor F. (Shagbaor Francis) Understanding and practising inculturation / Shagbaor F. Wegh. Published/Created: Ibadan, Nigeria: Caltop Publications (Nigeria), 1997. Description: 61 p.; 18 cm. Notes: Includes bibliographical references (p. 58-61). Subjects: Catholic Church--Africa. Christianity and culture--Africa. LC Classification: BR115.C8 W424 1997

Wei, Cho-min, 1888- The spirit of Chinese culture. Published/Created: New York, C. Scribner's Sons, 1947. Description: xii, 186 p. 20 cm. Notes: Delivered in 1946 at the Union Theological Seminary, New York, the Episcopal Theological School, Cambridge, Mass., and the Andover-Newton Theological School. Subjects: Christianity and other religions--Chinese. China--Civilization. China--Religion. Series: Hewett lectures, 1946 LC Classification: BR128.C4 W4 Dewey Class No.: 290.951

Weigel, Gustave, 1906-1964. The modern God; faith in a secular culture. Published/Created: New York, Macmillan [1963] Description: 168 p. 22 cm. Subjects: Christianity--20th century. LC Classification: BR123 .W4

Wellman, James K. The gold coast church and the ghetto: Christ and culture in mainline Protestantism / James K. Wellman, Jr.; foreword by Martin E. Marty. Published/Created: Urbana: University of Illinois Press, c1999. Description: xv, 257 p.: ill.; 24 cm. ISBN: 0252024893 (cloth: alk. paper) 0252068041 (pbk.: alk. paper) Notes: Includes bibliographical references (p. [243]-252) and index. Subjects: Fourth Presbyterian Church (Chicago, Ill.)--History. Protestant churches--United States--Case studies. Christianity and culture--United States--Case studies. Chicago (Ill.)--Church history. LC Classification: BX9211.C414 W48 1999 Dewey Class No.: 285/.177311 21

Wells, Colin, 1965- The Devil and Doctor Dwight: satire and theology in the early American Republic / Colin Wells. Published/Created: Chapel Hill: Published for the Omohundro Institute of Early American History and Culture, Williamsurg, Virginia, by the University of North Carolina Press, 2002. Related Authors: Omohundro Institute of Early American History & Culture. Description: p. cm. ISBN: 0807827150 (alk. paper) 0807853836 (pbk.: alk. paper) Notes: Includes index. Subjects: Dwight, Timothy, 1752-1817. Triumph of infidelity. Chauncy, Charles, 1705-1787 -- In literature. Christianity and literature--United States--Freethinkers--History--18th century. Christian poetry, American--Verse satire--History and criticism. Belief and doubt in literature. Theology in literature. Faith in literature. LC Classification: PS739.T75 W45 2002 Dewey Class No.: 811/.2 21

Wells, David F. God in the wasteland: the reality of truth in a world of fading dreams / David F. Wells. Published/Created: Grand Rapids, Mich.: W.B. Eerdmans, 1994. Description: x, 278 p.; 23 cm. ISBN: 0802837735 (pbk.) Notes: Includes bibliographical references (p. 257-270) and index. Subjects: Evangelicalism--United States--History--20th century. Christianity and culture. Theology--History--20th century. LC Classification: BR1642.U5 W44 1994 Dewey Class No.: 230/.046 20

Wells, David F. Losing our virtue: why the church must recover its moral vision / David F. Wells. Published/Created: Grand Rapids, Mich.: W.B. Eerdmans Pub., c1998. Description: xii, 228 p.; 24 cm. ISBN: 0802838278 (alk. paper) Notes: Includes bibliographical references (p. 211-222) and index. Subjects: Christianity and culture--United States. Christianity--United States--20th century. Christian ethics. United States--Moral conditions. LC Classification: BR115.C8 W43 1998 Dewey Class No.: 241/.0973 21

Wells, David F. No place for truth, or, Whatever happened to evangelical theology? / David F. Wells. Published/Created: Grand Rapids, Mich.: W.B. Eerdmans Pub. Co., c1993. Description: xii, 318 p.; 24 cm. ISBN:

0802837131 0802806503 Notes: Includes bibliographical references (p. 302-315) and index. Subjects: Evangelicalism--United States--History--20th century. Christianity and culture. LC Classification: BR1642.U5 W45 1993 Dewey Class No.: 230/.046 20

Weltin, E. G., 1911- Athens and Jerusalem: an interpretative essay on Christianity and classical culture / E.G. Weltin. Atlanta, Ga.: Scholars Press, c1987. Description: 257 p.; 24 cm. ISBN: 1555401430 (alk. paper) 1555401449 (pbk.: alk. paper) Notes: Includes index. Bibliography: p. [237]-245. Subjects: Christianity and culture--Early church, ca. 30-600. Christianity and other religions--Greek--Roman. Church history--Primitive and early church, ca. 30-600. Civilization, Classical. Series: AAR studies in religion; no. 49. LC Classification: BR166 .W43 1987 Dewey Class No.: 261 19

Wessels, Antonie. Europe, was it ever really Christian?: the interaction between gospel and culture / Anton Wessels. Edition Information: 1st British ed. Published/Created: London: SCM Press, 1994. Description: ix, 242 p.: ill.; 22 cm. ISBN: 0334025699 (pbk.) Notes: Includes bibliographical references (p. [197]-227) and index. Subjects: Christianity--Europe. Europe--Religion. LC Classification: BR735 W3713 1994 Dewey Class No.: 274 21

Westfield, N. Lynne. All quite beautiful / N. Lynne Westfield. Published/Created: New York: Friendship Press, c1996. Description: 23 p.: col. ill., music; 28 cm. ISBN: 0377003042 (pbk.) Summary: A study book from a Christian perspective with stories, poems, songs, and activities that explore differences in language, culture, foods, and religious beliefs and celebrations. Notes: Cover title. "Living in a multicultural society." Subjects: Multiculturalism--Religious aspects--Christianity Juvenile literature. Christian life. LC Classification: BR115.C8 W44 1996 Dewey Class No.: 261.8/34 20

What's God got to do with the American experiment? / E.J. Dionne, Jr., John J. DiIulio, Jr., editors. Published/Created: Washington, D.C.: Brookings Institution Press, c2000. Related Authors: Dionne, E. J. DiIulio, John J. Description: xvii, 188 p.; 23 cm. ISBN: 0815718691 (alk. paper) Partial Contents: God and the American experiment: an introduction / E.J. Dionne, Jr. and John J. DiIulio, Jr. -- America's ever-changing religious landscape / Richard N. Ostling -- America's changing political and moral values / Robert J. Blendon ... [et al.] Notes: Includes bibliographical references (p. 171-176) and index. Subjects: Religion and politics--United States. Christianity and politics--United States. United States--Religion--1960- LC Classification: BL2525 .W47 2000 Dewey Class No.: 200/.973/09045 21

Wheeler, Michael, 1947- Ruskin's God / Michael Wheeler. Published/Created: Cambridge, UK; New York, NY: Cambridge University Press, 1999. Description: xviii, 302 p.: ill.; 24 cm. ISBN: 0521574145 (hardback) Notes: Includes bibliographical references and index. Subjects: Ruskin, John, 1819-1900 --Religion. Christianity and literature--Religion and literature--Christianity and art--Art and religion--History--19th century. God in literature. God--Art. Series: Cambridge studies in nineteenth-century literature and culture; 24 LC Classification: PR5267.R4 W47 1999 Dewey Class No.: 828/.809 21

Whitehead, John W., 1946- Grasping for the wind: the search for meaning in the 20th century / John W. Whitehead. Published/Created: Grand Rapids, Mich.: Zondervan, c2001. Description: 320 p.: ill. (some col.); 25 cm. ISBN: 0310232740 (alk. paper) Notes: Includes bibliographical references (p. 277-302) and index. Subjects: Civilization, Western--20th century. Civilization, Modern--20th century. Twenty-first century--Forecasts. Philosophy, Modern. Christianity and culture. LC Classification: CB245 .W515 2001 Dewey Class No.: 909.82 21

Whitehead, John W., 1946- Truth under fire: a
call to Christian thought and action in all of
life / John W. Whitehead.
Published/Created: Wheaton, Ill.:
Crossway Books, c1998. Description: 219
p.; 22 cm. ISBN: 1581340095 (pbk.: alk.
paper) Subjects: Church and state--
Freedom of religion--Christianity and
culture--Civil rights--United States. Civil
rights--Religious aspects--Christianity.
United States--Moral conditions. United
States--Religion--1960- United States--
History--Religious aspects--Christianity.
LC Classification: BR516 .W443 1998
Dewey Class No.: 261/.0973 21

Whiteside, Elena Scott. God's word in culture /
by Elena Scott Whiteside.
Published/Created: New Knoxville, Ohio,
U.S.A.: American Christian Press, 1983.
Description: xi, 233 p., [1] leaf of plates:
col. ill.; 19 cm. ISBN: 0910068518 (pbk.)
Subjects: Christianity and culture. LC
Classification: BR115.C8 W48 1983
Dewey Class No.: 261.5 19

Wicker, Brian, 1929- Culture and theology: a
sketch for a contemporary Christianity.
Published/Created: London, Melbourne,
Sheed & Ward, 1966. Description: xi, 305
p. 18 cm. Notes: Bibliography: p. 279-291.
Subjects: Christianity and culture. LC
Classification: BR115.C8 W5 Dewey
Class No.: 230.01

Wicker, Brian, 1929- Toward a contemporary
Christianity. Edition Information: [1st
American ed. Published/Created: Notre
Dame, Ind.] University of Notre Dame
Press [1967] Description: xi, 305 p. 21 cm.
Notes: First published in 1966 under
Culture and theology. Bibliography: p.
279-291. Subjects: Christianity and culture.
LC Classification: BR115.C8 W5 1967
Dewey Class No.: 230.01

Wijsen, Frans Jozef Servaas, 1956- There is
only one God: a social-scientific and
theological study of popular religion and
evangelization in Sukumaland, Northwest
Tanzania / Frans Jozef Servaas Wijsen.
Published/Created: Kampen: Kok, 1993.
Description: xv, 338 p.: maps; 24 cm.

ISBN: 903900501X Notes: Summary in
Dutch. Thesis (Ph. D.)--Faculty of
Theology, University of Nijmegen, 1993.
Includes bibliographical references.
Subjects: Catholic Church--Evangelistic
work--Christianity and culture--Tanzania--
Sukumaland.--Religion--Church history.
Series: Kerk en theologie in context; nr. 8.
LC Classification: BX1682.T35 W55 1993

Wilder, Amos Niven, 1895- Modern poetry and
the Christian tradition; a study in the
relation of Christianity to culture.
Published/Created: New York, Scribner,
1952. Description: 287 p. 22 cm. Subjects:
Religion and literature. Poetry--History
and criticism. LC Classification: PN1077
.W5 Dewey Class No.: 809.1

Will Western civilization survive: challenging
readings for contemporary times / edited
by Edward Alcott. Published/Created:
Dubuque, Iowa: Kendall/Hunt Pub. Co.,
c1981. Related Authors: Alcott, Edward.
Description: v, 174 p.: ill.; 23 cm. ISBN:
0840323700 (pbk.) Partial Contents:
Introduction -- The unfinished business of
politics / Karl W. Deutsch -- Learning to
live in a technological society: toward a
world community / Harrison Brown.
Notes: Includes bibliographical references.
Subjects: Civilization, Western.
Civilization, Modern--20th century. LC
Classification: CB245 .W53 Dewey Class
No.: 909/.09821 19

Will, James E. The universal God: justice, love,
and peace in the global village / James E.
Will. Edition Information: 1st ed.
Published/Created: Louisville, Ky.:
Westminster John Knox Press, c1994.
Description: viii, 280 p.; 23 cm. ISBN:
0664255604 (pbk.: alk. paper) Notes:
Includes bibliographical references (p.
231-273) and index. Subjects: God.
Hermeneutics--Religious aspects--
Christianity. Christianity and culture.
Christianity and other religions.
Christianity and justice. Love--Peace--
Religious aspects--Christianity. LC
Classification: BT102 .W55 1994 Dewey
Class No.: 231 20

Williams, Lewin Lascelles, 1936- Caribbean theology / Lewin Williams. Published/Created: New York: P.Lang, c1994. Description: xiii, 231 p.; 24 cm. ISBN: 0820418595 Notes: Includes bibliographical references (p. [219]-231). Subjects: Theology, Doctrinal--Caribbean Area. Christianity and culture. Series: Research in religion and family; vol. 2 LC Classification: BT30.C27 .W55 1994 Dewey Class No.: 230/.09729 20

Williams, Lewin Lascelles, 1936- The Caribbean: enculturation, acculturation, and the role of the churches / Lewin L. Williams. Published/Created: Geneva, Switzerland: WCC Publications, c1996. Related Authors: World Council of Churches. Description: ix, 29, [1] p.; 21 cm. ISBN: 2825412015 Notes: Includes bibliographical references (p. [30]). Subjects: Christianity and culture. Christianity--Caribbean Area--Church history. Series: Gospel and cultures pamphlet; 10 LC Classification: BR655 .W55 1996 Dewey Class No.: 277.29 21

Williamson, Clark M. The teaching minister / Clark M. Williamson and Ronald J. Allen. Edition Information: 1st ed. Louisville, Ky.: Westminster/John Knox Press, c1991. Related Authors: Allen, Ronald J. (Ronald James), 1949- Description: 138 p.; 138 cm. ISBN: 0664251749 Notes: Includes bibliographical references (p. 125-133) and index. Subjects: Church--Teaching office. Clergy--Office. Tradition (Theology) Christianity and culture. Protestant churches--United States—Clergy--Church history--20th century. LC Classification: BR526 .W54 1991 Dewey Class No.: 262/.14 20

Wilson, John Frederick. Public religion in American culture / John F. Wilson. Philadelphia: Temple University Press, 1979. Description: ix, 198 p.; 22 cm. ISBN: 0877221596 : Notes: Includes bibliographical references and index. Subjects: Christianity--United States. United States--Religion. LC Classification: BR515 .W54 Dewey Class No.: 277.3

Wilson, Jonathan R. Gospel virtues: practicing faith, hope & love in uncertain times / Jonathan R. Wilson. Published/Created: Downers Grove, Ill.: InterVarsity Press, c1998. Description: 214 p.; 21 cm. ISBN: 0830815201 (pbk.: alk. paper) Notes: Includes bibliographical references (p. [183]-208) and indexes. Subjects: Theological virtues. Christianity and culture. LC Classification: BV4635 .W55 1998 Dewey Class No.: 241/.4 21

Wilson, Jonathan R. Theology as cultural critique: the achievement of Julian Hartt / by Jonathan R. Wilson. Published/Created: Macon, Ga.: Mercer, c1996. Description: xiv, 180 p.; 23 cm. ISBN: 0865545227 (pbk.: alk. paper) Notes: Includes bibliographical references (p. [173]-180). Subjects: Hartt, Julian Norris. Christianity and culture--History of doctrines--20th century. Series: Studies in American biblical hermeneutics; 12 LC Classification: BX8495.H2685 W55 1996 Dewey Class No.: 261/.092 21

Wilson, Wayne A. Worldly amusements: restoring the Lordship of Christ to our entertainment choices / Wayne A. Wilson. Published/Created: Mukilteo, WA: WinePress Pub., c1999. Description: viii, 297 p.; 22 cm. ISBN: 1579212131 Notes: Includes bibliographical references (p. 285-290) and indexes. Subjects: Jesus Christ--Lordship. Popular culture--Religious aspects--Christianity. Christianity and culture--United States--History--20th century. Motion pictures--Religious aspects--Christianity. Amusements--Religious aspects--Christianity. Christian life. LC Classification: BR526 .W57 1999 Dewey Class No.: 241/.65 21

Wingate, Andrew. Does theological education make a difference?: Global lessons in mission and ministry from India and Britain / Andrew Wingate. Published/Created: Geneva: WCC Publications, c1999. Description: ix, 116 p.; 21 cm. ISBN: 2825413208 Partial Contents: Foreword / Israel Selvanayagam -- A personal introduction -- The training experience at Tamilnadu -- Ministry to prisoners: learning from experience -- Six ministries in Tamilnadu -- Has TTS made a difference? Notes: Includes bibliographical references (p. [115]-116). Subjects: Tamilnadu Theological Seminary. Theology--Study and teaching. Christianity and culture. Missions. Church work. Missionaries--Training of. Theology--Study and teaching. Series: Risk book series; no. 87 Local Call/Shelving: BV4020 .W56 1999

Wingerd, Mary Lethert, 1948- Claiming the city: politics, faith, and the power of place in St. Paul / Mary Lethert Wingerd. Published/Created: Ithaca: Cornell University Press, 2001. Description: xiii, 326 p.: ill.; 24 cm. ISBN: 0801439361 (alk. paper) Partial Contents: The economy of culture: city building on the frontier -- Money, status, and power: the making of an Irish-Catholic town -- Delivering the goods: the social geography of a declining economy -- Raising the flag: the struggle to reshape civic identity -- Taking aim: enemies of the state -- The first volley: policing the social order. Notes: Includes bibliographical references (p. [277]-316) and index. Subjects: Catholic Church--Minnesota--Saint Paul--History--20th century. Political culture--Minnesota--Saint Paul--History--20th century. Regionalism--Political aspects--Minnesota--Saint Paul History--20th century. Working class--Minnesota--Saint Paul--Political activity History--20th century. Industrial relations--Minnesota--Saint Paul--History--20th century. Irish Americans--Minnesota--Saint Paul--Politics and government--20th century. Christianity and politics--Minnesota--Saint Paul--History 20th century. Saint Paul (Minn.)--Politics and government--20th century. Saint Paul (Minn.)--Social conditions--20th century. Saint Paul (Minn.)--Economic conditions--20th century. Series: Cushwa Center studies of Catholicism in twentieth-century America LC Classification: F614.S4 W77 2001 Dewey Class No.: 306.2/09776/5810904 21

Winter, Richard, 1945- Still bored in a culture of entertainment: rediscovering passion & wonder / Richard Winter. Published/Created: Downers Grove, Ill.: InterVarsity Press, c2002. Description: p. cm. ISBN: 0830823085 (pbk.: alk. paper) Partial Contents: Three yawns for boredom! -- Basics of boredom: under-stimulation, repetition, and disconnection -- Two types of boredom: the long and the short of it -- Entertained to excess: leisure, over-stimulation, and the entertainment industry -- Advertised to apathy: the stimulation and disappointment of desire -- Why some people are more likely to get bored: perception, personality, and proneness -- Negated to numbness: anxiety, disappointment, and emotional shutdown . Notes: Includes bibliographical references. Subjects: Boredom--Religious aspects--Christianity. Christian life. LC Classification: BV4599.5.B+

Wise, Isaac Mayer, 1819-1900. History of the Hebrews' second commonwealth with special reference to its literature, culture, and the origin of rabbinism and Christianity, by Isaac M. Wise. Published/Created: Cincinnati, Bloch & co., 1880. Description: 3 p. l., 386 p. 22 1/2 cm. Notes: The present volume, though a complete book in itself, is a continuation of the author's History of the Israelitish nation. Albany, 1854. cf. Pref. Subjects: Jews--History--586 B.C.-70 A.D. LC Classification: DS118 .W81

Witte, John, 1959- From sacrament to contract: marriage, religion, and law in the Western tradition / John Witte, Jr. Edition Information: 1. ed. Published/Created: Louisville, Ky.: Westminster John Knox Press, c1997. Description: xii, 315 p.; 23 cm. ISBN: 0664255434 (pbk.: acid-free paper) Notes: Includes bibliographical references (p. [274]-301) and indexes. Subjects: Marriage law--Religious aspects. Marriage--Religious aspects--Christianity. Marriage (Canon law) Series: The family, religion, and culture LC Classification: K675 .W57 1997 Dewey Class No.: 234/.165/09 21

Wogan-Browne, Jocelyn. Saints' lives and women's literary culture c. 1150-1300: virginity and its authorizations / Jocelyn Wogan-Browne. Published/Created: Oxford; New York: Oxford University Press, 2001. Description: xvi, 314 p.: ill., map; 24 cm. ISBN: 0198112793 (alk. paper) Notes: Includes bibliographical references (p. [266]-305) and index. Subjects: English literature--Middle English, 1100-1500--History and criticism. Women and literature--England--History--To 1500. Virginity--Religious aspects--Christianity--History of doctrines--Middle Ages, 600-1500. Christian literature, English (Middle)--History and criticism. English literature--Women authors--History and criticism. Women--Books and reading--England--History--To 1500. Christian women saints--Legends--History and criticism. Women--Religious life--England--History--To 1500. Christian saints in literature. Virginity in literature. Hagiography. LC Classification: PR275.W6 W64 2001 Dewey Class No.: 820.9/352042/0902 21

Wolf, Teresa Ann, 1943- Towards an inculturated local theology in the diocese of Crookston, Minnesota [microform] / by Teresa Ann Wolf. Published/Created: 1998. Description: xix, 233 leaves: maps. Notes: Thesis (D. Min.)--Catholic Theological Union of Chicago, 1998. Microfiche. Portland, Or.: Theological Research Exchange Network, 1998. 1 microfiche: negative. Subjects: Hispanic American Catholics--Minnesota--Crookston. Christianity and culture--Minnesota--Crookston. LC Classification: Microfiche 99/115 (B)

Women and men in spiritual culture, XIV-XVII centuries: a meeting of South and North / edited by Elisja Schulte van Kessel. Published/Created: The Hague: Netherlands Govt. Pub. Office, 1986. Related Authors: Schulte van Kessel, Elisja, 1937- Università degli studi di Roma "La Sapienza." Dipartimento di studi storici. Nederlands Instituut te Rome. Historical Dept. Description: 260 p.: ill.; 25 cm. ISBN: 901205222X (pbk.) Notes:

Papers presented at a meeting in Rome in Oct. 1984, organized by the Dipartimento di Studi Storici of the Università di Roma 'La Sapienza' and the Historical Department of the Netherlands Institute in Rome. Subjects: Spiritual life--Christianity--Congresses. Women--Religious aspects--Christianity--Congresses. Christian women--Religious life--Congresses. Man (Christian theology)--Congresses. Men--Religious life--Congresses. LC Classification: BV4485.5 .W65 1986 Dewey Class No.: 274/.05/088042 19

Women and religion in medieval and Renaissance Italy / edited by Daniel Bornstein and Roberto Rusconi; translated by Margery J. Schneider. Published/Created: Chicago: University of Chicago Press, 1996. Related Authors: Bornstein, Daniel Ethan, 1950- Rusconi, Roberto. Description: x, 334 p.: ill.; 23 cm. ISBN: 0226066371 0226066398 (pbk.) Notes: Includes bibliographical references and index. Subjects: Catholic Church--Italy--History. Women in Christianity--Italy--History. Women mystics--Italy--History. Spirituality--Italy--History. Spirituality--Catholic Church--History. Monasticism and religious orders for women--Italy--History Middle Ages, 600-1500. Christian women saints--Italy--History. Italy--Church history--476-1400. Italy--Church history--15th century. Series: Women in culture and society LC Classification: BX1544 .M5713 1996 Dewey Class No.: 282/.082 20

Women of faith in Victorian culture: reassessing the angel in the house / edited by Anne Hogan and Andrew Bradstock. Published/Created: New York, N.Y.: St. Martin's Press, 1998. Related Authors: Hogan, Anne. Bradstock, Andrew. Description: xv, 230 p.: ill.; 23 cm. ISBN: 0312212178 0333694554 Notes: Includes bibliographical references and index. Subjects: English literature--19th century--History and criticism. Christianity and literature--Great Britain--History--19th century. Women and literature--Great Britain--History--19th century. Women and religion--Great Britain--History--19th century. Christian literature, English--History and criticism. Angels in literature. Great Britain--History--Victoria, 1837-1901. LC Classification: PR468.R44 W6 1998 Dewey Class No.: 820.9/352042 21

Won, Ui-bom. A history of Korean Buddhist culture and some essays: the Buddhist Pure Land & the Christian Kingdom of Heaven / by Won Yi Beom and Lim Byeong Ho. Published/Created: Seoul, Korea: Jip Moon Dang Pub., 1992. Related Authors: Lim, Byeong Ho. Description: xix, 197 p.: ill., map; 21 cm. ISBN: 893030074X Notes: Includes bibliographical references (p. 161-164) and index. Subjects: Buddhism--Korea--History. Pure Land Buddhism--Relations--Christianity. Christianity and other religions--Pure Land Buddhism LC Classification: BQ656 .W66 1992 Dewey Class No.: 294.3/09519 21

Wong, Wai-Ching Angela, 1959- The poor woman: a critical analysis of Asian theology and contemporary Chinese fiction by women / Wai-Ching Angela Wong. Published/Created: New York: P. Lang, c2002. Description: viii, 176 p.; 24 cm. ISBN: 0820448990 (alk. paper) Notes: Includes bibliographical references (p. [165]-176). Subjects: Feminist theology--Asia. Women authors, Chinese. Christianity and culture. Christianity in literature. Series: Asian thought and culture; v. 42 LC Classification: BT83.55 .W654 2002 Dewey Class No.: 230/.082/095 21

Woodley, Randy, 1956- Living in color: embracing God's passion for diversity / Randy Woodley; foreword by John Dawson. Published/Created: Grand Rapids, Mich.: Chosen Books, c2001. Description: 205 p.; 23 cm. ISBN: 0800792912 (pbk.) Notes: Includes bibliographical references (p. 196-199) and index. Subjects: Christianity and culture. Multiculturalism--Religious aspects--Christianity. LC Classification: BR115.C8 W66 2001 Dewey Class No.: 261.8/34 21

World catechism or inculturation? / edited by Johann-Baptist Metz and Edward Schillebeeckx; English language editor, Philip Hillyer. Published/Created: Edinburgh: T&T Clark, 1989. Related Authors: Metz, Johannes Baptist, 1928- Schillebeeckx, Edward, 1914- Hillyer, Philip. Description: xviii, 130 p.; 22 cm. ISBN: 0567300846 (pbk.) Notes: Includes bibliographical references. Subjects: Catechisms. Christianity and culture. Series: Concilium (Glen Rock, N.J.); v. 204. LC Classification: BT990 .W67 1989 Dewey Class No.: 238/.2 20

World order and religion / edited by Wade Clark Roof. Published/Created: Albany: State University of New York Press, c1991. Related Authors: Roof, Wade Clark. Description: 320 p.; 24 cm. ISBN: 079140739X (alk. paper) 0791407403 (pbk.: alk. paper) Notes: Includes bibliographical references and index. Subjects: Religion and international affairs. Christianity and international affairs. Religions--Relations. Missions--Theory. World politics--20th century. United States--Religion--20th century. Series: SUNY series in religion, culture, and society LC Classification: BL65.I55 W68 1991 Dewey Class No.: 291.1/7 20

Worldwide perspectives: understanding God's purposes in the world from Genesis to Revelation / Meg Crossman, editor. Published/Created: Pasadena, Calif.: William Carey Library, c1995. Related Authors: Crossman, Meg. Description: 1 v. (various pagings): ill., maps; 30 cm. ISBN: 0878087656 (alk. paper) Notes: "A text for use with Perspectives on the world Christian movement." Includes bibliographical references. Subjects: Missions. Missions--Theory. Missions--Biblical teaching. Christianity and culture. LC Classification: BV2061 .W67 1995 Dewey Class No.: 266 20

Worshipping God as Africans: report on the AFALMA-Namibia Workshop and Festival, Windhoek, 7-12 December 1993 / editor, Christo Lombard, sub-editor, Petro Rabe. Published/Created: Windhoek,

Namibia: EIN Publications, 1995. Related Authors: Lombard, C. Rabe, Petro. Description: 100 p.: ill.; 29 cm. ISBN: 9991673229 Notes: Includes bibliographical references (p. 92-96). Subjects: Christianity--Namibia--Congresses. Public worship--Congresses. Christianity and culture--Namibia--Congresses. Namibia--Religious life and customs--Congresses. LC Classification: BR1458 .A43 1993

Worth, Roland H., 1943- The seven cities of the apocalypse and Greco-Asian culture / Roland H. Worth, Jr. Published/Created: New York: Paulist Press, c1999. Description: iii, 377 p.; 23 cm. ISBN: 0809138778 (alk. paper) Notes: Includes bibliographical references (p. 316-363) and index. Subjects: Seven churches. Christianity and culture--Turkey--History--Early church, ca. 30-600. LC Classification: BR185 .W68 1999 Dewey Class No.: 228/.067 21

Worth, Roland H., 1943- The seven cities of the Apocalypse and Roman culture / Roland H. Worth, Jr. Published/Created: New York: Paulist Press, c1999. Description: iii, 258 p.; 23 cm. ISBN: 0809138743 (pbk.: alk. paper) Notes: Includes bibliographical references (p. 198-248) and index. Subjects: Seven churches. Christianity and culture--Turkey--History--Early church, ca. 30-600. LC Classification: BR185 .W67 1999 Dewey Class No.: 275.61/01 21

Wright, Robin. Cosmos, self, and history in Baniwa religion: for those unborn / Robin M. Wright. Edition Information: 1st ed. Published/Created: Austin: University of Texas Press, 1998. Description: xx, 314 p.: ill., maps; 24 cm. ISBN: 0292791224 (cloth: alk. paper) Contents: Cosmogony: perspectives on the beginning and its legacy -- Guardians of the cosmos -- Indians and whites in Baniwa history -- Music of the ancestors -- The times of death -- Spiritualities of death and birth -- From rubber to the gospel -- Deo iako: the creation of a new generation of believers. Notes: Includes bibliographical references (p. [305]-310) and index. Subjects: Baniwa

Indians--Religion. Baniwa philosophy. Baniwa Indians--Social life and customs. Shamanism--Amazon River Valley. Nativistic movements--Amazon River Valley. Christianity and culture--Amazon River Valley. Amazon River Valley--Social life and customs. LC Classification: F2520.1.B35 W75 1998 Dewey Class No.: 299/.8839 21

Wright, Tim, 1957- The prodigal hugging church: a scandalous approach to mission for the 21st century / Tim Wright. Published/Created: Minneapolis, MN: Joy Resources, c2001. Description: 63 p.; 20 cm. ISBN: 0806642785 (alk. paper) Subjects: Church growth. Evangelistic work. Christianity and culture. LC Classification: BV652.25 .W75 2001 Dewey Class No.: 253 21

Yang, Nak Heong, 1956- Reformed social ethics and the Korean church / Nak Heong Yang. Published/Created: New York: P. Lang, c1997. Description: 199 p.; 23 cm. ISBN: 0820426229 Notes: Includes bibliographical references (p. [191]-199). Subjects: Presbyterian Church--Korea--Doctrines--History. Christian ethics--Social ethics--Korea--History. Sociology, Christian (Reformed Church)--Reformed Church--Korea--Doctrines--History. Christianity and politics--Presbyterian Church--History. Korea--Church history. Series: Asian thought and culture; vol. 21 LC Classification: BX9151.K8 Y36 1997 Dewey Class No.: 261.7/09519 20

Yeo, Khiok-Khng. Rhetorical interaction in 1 Corinthians 8 and 10: a formal analysis with preliminary suggestions for a Chinese, cross-cultural hermeneutic / by Khiok-Khng Yeo. Published/Created: Leiden; New York: E.J. Brill, 1995. Description: xvi, 275 p. ′ 24 cm. ISBN: 9004101152 Notes: Revision of the author's thesis, Northwestern University, 1990. Includes bibliographical references (p. [223]-269) and indexes. Subjects: Yeo, Khiok-Khng. Bible. N.T. Corinthians, 1st, VIII--Criticism, interpretation, etc. Bible. N.T. Corinthians, 1st, X--Criticism, interpretation, etc. Bible--Hermeneutics.

Christianity and culture. Series: Biblical interpretation series, 0928-0731; v. 9 LC Classification: BS2675.2 .Y46 1995 Dewey Class No.: 227/.206 20

Yoder, John Howard. For the nations: essays evangelical and public / John H. Yoder. Published/Created: Grand Rapids, Mich.: W.B. Eerdmans, c1997. Description: vi, 251 p.; 23 cm. ISBN: 0802843247 (pbk.: alk. paper) Notes: Includes bibliographical references and indexes. Subjects: Church and the world. Mission of the church. Christianity and culture. Christian ethics--Mennonite authors. Sociology, Christian (Mennonite) LC Classification: BR115.W6 Y63 1997 Dewey Class No.: 261 21

Yohannan, K. P. The road to reality: coming home to Jesus from the unreal world / K.P. Yohannan; [foreword by Erwin Lutzer]. Published/Created: Altamonte Springs, Fla.: Creation House, c1988. Description: 203 p.; 23 cm. ISBN: 0884192504 Subjects: Christianity and culture. Christian life. United States--Moral conditions. LC Classification: BR115.C8 Y55 1988 Dewey Class No.: 248.4 20

Young, Frances M. (Frances Margaret) Biblical exegesis and the formation of Christian culture / Frances M. Young. Published/Created: Peabody, Mass.: Hendrickson Publishers, [2002] Description: p. cm. ISBN: 1565637356 (pbk.: alk. paper) Notes: Originally published: Cambridge; New York: Cambridge University Press, 1997. Includes bibliographical references (p.) and indexes. Subjects: Bible--Hermeneutics. Civilization, Christian. Christianity and culture. LC Classification: BS476 .Y 68 2002 Dewey Class No.: 220.6/09/015 21

Young, Frances M. (Frances Margaret) Biblical exegesis and the formation of Christian culture / Frances M. Young. Published/Created: Cambridge; New York: Cambridge University Press, 1997. Description: xiv, 325 p.: ill.; 24 cm. ISBN: 0521581532 (hardcover) Notes: Includes bibliographical references (p. 300-316) and

indexes. Subjects: Bible--Hermeneutics. Civilization, Christian. Christianity and culture. LC Classification: BS476 .Y68 1997 Dewey Class No.: 220.6/09/015 20

Young, Mildred Binns. What doth the Lord require of thee? Published/Created: [Wallingford, Pa., Pendle Hill Publications, 1966] Description: 32 p. 20 cm. Notes: Bibliographical references included in "Notes" (p.32) Subjects: Christianity and culture. LC Classification: BR115.C8 Y6 Dewey Class No.: 261

Yu, Jose Vidamor B. Inculturation of Filipino-Chinese culture mentality / Jose Vidamor B. Yu. Published/Created: Roma: Pontificia università gregoriana, 2000. Description: x, 276 p.; 24 cm. ISBN: 8876528482 Notes: Includes bibliographical references (p. 253-276). Subjects: Chinese--Philippines. Chinese--Philippines--Religion. Christianity and culture--Philippines. Series: Interreligious and intercultural investigations; 3 LC Classification: DS66.C5 Y8 2000

Yuen, Wai Man, 1958- Religious experience and interpretation: memory as the path to the knowledge of God in Julian of Norwich's Showings / Wai Man Yuen. Published/Created: New York: P. Lang, 2002. Description: p. cm. ISBN: 0820458325 (alk. paper) Notes: Includes bibliographical references (p.). Subjects: Julian, of Norwich, b. 1343. Revelations of divine love. Augustine, Saint, Bishop of Hippo--Contributions in memory. Devotional literature, English (Middle)--History and criticism. Memory--Religious aspects--Christianity. Experience (Religion) Series: Feminist critical studies in religion and culture; v. 1 LC Classification: BV4831.J8 Y84 2002 Dewey Class No.: 248.2/2/092 21

Zacharias, Ravi K. Deliver us from evil: restoring the soul in a disintegrating culture / Ravi Zacharias. Published/Created: Dallas: Word Pub., 1996. Description: xviii, 234 p.; 25 cm. ISBN: 0849913950 Notes: Includes bibliographical references (p. 227-228). Subjects: Christianity and culture--History--20th century. Moral conditions. Apologetics. LC Classification: BR115.C8 Z33 1996 Dewey Class No.: 270.8/2 20

Zahniser, A. H. Mathias, 1938- Symbol and ceremony: making disciples across cultures / A.H. Mathias Zahniser. Monrovia, Calif.: MARC, c1997. Description: x, 236 p.: ill.; 23 cm. Notes: Includes bibliographical references (p. 221-230) and indexes. Subjects: Discipline (Christianity) Missions--Cross-cultural studies. Christianity and culture. Religion and culture. Series: Innovations in mission; 6th LC Classification: IN PROCESS

Zemka, Sue, 1958- Victorian testaments: the Bible, christology, and literary authority in early-nineteenth-century British culture / Sue Zemka. Published/Created: Stanford, Calif.: Stanford University Press, c1997. Description: viii, 279 p.; 24 cm. ISBN: 0804728488 (cloth: alk. paper) Notes: Based on the author's thesis (doctoral)-- Stanford University, 1989. Includes bibliographical references (p. [261]-274) and index. Subjects: Jesus Christ--In literature. Bible--Criticism, interpretation, etc. Bible--In literature. English literature-- 19th century--History and criticism. Christianity and literature--Great Britain-- Authority--Religious aspects--Christianity- -History--19th century. Christian literature, English--History and criticism. Popular culture--Spirituality--Great Britain-- History--19th century. Authority in literature. Great Britain--Civilization--19th century. LC Classification: PR468.B5 Z45 1997 Dewey Class No.: 820.9/3823 21

AUTHOR INDEX

Azevedo, Marcello de Carvalho, 8

A

Aaseng, Rolf E., 2
Abhishiktananda, Swami, 2
Abraham, K. C., 166
Abregana, Betty C., 128
Adams, Daniel J., 59
Adams, Lawrence E., 2
Adappur, Abraham, 3
Adeney, Bernard T., 3
Adibe, Gregory E. M., 3
Adler, Felix, 3
African Synod, 118, 148
Aigbe, Sunday A., 3
Akaabiam, Terwase H., 3
Alcott, Edward, 178
Alderson, David, 4
Allen, Ronald J. (Ronald James), 179
Amaladoss, M. (Michael), 4
Ambler, R. A., 4
Anderson, Leith, 5
Andolsen, Barbara Hilkert, 137
Andriacco, Dan, 5
Angrosino, Michael V., 5
Anshen, Ruth Nanda, 6
Anthony, Francis-Vincent, 6
Apel, Pat, 6
Aragon, Lorraine V., 7
Arbuckle, Gerald A., 7
Ariarajah, S. Wesley, 7
Armerding, Hudson T., 7
Armstrong, John H. (John Harper), 162
Arnold, Duane W. H., 43
Arnold, Eberhard, 7
Arthur, C. J. (Christopher John), 7
Asher, Kenneth George, 8
Astell, Ann W., 45
Aymes, María de la Cruz, 48

B

Bacon, Leonard, 9
Bacon, Samuel Frederick, 9
Bakare, Sebastian, 9
Baker, Archibald G. (Archibald Gillies), 9
Bakke, Corean, 9
Balasuriya, Tissa, 166
Baldwin, J. F., 9
Bamat, Tomás, 126
Barbour, John D., 9
Barbour, Reid, 9
Barr, William R., 36
Bascom, Tim, 10
Bassard, Katherine Clay, 10
Batalov, A. L. (Andrei Leonidovich), 82
Bate, Stuart C., 10
Batson, E. Beatrice, 7
Baue, Frederic W., 10
Bauer, Bruno, 10
Bayer, Charles H., 10
Beard, Charles, 133
Beatty, Charles, 11
Beckwith, Sarah, 11
Bediako, Kwame, 11
Bell, Dean Phillip, 11
Belsey, Catherine, 11
Belz, Joel, 119
Beniston, Judith, 23
Benne, Robert, 12
Benoit, David, 12
Berdiaev, Nikolai Aleksandrovich, 12
Berger, Peter L., 12
Berinyuu, Abraham Adu, 12
Berkey, Robert F., 30
Bernstein, Eleanor, 97
Berthrong, John H., 13

Best, Thomas F., 11
Betz, Hans Dieter, 5
Bevans, Stephen B., 13
Biebuyck, Benjamin, 53
Binion, Rudolph, 14
Bird, Warren, 32
Bjork, David E., 14
Black, Jim Nelson, 14, 15
Blamires, Harry, 15
Blanchette, Manon, 134
Bleeker, Claas Jouco, 15
Blincoe, Robert, 15
Blodgett, Jan, 15
Bloesch, Donald G., 59
Blount, Brian K., 15
Blumhofer, Edith Waldvogel, 16, 133
Boa, Kenneth, 16
Boesak, W., 16
Boice, James Montgomery, 16
Bonk, Jon, 16
Boonprasat-Lewis, Nantawan, 134
Bornstein, Daniel Ethan, 181
Bosch, David Jacobus, 16, 31
Bottignole, Silvana, 17
Bouma-Prediger, Steven, 17
Bouyer, Louis, 23
Bowers, Russell H., 17
Bowman, Robert M., 16
Boyd, Jeffrey H., 17
Boyer, Paul S., 17
Bozeman, Theodore Dwight, 17
Braaten, Carl E., 165
Bradley, Terris Wade, 17
Bradshaw, Bruce, 18
Bradstock, Andrew, 102, 181
Brady, Veronica, 18
Bragt, Jan van, 110
Brailsford, William, 1
Bramadat, Paul A., 18
Brauer, Jerald C., 163
Bravman, Bill, 18
Breen, Quirinus, 163
Breese, Dave, 18
Brekus, Catherine A., 18
Brent, Allen, 18
Bria, Ion, 19
Bright, Pamela, 43
Brimlow, Robert W., 160
Briner, Bob, 19
Brinsmead, Robert D., 19
Brookes, Norman E., 175
Brosnan, Declan, 19
Brown, Delwin, 20, 36

Brown, Neil, 20, 53
Brown, Peter Robert Lamont, 20
Browning, Don S., 58
Brumbaugh, Thoburn Taylor, 20
Buckley, Francis J., 20
Budde, Michael L., 20, 160
Buddenbaum, Judith Mitchell, 130, 131
Bujo, Bénézet, 20, 21
Bulman, Raymond F., 21
Bumpus, Harold B., 52
Burkhart, Louise M., 21
Burkholder, John Richard, 87
Burt, Ben, 90
Bush, Harold K. (Harold Karl), 21
Busséll, Harold L., 21

C

Cailliet, Émile, 21
Caird, Edward, 22
Caird, John, 21
Cairns, George F., 13
Caldwell, Patricia, 22
Calhoun, Arthur W. (Arthur Wallace), 22
Camenisch, Paul F., 137
Camps, Arnulf, 40
Carlson, Ron, 22
Carnes, John Robb, 22
Carr, Anne E., 132
Carr, Steven A., 22
Carrier, Hervé, 23
Carro, Daniel, 36
Carson, D. A., 14, 63
Casanova, Judith Boice, 23
Casarella, Peter J., 27
Cassidy, Eoin G., 53
Castell, Alburey, 77
Cataldo, Peter J., 162
Cavarnos, Constantine, 24
Cavarnos, John P. (John Peter), 24
Cell, Edward, 24
Chagall, David, 24
Chandler, Paul Gordon, 24
Chandy, K. K., 24
Chatterji, Saral Kumar, 41, 151
Chaves, Mark, 25
Cheadle, Rand, 74
Chibuko, Patrick Chukwudezie, 25
Chidili, Barth, 25
Choi, Myung-Keun, 25
Choong, Chee Pang, 31
Chupungco, Anscar J., 30, 31
Clammer, J. R., 31

Clapp, Rodney, 32, 162, 175
Clarke, B. J., 41
Claussen, Janet, 32
Clegg, Tom (Thomas T.), 32
Clement, Atchenemou Hlama, 39
Clouse, Robert G., 32
Coates, R. (Ruth), 162
Cobb, John B., 32
Cochran, Mary E., 33
Cochrane, Charles Norris, 33
Coffey, David (David Michael), 33
Cohen, Arthur Allen, 33
Coleman, Simon, 33
Colledge, Edmund, 127
Collier, Jane, 34
Collins, Adela Yarbro, 5
Collins, John Joseph, 162
Colson, Charles W., 34, 127
Conger, Jay Alden, 152
Conkin, Paul Keith, 35
Conlon, James, 35
Connell, Martin F., 159
Conway, Ruth, 37
Cook, Anthony E., 37
Cook, Guillermo, 39
Cook, Kaye V., 37
Cooper, Charles Champlin, 37
Coote, Robert T., 46, 64
Copley, A. R. H. (Antony R. H.), 37
Cornille, C. (Catherine), 37, 38
Corwin, Gary, 109
Costa, Ruy O., 119
Costas, Orlando E., 38
Cote, Richard G., 38
Couch, Mal, 38
Coudert, Allison, 83
Covert, William Chalmers, 38
Cowling, Maurice, 36
Cox, James L. (James Leland), 135
Cragg, Kenneth, 38
Craig, Clarence Tucker, 39
Crist, Terry M., 39
Crossman, Meg, 182
Crowe, Jerome, 40
Cruz, Anne J., 40
Cunningham, Sarah, 51
Currie, Thomas W., 41

D

Dah, Jonas N. (Jonas Nwiyende), 41
Daly, Robert J., 78
Daniélou, Jean, 41

Darby, James Ezra, 41
Darevych, Dariia, 2
Davaney, Sheila Greeve, 25, 36
Davidson, Allan K., 42
Dawn, Marva J., 42
Dawson, Christopher, 42, 43, 51
Dayal, Har, 43
Dayton, Edward R., 43
D'Costa, Gavin, 132
De Gruchy, John W., 45
De Sherbinin, Julie W., 43
De Souza, Teotonio R., 45
De Vos, Craig Steven, 43
Deacy, Christopher, 44
Deats, Richard L., 64
Deck, Allan Figueroa, 125
Dempsey, Corinne G., 44
Dennis, Barbara, 44
Dennis, Lane T., 44
DeParrie, Paul, 44
Derrick, Christopher, 44
Desai, Ram, 44
Dhavamony, Mariasusai, 45
Dialog der Bilder, 120
Díaz-Stevens, Ana María, 5
Dickson, Kwesi A., 45
Diehl, Carl Gustav, 45
DiIulio, John J., 177
Dionne, E. J., 177
Dirven, René, 53
DomNwachukwu, Peter Nlemadim, 46
Donaldson, Devlin, 46
Donovan, Mary Ann, 20
Dooyeweerd, H. (Herman), 46
Doran, Robert M., 46
Drane, John William, 47
Dreisbach, Daniel L., 132
D'Souza, Jerome, 47
DuCille, Frank O. (Frank Olivier), 47
Ducruet, Jean, 53
Dudley, Roger L., 47
Duffy, Regis A., 47
Dumais, Marcel, 47
Durant, Ariel, 47
Durant, Will, 47
Dyrness, William A., 47, 48, 50

E

Eagleton, Terence, 48
Eagleton, Terry, 48
Eakin, Frank E., 48
Eckman, James P., 48

Edington, Carol, 48
Edwards, D. Miall (David Miall), 48
Edwards, David Lawrence, 48
Edwards, Sarah A., 30
Eich, David, 49
Ejizu, Christopher I., 49
Elavathingal, Sebastian, 49
Eliot, T. S. (Thomas Stearns), 49
Elizondo, Virgilio P., 49
Ellenwood, Cynthia, 149
Ellingsen, Mark, 49
Elliot, Elisabeth, 49
Elliott, Michael C., 50
Ellul, Jacques, 50
Elmer, Duane, 50
Emilsen, William W., 50
Ernst, Eldon G., 50, 51
Erskine, Thomas, 51
Eskidjian, Salpy, 150
Eslinger, Ellen, 51
Esteban, Rafael, 34
Evans, Alice F., 163
Evans, Robert A., 163
Everett, William Johnson, 52
Eversole, Finley, 52
Eyre, Stephen D., 52
Ezugwu, Tony Ifeanyi, 52

F

Fabella, Virginia, 174
Fagan, Seán, 3
Farrell, Thomas J., 35
Feeley-Harnik, Gillian, 54
Feister, John Bookser, 137
Fenn, Richard K., 54
Fernández-Armesto, Felipe, 54
Fernando, Peter, 79
Feuerbach, Ludwig, 54
Fiala, Edward, 126
Ficker, Victor B., 54
Fiddes, Paul S., 53, 164
Fiddes, Paul S., 55
Fiedler, Klaus, 55
Figgis, John Neville, 55
Finney, Paul Corby, 55
Finucane, Ronald C., 55
Fischer, John, 56
Fisher, James Terence, 56
Fishwick, Marshall William, 56
Fitch, Robert Elliot, 56
Fitzgerald, Timothy, 159
Fitzpatrick, Joseph P., 56

Flake, Carol, 56
Flanagan, Kieran, 56
Fleming, Bruce C. E., 57
Flint, Thomas P., 27
Florovsky, Georges, 57
Fong, Bobby, 27
Fore, William F., 57
Forell, George Wolfgang, 57
Forristal, Desmond, 57
Foster, Durwood, 167
Fountain, Oswald G., 104
Fowler, Richard A., 57, 58
Fox, Matthew, 58
Francis, Leslie J., 85
Francis, Mark R., 58
Franklin, Simon, 58
Free, Katharine B., 163
Friend, William B., 52
Friesen, Duane K., 58
Frontain, Raymond-Jean, 130
Fussell, Edwin S., 59

G

Gaede, S. D., 59
Gaggawala, Paul O., 59
Gaillardetz, Richard R., 59
Gallagher, Michael Paul, 59
Galloway, Allan Douglas, 60
Gameson, Richard, 11
García-Rivera, Alex, 60
Garnett, Lucy Mary Jane, 60
Garrison, Charles E., 60
Garsoïan, Nina G., 60
Gasparov, B., 28
Gatta, John, 60
Gay, Craig M., 60
Geering, Lloyd George, 61
Gelpi, Donald L., 61
Geoghegan, Arthur Turbitt, 61
George, Marie I., 53
Gerami, Shahin, 61
Gerhart, Mary, 111
Giffin, Michael, 61
Gilchrist, Roberta, 61
Giles, Paul, 62
Gilkey, Langdon Brown, 62
Gill, Kenneth D., 62
Gill, Sean, 132
Gilliland, Dean S., 166
Girard, René, 62, 137
Gittins, Anthony J., 62, 94
Gladden, Washington, 62

Goa, David J., 63
Goetz, William R. (William Ralph), 63
Gofwen, Rotgak I., 63
Goldewijk, Berma Klein, 40, 127
Goldie, R. M. (Rosemary M.) 'Swiecicki,
   Andrzej, 47
González, Justo L., 63, 64
Goodich, Michael, 64
Goosen, Gideon, 64
Gorospe, Vitaliano R., 64
Gostwick, Joseph, 64
Gottwald, Norman K. (Norman Karol), 64
Graggs, Charles Randall, 65
Graham, Gael, 65
Grant, George, 65
Grant, Judith, 127
Grant, Patrick, 65
Graves, Herbert S., 54
Graveson, Caroline Cassandra, 65
Green, John Clifford, 132
Greenspahn, Frederick E., 129
Gregory of Nazianzus, Saint, 65
Greinacher, Norbert, 27
Gremillion, Joseph, 160
Grey, Mary C., 65
Griffith, Leonard, 66
Griffiths, Michael, 66
Griffiths, Nicholas, 152
Grimstead, Jay, 39
Groothuis, Rebecca Merrill, 66
Grunlan, Stephen A., 66
Guibbory, Achsah, 66
Guinness, Os, 67
Gundry Volf, Judith M., 67
Gunton, Colin E., 67
Guroian, Vigen, 67
Gushee, David P., 30
Gutiérrez, Gustavo, 143

H

Habito, Ruben L. F., 108
Hague, Daryl, 87
Hall, Donald E. (Donald Eugene), 113
Hall, Douglas John, 67, 68
Hambrick-Stowe, Charles E., 68
Hammond, David M., 166
Hammond, Jeffrey, 68
Hammond, Phillip E., 69
Handy, Robert T., 69
Hangen, Tona J., 69
Hankins, Barry, 69
Hanley, Mark Y., 69

Hanratty, Gerald, 70
Happel, Stephen, 70
Häring, Bernhard, 70
Harnack, Adolf von, 70
Harrison, Mark, 72
Hart, Ray L., 70
Hartt, Julian Norris, 70
Hasman, Melvin, 70
Hastings, Adrian, 28, 70
Hatch, Edwin, 71
Hauerwas, Stanley, 71
Hay, Donald A., 28
Hayward, John, 49
Healey, Joseph, 71
Hedlund, Roger E., 40
Heesters, Cornelius, 1
Hefferan, Gerry, 2
Hefner, Robert W., 36
Hegland, Martin, 72
Heick, Otto William, 4
Helleman, Wendy E., 28, 72
Heller, Dagmar, 11
Henderson, David W., 72
Hendriks, Joan, 2
Hendrix, Raymond F., 72
Henry, Bill, 34
Henry, Carl Ferdinand Howard, 63, 72, 73, 130
Henry, Rodney L., 73
Herbert, Beulah, 40
Hereford, Marie Judith, 73
Hershberger, Guy F. (Guy Franklin), 87
Hesselgrave, David J., 73
Hibbert, Giles, 73
Hiebert, Paul G., 73
Hill, Jim, 74
Hillman, Eugene, 74
Hillyer, Philip, 182
Hirudayam, Ignatius, 74
Hluvko, Rostyslav, 2
Hocking, William Ernest, 160
Hoekema, David A., 27
Hogan, Anne, 181
Holditch, W. Kenneth, 78
Holeton, David, 96
Holland, J. G. (Josiah Gilbert), 74
Hollar, Barry Penn, 74
Hollenweger, Walter J., 124
Holley, Linda Tarte, 32
Holmes, Barbara Ann, 74
Holsinger, Bruce W., 74
Holsworth, Robert D., 75
Hong, Edna Hatlestad, 86
Hong, Harold S., 89

Hong, Howard Vincent, 86
Hood, Ralph W., 116
Hood, Robert E. (Robert Earl), 75
Hoole, Charles R. A., 75
Hopkins, Dwight N., 25
Hopler, Marcia, 75
Hopler, Thom, 75
Hopper, Jeffery, 75
Horn, Thomas R., 75
Horton, Michael Scott, 76, 127
Hostetler, Bob, 104
Hotchkiss, Valerie R., 76
House, H. Wayne, 57, 58
Hoxie, Frederick E., 157
Hsia, Adrian, 158
Huber, Carlo, 76
Huff, Peter A., 77
Huffstetter, Stephen, 77
Hughes, Robert P., 140
Hughson, D. Thomas, 77
Hunsberger, George R., 77, 161
Huxley, Thomas Henry, 77

I

Ifie, Egbe, 37
Igboaja, Eugene Ugonna, 80
Ike, Obiora F., 80
Ilogu, Edmund, 78
Inch, Morris A., 79
Irarrázaval, Diego, 80
Iroegbu, Pantaleon, 80
Irvine, Gerald, 29
Isasi-Díaz, Ada María, 80, 81
Iwe, Nwachukwuike S. S. (Nwachukwuike Sonde
    Sylvanus), 81

J

Jacobs, Alan, 81
James, Wendy, 171
Janssen, Gretchen, 81
Jeffrey, David L., 81
Jelsma, Auke, 82
Jenson, Robert W., 82, 165
Jewett, Robert, 82
Ji, Won Yong, 89
Jo, Yung-hwan, 82
John Chrysostom, Saint, 91
Johnson, Douglas Hamilton, 171
Johnson, Eric, 83
Johnson, Robert Leon, 83
Johnston, Jon, 83

Jones, Timothy S., 102
Jongeneel, J. A. B., 124
Jordan, James B., 163
Jorstad, Erling, 83
Jurjevich, Ratibor-Ray M., 84

K

Kabasele Lumbala, François, 84
Kallestad, Walther P., 84
Kamensky, Jane, 84
Kamu, Lalomilo, 84
Kan, Sergei, 84
Kanyoro, Rachel Angogo, 157
Kaplan, Steven, 80
Karamaga, André, 128
Kastfelt, Niels, 84
Kaufman, Gordon D., 85
Kay, William K., 85
Kee, Howard Clark, 30
Keidel, Levi O., 85
Kelly, Joseph F. (Joseph Francis), 85
Kelsay, John, 96
Kenny, Mary, 85
Kessler, Aharon, 85
Kessler, Sanford, 85
Khabela, M. Gideon, 86
Kidwell, Clara Sue, 86
Kierkegaard, Søren, 86
Killinger, John, 86
Kim, Chung Choon, 89
Kim, Dong-Sun, 86
Kim, Heup Young, 86
Kim, Jung Ha, 87
Kim, Kyong-jae, 87
Kimball, Robert C., 167
King, Arthur Henry, 87
King, Ursula, 132
Kintz, Linda, 106
Kirby, John P., 87
Kirst, Nelson, 134
Klingshirn, William E., 164
Knight, Frances, 88
Kniss, Fred Lamar, 88
Knitter, Paul F., 126
Knox, John, 88
Koester, Helmut, 88
Koschorke, Klaus, 1
Kraft, Charles H., 89
Kraus, C. Norman (Clyde Norman), 89
Krawchuk, Andrii, 89
Kreeft, Peter, 89
Kreider, Alan, 28, 89

Kromkowski, John, 2
Krondorfer, Björn, 106
Kronenfeld, Judy, 90
Kruithof, Bastian, 90
Kuenning, Larry, 90
Kuhns, William, 90
Kurewa, John Wesley Zwomunondiita, 90
Küster, Volker, 90
Kwa'ioloa, Michael, 90
Kwawe, Daniel Badu, 91
Kwok, Pui-lan, 91
Kwong, Chungwah, 91

L

Laistner, M. L. W. (Max Ludwig Wolfram), 91
Lamle, Elias Nankap, 91
Lançon, Bertrand, 91
Lande, Aasulv, 109
Lane, Dermot A., 131
Lange, Maurice de, 91
Langston, Richard L., 92
Lapiz, Ed, 92
Larkin, William J., 92
Larousse, William, 92
Larson, Duane H. (Duane Howard), 93
LaVerdiere, Eugene, 1
Law, Eric H. F., 93
Lawhead, Steve, 93
Lawrence, Irene, 146
Lawrie, Ingrid, 28
Leahy, William P., 93
Lee, Jung Young, 93
Lee, Lance (Lance L.), 37
Lee, Philip J., 35
Lee, Robert, 93
Leeuwen, Arend Theodoor van, 94
Lefort, Guy, 62
Legrand, Lucien, 94
Lesage, Julia, 106
Levison, John R., 126, 134
Lewy, Guenter, 94
Leyser, Henrietta, 11
Liankhohau, T., 94
Lidov, Aleksei, 82
Lim, Byeong Ho, 182
Limberis, Vasiliki, 94
Lindberg-Seyersted, Brita, 116
Lindenauer, Leslie J., 95
Lindsell, Harold, 95
Lingenfelter, Sherwood G., 95
Linn, Jan, 95
Lints, Richard, 95

LiPuma, Edward, 95
Little, David, 96
Little, Joyce A., 96
Little, Lawrence S., 96
Llywelyn, Dorian, 97
Lockerbie, D. Bruce, 97
Loewen, Jacob A. (Jacob Abram), 97
Logan, Oliver, 97, 98
Lombard, C. Rabe, Petro, 183
Lonergan, Bernard J. F., 165
Long, D. Stephen, 98
Long, Loretta M. (Loretta Marie), 98
Lowber, James W, 98
Lowber, James William, 98
Lowrie, Donald Alexander, 12
Lundin, Roger, 98
Luttikhuizen, Henry, 126
Luzbetak, Louis J., 98, 99
Lynch, Christopher Owen, 99
Lyon, K. Brynolf, 158

M

MacArthur, John, 99
Macchioro, Vittorio, 99
Machin, G. I. T., 99
Mack, Burton L., 99
MacKenzie, Charles Sherrard, 99
MacMullen, Ramsay, 100
Maddux, Bob, 100
Madigan, Patrick, 100
Madison, James, 100
Magliola, Robert R., 100
Mallard, William, 100
Manathodath, Jacob, 100
Manus, Ukachukwu Chris, 101
Maritain, Jacques, 51
Markus, R. A. (Robert Austin), 101, 164
Marler, J. C., 127
Marsden, George M., 101
Marsh, Joss, 101
Martin, Lloyd, 101
Martin, Margaret Reid, 175
Marty, Martin E., 129
Mason, Debra L., 130
Massa, Mark Stephen, 102
Massey, Lesly F., 102
Mastroeni, Anthony J., 80
Matovina, Timothy M., 125
Matsoukas, George, 129
Maxwell, David (David James), 103
Maxwell, David, 28
Maxwell, John C., 113

Mayers, Marvin Keene, 66, 103
Mayr-Harting, Henry, 11
Mbachu, Hilary, 103
Mbanda, Laurent, 103
Mbefo, Luke Nnamdi, 103
McAlpine, Thomas H., 104
McCallum, Dennis, 162
McCarron, D. Michael, 52
McCullough, Donald W., 104
McDannell, Colleen, 104
McDowell, Josh, 104
McEachern, Claire Elizabeth, 131
McGavran, Donald Anderson, 104
McGinn, Bernard, 162
McGinness, Frederick J., 104
McGregor, Donald E., 104
McIntosh, John A., 104
McKay, Stan, 105
McKenzie, John L., 105
McLean, George F., 2, 105, 134
McShane, Philip, 105
McTighe, Michael J., 105
Meek, Donald E., 106
Meilaender, Gilbert, 106
Melling, Philip H., 106
Mendes-Flohr, Paul R., 33
Menuge, Angus J. L., 26
Mercado, Leonardo N., 107
Merrill, Dean, 107
Merton, Thomas, 7
Mette, Norbert, 27
Metuh, Emefie Ikenga, 107
Metz, Johannes Baptist, 182
Meyer, Ben F., 146
Meyer, Franklin A., 22
Middleton, J. Richard, 173
Mielke, Arthur J., 107
Milbank, John, 107
Miles, Margaret Ruth, 108
Miller, Haskell M., 108
Mills, Kenneth (Kenneth R.), 108
Minahane, John, 108
Minnery, Tom, 108
Miranda-Feliciano, Evelyn, 109
Mitchell, Michael A., 109
Mitchell, William, 109
Molnar, Thomas Steven, 109
Moloney, Francis J., 109
Moltmann, Jürgen, 110
Mommaers, Paul, 110
Montgomery-Fate, Tom, 110
Moore, Stephen D., 110
Moreland, James Porter, 110

Morgan, D. Densil, 110
Morgan, Donn F., 111
Mousalimas, S. A., 111
Mouw, Richard J., 111
Muck, Terry C., 108
Mueller, J. J. (John J.), 111
Mueller, Walt, 111, 112
Mugambi, J. N. Kanyua (Jesse Ndwiga Kanyua), 112, 160
Mughogho, Kelvin K., 112
Mukonyora, Isabel, 135
Mullins, Edgar Young, 112
Mullins, Mark, 112, 125
Mulloor, Augustine, 53
Mulrain, George MacDonald, 112
Murphy, J. Stanley (Joseph Stanley), 112
Muzorewa, Gwinyai H., 113
Myers, Ken, 113

N

Nappa, Mike, 113
Nariculam, Antony, 79
Nash, Kimberley, 113
Ndiokwere, Nathaniel I., 113
Neckebrouck, V., 37, 113
Nevill, Antonia, 91
Neville, Gwen Kennedy, 113
Newbigin, Lesslie, 114
Ng, David, 124
Nicholls, Bruce, 45
Nicholls, Kathleen D., 114
Nichols, Aidan, 114
Niebuhr, H. Richard (Helmut Richard), 115, 145, 153
Niebuhr, H. Richard (Helmut)
Niehaus, Carl, 101
Nieman, James R., 115
Nieuwenhove, Jacques van, 127
Nieuwenhove, Jacques van, 40
Nimmo-Smith, Jennifer, 65
Nineham, D. E. (Dennis Eric), 115
Nobili, Roberto de', 116
Nolan, Albert, 116
Noley, Homer, 86
Noll, Mark A., 116
Noorbergen, Rene, 116
North, Gary, 165
Novak, Michael, 1
Novalis, 117
Nowaczyk, Miroslaw, 92
Nuovo, Victor, 167
Nwaigbo, Ferdinand, 117

Nygren, Anders, 117

O

Ó Murchú, Diarmuid, 117
Oates, Lynette Frances, 117
Obeng, J. Pashington, 117
Obi, Obioma Des, 117
O'Brien, Conor Cruise, 118
O'Brien, William James, 164
O'Donnell, Michael (Michael Alan), 118
O'Donovan, Wilbur, 118
Oduyoye, Mercy Amba, 157
Ogbajie, Chukwu, 118
Okere, Theophilus, 78
Okolo, Chukwudum Barnabas, 118
Okure, Teresa, 1
Oladipo, Caleb Oluremi, 119
Olasky, Marvin N., 119
Olukoju, Ayodeji, 115
Olurode, 'Lai, 115
O'Malley, John W., 119, 164
Onuh, Charles Ok, 119
Onwubiko, Oliver Alozie, 119, 120
Onyeneke, Augustine O., 120
Opocenský, Milan, 120
Ostrander, Richard, 120
O'Sullivan, Owen, 120
Osuntokun, Akinjide, 115
Ott, Martin, 120
Ottati, Douglas F., 121
Oughourlian, Jean-Michel, 62
Overman, Christian, 121
Ovitt, George, 121
Owens, Virginia Stem, 121
Owoahene-Acheampong, Stephen, 121

P

Pacini, Andrea, 26
Pahl, Jon, 121
Palma, Robert J., 122
Palmer, Michael F., 168
Pamer, Nan, 122
Panikkar, Raimundo, 126
Paperno, Irina, 140
Parani, Maria G., 122
Pardini, David A., 122
Parent, Mark, 122
Park, Sun Ai Lee, 174
Parshall, Craig, 122
Parshall, Janet, 122
Parshall, Phil, 122

Pati, Biswamoy, 72
Pattel-Gray, Anne, 102
Patterson, Philip D., 123
Pattison, George, 123
Pattison, Robert, 123
Paz, D. G. (Denis G.), 116
Peachey, Paul, 2
Pearce, Tariq Safina, 123
Pearcey, Nancy, 34
Pecherskaya, Natalia A., 162
Peel, J. D. Y. (John David Yeadon), 123
Peelman, Achiel, 124
Pelikan, Jaroslav Jan, 124
Perrotta, Kevin, 29
Perry, Mary Elizabeth, 40
Perry, Paul E., 175
Persaud, Winston D., 124
Peters, Ted, 125
Peterson, Anna Lisa, 30
Petro, Nicolai N., 28
Phelps, Jamie T. (Jamie Therese), 14
Phillips, Henry, 125
Pierard, Richard V., 32
Pierce, Lorne Albert, 125
Pietrasiewicz, Bogumil, 126
Pike, Kenneth Lee, 125
Pinto, Joseph Prasad, 125
Pishchik, Yuri B., 140
Pittman, Don Alvin, 108
Plou, Dafne Sabanes, 126
Pobee, J. S., 126
Poewe, Karla O., 25
Pool, Jeff B., 62
Pope-Levison, Priscilla, 126, 134
Porete, Marguerite, 127
Pounds, Norman John Greville, 127
Poupard, Paul, 127
Power, David Noel, 96, 127
Price, Maurice Thomas, 127, 128
Principe, Walter H. (Walter Henry), 128
Prior, Randall, 128
Puckett, Walter, 129
Pudaite, Lien Jacob, 129
Purves, Alan C., 129
Pyron, Bernard, 129

R

Raja, John Joshva, 130
Ramos, Alice, 53
Rapisarda, Philip A., 130
Raschke, Carl A., 130
Ratzinger, Joseph, 23

Raybin, David, 32
Redekop, Calvin Wall, 87
Reeves, Dale, 153
Regan, Hilary D., 26
Reid, David, 131
Reisinger, Ernest C., 131
Reist, Benjamin A., 131
Renan, Ernest, 133
Renck, G. L., 133
Rhee, Jung Suck, 135
Rhodes, Stephen A., 135
Riamela, Daniel Odafetite, 135
Richardson, Tommy G., 135
Ridings, Daniel, 135
Ries, John, 53
Robb, John D., 136
Roberts, J. Deotis (James Deotis), 136
Roberts, Jon H., 136
Robertson, Ritchie, 23
Robinson, Gnana, 137
Roels, Shirley J., 137
Roembke, Lianne, 137
Rogers, Bruce, 22
Rogers, Thomas G., 115
Rohr, Richard, 137
Romanowski, William D., 137
Rommen, Edward, 73, 109
Roof, Wade Clark, 182
Roozen, David A., 163
Roper, Lyndal, 145
Rosio, Bob, 138
Rosman, Doreen M., 138
Ross, Kenneth R., 138
Rotholz, James M., 138
Rouner, Leroy S., 138
Roxburgh, Alan J., 138, 139
Ruckman, Peter S., 139
Rudy, Gordon, 139
Rueschhoff, Norlin G., 26
Ruether, Rosemary Radford, 139
Rupp, George, 139
Rusconi, Roberto, 181
Rushdoony, Rousas John, 140
Russello, Gerald J., 42
Russo, Steve, 140
Rutler, George W. (George William), 140
Ryken, Leland, 140, 141
Ryken, Philip Graham, 141

S

Sabatier, Auguste, 141
Sack, Daniel, 141

Sahay, Keshari N., 141
Sait̄o, S̄oichi, 141
Samartha, S. J. (Stanley J.), 141
Sample, Tex, 142
Samuel, Vinay, 161
Sánchez, Julio A., 142
Sanneh, Lamin O., 142
Saunders, George R., 40
Schaeffer, Francis A. (Francis August), 143
Schapera, Isaac, 143
Scharlemann, Robert P., 70
Schaum, Konrad, 26
Scheinberg, Cynthia, 143
Schenck, Paul C., 143
Schenck, Robert L., 143, 144
Schidlovsky, Nicolas, 63
Schilder, K. (Klaas), 144
Schillebeeckx, Edward, 182
Schindler, David L., 23
Schineller, Peter, 144
Schlieper, Heiko C., 63
Schmidt, Alvin J., 144
Schmidt, Herman A. P., 96
Schneider, John R., 144
Schner, George P., 27
Schreiter, Robert J., 144
Schuller, David S., 144
Schulte van Kessel, Elisja, 181
Schultz, Erich R. W., 4
Schultze, Quentin J. (Quentin James), 41, 144
Schwarz, John E., 145
Scott, Nathan A., 111
Scott, Steve, 145
Scoville, Gordon, 145
Scribner, Robert W., 145
Scriven, Charles, 145
Seel, John, 146
Seerveld, Calvin, 126
Senior, John, 146
Senn, Frank C., 146
Sernau, Scott, 146
Sfekas, Stephen J., 129
Shairp, John Campbell, 146
Shastri, Hermen P., 146
Shaull, Richard, 134
Shaw, Chandler, 147
Shaw, Charles Gray, 147
Shaw, Joseph M., 130
Shaw, R. Daniel (Robert Daniel), 147
Sheen, Fulton J. (Fulton John), 147
Sheets, Dutch, 147
Sheldon, Garrett Ward, 132
Shelley, Bruce L. (Bruce Leon), 147

Shenk, David W., 147
Shenk, Joseph C., 147
Short, Robert L., 147
Shorter, Aylward, 148
Shuger, Debora K., 131
Siddiqui, Abdul Hameed, 148
Signorotto, Gianvittorio, 38
Sih, Paul K. T. (Kwang Tsien), 148
Simons, Gerald, 148
Sindima, Harvey J., 149
Sine, Tom, 149
Sire, James W., 149
Sittler, Joseph, 149
Skard, Sigmund, 116
Slosser, Bob, 149
Slusser, Gerald H., 149
Smalley, William Allen, 150
Smith, Archie, 158
Smith, Christian (Christian Stephen), 150
Smith, Debbie, 150
Smith, Gregory A., 26
Smith, Oran P., 151
Smith, Robert Wayne, 25
Smith, Theophus Harold, 151
Smith-Christopher, Daniel L., 159
Sng, Bobby E. K. (Bobby Ewe Kong), 31
Snyder, Graydon F., 139, 151
Sockman, Ralph W. (Ralph Washington), 151
Solomon, Jerry, 8
Song, Choan-Seng, 151
Sorokowski, Andrew, 2
Soukup, Paul A., 35, 106
Spae, Joseph John, 152
Spinka, Matthew, 152
Sproul, R. C. (Robert Charles), 152
Sprunger, David A., 102
Squire, Aelred, 153
St. James, Rebecca, 153
St. Kilda, Martin, 153
Stachowski, Zbigniew, 92
Stackhouse, Max L., 137, 153
Stassen, Glen Harold, 153
Staunton, Michael, 153
Stein, Stephen J., 162
Steinmetz, Paul B., 154
Stern, David, 33
Sterner, Douglas W., 154
Stevens Arroyo, Antonio M., 5
Stewart, James Livingstone, 154
Stone, Charles J., 154
Stone, Ronald H., 131, 164
Storck, Thomas, 154
Stott, John R. W., 46, 64

Stout, Daniel A., 131
Streit, Jakob, 154
Stürzenhofecker, G. (Gabriele), 155
Sugden, Chris, 161
Sugirtharajah, R. S. (Rasiah S.), 171, 172
Sullivan, Timothy, 155
Sumithra, Sunand, 45
Suttles, Virgil, 155
Sweet, Leonard I., 155, 156
Swimme, Brian, 58
Sybertz, Donald, 71
Syrjänen, Seppo, 156
Szarmach, Paul E., 8

T

Taber, Charles Russell, 30, 156
Takatemjen, 156
Takenaka, Masao, 156
Tamney, Joseph B., 157
Tang, Yijie, 157
Tanner, Kathryn, 36, 157
Tano, Rodrigo D., 157
Tarango, Yolanda, 125
Tarr, Delbert Howard, 158
Tate, Allen, 158
Taylor, Mark L. (Mark Lewis), 158
Taylor, Richard Warren, 41, 158
Terrell, Richard, 158
Terry, Randall A., 158
Tesfai, Yacob, 165
Teyegaga, B. D., 159
Thistlethwaite, Susan Brooks, 13
Thomas, Corrine, 73
Thomas, George Finger, 166
Thomas, George M., 166
Thomas, T. Jacob (Thannikapurathoot Jacob), 167
Thompson, James, 167
Thompson, T. Jack, 167
Thornhill, John, 167
Tigner, Hugh Stevenson, 167
Tillich, Paul, 167, 168
Tinker, George E., 86
Tippit, Sammy, 168
Tobin, Greg, 141
Tonucci, G. M. (Giovanni Mwenda), 163
Torrance, Alan J., 26
Torrance, Thomas Forsyth, 168
Torwesten, Hans, 168
Tovey, Phillip, 168
Towns, Elmer L., 169
Trace, Arther S., 169

Transformation (Organization), 36
Troeger, Thomas H., 169
Trueblood, Elton, 169
Turkson, Peter, 79
Tuttle, Robert G., 169
Twiss, Richard, 169
Tyloch, Witold, 92

U

Udeafor, Ndubisi Innocent, 170
Udoidem, S. Iniobong, 170
Ugolnik, Anthony, 170
Ustorf, Werner, 109
Uzukwu, E. Elochukwu, 107, 170

V

Van der Peet, G., 170
Van der Walt, B. J., 170
Van Dyke, Henry, 170
Van Gelder, Craig, 35, 161
Van Leeuwen, Mary Stewart, 132
Van Rheenen, Gailyn, 171
VanderVennen, Robert E., 31
Vanhoozer, Kevin J., 165
Vaporis, N. M. (Nomikos Michael), 136
Varacalli, Joseph A., 171
Vásquez, Manuel A., 30
Vaughn, Ellen Santilli, 34
Vecsey, Christopher, 171
Veith, Gene Edward, 171
Vennen, Mark Vander, 46
Verstraelen, F. J., 135
Vessey, Mark, 164
Villa-Vicencio, Charles, 45, 101
Visceglia, Maria Antonietta, 38
Volf, Miroslav, 67
Von Holzen, Walter, 3
Vööbus, Arthur, 172
Voshaar, Jan, 172

W

Waldecker, Gary, 172
Waliggo, John Mary, 79
Walker, Keith, 172
Walls, Andrew F. (Andrew Finlay), 173
Walsh, Andrew D., 173
Walsh, Brian J., 173
Wamberg, Steve, 46
Wang, Xiaochao, 173
Ward, Lionel O., 173

Ward, Merrill, 173
Warhola, James W. (James Walter), 174
Wariboko, Waibinte E. (Waibinte Elekima), 174
Warren, Michael, 24, 174
Watson, David Lowes, 174
Weakland, Rembert, 175
Weaver, Rufus W. (Rufus Washington), 175
Webb, William J., 175
Webber, Robert, 175
Webster, A. C. (Alan C.), 175
Webster, Douglas D., 175
Wegh, Shagbaor F. (Shagbaor Francis), 176
Wei, Cho-min, 176
Weigel, Gustave, 176
Wellman, James K., 176
Wells, Colin, 176
Wells, David F., 176
Weltin, E. G., 177
Wessels, Antonie, 177
Westfield, N. Lynne, 177
Wethersfield Institute, 29
Wheeler, Michael, 177
Whitehead, John W., 177, 178
Whiteside, Elena Scott, 178
Wicker, Brian, 178
Wiest, Jean-Paul, 126
Wijsen, Frans Jozef Servaas, 79, 178
Wilbanks, Dana W., 164
Wilder, Amos Niven, 178
Wilkes, Peter, 29
Will, James E., 178
Willard, Dallas, 110
Williams, Lewin Lascelles, 179
Williams, Philip J., 30
Williams, Rhys H., 40
Williamson, Clark M., 179
Williamson, Peter, 29
Willimon, William H., 71
Wilson, Derek A., 54
Wilson, John Frederick, 179
Wilson, Jonathan R., 179
Wilson, Richard Francis, 36
Wilson, Wayne A., 179
Wingate, Andrew, 179
Wingerd, Mary Lethert, 180
Winter, Richard, 180
Wise, Isaac Mayer, 180
Witte, John, 180
Wogan-Browne, Jocelyn, 181
Wolf, Teresa Ann, 181
Won, Ui-bom, 182
Wong, Wai-Ching Angela, 182
Wood, G. A., 26

Woodbridge, John D., 63
Woodley, Randy, 182
Woodside, Sarah, 150
World Council of Churches, 7, 9, 42, 106, 126,
    179
World Religions Curriculum Development
    Center, 159
Worth, Roland H., 183
Wright, Robin, 183
Wright, Tim, 183
Wust, Peter, 51

Yoder, John Howard, 153, 184
Yohannan, K. P., 184
Young, Frances M. (Frances Margaret), 184
Young, Mildred Binns, 184
Young, Richard Fox, 125
Ysaac, Walter L., 165
Yu, Anthony C., 111
Yu, Chai-Shin, 88
Yu, Jose Vidamor B., 184
Yuen, Wai Man, 184
Yuhaus, Cassian J., 159

Y

Z

Yamamori, Tetsunao, 30
Yamauchi, Edwin M., 32
Yang, Nak Heong, 183
Yap, Kim Hao, 8
Yeager, Diane M., 153
Yeo, Khiok-Khng, 183
Yeow, Choo Lak, 46

Zacharias, Ravi K., 184
Zahniser, A. H. Mathias, 185
Zemka, Sue, 185
Zuidervaart, Lambert, 126
Zyci´nski, Józef, 163
Zylstra, Bernard, 46

Subject Index

#

17th century, 116
19th century, 120, 174
20th century, 15, 16, 35, 55, 65, 69, 93, 95, 110, 120, 124, 134, 177, 180

A

Advertising, 20
Africa, 1, 3, 10, 11, 12, 18, 21, 25, 28, 31, 36, 44, 45, 49, 55, 59, 70, 71, 74, 75, 78, 79, 81, 83, 84, 90, 94, 96, 101, 107, 112, 113, 116-118, 120, 121, 126, 128, 143, 148, 150, 158, 160, 161, 163, 168
Africa, Sub-Saharan, 12, 74, 75, 90, 94, 101, 112, 113, 118, 121, 168
Africa, West, 126, 158
African American women, 10
African American women in literature, 10
African Americans, 74
African Methodist Episcopal Church, 96
African poetry, 92
African Synod, 118, 119, 120, 148, 161, 169
Afro-American Catholics, 14
Afro-American Presbyterians, 47
Afro-Americans, 65
Afro-Americans.United States, 65
Agape., 117
Aguilar, Grace, 1816-1847, 143
Akan (African people), 117, 121
Alaska, 111
Aluni (Papua New Guinea), 155
Amazon River Valley, 183
America, 2, 3, 9, 14, 15, 18, 20, 23, 28, 31, 32, 35, 38, 40, 42, 47, 48, 51, 53, 56, 58, 59, 60, 61, 65, 67, 68, 69, 72, 76, 80, 82, 83, 86, 92, 93, 94, 104, 105, 106, 107, 111, 120, 126, 128,

131, 134, 136, 138, 139, 142, 143, 147, 149-152, 158, 160-162, 164, 168, 170, 177, 180
American fiction, 15
American literature, 8, 10, 21, 22, 59, 60, 62, 69, 77, 116
American poetry, 68
Anabaptists, 58, 145
Ancestor worship, 122, 131
Angas (African people), 63
Angels in literature, 182
Anglican Church of Australia, 2
Anglican Communion, 2, 19, 22, 88, 96
Anglo-Catholicism in literature, 44
animals, mythical, 102
anthropology, 66, 89, 150
anti-apartheid movements, 101
antinuclear movement, 75
Antioch (Turkey), 40
apocalyptic literature, 163
apologetics, 8, 34, 41, 95, 110, 112, 114, 125, 143, 153, 185
Arab countries, 26
Archdiocese of Lima (Peru), 108
Armenia, 60
Armenian Church, 60
Arnold, Matthew, 1822-1888, 154
art and religion, 52, 123, 132, 177
Art, American, 134
Art, Byzantine, 122
Art, Early Christian, 55
Art, Modern, 52
Arts, American, 62, 79
Arts, Indic, 114
Arts, Russian, 82
Ashanti (African people), 117
Asia, 4, 8, 32, 36, 46, 72, 107, 151, 156, 157, 169, 175
Assemblies of God, 3, 16
atonement, 110

Augustine, Saint, Bishop of Hippo, 8, 16, 20, 43,
    184
Austen, Jane, 1775-1817, 61
Australia, 20, 33, 43, 117, 128, 150, 152
Australian aborigines, 2, 102
Austria, 23, 97, 98, 170
authority in literature, 185
Authors, American, 62
Authors, Scottish, 48
axioms, 22

B

baby boom generation, 142
Baniwa Indians, 183
Baniwa philosophy, 183
baptism, 11
Baptists, 69
Barge family, 147
Barth, Karl, 1886-1968, 86, 122, 135
Bascom, Tim, 1961-, 10
Batak (Indonesian people), 105
belief and doubt in literature, 176
Bernard, of Clairvaux, Saint, 139
Best books, 149
Bible, 4, 5, 13, 16, 27, 40, 47, 49, 53, 63, 74, 82,
    85, 88, 91, 94, 97, 99, 101, 103, 110, 111, 120,
    130, 134, 139, 151, 159, 167, 171, 172, 183,
    185
Bible as literature, 82
Binumarien (Papua New Guinea people), 117
biography, 51
Bishops, 107, 114, 128, 161, 164
black theology, 16, 75, 96, 136
blasphemy in literature, 101
Blatty, William Peter, 148
body, human, 11, 29, 74, 107, 110, 113
body, human, in literature, 74, 113
body, human, in music, 74
Bosnia and Hercegovina, 67
Brendan, Saint, the Voyager, ca, 154
Brigid, of Ireland, Saint, ca, 154
Browne, Thomas, Sir, 1605-1682, 66
Browning, Elizabeth Barrett, 1806-1861, 143
Buddhism, 91, 100, 132, 157, 182
Bukidnon (Philippine people), 21
Bukidnon, Philippines, 21
burning bush, 93
Byzantine Empire, 95

C

Caird, John, 1820-1898, 21, 22

Cameroon, 41
camp meetings, 51
Campbell, Selina Huntington, 98
Canada, 12, 28, 31, 63, 105, 122
Capitalism, 155
Cappadocian Fathers, 124
Caribbean Area, 75, 125, 179
Catechisms, 182
Catholic Church, 1-4, 9, 14, 17, 20, 23-25, 31, 33,
    34, 38, 39, 44, 46, 49, 51- 54, 56-60, 62, 71,
    74, 76, 77, 79-81, 84, 94, 96-99, 102, 103,
    106-108, 114-119, 125, 127, 128, 133, 140,
    141, 143, 144, 147, 148, 152, 154, 159-161,
    164, 170, 171, 174-176, 178, 180, 181
Catholic converts, 77
Catholic learning and scholarship., 134
Catholic universities and colleges, 53, 93
Catholics, 32, 52, 56, 62, 93, 102, 125, 171
Catholics in literature, 62

chastity, 153
Chauncy, Charles, 176
Chekhov, Anton Pavlovich, 43
Chicago (Ill.), 176
Chicago Theological Seminary, 13
child rearing, 49, 87, 104, 109, 123
Chile, 172
China, 42, 65, 128, 148, 152, 154, 158, 169
choice of church, 169
Christ and culture, 26, 38, 42, 115, 144, 145, 153,
    156, 176
Christian antiquities, 61, 62, 154, 155
Christian art and symbolism, 11, 49, 55, 108,
    121, 123, 172
Christian biography, 19
Christian Brothers, 136
Christian college students, 18
Christian communities, 7, 26, 125
Christian converts, 37, 156
Christian converts from Islam, 156
Christian education, 20, 42, 130, 174
Christian education of children, 42
Christian ethics, 3, 16, 20, 21, 23, 27, 48, 67, 71,
    78, 99, 106, 115, 137, 145, 153, 175, 176, 183,
    184
Christian fiction, American, 15
Christian fiction, English, 61
Christian life, 5, 10, 15, 19, 32, 34, 44, 52, 56, 59,
    70, 71, 76, 100, 104, 109, 113, 122, 125, 147,
    169, 177, 179, 180, 184
Christian literature, American, 22, 62
Christian literature, English, 181, 182, 185
Christian literature, English (Middle), 181

Christian literature, Welsh, 97
Christian pilgrims and pilgrimages, 55, 114
Christian poetry, American, 176
Christian poetry, English, 143
Christian poetry, Irish, 108
Christian saints, 44, 55, 60, 181
Christian saints in literature, 60, 181
Christian sects, 21, 31, 107, 112
Christian shrines, 55
Christian union, 163
Christian women, 181
Christian women saints, 181
Christianity and antisemitism, 8, 85
Christianity and art, 122, 177
Christianity and economics, 42
Christianity and international affairs, 4, 138, 182
Christianity and justice, 2, 50, 59, 158, 174, 178
Christianity and literature, 8, 10, 15, 21, 32, 44, 48, 60, 61, 62, 65, 66, 69, 77, 82, 90, 100-102, 108, 111, 113, 126, 130, 143, 154, 176, 177, 181, 185
Christianity and other religions, 2, 4, 9, 12, 13, 15, 17, 20, 26, 28, 30, 33, 37-39, 41, 44, 45, 50, 52, 72, 79, 82, 83, 85-87, 92, 94, 97, 99-101, 105,-111, 118, 122, 124, 128, 133, 138, 142, 147, 152, 154, 158, 166, 168, 176-178, 182
Christianity and politics, 3, 7, 16, 20, 30, 33, 36, 37, 38, 40, 50, 52, 56, 65, 69, 74, 75, 76, 77, 86, 96, 107, 131, 132, 133, 139, 144, 149-151, 158, 160, 165, 175, 177, 180, 183
Christianity and the arts, 1, 2, 19, 62, 126, 132, 141, 145
Christianity and the social sciences, 60, 156
Christianity and the world, 7, 54, 135
Christianity History France, 116
Christianity in literature, 43, 182
Christianity, Modern, 42
Christians, 3, 12, 16, 20, 21, 22, 23, 24, 30, 45, 55, 56, 65, 85, 95, 98, 103, 107, 109, 113, 122, 128, 155
Christians (Disciples of Christ), 98
Christians in India, 45
chronic fatigue syndrome, 138
church and college, 54, 93, 169
church and education, 72, 111
church and labor, 61
church and social problems, 23, 25, 35, 37, 39, 45, 55, 57, 58, 82, 99, 119, 128, 151, 161, 175
church and state, 3, 10, 28, 65, 71, 88, 120, 131, 132, 139, 163, 174, 178
church and the world, 18, 19, 39, 56, 65, 66, 68, 70, 71, 74, 76, 109, 122, 129, 144, 145, 184

church attendance, 169
church development, new, 91
church group work with teenage girls, 32
church growth, 66, 67, 91, 183
church history, 10, 25, 30, 32, 33, 40, 43, 57, 71, 75, 85, 91, 95, 100, 101, 120, 133, 135, 163, 164, 170, 177
church membership, 169
Church Missionary Society, 174
Church of England, 44, 55, 88
Church of Jesus Christ of Latter Day Saints, 87
church polity, 19
church relations, 125
church renewal, 12, 47, 86, 95, 129, 155, 156, 159, 174
church work with children, 42
church work with families, 158
church work with Hispanic Americans, 125
church work with the poor, 149, 161
church work with the sick, 12
church work with young adults, 142
Churches Interiors Decoration Great Britain, 173
Ciskei (South Africa), 162
civil religion, 85, 138, 170
civil rights, 110, 178
Civilization, Ancient, 147
Civilization, Celtic, in literature, 108
Civilization, Christian, 22, 29, 33, 43, 46, 52, 88, 95, 100, 109, 125, 128, 130, 146, 147, 158, 166, 175, 184
Civilization, Classical, 124, 135, 177
Civilization, Greco-Roman, 33
Civilization, Medieval, 42, 102, 106
Civilization, Modern, 14, 15, 23, 48, 67, 84, 85, 95, 109, 114, 118, 123, 140, 149, 155, 168, 173, 177, 178
Civilization, Oriental, 128
Civilization, Secular, 42, 130
Civilization, Western, 29, 115, 148, 177, 178
classical literature, 28
Clement, of Alexandria, Saint, ca, 135
clergy, 32, 54
Cleveland (Ohio), 105
college students, 34
Collegium Cardinalium, 38
colonies, 22
colonization., 81
Columba, Saint, 154
Columban, Saint, 154
commitment to the church, 43, 168
common sense, 49
communication, 7, 8, 35, 106, 126, 129
communication and culture, 126, 129

communism, 84, 147, 152
communism and Christianity, 84, 152
community in literature, 66
community life, 10, 18
comparative studies, 163
conduct of life, 32, 74
Confucianism, 91, 157
Conservative Party (Great Britain), 36
Consumption (Economics), 28, 162
control (Psychology), 40
conversion, 36, 150
Corinth (Greece), 43
Corinthians, 1st, VIII, 183
Corinthians, 1st, X, 183
corporate culture, 26, 152
cosmology, 74
Council of Jerusalem, 103
Counter-Reformation, 104
country life, 44
criticism, 49, 99
Crookston, 181
cross-cultural orientation, 81
cross-cultural studies, 63, 147, 155
cults, 21, 84
cultural industries, 20
cultural relativism, 60
culture conflict, 21, 40, 63, 66, 96, 129, 132, 137,
    138, 149
culture shock, 50, 81

D

Darwin, Charles, 35
Dawson, Christopher, 29, 42, 43, 51, 162
death, 69
death in literature, 69
deconstruction, 98
Democracy, 118
Derrida, Jacques, 100
Desire for God, 175
developing countries, 50, 134, 165, 166
devil, 84, 176
devotional literature, 11, 184
Dewey, John, 37
dialogue, 49
Discipline (Christianity) Missions, 185
discourse analysis, Narrative, 18
Dissenters, Religious, in literature, 90
doctrines, 7
dogma, 141
domestic drama, English, 12
druids and druidism, 108
Duna (Papua New Guinea people), 155

Dupré, Louis K., 27
Dwight, Timothy, 176

E

early church, 20, 43, 100, 177
East and West, 4, 16, 59, 93, 94, 152, 157
East Asia, 4, 46, 87, 125, 148
Eastern question (Balkan), 19
economic development, 161
economic justice for all, 77
ecumenical movement, 3, 7, 124
education, 4, 6, 46, 64, 149, 173
El Salvador, 30
Elegiac poetry, American, 68
Eliot, T, 8, 49
Elliott, Michael C, 50
Elwin, Verrier, 50
end of the world, 163
England, 4, 8, 9, 16, 17, 19, 22, 43, 55, 58, 59,
    61, 63, 66, 68, 82, 84, 88, 101, 109, 113, 131,
    133, 143, 159
English language, 84, 90, 101, 182
English literature, 10, 65, 66, 101, 102, 130, 131,
    181, 185
Enlightenment, 95, 118
Enugu State, 52, 168
Episcopacy and Christian union, 19
Episcopal Church, 33, 96, 100
Epistles of Paul, 40, 53, 82
ethical culture movement, 3, 9
ethics, 3, 67, 92
ethics in the Bible, 92
ethics, Comparative, 3
Ethiopia, 51
ethnic relations, 2
ethnicity, 2, 9, 18, 49, 75
ethnology, 97, 159
Europe, 19, 40, 50, 72, 76, 82, 96, 126, 132, 148,
    149, 163, 177
Europe, Eastern, 19, 50, 163
European influences, 143
evangelicalism, 15, 59, 66, 76, 83, 95, 110, 125,
    127, 149, 162
evangelistic work, 7, 10, 20, 23, 32, 35, 38, 39,
    41, 52, 72, 75, 80, 84, 89, 91, 95, 100, 101,
    103, 107, 114, 119, 136, 143, 161, 164, 165,
    169, 178, 183
evolution, 78
excavations (archaeology), 61, 62, 172
Ex-church members, 9
exorcist, 148

F

faith, 11, 12, 13, 20, 21, 23, 27, 29, 33, 34, 41,
   48, 53, 54, 57, 60, 70, 71, 80, 84, 105, 110,
   111, 114, 120, 123, 124, 127, 128, 134, 136,
   142, 144, 160, 163, 174, 176
faith and reason, 54, 105, 110, 124
faith movement (Hagin), 34
fall of man in literature, 12
family, 12
fantasy in mass media, 100
fascism, 158
fasts and feasts, 108
fathers of the church, 55
femininity in literature, 60
feminism, 107
feminist theology, 81, 91, 182
folk literature, african, 158
folklore, 154
foreign relations, 19
Foucault, Michel, 110
Fourth Presbyterian Church (Chicago, Ill.), 176
France, 11, 14, 125, 171
Francis, of Assisi, Saint, 1182-1226, 137
Fraser, Donald, 1870-1933, 167
Free will and determinism, 121
Freedom of religion, 178
Fundamentalism, 54, 67, 76, 101, 106, 132, 149
Fur trade, 105
Future life, 14, 135

G

Gandhi, Mahatma, 50
Gay men, 130, 173
Gay men in literature., 130
Gender identity, 4
Generation X, 142
Germany, 1, 7, 11, 41, 88, 133, 145
Ghana, 19, 87, 94, 117, 121
Globalization, 7, 163
God, 8, 14, 16, 20, 24, 26, 34, 35, 41, 42, 48, 50,
   52, 55, 60, 63, 67, 70, 72, 75, 76, 83, 85, 90,
   101, 110, 113, 116, 122, 129, 135, 137, 138,
   142, 143, 144, 147, 149, 150, 156, 164, 167,
   174, 175, 176, 177, 178, 182, 184
God in literature, 177
Godfrey) Christianity and culture, 171
Government relations, 108
Grace, 23, 41, 149
Great Britain, 2, 4, 10, 55, 61, 101, 102, 113, 117,
   119, 142, 173, 182, 185
Great Plains, 33

Greek, 10, 24, 57, 65, 71, 75, 136, 147
Gregory, of Nazianzus, Saint, 65
Grief, 69
Grief in literature, 69
Group identity, 40
Guilt, 54
Guilt and culture, 54

H

Hagiography, 64, 181
Halloween, 140
Hellenism, 41, 124, 135
Heroic virtue, 140
Hesperides, 66
Highlands (Scotland), 106
Hinduism, 132
Hispanic American Catholics, 56, 125, 181
Hispanic American women, 80, 81
Hispanic Americans, 5
Historic sites, 172
History, 5, 15, 17, 19, 22, 23, 25, 30, 38, 57, 60,
   68, 74, 75, 84, 87, 88, 92, 95, 96, 97, 98, 103,
   107, 120, 128, 133, 136, 143, 144, 151, 152,
   157, 164, 165, 176, 180, 181, 183
History and criticism, 22, 84, 92, 95, 143
History of doctrines, 19, 30, 107
Holism, 18
Holocaust (Jewish theology), 33
Holy Cross, 136, 165
Holy Spirit, 4, 119, 142, 174
Holy, The, in literature, 130
Homiletical illustrations, 19, 87
Homosexuality, 130, 173, 175
Homosexuality and literature, 130
Homosexuality in the Bible, 175
Homosexuality, Male, 173
Hong Kong (China), 91
Honiara (Solomon Islands), 91
Hope, 8, 137
Huao Indians, 50
Human beings, 90
Human ecology, 4, 17, 23, 35, 138
Human evolution, 35
Human genetics, 29
Human reproductive technology, 125
Human rights, 96, 110
Humanism, 42, 84, 130, 169
Humanities, 77, 105, 131
Hutterian Brethren, 7
Hwesa (African people), 103
Hwesaland, 103
Hwesaland (Zimbabwe), 103

Hymns, 9, 95
Hymns, Greek, 95
Hypertext systems, 129

I

Identification (Religion), 20, 50, 51, 71, 82, 163, 173
Identity (Psychology), 78
Ideology, 96, 153
Igbo (African people), 3, 46, 52, 78, 103, 117, 118, 119, 120, 170
Ignatius, of Loyola, Saint, 164
Illinois, 16, 21, 176
Imaginary letters, 49
Imitation, 62
Independent churches, 138
India, 3, 4, 5, 24, 37, 40, 44, 45, 50, 53, 71, 72, 94, 116, 129, 141, 151, 156, 167, 179
India, Northeastern, 151
Indian Catholics, 171
Indian mythology, 86
Indians, 11, 72, 86, 97, 105, 108, 124, 157, 169, 171, 183
Indians of North America, 11, 86, 105, 124, 157, 170, 171
Indians of South America, 97, 108
Indians, Treatment of, 105, 157
Indigenous church administration, 19
Indigenous peoples, 1, 111, 143, 170
Individuality, 70
Indonesia, 7, 53, 105, 156
Industrial relations, 180
Influence, 28, 115
Information technology, 8
Institute of African Women in Religion and Culture Congresses, 157
Intellectual life, 138
Intercultural communication, 26, 39, 50, 73, 85, 89, 93, 95, 102, 103, 137
International business enterprises, 20
International cooperation, 6
Internationalism, 153
Interpersonal relations and culture, 85
Inter-Varsity Christian Fellowship, 18
Ireland, 59, 108, 153, 154
Irish Americans, 180
Isaiah LX, 111
Islam, 2, 44, 60, 61, 105, 132, 138, 150, 165
Islamic countries, 105, 166
Islamic fundamentalism, 61
Israel, 145, 150, 166, 172, 179
Istanbul (Turkey), 95

Italy, 118, 119, 148, 158, 161, 169, 181

J

Japan, 20, 77, 94, 112, 125, 131, 141
Jefferson, Thomas, 132
Jerusalem, 8, 13, 40, 82, 103, 111, 177
Jerusalem in Christianity, 82
Jerusalem in the Bible, 40
Jesuits, 8, 93, 164
Jesus Christ, 5, 11, 16, 26, 30, 42, 53, 67, 84, 90, 97, 101, 102, 107, 110, 119, 124, 126, 128, 139, 142, 144, 147, 148, 151, 158, 168, 179, 185
Jesus Christ superstar [Motion picture], 148
Jewish families, 132
Jewish poetry, 143
Jews, 129
Jimi River Valley (Papua New Guinea), 96
John Paul II, Pope, 170
John XIII-XVI, 99
Journalism, Religious, 164
Judaism, 2, 3, 4, 8, 33, 43, 48, 85, 129, 132, 143, 145, 162, 172
Judaism and art, 8
Judaism and literature, 143
Judaism., 2, 33, 48, 172
Julian, of Norwich, 184
Justice, 27, 168
Juvenile literature, 177

K

Kentucky, 51, 99
Kenya, 1, 17, 18, 21, 25, 71, 118, 128, 148, 172
Kerala (India), 44
Kierkegaard, Søren, 86, 123
Kievan Rus, 28, 58, 140
King Lear, 90
King, Arthur Henry, 87
King, Martin Luther, Jr., 37
Kingdom of God, 8, 16
Kings and rulers, 101
Knowledge, 4, 22, 143, 156
Knowledge, Theory of, 22, 143
Korea, 82, 86, 87, 88, 89, 125, 182
Korean American women, 87
Krobo (African people), 159
Kurdistan, 15

L

Labor and laboring classes, 61

Laity, 111, 128
Land tenure, 2
Landis family, 147
Language, 22, 37, 76, 84, 90, 92, 101, 107, 108, 125, 129, 133
Language and culture, 37, 84, 90, 101, 108
Language and languages, 22, 76, 107, 125, 133
Language question in the church, 129
Lao-tzu, 158
Latin America, 30, 36, 39, 40, 59, 60, 80, 108, 114, 134, 143, 150, 160, 164
Latin Americans, 30
Law (Theology) Christianity and culture, 131
Law and gospel, 131
Lear, King (Legendary character), in literature, 90
Learning and scholarship, 25
Lee, Jung Young, 93
Lesbians in literature, 130
Lesotho, 36
Liberalism, 20, 74, 121, 123, 130, 140
Liberalism (Religion), 74, 121, 123, 130, 140
Liberation theology, 16, 38, 40, 75, 127, 139, 14), 166
Liberty, 96
Library, 9, 14, 22, 26, 30, 57, 64, 73, 89, 97, 98, 100, 109, 115, 137, 145, 147, 172, 182
Life, 22, 94, 99
Life and death, Power over, 22
Life is worth living (Television program), 99
Lindsay, David, Sir, 48
Literary form, 15
Literature, 8, 9, 14, 15, 20, 21, 33, 40, 44, 55, 61, 65, 68, 88, 90, 109, 113, 120, 126, 137, 154
Literature and anthropology, 65, 68
Literature and history, 21, 90
Literature and society, 8, 15, 44, 61, 113
Literature, Comparative, 154
Literature, Modern, 14, 33
Liturgical adaptation, 2, 84
Liturgics, 93, 127, 142, 146
Liturgy, 25, 31, 58, 59, 79, 96, 159
Lordship, 179
Los Angeles (Calif.), 93
Loss (Psychology) in literature, 12
Loughman, Graham, d, 128
Love, 27, 79, 110, 135, 137, 153
Luke XXIV, 4
Luther, Martin, 54, 134
Lutheran Church, 55, 86, 134

M

Macrina, the Younger, Saint, 124
Madison, James, 100, 132
Malachy, Saint, 154
Malaita (Solomon Islands), 91
Malawi, 55, 112, 120, 138
Malaysia, 146
Man (Christian theology), 23, 29, 46, 77, 124, 130, 181
Man (Theology), 13
Manipulative behavior, 24
Manipur (India), 94
Man-woman relationships, 37
Maori (New Zealand people), 102
Marginality, Social, 93
Maring (Papua New Guinea people), 96
Mark XIV, 16
Marketing, 20
Marriage, 180
Marriage (Canon law), 180
Marriage law, 180
Martín, de Porres, Saint, 60
Marx, Karl, 124
Mary Magdalene, Saint, 43
Mary, Blessed Virgin, Saint, 43, 45, 60, 94, 117
Mary, of Egypt, Saint, 43
Masai (African people), 74, 113, 172
Masculinity, 102, 110, 113
Masculinity in literature, 102, 113
Masculinity of God, 110
Mass media, 5, 8, 20, 24, 41, 57, 73, 93, 100, 106, 112, 121, 122, 123, 130, 132, 142, 169
Mass media and children, 24, 123
Mass media and teenagers, 112
Mass media and youth, 41
Mass media in religion, 106, 121, 130, 132
Massachusetts, 48
Material culture, 122
Material culture in art, 122
Maya philosophy, 39
Medicine, 72
Medieval, 500-1500, 11
Mediterranean Region, 5, 13
Megalithic monuments, 154, 155
Memory, 84
Men, 76, 102, 106, 113
Men (Christian theology), 106
Men in literature, 102, 113
Mentoring in church work, 13
Mestizaje, 60
Metaphor, 53
Methodist Church, 147

Methodology, 85
Mexican Americans, 49
Mexico, 21, 62, 166
Michigan, 32, 95, 164
Middle Ages, 8, 11, 28, 62, 76, 139, 149, 181
Middle Ages, 600-1500, 62, 181
Middle Belt (Nigeria), 85
Middle East, 13, 26
Millennium of Christianity in Kievan Rus, 988-1988, 28
Milton, John, 66
Ministry and Christian union, 107
Minjung theology, 86
Minnesota, 40, 106, 181
Miracles, 55
Mission of the church, 17, 18, 65, 76, 114, 127, 135, 145, 174, 184
Missions, 9, 16, 18, 45, 50, 55, 66, 75, 79, 85, 97, 104, 110, 114, 118, 120, 123, 124, 128, 137, 142, 167, 171, 180, 182
Missions to Muslims, 123
Missions, Portuguese, 45
Missions, Scottish, 167
Modernism (Christian theology), 67, 167
Modernism (Literature), 77, 154
Monasticism and religious orders for women, 61, 62, 142, 181
Monotheism, 115
Monsters, 102
Montgomery-Fate, Tom, 110
Moral and ethical aspects, 123
Moral conditions, 5, 185
Moral education, 9, 78, 173
Mormon Church, 87
Motherhood, 118
Motion pictures, 44, 82, 179
Mujerista theology, 81
Multicultural education, 93, 170
Multiculturalism, 26, 162
Music, 1, 74, 172, 183
Music facilities, 172
Muslim converts from Christianity., 123
Muslim women, 61
Mystical union, 139
Mysticism, 83, 110
Myth, 7, 21, 109
Myth in literature, 21
Mythology, African, 37
Mythology, Masai, 172

N

Namibia, 183

Nankhwali (Malawi), 112
Narrative theology, 71
National characteristics, American, 7, 21
National characteristics, American, in literature, 21
National characteristics, Nigerian, 78
National Conference of Catholic Bishops, 77
Nationalism, 12
Nativistic movements, 183
Natural theology, 124
Nature, 23
Naudé, Beyers, 101
Neo-Confucianism, 13, 86
Neo-Confucianism., 13, 86
Neopaganism, 95, 109
Netherlands, 79, 127, 132, 135, 181
New Age movement, 12
New Calabar (Nigeria), 174
New England, 11, 17, 22, 68, 84
New Orleans, 78
New Zealand, 26, 42, 102, 175
Ngoni (African people), 167
Nigeria, 3, 39, 52, 74, 78, 80, 81, 83, 84, 85, 91, 103, 107, 113, 115, 118, 120, 128, 164, 168, 170, 176
North America, 5, 35, 61, 67, 68, 86, 105, 124, 139, 158, 161, 170, 171
North and South, 4, 21, 136
Northeast India Theological Seminary (Manipur, India) Curricula, 129
Northern Ireland, 65
Nuclear warfare, 75
Nudity in literature., 90

O

Office, 136, 159, 160, 174, 181
Oglala Indians, 154
Oglala mythology, 154
Ohio, 5, 17, 30, 34, 54, 68, 86, 137, 167, 178
Oneness Pentecostal churches, 62
Ontario, 28, 31
Opocenský, Milan, 120
Oral communication, 84
Oraon (Indic people), 141
Ordination of women, 25
Orpheus (Greek mythology) Mysteries, Religious, 99
Orthodox Eastern Church, 19, 28, 57, 63, 82, 84, 94, 111, 129, 136, 140, 152, 162, 170, 174
Oxford movement, 44

P

Pacific Gulf Yupik Eskimos, 111
Paganism, 91, 135
Paite (Asian people), 94
Pakistan, 28
Palestine, 13
Papal courts, 38
Papua New Guinea, 96, 104, 117, 133, 155
Parables, 19, 87
Parent and teenager, 112
Paschal mystery, 25
Passover, 54
Pastoral counseling, 13, 77
Pastoral theology, 49, 71, 117, 142
Patrick, Saint,, 154
Paul VI, Pope, 1897-1978, 101
Paul, the Apostle, Saint, 99
Peace, 24, 158, 168
Penal laws in Ireland, 154
Pentecostal churches, 3
Pentecostalism, 25, 62, 124, 127
Periodicals, 5, 24, 39, 40, 52, 64, 77, 82, 83, 98,
    106, 132, 155, 159
Peru, 108
Peter, 1st, 167
Philippi (Extinct city), 44
Philippines, 9, 64, 92, 107, 128, 142, 157, 165
Philosophical anthropology, 78, 163
Philosophical theology, 76
Philosophy, 2, 5, 13, 27, 28, 41, 48, 51, 52, 74,
    76, 78, 83, 86, 100, 105, 124, 134, 139, 140,
    143, 154, 155, 157, 162, 174, 177
Philosophy and religion, 5, 41, 48, 83, 100, 139
Philosophy, Ancient, 5, 28
Philosophy, Chinese, 154, 157
Philosophy, Comparative, 86
Philosophy, Confucian, 13
Philosophy, Duna, 155
Philosophy, Modern, 143, 177
Philosophy, Nigerian, 78
Pluralism (Social sciences), 2, 20, 109, 170
Polish literature, 126
Political aspects, 84
Political correctness, 59
Political culture, 115, 121, 180
Political theology, 110, 158
Politics and culture, 40, 84
Politics and government, 21, 59, 63, 65, 85, 132,
    138, 148, 157, 167, 174, 180
Politics and literature, 48

Popular culture, 16, 41, 44, 55, 56, 64, 70, 79, 83,
    84, 100, 102, 111, 112, 113, 137, 142, 143,
    144, 148, 154, 169, 179, 185
Popular literature, 15
Positivism., 43
Postliberal biblical narrative model of theology,
    49
Postmodern theology, 32
Postmodernism, 32, 162
Power, 41, 96, 127, 139, 144
Power (Christian theology), 139
Preaching, 86, 90, 115, 116, 169
Presbyterian Church, 15, 47, 51, 128, 130, 131,
    160, 164, 165, 183
Pride and vanity, 91
Process theology, 111, 131
Pro-choice movement, 18
Progressivism (United States politics), 157
Pro-life movement, 18, 80, 159
Prophecy (Christianity), 17
Proselytes and proselyting, Jewish, 129
Protestant churches, 37, 65, 69, 70, 84, 86, 95,
    105, 120, 140, 156, 176, 179
Protestantism, 10, 15, 39, 88, 121, 176
Protestantism and literature, 10, 15
Protestants, 105, 120, 132, 141
Psychiatry and religion, 17, 84
Psychoanalysis and culture, 13
Psychology, 9, 54, 62
Psychology, Religious, 9, 54, 62
Puberty rites, 159
Public health, 72
Public worship, 42, 146, 169, 175, 183
Publishing, 63, 81, 99, 118
Puerto Rico, 142
Pure Land Buddhism, 182
Puritan movements in literature, 21

Q

Quality of work life, 152
Quechua Indians, 108

R

Race, 47, 74
Race relations, 16, 47, 65, 101, 102, 143, 157
Radio in religion, 69
Ramakrishna, 1836-1886, 168
Reconciliation, 52
Reconstruction (1939-1951), 6, 151
Redemption in motion pictures, 44
Reformation, 19, 54, 82, 104, 145

Reformed Church, 120, 156, 163, 165, 183

Relations, 114, 141, 143

Religion and civilization, 101

Religion and culture, 5, 8, 13, 37, 45, 51, 61, 62, 65, 70, 100, 101, 108, 110, 113, 115, 131, 132, 142, 145, 151, 170, 185

Religion and ethics, 94

Religion and international affairs, 182

Religion and literature, 10, 59, 65, 66, 102, 130, 177, 178

Religion and politics, 37, 84, 115, 177

Religion and science, 35, 54, 70, 93, 115, 124, 125, 139, 143, 159, 168

Religion and sociology, 5, 25, 31, 56, 87

Religion and state, 131

Religion and the social sciences, 109

Religion in literature, 14, 61, 106

Religion Psychology, 85

Religions, 8, 10, 37, 43, 48, 53, 92, 101, 113, 129, 159

Religious articles, 104

Religious aspects, 3, 8, 29, 44, 63, 88, 107, 138, 179

Religious broadcasting, 69, 144

Religious education, 9, 91

Religious education of children, 91

Religious fundamentalism, 19, 61, 106

Religious life, 112, 132

Religious life and customs, 112

Religious pluralism, 20, 22, 54, 85, 109, 119, 138, 142, 165

Religious poetry, English, 143

Religious thought, 175

Religious tolerance, 45, 104

Renaissance, 8, 48, 131, 181

Repentance, 21, 32

Repentance in literature, 21, 32

Repetition (Philosophy), 155

Republican Party, 151, 166

Research, 2, 40, 76, 77, 78, 82, 92, 105, 118, 122, 128, 129, 134, 152, 155, 157, 165, 172, 175, 179, 181

Revelation, 63, 131, 182

Revelations of divine love, 184

Rhetoric, 32, 96, 104

Rhetoric, Medieval, 32

Richard (Helmut Richard), 115, 145, 153

Richmond (Va.), 75

Rites and ceremonies, 66

Rites and ceremonies in literature, 66

Ritual in literature, 66

Roman, 91, 101, 129, 150, 151, 170, 183

Romania, 19

Rome, 3, 4, 8, 10, 38, 47, 48, 49, 53, 91, 104, 113, 118, 119, 133, 148, 161, 169, 181

Rome (Italy), 104

Rossetti, Christina Georgina, 1830-1894, 143

Rural development, 142

Ruskin, John, 1819-1900, 177

Russia, 6, 28, 63, 82, 140, 162, 174

Russia (Federation), 28, 82, 140, 162, 174

Russian literature, 28, 43

Russkaia pravoslavnaia tserkov´, 82, 111, 140, 162, 170, 174

Rwanda, 103

S

Sacramentals, 31

Sacred space, 97

Sacrifice, 62

Saint Paul (Minn.), 180

Saints, 141, 181

Samaritan woman (Biblical figure), 67

Sandaun Province, 104

Sandaun Province (Papua New Guinea), 104

Sannyasi, 75

Santee Indians, 33

Scapegoat, 62

Schenk family, 147

Science, 6, 29, 78, 122, 139, 161

Science and religion, 122

Scotland, 48, 124, 150, 155

Secularism, 15, 22, 60, 70, 71, 84, 96, 97, 121, 135, 169

Secularization (Theology), 14, 135

Self, 56

Sermons, 18, 65

Sermons, American, 18

Sermons, Early Christian, 65

Seven churches, 183

Seventh-Day Adventists, 47

Sex, 37, 61, 62, 65, 113, 137, 155

Sex differences, 65

Sex differences in education, 65

Sex discrimination in employment., 137

Sex role, 37, 61, 62, 113, 137, 155

Sex role in literature, 113

Sexual abstinence, 153

Shakespeare, William, 12, 90

Shamanism, 111

Sin, Original, 14

Singapore, 8, 31, 46

Sitka (Alaska), 84

Slavery in the Bible, 175

Slavs, 28, 140, 152

Slavs, Eastern, 28
Slavs, Southern, 152
Sobo (African people), 135
Social change, 18, 25, 37, 99, 117, 143, 161
Social change Role of Catholicism South
    America Central America, 143
Social conditions, 18
Social conflict, 24, 65, 88, 137
Social conflict in literature, 65
Social conflict., 137
Social ethics, 20, 21, 23, 90, 110, 144, 145, 175,
    183
Social ethics in literature, 90
Social history, 11, 18
Social life and customs, 151
Social problems, 40, 63
Social sciences and ethics, 175
Social structure, 104
Social values, 12, 89
Social values in literature, 12
Socialism, 139, 155
Sociolinguistics, 16
Sociology, Christian, 1, 12, 24, 25, 29, 30, 31, 46,
    47, 49, 52, 54, 56, 57, 58, 61, 77, 85, 99, 102,
    124, 125, 130, 137, 138, 139, 142, 153, 154,
    157, 165, 166, 171, 175, 183, 184
Sociology, Christian (Catholic), 1, 46, 54, 56, 77,
    125, 154, 171
Solomon Islands, 90
Soul, 17
South Africa, 10, 16, 31, 45, 101, 116, 143, 150,
    161, 162, 170
South Dakota, 77
Southern Baptist Convention, 69, 151
Southern States, 77, 114
Soviet Union, 15, 28, 170
Spain, 40
Special and Rare Books Collection, 89
Spiritual life, 10, 22, 39, 58, 68, 70, 100, 127,
    129, 137, 152, 153, 181
Spiritual warfare, 75, 87, 100
Spirituality, 45, 55, 102, 136, 138, 164
Spirituality in literature, 55, 102, 164
Spirituals (Songs), 10
Sri Lanka, 75
Stokes, Samuel, 1882-1946, 50
Storytelling, 19, 87
Students, 101
Study and teaching, 32
Sukumaland (Tanzania), 178
Sulawesi Tengah (Indonesia), 7
Sweden, 135
Symbolism, 109

Syrophoenician woman (Biblical figure), 67

T

Taita (African people), 18
Taita Hills (Kenya), 18
Tamil (Indic people), 74, 75
Tamilnadu Theological Seminary, 180
Tanzania, 55, 178
Tao te ching, 158
Taoism, 91, 158
Taoism in literature, 158
Taoism., 158
Tate, Allen, 1899-, 77, 158
Technology, 29, 90
Technology and civilization., 90
Teenage girls, 32
Television in religion, 99, 144
Ten commandments, 131, 144
Teton Indians, 77
Theodoret, Bishop of Cyrrhus, 135
Theological seminaries, 129
Theological virtues, 179
Theology, 8, 10, 14, 16, 20, 22, 23, 33, 36, 41,
    45, 46, 48, 49, 50, 51, 52, 55, 57, 59, 61, 62,
    64, 67, 68, 71, 74, 75, 80, 82, 83, 85, 86, 87,
    93, 95, 100, 103, 107, 111, 112, 115, 116, 118,
    119, 120, 124, 125, 126, 128, 130, 131, 136,
    138, 146, 148, 151, 152, 153, 156, 157, 162,
    163, 164, 165, 166, 167, 174, 175, 176, 178,
    179
Theology in literature, 59, 176
Theology, Doctrinal, 8, 10, 16, 20, 22, 33, 36, 41,
    45, 46, 48, 49, 50, 59, 61, 64, 67, 68, 71, 75,
    80, 83, 85, 86, 87, 93, 95, 107, 115, 116, 118,
    119, 120, 124, 131, 136, 151, 156, 157, 166,
    167, 175, 179
Theology, Practical, 166
Theology., 51, 55, 57, 62, 67, 82, 83, 111, 148,
    153, 162, 174
Theory, 3, 77, 120
Thessalonik̄e (Greece), 43
Tiv (African people), 4
Tlingit Indians, 84
Tocqueville, Alexis de, 1805-1859, 85
Toleration, 59
Torres Strait Islanders, 2
Tradition (Theology), 20, 179
Traditional medicine, 121
Translating, 147
Translating and interpreting, 147
Travel, Medieval, 55
Trials (Blasphemy), 101